PENGUIN VEER

LEADERSHIP IN THE INDIAN ARMY

Major General V.K. Singh graduated from the National Defence Academy, Khadakwasla in May 1964. He passed out from the Indian Military Academy, Dehradun, in May 1965 and was commissioned into the Corps of Signals. In his career spanning thirty-seven years in the Indian Army, he held several important posts, including that of Chief Signal Officer of the Western Command. He also raised the signal regiment of the Indian Army's first mechanised division in 1982.

General Singh is an alumnus of the Staff College, Wellington; the College of Defence Management, Secunderabad; and the National Defence College, New Delhi. He served as an instructor at the Military College of Telecommunication Engineering, the Army War College, and the Staff College. He retired from active service in June 2002.

Among his varied interests are adventure sports, military history and journalism. A keen rallyist, General Singh has participated in three Himalayan Car Rallies (1982–84). A regular contributor to magazines, newspapers and journals, many of his short stories and poems have been published in the *Illustrated Weekly*, *Filmfare*, *Femina* and *Eve's Weekly* in the seventies and eighties. In later years he took to professional writing and has authored ten books.

PRAISE FOR THE BOOK

'Immaculately researched . . . the book flows with an easy style that makes it as relevant to the man at the battlefront as it does to the one who battles it out in the boardroom and indeed, even today's youth who often look for real life heroes'—*Hindustan Times*

'To a large milieu of youth aspiring to be members of India's armed forces, an intense reading of this book is very strongly recommended'—Prashant Dikshit, former deputy director, IPCS

MAJOR GENERAL
V. K. SINGH

LEADERSHIP
IN THE
INDIAN ARMY

BIOGRAPHIES OF
TWELVE SOLDIERS

PENGUIN
VEER
An imprint of Penguin Random House

PENGUIN VEER

USA | Canada | UK | Ireland | Australia
New Zealand | India | South Africa | China | Singapore

Penguin Veer is part of the Penguin Random House group of companies
whose addresses can be found at global.penguinrandomhouse.com

Published by Penguin Random House India Pvt. Ltd
4th Floor, Capital Tower 1, MG Road,
Gurugram 122 002, Haryana, India

Penguin
Random House
India

First published in Penguin Veer by Penguin Random House India 2023

Copyright © V. K. Singh 2023

All rights reserved

10 9 8 7 6 5 4 3 2

The views and opinions expressed in this book are the author's own and the
facts are as reported by him which have been verified to the extent possible,
and the publishers are not in any way liable for the same.

ISBN 9780143462439

Typeset in Sabon by Manipal Technologies Limited, Manipal
Printed at Manipal Technologies Limited, India

www.penguin.co.in

MIX
Paper | Supporting
responsible forestry
FSC® C043100

This is a legitimate digitally printed version of the book and therefore might not
have certain extra finishing on the cover.

Contents

List of Abbreviations   vii
Foreword   xi
Preface   xiii
Acknowledgements   xix

1. Field Marshal K.M. Cariappa, OBE   3
   First Indian Commander-in-Chief

2. Lieutenant General Thakur Nathu Singh   41
   A Fearless Nationalist

3. General K.S. Thimayya, DSO   83
   Timmy Sahib, India's Most Popular General

4. Lieutenant General S.P.P. Thorat, KC, DSO   123
   A Professional to the Core

5. Brigadier Mohd Usman, MVC   159
   The Epitome of Valour

6. Field Marshal S.H.F.J. Manekshaw, MC   195
   The Architect of India's Victory Over Pakistan

7. Lieutenant General R.N. Batra, PVSM, OBE   243
   Communicator par Excellence

8. Lieutenant General P.S. Bhagat, PVSM, VC   285
   The Soldiers' General

9. Lieutenant General Sagat Singh, PVSM   325
   India's Finest Combat Leader

10. Lieutenant General Z.C. Bakshi, PVSM, MVC,
    VrC, VSM   365
    India's Most Decorated General

11. Lieutenant General S.K. Sinha, PVSM   399
    The Solider–Statesman

12. Lieutenant General Hanut Singh, PVSM, MVC   431
    A Brilliant Tactician

Select Bibliography   467

List of Abbreviations

2/Lt	Second Lieutenant
2ic	Second-in-Command
AA & QMG	Assistant Adjutant & Quarter Master General
ADC	Aide-de-Camp
AFHQ	Armed Forces Headquarters
AG	Adjutant General
AOC	Air Officer Commanding *or* Army Ordnance Corps
AOC-in-C	Air Officer Commanding-in-Chief
AQMG	Assistant Quarter Master General
AREN	Army Radio Engineered Network
AVSM	Ati Vishisht Seva Medal
BAOR	British Army on the Rhine
BCF	British Commonwealth Force
BIO	Brigade Intelligence Officer
BJP	Bharatiya Janata Party
BM	Brigade Major
BOR	British Other Rank(s)
BSF	Border Security Force
CDS	Chief of Defence Staff
CFI	Custodian Force in India
CGS	Chief of General Staff
C-in-C	Commander-in-Chief
CO	Commanding Officer

COAS	Chief of Army Staff
COS	Chief of Staff
COSC	Chiefs of Staff Committee
CPV	Chinese People's Volunteers
CRPF	Central Reserve Police Force
DAAG	Deputy Assistant Adjutant General
DAA & QMG	Deputy Assistant Adjutant & Quarter Master General
DAQMG	Deputy Assistant Quarter Master General
DCB	Ditch-cum-Bund
DCGS	Deputy Chief of General Staff
DEP	Delhi and East Punjab Command
DMI	Director of Military Intelligence
DMO	Director of Military Operations
DSI	Director of Signal Intelligence
DSO	Distinguished Service Order
DTL	Deep Trench Latrine
DVC	Damodar Valley Corporation
ECO	Emergency Commissioned Officer
FOO	Forward Observation Officer
FFR	Frontier Force Regiment
GCB	Knight Grand Cross of the Order of Bath
GCSI	Knight Grand Commander of the Most Exalted Order of Star of India
GHQ	General Headquarters
GOC	General Officer Commanding
GOC-in-C	General Officer Commanding-in-Chief
GS	General Staff
GSO 1	General Staff Officer, Grade 1 (Lieutenant Colonel)
GSO 2	General Staff Officer, Grade 2 (Major)
GSO 3	General Staff Officer, Grade 3 (Captain)
HLI	Highland Light Infantry
HQ	Headquarters
IAF	Indian Air Force

IAS	Indian Administrative Service
IB	Intelligence Bureau, International Border
ICO	Indian Commissioned Officer
ICS	Indian Civil Service
IESL	Indian Ex-Servicemen's League
IGP	Inspector General of Police
IMA	Indian Military Academy
INA	Indian National Army
IOM	Indian Order of Merit
IOR	Indian Other Rank(s)
IPS	Indian Police Service
JAKF	Jammu and Kashmir Force
JCO	Junior Commissioned Officer
JSSC	Joint Services Staff College
KC	Kirti Chakra (formerly Ashoka Chakra Class II)
KCIO	King's Commissioned Indian Officer
KCMG	Knight Commander of the Order of St. Michael and St. George
KPVA	Korean People's Army
MBE	Member of (the Order of) the British Empire
MC	Military Cross
MCTE	Military College of Telecommunication Engineering
MES	Military Engineering Service
MLI	Mahratta (now Maratha) Light Infantry
MI	Military Intelligence
MNA	Mizo National Army
MO	Military Operations
MVC	Maha Vir Chakra
NCO	Non Commissioned Officer
NDA	National Defence Academy
NDC	National Defence College
NEFA	North East Frontier Agency
NNRC	Neutral Nations Repatriation Commission
NWFP	North-West Frontier Province

OBE	Officer of (the Order of) the British Empire
ONUC	Opération des Nations Unies au Congo
OP	Observation Post
OR	Other Rank(s)
PBF	Punjab Boundary Force
POW	Prisoner of War
PRC	Permanent Regular Commission
PVSM	Param Vishisht Seva Medal
PVC	Param Vir Chakra
PWRIMC	Prince of Wales Royal Indian Military College
QMG	Quarter Master General
QVOLI	Queen Victoria's Own Light Infantry
RIMC	Rashtriya Indian Military College
RQMS	Regimental Quarter Master Sergeant
SC	Shaurya Chakra (formerly Ashoka Chakra class III)
SD & WE	Staff Duties & Weapons and Equipment
SHBO	Special Helicopter-borne Operation
SITREP	Situation Report
TSIC	Temporary School for Indian Cadets
UNCIP	United Nations Commission for India and Pakistan
UO	Under Officer
UPASI	United Planters' Association of South India
VC	Victoria Cross
VCO	Viceroy's Commissioned Officer
VrC	Vir Chakra
VSM	Vishisht Seva Medal

Foreword

Without apologising for beginning with a rather clichéd phrase, because it is true, I would like to say that it is a pleasure and a privilege to write this. A pleasure, as the author is one whose talent and friendship I cherish. A privilege, as the motives impelling the book are laudable.

A trifle too often our heroes tend to be men in white, whereas the ones in fatigues are all but ignored. The soldier's exploits are expected to be confined to the battlefield; similarly his honours. Yet written history is, unfortunately, rarely accurate, and the contributions of such men towards nation-building are often conveniently glossed over. Moreover, the soldier is confined to a stereotype whose human face is often to be seen only in mess-hall lore, and never outside military circles.

Setting right the historical perspective, analysing qualities that give these men the right to be honoured, both for their leadership and their vision, giving credit where it is due and, most of all, bringing out the human face behind the military façade is what the author has succeeded in doing here. This is important as, without knowledge of the truth, history degenerates into a story with little significance for those who seek to better the future from the lessons of the past.

Nor does the task seem to have been an easy one. To gather information traditionally never archived is a daunting task. It involves identifying, locating, contacting and interviewing people scattered all over the nation, or even the world. Then, of course, lies the equally, if not more, daunting task of verification and cross-verification. A painstaking process and a long one! In this particular case, all of five years!

I sincerely hope that this book will prove invaluable to academics and to the average Indian who seeks to serve his motherland better by acquainting himself with unknown facts and facets of those who have shaped her history. Moreover, if it inspires the youth of the nation to follow the footsteps of the great men whose lives have been detailed here, the author's pains will not have been in vain.

Lieutenant General (Retd) Ajai Singh, PVSM, AVSM
Former governor, Assam
Raj Bhavan
Guwahati

Preface

In times of yore, history was often nothing more than a record of battles between kings and warlords. The effects of wars on human civilisation were more profound than that of any other activity of man or God. Wars, and those who directed them, decided the fates of people. Military leaders were revered and feared, and tales of their valour were passed on from generation to generation, forming the bedrock on which histories were written. The growth of science and technology, trade, industry and economy has begun to overshadow the importance of wars and of those who fight them. Such thoughts and ideas were propounded after the Industrial Revolution two centuries ago and the Technological and Economic Revolutions which are of more recent vintage. However, the world witnessed two great wars in the last century, which together lasted 10 years. Even today, the threat of war has not receded. And as long as there are wars, there will be soldiers to fight them. In the ultimate analysis, it is the soldier and those who lead him who will decide the fate of peoples and of nations.

The Indian Army is over 250 years old. However, it was only 50 years ago that it began to be led by Indians and became truly and completely Indian. Fifty years is not a long time in the history of a nation or an army. But nations and armies have had shorter life spans, and 50 years equal two human generations. Today, because of the growing distance between the soldier and the common man, there is a lack of awareness in the general public about military leaders and their contribution towards maintaining the integrity of the country. It is well to remember that military leaders serve the nation not only during war but also in times of peace, by helping to maintain stability and harmony. Indians have only to look in their neighbourhood to realise that soldiers cannot only be protectors, but also the plunderers of democracy. The record of the Indian Army in this regard has been impeccable and the credit for this must go to leaders like Cariappa, who kept the Army away from politics and welded it into a force that exemplifies national integration. The Indian public must recognise the sterling contributions of its military leaders, not only in protecting the Nation's sovereignty, but also its social fabric, cultural identity and democratic traditions.

The generals included in this book were all leaders. It should be remembered that the government appoints generals while leaders have to prove themselves. Not all generals are leaders— if they were, Norman Dixon would have had a difficult time finding subjects for his book, *On the Psychology of Military Incompetence*. Unlike other callings, the military profession provides the ideal platform for a good leader to prove himself, as it does for the incompetent one to be exposed. One quality which all these leaders share is strength of character—a virtue which has all but vanished from public life; even among soldiers, only vestiges remain. It is hoped that their stories will inspire our youth, especially those who intend to join the profession of arms.

I must confess that the major difficulty was not in deciding which general to include, but the ones to be left out. There are scores of others who merit inclusion, if the criteria of good leadership and strength of character alone were to be applied. The only reason that I can offer for keeping the list short is space and time. To those who have not found a place in this book and their admirers, I can only say that this in no way reflects on their leadership and standing in the Indian Army. I am certain that their valuable contributions will be recognised and documented, if they have not already been done.

Work on this book had begun more than ten years ago, and it was not an easy task to get information about the leaders who are no more. Since the intention was not to write a purely professional biography but also to bring out characteristic traits, reliance had to be placed on personal accounts of people who knew these leaders, rather than written records such as regimental histories, war diaries, etc. Of course, biographies have been written of Cariappa, Thimayya and Bhagat, and autobiographies of Thorat and Sinha. These have been extensively relied upon and quoted. But for the rest, whatever appears in this book has been culled from various sources, including books, articles and personal narratives. Some of these leaders are legendary figures and their exploits are part of the folklore of the Indian Army. Many of the incidents and anecdotes described in this book are based on stories that have been told and heard in mess halls and ante-rooms for several decades and it is difficult to vouch for their veracity. Wherever the subjects are still alive, it was possible to get such accounts authenticated. Otherwise, an attempt was made to cross-check with those who have served with them or know them well. However, there may be inaccuracies for which I alone am responsible, and for these I offer my sincere apologies.

Though this may appear strange, another reason for relying on personal accounts rather than written records is veracity. Most regimental histories tend to glorify the actions of battalions as well as individuals. Hence successes are highlighted but failures rarely mentioned. In battle, cases of units fighting to the last man are matched by instances of units breaking up and of brilliant generalship by incompetent leadership. Not surprisingly, some earn medals and promotions while others are sacked. Like in any two-sided match, the odds of winning and losing in battle are equal and one would expect that the performance of units and commanders would conform to this pattern. The military profession has always placed a greater premium on valour, rather than on victory. This is especially true in India, where the most famous military leaders—Porus, Prithvi Raj Chauhan, Rana Pratap, and Rani Laxmi Bai—lost their battles. Yet, their stories make up for legends and have acted as an inspiration to generations of Indians. Unfortunately, military historians today have different views and failure in battle seems to carry with it a stigma and guilt, which is totally unwarranted. Today, a misplaced sense of honour and *izzat* impels units to hide mistakes and failures, and magnify achievements. In several cases, when I interviewed the superior formation commanders or staff officers, I found that their accounts were at variance with those recorded in regimental histories. Perhaps there is a need for the Colonels of Regiments to have a closer look at this aspect. If not corrected, this may seriously impinge on the integrity of the post-Independence military history of India.

The leaders selected represent a cross-section of the Indian Army. Of the twelve, nine are from the Infantry and one each from the Cavalry, Engineers and Signals. There are three Chiefs (Cariappa, Thimayya and Manekshaw); four Army Commanders (Nathu Singh, Thorat, Bhagat and Sinha); three Corps Commanders (Sagat, Bakshi and Hanut); one Head of Arm (Batra); and one Brigade Commander (Usman). If one were to go by valour, there were seven who were decorated for gallantry. There was one VC (Bhagat); three MVCs (Bakshi, Hanut and Usman); two DSOs (Thimayya and Thorat); one VrC (Bakshi); and one MC (Manekshaw).

In most nations, the contributions of famous military leaders are recognised by national awards. In Britain, they are elevated to the peerage, or knighted. Even Indian military leaders were given such honours, for example, Cariappa and Batra were given the Order of the British Empire (OBE). After Independence, a new series of awards was instituted. Starting from the Bharat Ratna, in descending order, they are the Padma Vibhushan, the Padma Bhushan and the Padma Shri. Of the military leaders profiled in this book, Manekshaw and Sagat were awarded the

Padma Vibhushan; Thimayya the Padma Bhushan; and Thorat the Padma Shri. Strange as it may seem, none of our military leaders was awarded the Bharat Ratna. Are the contributions of Cariappa and Manekshaw towards the Indian nation in any way less than those of the politicians, scientists, academics, industrialists and musicians who have been honoured with the nation's highest award? The adage about soldiers being remembered only during adversity and being quickly forgotten afterwards was never so true.

Major General V.K. Singh
New Delhi
March 2004

Acknowledgements

It is virtually impossible to record, or even remember, the name of every person who related an anecdote, or gave some titbit of information about the personalities covered in this book. I am grateful to each of the many people who came forward to help me in this venture. In particular, I wish to acknowledge my debt to the authors of those biographies and autobiographies that provided the foundation of some of the profiles. These are Humphrey Evans (*Thimayya of India*); Brigadier C.B. Khanduri (*Field Marshal Cariappa—His Life And Times*); Lieutenant General S.K. Sinha (*A Soldier Recalls*); Lieutenant General S.P.P. Thorat (*From Reveille to Retreat*); and Lieutenant General Mathew Thomas and Jasjit Mansingh (*Lt. Gen. P.S. Bhagat, PVSM, VC*). I am particularly indebted to Mrs Priyo Batra, who parted with the papers of Late Lieutenant General R.N. Batra; to Lieutenant General Prakash Gokarn, who had started work on the biography of Late Lieutenant General R.N. Batra and handed over to me the responses of a large number of people to whom he had written; to Mrs Mohini Bhagat for her impressions and a copy of the Commemorative Issue of the Bombay Sappers Newsletter devoted to Prem Bhagat; to Thakur Amarjeet Singh and Colonel Maharaj Guman Singh, for sending me the papers of Late Lieutenant General Nathu Singh; and to Lieutenant General A.M. Sethna, Dr Shernaz Cama and Brigadier Adi Sahukar of the UNESCO Parzor Project, for making available a copy of the souvenir and film produced on the occasion of the 90th birthday of Field Marshal S.H.F.J. Manekshaw. Finally, I must acknowledge my debt to Field Marshal S.H.F.J. Manekshaw, Lieutenant General Sagat Singh, Lieutenant General Z.C. Bakshi, Lieutenant General S.K. Sinha and Lieutenant General Hanut Singh, for having spared their precious time in going through the drafts and making corrections. Sadly, Lieutenant General Sagat Singh passed away before this book could be published.

To uncover little-known details about the lives of these 'Twelve Soldiers', I interacted with a large number of people through correspondence, personal interviews, and on telephone. To each one of them, I would like to express my heartfelt thanks. These people, in addition to the names already mentioned, include:

Lieutenant General M.N. Batra
Lieutenant General I.D. Verma, PVSM
Lieutenant General A.M. Sethna, PVSM, AVSM
Lieutenant General Ajai Singh, PVSM, AVSM
Vice Admiral R.N. Batra, PVSM
Major General J. Mayadas, PVSM
Major General B.S. Paintal
Major General S.C. Sinha, PVSM
Major General Niranjan Prasad
Rear Admiral R.V. Singh
Brigadier T.B. Kapur, AVSM
Brigadier Lakhpat Singh
Brigadier Apar Singh, MBE
Brigadier N.S. Pathania
Colonel Maharaj Guman Singh
Colonel Mustasad Ahmed
Colonel A.B. Jadhav
Colonel P.N. Luthra, Padma Bhushan
Lieutenant Colonel Ram Singh
Lieutenant Colonel Teja Singh

Commander R.N. Batra, VSM
Mrs Guddo Dewan
Mrs Mira Paintal
Mrs Preminda Langer
Mr Y.S.P. Thorat
Mr Har Mander Singh
Thakur Amarjeet Singh
Mr G.H. Keswani
Mr Upendra Sood

1

Field Marshal
K.M. Cariappa,
OBE

1

Field Marshal K.M. Cariappa, OBE

First Indian Commander-in-Chief

Kodandera Madappa Cariappa was the country's first Indian Commander-in-Chief of the Army. Considered the epitome of military leadership by generations of Indians, he was responsible for laying the foundations of what we today recognise as the modern Indian Army. Kipper, as he was affectionately called, was a 'pucca' sahib, even more so than the British themselves. Though many Indians considered him a WOG (Westernised Oriental Gentleman), he was fiercely patriotic. His iron discipline, integrity and forthright views won him many admirers. However, what he was known for best was his love for the Indian soldier or jawan. It is no wonder, then that the troops loved and worshipped him. For a military leader, there can be no greater approbation.

Kipper was born on 28 January 1900, in Madikeri (Mercara), Kodaga (Coorg), a small state on the western coast of South India. Inhabited by the Kodavus (Coorgs)—a warlike race—Kodaga is a picturesque region, famous for its coffee plantations. Cariappa came from a family of prosperous farmers belonging to the Kodandera clan. His father, Madappa, was an official of the revenue department who lived in Madikeri in a house called Lime Cottage. Madappa had four sons—Aiyanna, Cariappa, Nanjappa and Bopaiah and two daughters, the

3

elder being Bollu. In 1917, after finishing his schooling at the Centre School in Madikeri, Cariappa joined Presidency College, Madras. It was here that he learnt that Indians were being selected for commissions in the Indian Army. At that time, the Indian Army was being led by British officers, who had been trained in Britain. The Royal Military College at Sandhurst was the premier institution imparting pre-commission training to officers of the British and Indian armies, as well as those of several other Dominions. On successful completion of the course at Sandhurst, officers were granted the King's Commission. To tide over the shortage of officers in the Indian Army during World War I, the British government had decided to open a Temporary School for Indian Cadets (TSIC) for the duration of World War I at the Daly College, Indore. Candidates were to be selected from families that had proved their loyalty to the Crown, particularly at the time when soldiers were being recruited for the War. The age limit was fixed at 25 years, and there was to be a written test followed by an interview. The period of training was not to exceed one year, at the end of which cadets would be granted temporary King's commissions. As an incentive, it was stated that these officers would be eligible for confirmation as permanent commissioned officers after the end of the War. The first batch was to comprise 50 cadets, with another of the same size to follow after six months.

Cariappa, who had always wanted to be a soldier, decided to apply. Of the 50 vacancies, only one was reserved for Coorg. Seventy candidates applied, of whom 42 were selected and granted admission. Fortunately, Cariappa was one of them and he joined the TSIC, also known as the Daly Cadet College. Keenly interested in all college activities, Cariappa did well during his time there. However, his shy and reticent nature limited his interaction with his fellow students. But this may also have been due to the fact that most of the other cadets came from aristocratic families, and included the sons of rulers of Indian states such as Jamnagar, Jind, Kapurthala and Baroda. Unable to match them in wealth and lifestyle, Cariappa nevertheless was able to hold his own in all activities concerned with training, including hockey and cricket. When he passed out, he was placed seventh in the overall order of merit.

It was initially planned that the training would span only six months. However, after World War I ended, it was decided to extend the training period by one year. Hence, instead of December 1918, Cariappa's batch finished on 1 December 1919 and the 39 cadets who passed out, were granted temporary commissions. Subsequently, vide a Gazette Notification issued on 9 September 1922, 33 were granted permanent commissions with effect from 17 July 1920 (one died, two were found unsuitable and three resigned). This date of commission was deliberately chosen by the War Office to ensure that the Indore batch remained junior to a batch that had passed out from the Sandhurst on 16 July 1920. In fact, 27 officers had been commissioned into the Indian Army from Sandhurst on 17 December 1919; 104 from Wellington on 29 January 1920; and 57 from Sandhurst on 16 July 1920. By delaying the date of commission, the Indian officers effectively became junior to the 188 British officers who had passed out after them. This was done due to the fact that unlike the Sandhurst-trained officers, who had undergone two-and-a-half years of training, the Indore batch had received training for only 18 months. There were loud protests from the affected officers, who felt that the decision was discriminatory and unfair. Some of them even resigned. As it happened, Cariappa's batch was the only one to pass out from Indore because subsequent batches were trained at Sandhurst. Before this, nine Indians serving in the Imperial Cadet Corps, who had rendered service during the War, had been granted King's commissions in August 1917. These were Zorawar Singh, Kunwar Amar Singh, Aga Kasim Shah, Khan Muhammad Akbar Khan, Malik Mumtaz Muhammad Khan, Kunwar Prithi Singh, Bala Saheb Daphle, Rana Jodha Jung Bahadur and Kanwar Savai Sinhji. The first batch of Indians to join Sandhurst in

January 1919 had five cadets, of whom two died and one was withdrawn. Of the two who passed out on 16 July 1920, Syed Iskander Ali Mirza and Iqbal Ali Beg, the latter did not join. The sole survivor, Syed Iskander Ali Mirza, did not stay with the army for long, transferring to the political service instead.

Cariappa's first posting was to the 2nd Battalion of the 88th Carnatic Infantry, which was then stationed in Bombay. Within three months, he was transferred to 2/125 Napier Rifles, which moved to Mesopotamia in May 1920. On his return to India in June 1922, Cariappa was again transferred to the 7th Prince of Wales' Own Dogra Regiment. The battalion was then located at Khirgi in Waziristan, its main tasks being to keep the Pathan tribesmen under control and maintain law and order. Within a few months of his arrival, Cariappa received his baptism by fire. He was leading a convoy of 20 lorries, when he was ambushed a few miles outside the post. Rallying his men together Cariappa immediately led an assault against the tribesmen, who were firing from a hilltop, and succeeded in driving them away. Due to his quick thinking and action the convoy suffered very little damage and by the time reinforcements arrived, Cariappa had the situation well under control.

In 1923, the process of Indianising the army began with the nomination of two units of Cavalry (7th Light Cavalry and 16th Cavalry) and six of Infantry (2/1 Madras Pioneers, 4/19 Hyderabad, 5/5 Mahratta Light Infantry, 1/7 Rajput, 1/14 Punjab and 2/1 Punjab) to which Indian officers were to be posted. In June 1923, Cariappa was transferred to the 1st Battalion of the 7th Rajput Regiment (Queen Victoria's Own Light Infantry), or 1/7 Rajput (2 QVOLI) as it was generally called, which became his parent unit. The battalion had just moved to Waziristan and was engaged in duties similar to those of his erstwhile unit. Life on the frontier was monotonous but not free of danger. The tribesmen were quick to exploit the slightest sign of laxity in vigil, and the frequent skirmishes often resulted in casualties. The North West Frontier (NWF) was the best training ground for young officers, and Cariappa mastered the basics of his profession during the three years he spent there. He developed an excellent eye for ground, and learned the importance of good administration, both of which were to stand him in good stead in later years.

In 1925, Cariappa decided to go on a grand tour. He had saved up enough money, and the General Headquarters (GHQ) in Delhi not only accorded him permission but also arranged for his stay with British units wherever possible. Cariappa visited Europe, USA, Japan, China and several other countries, where he met a large number of soldiers as well as civilians of different nationalities. He was able to see for himself the reason why some of them were far ahead of India in many fields. The trip was a highly educative one for him and he returned a much wiser and better man. He rejoined his battalion which had now moved to Fatehgarh. Here for the first time in his career, Cariappa was able to settle down. It was in Fatehgarh that he acquired his nickname 'Kipper'. It is said that a British officer's wife found his name difficult to pronounce and insisted on calling him Kipper.

As a young officer, Cariappa took his soldiering seriously. A stickler for rules, he rarely got into trouble. There is an interesting anecdote about Cariappa and Mussoorie, which was then a popular holiday resort for British officers. Cariappa had applied for a few days' leave to visit the hill-station. When his Commanding Officer (CO) heard about it, he told Cariappa to go somewhere else. Cariappa was surprised and wanted to know why. The 'Old Man' (euphemism in the army for Commanding Officer or Commander) told him that Mussoorie was full of disreputable women, and it was a regimental tradition that bachelors did not visit the place. Cariappa took his word seriously and did not go to Mussoorie till well after he was married and had a son.

In those days, cantonment life in peace stations was staid and leisurely. Intended to provide a respite from the rigorous activity on the frontier, sojourns to these stations were short and when posted there, officers and men tried to make the most of them. Fatehgarh was a small town with little to offer in terms of entertainment or sightseeing. Cariappa thus had plenty of time on his hands, which he spent reading books on history and tactics, as well as some classics. He also began writing for military journals and newspapers. This provided him not only the pleasure of seeing his name in print but also some additional income. He enjoyed music and theatre, and was an avid fan of Prithvi Raj Kapoor, K.L. Saigal, and M.S. Subbulakshmi. In fact, Prithvi Raj Kapoor became a close friend and in subsequent years often stayed with Cariappa, in both Delhi and Coorg.

Cariappa was a man of frugal habits and did everything in moderation. His cigarettes were made especially for him by a firm in England and had the letter 'C' embossed on them. In later years though, he gave up cigarettes and switched to cigars, and still later to a pipe. He drank moderately and never exceeded two pegs, even during formal functions and parties. Fussy about his attire, he took pride in always appearing immaculately dressed. He never wore casual clothing, not even in his own home. He was fastidious about punctuality, etiquette and table manners, and there are many stories and anecdotes about his obsession with them.

In those days, as it is even now, the Staff College was considered a stepping stone to higher ranks in the army. The Staff College at Camberley trained officers of the British Army, whereas the one in Quetta had been established primarily for the Indian Army. Once Indian officers began to get commissions, a few vacancies were earmarked for them in Quetta, but these remained unfilled, as the Indian officers were still too junior and none had passed the entrance examination. In July 1931, Cariappa was posted to HQ Peshawar District as DAQMG. This was a non-graded staff appointment, and gave him some experience of the functioning of administrative staff at higher headquarters. His superiors and colleagues urged him to take the Staff College examination, and offered to provide some coaching. Through the efforts of one of his friends, in January 1932, he went to England for tuition, by the Royal United Service Institution (RUSI). He was also able to get a month's attachment with a British battalion, the Coldstream Guards. In addition, to round off his preparations he attended two short courses at the Small Arms School and the Royal Artillery School. As a result of the hard work put in by him, Cariappa passed the entrance examination, and became the first Indian officer to attend the course at the Staff College, Quetta.

Cariappa's presence at the Staff College was regarded by his colleagues with some amusement. British officers tended to treat men from the colonies with contempt and disdain. Cariappa tried to take the sarcasm and discriminatory behaviour in his stride, and rarely challenged them. On one occasion, however, he could not contain himself. In a large gathering held towards the end of the training, student officers were invited to comment on the course and suggest improvements. Cariappa pointed out that the number of vacancies for Indian officers at the Staff College was too small. This deprived a large number of deserving Indians of the opportunity to attend the course. In the ultimate analysis, this would affect the quality of the Imperial Army and might even prove to be its undoing in a major war. Everyone, including the Commandant, was stunned by the audacity of the young Indian officer.

Later, the Commandant told Cariappa that his remarks seemed to have been politically motivated. Cariappa was advised to broaden his views and think of the army as a whole, rather than in terms of 'Indianisation', which reflected a narrow vision. After the course, Cariappa asked for an appointment at the India House or the War Office in London, but was refused. In 1934 he rejoined his unit at Kohat for a third tenure of regimental service on the North West Frontier.

After successful completion of the staff course, officers were normally given staff appointments, which carried higher emoluments. Cariappa also tried for a staff job. But it was two years before he succeeded and was posted to Secunderabad as Staff Captain of the Deccan Area in March 1936. It was a non-graded appointment, but Cariappa did not complain. Finally, in 1938, he was promoted Major and appointed DAA & QMG in the same HQ. In 1939, when World War II began, he was posted as Brigade Major to 20 Indian Brigade in Derajat. At this point, one cannot help making a comparison between Cariappa and General K.S. Thimayya. Both joined the army at a time when very few Indians held commissioned ranks, and discrimination between them and their British colleagues in terms of promotions and appointments was common, though not officially sanctioned. Thimayya always rebelled against such discrimination and usually got what he wanted. Cariappa, on the other hand, rarely displayed any ambition, and accepted whatever came his way.

While at Secunderabad, Cariappa was married in March 1937, to Muthu Machia, the daughter of a forest officer. A Kodavu (Coorg) like him, Muthu was a well-educated and sociable girl. At that time, Cariappa was still a captain. He was 37 years old and at 20, his wife was a little over half his age. Muthu was a very beautiful woman, known as the Ava Gardner of Coorg. Their first few years together were happy and resulted in two children, a son and a daughter. Their son, K.C. Cariappa, affectionately called Nanda, was born on 4 January 1938, followed by their daughter Nalini, on 23 February 1943. Nanda later joined the Indian Air Force (IAF) and rose to become an Air Marshal. Unfortunately, Cariappa and Muthu were an ill-matched pair. Muthu was an extrovert, fond of parties and dancing, while Cariappa had no time for such trivialities. Before long, cracks began to appear in their marriage. Cariappa's frequent transfers, coupled with his total involvement with his profession, increased the rift between them. Muthu began to feel neglected. She turned to drink to assuage her resentment and pain. The alienation soon turned into bitterness, and in September 1945 they separated. There was no formal divorce—

Muthu simply left the children with him and began living with a friend. She did not live long, though. Three years later, she met with a fatal accident. Cariappa never remarried, preferring to live alone with his children. In later years, his sister, Bolu Chengappa, or her daughter, Sagari, often stayed with him to act as his official hostess when he was the C-in-C in Delhi, and later High Commissioner in Australia.

In 1939, in response to the demand of a large section of Indians, and heated discussions in the Assembly as well as in the Council of States, the government formed the Committee on the Indianisation of the Officer Ranks of the Indian Army. The Skeen Committee, as it came to be known, issued a long questionnaire to officers commissioned after 1919, asking for their views on the progress of Indianisation. A large number of them were called as witnesses to give evidence before the committee. One of them was Major K.M. Cariappa, who was called in June 1939 as the 26th witness. He was then a senior Indian officer with 19 years of service, and the committee held detailed discussions with him over several days.

Cariappa was dissatisfied with the pace of Indianisation and he indicated this in no uncertain terms. In the last 20 years, only 250 Indians had been granted commissions, including the King's Commissioned Indian Officers (KCIOs) from Sandhurst and the Indian Commissioned Officers (ICOs) from Dehradun. He felt that the ICOs made better regimental officers and were better suited to the Indian Army than KCIOs. As to the type of entry, he felt that the 'O' (open entry) cadets were much better than the other two—the 'A' cadets who came from the ranks, and the 'S' cadets who came from State families. The latter provided a backdoor entry to those who could not get admission through open competition and resulted in the induction of officers of lower quality and higher age group, who would have to be wasted out, and could not aspire to command a battalion someday.

Cariappa was also against the Eight Unit Scheme, which he felt was segregative. The units were top heavy, with the British officers being very senior and the Indians all very junior. This precluded the development of camaraderie and harmonious relations between officers. Worse, these units were considered inferior and looked down upon, not only by those within the army but also by civilians. He remarked:

> There are too many critical eyes set on these units, and naturally so—but is it fair on the young Indians? In these circumstances, they will have to be 100 per cent perfect to be considered average— quite an impossibility.

When questioned about the paucity of good cadets, Cariappa suggested that this was because people lacked education about career prospects in the army. When asked what could be done to improve matters, he said, '. . . no Indian has as yet been placed in a position of responsibility to demonstrate whether he can run the show properly or not.' Another point to be discussed was the use of ICOs to replace the Viceroy's Commissioned Officers (VCOs) as platoon commanders; the KCIOs, on the other hand, were appointed company officers. Cariappa likened this to using a Rolls Royce instead of a Ford car. He also had very strong feelings about the difference in the KCIO and ICO salary scales. Other anomalies related to the overseas and marriage allowances, to which only KCIOs were entitled. The ICO, who was drawing less than half the pay of a KCIO, had to dine in the same mess and pay the same charges as a KCIO, which put a severe strain on his finances. All this, coupled with the fact that ICOs were made to carry out tasks which only VCOs performed in non-Indianised units, made them feel that they were inferior to KCIOs. The Skeen Committee adjourned on 24 August 1939, but could never reassemble due to the outbreak of World War II. However, the records of its deliberations make interesting reading and provide an insight into Cariappa's mind and the opinions he held at that time.

In January 1941, Cariappa was posted as the DAQMG of 10 Indian Division, which was then in Iraq. The general officer commanding (GOC), 'Bill' Slim, was overjoyed when Cariappa joined his staff in Baghdad. World War II had begun and the division spent the next one year in Iraq, Iran, Syria and North Africa. While it was advancing through a town called Deir ez Zor in Syria, the mayor came to meet Cariappa, and asked him if it was safe to let the women out. On enquiry, he revealed that having heard rumours about the way Indians treated women, he had ordered all the women of the town to stay indoors. Cariappa was both amused and angry. He told the mayor that Indians never misbehaved with women and if there was any instance of untoward behaviour, strict action would be taken against the offenders. The mayor returned after a few days to apologise. As Cariappa had predicted, there was not a single instance of misbehaviour with women that involved Indian troops.

In March 1942, Cariappa was posted as second-in-command of 7 Rajput Machine Gun Battalion, which was a new raising, at Fatehgarh. On 15 April 1942, he was promoted Lieutenant Colonel and given command of the battalion, thus becoming the first Indian to command a battalion in the Indian Army. In a way, his promotion was a sign that the British had finally come to accept Indians in the officer cadre. The way was now open for Indians to reach the top echelons of the military, and Cariappa's appointment was widely acclaimed not only by his compatriots but also by several Englishmen, including Slim who was now commanding 15 Corps, which had just retreated from Burma. Major (later General) Maharaj Rajendra Sinhji, who had been commissioned into the 2nd Lancers from Sandhurst on 14 July 1921, and was destined to succeed Cariappa as the C-in-C in 1953, wrote: '. . . VCs, DSOs are a flash in the pan. A bit of luck, and there it is. But the command of a battalion is not mere luck.'

Cariappa's battalion comprised Muslims and Rajputs in the ranks. Among officers, two-thirds were British and one-third Indian. The unit was equipped with Vickers machine-guns, which required considerable skill in handling. A battalion under raising has to start from scratch, not only in terms of administration and training but also in terms of building up esprit de corps. Cariappa soon welded his men into an effective fighting force. He was a hard taskmaster and always on his feet, training and motivating his troops. After three months, the unit was redesignated as 52 Rajput and moved to Lahore as part of 43 Indian Armoured Division. It was converted into an Armoured Corps unit and its machine-guns were replaced by tanks. But this did not last long, and within two months the unit was reverted to Infantry, redesignated 17/7 Rajput and moved to Secunderabad in the Deccan. With two conversions and two moves within as many months, the unit and its CO were confused and tired. They breathed a sigh of relief when they reached Secunderabad.

On 1 April 1943, Cariappa handed over command of his battalion and proceeded to HQ Eastern Command as Assistant Quarter Master General (AQMG). Though he had been given command of a battalion, he would miss the opportunity to lead it in battle against the Germans or the Japanese. Several other Indians, such as Rajendra Sinhji, Thimayya, Thorat and Sen had this chance. Thimayya even commanded a brigade in Burma. As a result, Cariappa could not earn a decoration as most of the others did. This was a pity, and Cariappa remained bitter at the injustice, though he accepted it as always.

As AQMG of Eastern Command Cariappa was involved with the logistics of several formations, including the Fourteenth Army which was now being commanded by Slim. He was not very happy cooling his heels in a staff job while most others were on active service. He knew that experience in battle was essential, not only for personal satisfaction but also for further promotion. In August 1943, the South East Asia Command was formed and the Fourteenth Army was placed under its command. There were several changes, and Cariappa volunteered to serve in an active formation. He was again posted as AQMG, this time of 26 Indian Division, then located near Buthidaung in Burma. It was a staff job, but at least it was on the battle front. The division was being commanded by Major General C.E.N. Lomax, who was in fact junior to Cariappa. It was in the thick of fighting and was instrumental in pushing the Japanese back from the Arakan. Cariappa did an excellent job and was awarded the Order of the British Empire (OBE), for his services. Though it could not be compared to a DSO or an MC—which were awarded for gallantry—it was some compensation for his efforts.

On 1 November 1944, Cariappa was promoted Brigadier. However, instead of being given command of a brigade, which he expected and deserved, he was posted as a member of the Reorganisation Committee. Cariappa protested to the Military Secretary, but to no avail. Again, one cannot help but make a comparison with Thimayya, who kicked up a shindy and offered to resign when told that he was not being sent back to his brigade after his recovery from an illness; he got back his command, though he was only officiating as a brigade commander. Cariappa did not believe in making an issue of personal matters, such as promotion or posting. If he could get what he wanted by using the designated channels, well and good; if he could not, he accepted it like a good soldier.

Cariappa spent about a year on the Reorganisation Committee, which had six British officers and one Indian officer, with Lieutenant General Sir Henry Wilcox as the Chairman. Stationed in Delhi, he had the opportunity to observe at close quarters the workings of General Headquarters and the Viceroy's Secretariat. This was to prove invaluable when he took over as C-in-C after four years. It also provided the British hierarchy, which included Lord Wavell, the Viceroy, and Field Marshal Auchinleck, the C-in-C, the opportunity to assess Cariappa. The committee was the brainchild of Auchinleck, who knew that after the war the Army would need to be reorganised. He wanted the committee to come up with a perspective plan for Indianising the army over the next 15–20 years. When the committee submitted its report, it was found that only 50 per cent Indianisation had been recommended, and that too by 1960. The VCO, peculiar to the Indian Army, was also to go. Cariappa did not agree with these recommendations and put his dissent on record. Auchinleck was also unhappy with the report, and felt that it had not examined the issues in sufficient depth. However, before any action could be taken, the issue was overtaken by events and instead of reorganisation, the Indian Army had to undergo division along with the country.

In November 1945, Cariappa was finally given command of a brigade, and posted as Commander of the Bannu Frontier Brigade, in Waziristan. Having served in the NWFP as a young officer, Cariappa was conversant with the terrain, as well as the habits of the Pathan tribesmen who lived in the area. Since he had seen that the British policy of trying to keep them under control by force had not succeeded, he resolved to adopt a different approach. He decided to win the hearts and minds of the tribesmen, by extending a hand of friendship. He knew that they could be warm and hospitable if treated with respect and as equals.

One day, while passing through a village, he saw a group of Pathan women carrying pitchers of water. When he discovered that they had to fetch water daily from another village four miles away, he immediately ordered a well to be dug near their own village. The Pathans were overwhelmed by this gesture and started calling him 'Khalifa'. Later, when the region was torn by communal strife, Bannu remained a haven of peace, thanks to the goodwill generated by Cariappa. When Jawaharlal Nehru visited Bannu as Head of the Interim Government, Cariappa organised a public meeting which was attended by all tribal leaders. On the following day, when he visited Razmak where another brigade was stationed, Nehru was fired upon by the tribesmen and the visit had to be called off. Nehru was impressed by Cariappa's leadership qualities and rapport with the tribesmen.

Along with his efforts to win over the locals, Cariappa also paid attention to the living conditions of his troops. He improved medical and canteen facilities for the men and ensured that they were given adequate time and opportunity for games and entertainment. One of his innovations was to establish a separate mess for VCOs. After Independence, the VCOs were redesignated as Junior Commissioned Officers (JCOs). When Cariappa became the first Indian C-in-C, he retained the system of separate messes for JCOs that he had initiated in Bannu, and it continues to this day.

In February 1946 he was appointed Presiding Officer of one of the General Court Martials constituted to try members of the Indian National Army (INA). Before the trial, he visited some of the detention camps where the prisoners were lodged. He found them full of rancour and hatred against the British for treating them badly and holding them without trial. Cariappa was moved by their plight and wrote to the Adjutant General, requesting him to expedite the trials. He also recommended that some of them, such as Shah Nawaz Khan, G.S. Dhillon and P.K. Sehgal, be pardoned. Cariappa pointed out that there was a considerable amount of sympathy and support for the prisoners among the political leaders who would, at a later date, be ruling the country. He felt that their attitude towards the Indian Army would be affected by the treatment meted out to the INA prisoners, and the government should take this factor into consideration. It would be fair to assume that the British decision to let off most of the prisoners was prompted as much by the impassioned pleas of soldiers like Cariappa and Nathu Singh, as it was by the strong reaction from the general public and the political leaders.

Notwithstanding his feelings, Cariappa performed his duties in the Court Martial without fear or favour. One of the officers tried by his court was Captain Burhanuddin of 2/10 Baluch Regiment. He was found guilty and Cariappa had to announce the sentence which was seven years of rigorous imprisonment. After reading out the sentence, he went up to the accused and shook hands with him and his counsel. There were raised eyebrows and Cariappa was later asked by the Adjutant General to explain his conduct. Cariappa felt that he had done nothing wrong. He said, 'I sentenced him as the President of the Court and shook hands with him as a gentleman.'

In January 1947 Cariappa was sent to the UK to attend the Imperial Defence College along with J.N. Chaudhury, who was then only a colonel. This was the first time that Indian officers had been given the opportunity to attend this prestigious course, thanks mainly to the foresight of Auchinleck. The 'Auk' knew that the British would soon be leaving India and appreciated the necessity of training Indian officers to fill senior appointments in the government and the army. Cariappa's old commander and mentor, Bill Slim, was the Commandant of the Imperial Defence College. He saw Cariappa as the future C-in-C of the Indian Army and often invited him for discussions on the situation then unfolding in the subcontinent.

At the Imperial Defence College Cariappa was exposed to a much wider canvas than the one to which he had been accustomed. He realised that officers of the Indian Army had a long way to go before they could achieve the levels of those from the developed nations. During this time, there was a lot of talk about the impending division of India and the Indian Army. Cariappa, who realised the dangers of dividing the army and was aware of the inexperience of officers at senior levels, said that it would take at least five years before the Indian Army could stand on its feet without the help of British officers. This was picked up by the press and caused a furore in India. Liaquat Ali Khan of the Muslim League felt that Cariappa's intentions in keeping an undivided army were suspect, and took up the issue with Lord Mountbatten. Cariappa was summoned to India House in London, where Lord Ismay, Mountbatten's Chief of Staff, was present. Cariappa explained that he had made the suggestion only because he felt that an undivided army could help the two newly independent nations overcome their teething problems. He was admonished, and told to dismiss the idea from his mind, never to mention it again. In a telegram to Mountbatten on 4 May 1947, Ismay wrote, 'It is hard to know whether Cariappa in putting forward his idea was ingenious and ignorant or disingenuous and dangerous, or both.' Cariappa took the advice and did not talk about it again. However, he was not the only one who was against the division of the army. Brigadier Nathu Singh, who belonged to the same regiment as Cariappa had already taken up the matter with Defence Minister Sardar Baldev Singh several months earlier. Cariappa could not complete the course at the Imperial Defence College as he was recalled in July to supervise the reorganisation of the army before partition. Immediately on his return, he wrote to Nehru, making another fervent appeal to prevent the division of the army. Nehru's reply was non-committal. On one occasion, he collared Jinnah at a social function, and told him categorically that if the army was split, both India and Pakistan would be vulnerable to outside attack. Jinnah laughed it off, saying that if this happened, both countries would get together and face the enemy.

On 15 August 1947, the day India became independent, Cariappa was promoted Major General and appointed Deputy Chief of General Staff (DCGS) at Army HQ. He saw from close quarters the traumatic events which followed the partition of the country. The Indian Army was also partitioned, and there was considerable wrangling and heart-burning over the division of regiments, military establishments and weaponry. But worse was to follow. On 22 October 1947, hordes of Pakistani tribesmen entered Kashmir. After dithering for a few days, Maharaja Hari Singh signed the Instrument of Accession on 26 October, and Indian troops were airlifted to Srinagar just before the raiders could capture the town. Then began the long and difficult struggle to drive them out of Kashmir.

In November 1947, Cariappa took over as GOC-in-C Eastern Command, relieving Lieutenant General Sir Francis Tuker. He was in Ranchi for just over a month. As the Kashmir situation worsened, he was moved to replace Lieutenant General Dudley Russel, who resigned as GOC-in-C, Delhi and East Punjab (DEP) Command in January 1948 after he was denied entry into Kashmir, which formed part of his command. HQ DEP Command was then located at Delhi, and one of Cariappa's first acts was to rename it as Western Command. He soon took control of the situation and selected Thimayya to replace Kalwant Singh as GOC JAK (Jammu and Kashmir) Force, which was renamed as Sri Division (later 19 Division), at Srinagar. Atma Singh was appointed GOC of Jammu Division (later 25 Division), at Jammu. Cariappa also moved his own HQ to Jammu and raised a Corps HQ at Udhampur, under Shrinagesh, to command all operations in Jammu and Kashmir.

Cariappa experienced some of his finest moments during the Kashmir operations. Operation Kipper, which successfully captured Naushera and Jhangar, was planned by him. This was followed by Operation Easy for the link-up with Punch, and Operation Bison for the capture of Zojila, Dras and Kargil. Had he been given additional troops and the necessary permission, he would have succeeded in pushing the Pakistanis out of Kashmir, plans for which had already been made. Unfortunately, this did not come about due to the intervention by the United Nations after an appeal from India. Characteristically, Nehru took the decision to appeal to the UN Security Council without consulting the armed forces.

India's report to the UN Security Council was lodged on 1 June 1948 under Article 35 of the UN Charter. On 15 June, Pakistan replied to the UN, denying that she was aiding the raiders. After several meetings, the Security Council adopted a resolution on 21 April 1948, calling for a ceasefire, a plebiscite and the appointment of a commission. Both India and Pakistan rejected the resolution, but agreed to receive the commission. The United Nations Commission for India and Pakistan (UNCIP) was then formed. The UNCIP adopted a resolution, asking both countries to agree to a ceasefire and conclude a truce agreement for further consultations for a plebiscite. India accepted the resolution, while Pakistan refused.

On 6 July 1948, Army HQ issued instructions that no major operations were to be undertaken without its sanction. Cariappa was told to concentrate on stabilising the existing positions and not expect any additional troops as none could be spared, given the Hyderabad operations and overall situation in the country. Cariappa protested that such a defensive policy would be harmful, since the enemy was on the offensive in Tithwal, Punch and Hajipir pass. There was a threat to Leh, and if it fell, Kargil could not be reinforced, posing a serious threat to the Kashmir valley. He pleaded for permission to · continue the offensive operations for the capture of Kargil, Domel and Mirpur, and asked for two additional brigades. With great reluctance, he was granted permission but only for the advance to Kargil, and allotted a brigade for the task. To make matters worse, the Indian Air Force was forbidden to attack installations near the border, to avoid receiving adverse reports from the UNCIP.

Given the restrictions placed on him by his own government, and the lack of support in terms of troops, it is indeed commendable that Cariappa succeeded in achieving what he did. Due to political considerations, a defensive policy was imposed on the army. That he did not allow this to be transformed into a defensive mentality was a major achievement. As a result of this policy, India lost several key objectives in the Uri and Tithwal sectors. Since the road to Ladakh could not be opened until Zojila, Dras and Kargil were captured, Cariappa decided to go ahead and do exactly that. By disobeying orders—which forbade all offensive operations—he took a grave risk. But had he not done so, Ladakh may not have been part of India today. As it happened, these key objectives were captured after a brilliant manoeuvre, including the use of tanks, which were deployed for the first time at such altitudes. The country owes an eternal debt to Cariappa for the risks he took. Had he failed, his career would most certainly have ended.

There were several incidents during the Kashmir operations which offer insight into Cariappa's character. Utterly fearless, he was a frequent visitor to the front lines. Once, while travelling from Srinagar to Uri, Brigadier L.P. 'Bogey' Sen who was driving the jeep suggested that they remove the flag and star plates to avoid being sniped at by the enemy. Cariappa refused, saying that it would be bad for the men's morale if they saw the Army Commander travelling without a flag out of fear. Sure enough, they soon came under sniper fire, but fortunately no one was hurt. Cariappa remarked that the snipers were not genuine tribesmen. The ones he knew from his days in NWFP were not such poor marksmen. On the return journey, the Pathans fired at his jeep again and managed to puncture a tyre, but Cariappa was unperturbed.

On another visit, this time to Tithwal, he showed a similar disregard for enemy fire. He climbed a hill which was under enemy observation and much to the distress of the local commander stood with his red tabs and peak cap with the red band, in full view of the enemy. Within minutes of his moving away, a shell landed at the exact spot where he had been standing. Cariappa was unruffled and made light of the incident, remarking that even enemy shells respected a general!

Soon after taking over as Army Commander, he visited Naushera, which was held by 50 Parachute Brigade, commanded by Brigadier Mohammed Usman. Cariappa told Usman that he wanted a present from him. When Usman asked him what he wanted, Cariappa said, 'I want you to capture Kot.' This feature overlooked the Naushera Tavi valley, and was the key to the defence of Naushera. Usman readily accepted the task assigned by his Army Commander and captured Kot. When Naushera was attacked by raiders a few days later, Kot was held by Indian troops and played a major role in the successful defence of the town. Cariappa had spent many years in the NWFP, and had a good eye for the ground. He appreciated the tactical importance of Kot as soon as he saw it.

Another of Cariappa's endearing qualities was his broadmindedness. He treated all troops equally and was utterly devoid of parochial feelings. After the battle of Naushera, he visited 1 Rajput, which had suffered heavy casualties and won several decorations. When he was shaking hands with the officers and JCOs who had lined up to meet him, the CO, Lieutenant Colonel Guman Singh said; 'Sir, this is your battalion,' (since Cariappa was from the Rajput Regiment). Cariappa replied; 'All the troops here are mine too.'

During the same period, Air Commodore Mehar Singh performed the unique feat of landing a Dakota packed with weapons at Punch, and that too at night. A few months later, he landed a Dakota at Leh, with Thimayya on board. Cariappa personally recommended Mehar Singh for a Maha Vir Chakra (MVC) and made sure he got it. Strangely enough, the Air Force brass were not very happy with 'Baba' Mehar, and he got no promotion after this.

When India became independent on 15 August 1947, Field Marshal Claude Auchinleck was appointed the Supreme Commander and General Sir Rob Lockhart the C-in-C of the Indian Army. At the request of the Government of India, several British officers in critical appointments agreed to serve for another few years. On 1 January 1948, General Sir Roy Bucher took over as C-in-C. His one-year engagement was to expire in January 1949, and the government decided to replace him with an Indian. At that time, the three seniormost officers were Cariappa, Rajendra Sinhji and Nathu Singh. All three were lieutenant generals and army commanders. Rajendra Sinhji was a year junior but six months older than Cariappa. Nathu Singh was two-and-a-half years junior, in service as well as age. Being seniormost Cariappa should have been the natural choice for the appointment of C-in-C, but this was not so. In fact, Sardar Baldev Singh, the Defence Minister in the interim government in 1946, had informed Nathu Singh—who was then just a brigadier—that he had been selected to be the first Indian C-in-C. Cariappa and

Nathu Singh were from the same regiment but shared little in common, including their views about the British. Nathu Singh is reported to have declined the offer, as he felt that Cariappa had a greater claim on the job. In 1948 the most serious contender was Rajendra Sinhji, who came from a princely family of Gujarat. He had an impressive war record and had won the DSO. One reason why some people did not favour Cariappa for the coveted appointment was that apart from being 'anglicised' he was considered to be too strong and outspoken. There was also some criticism of his fraternising with Pakistani officers. Whenever he visited Pakistan, he stayed with his erstwhile colleagues, who did the same when they visited India. This naturally provoked anger in certain quarters and led some people to even doubt his patriotism. Fortunately, Cariappa's merit and seniority, along with the support of his colleagues, won the day. Rajendra Sinhji also declined the coveted appointment in deference to Cariappa and on 4 December 1948, the government announced that Cariappa would be the next C-in-C.

On 15 January 1949, Cariappa succeeded General Sir Roy Bucher as Chief of Army Staff (COAS) and Commander-in-Chief of the Indian Army. (The designation 'Commander-in-Chief' was discontinued from 1 April 1955.) At precisely 9 a.m., Cariappa entered the office of the C-in-C at South Block. General Sir Roy Bucher welcomed him and led him to his chair. They shook hands, after which General Bucher left. There was no other ceremony. Cariappa was wearing the badges of rank of a full general, and was 13 days short of his 49th birthday. After almost 200 years of British rule, an Indian had finally assumed command of the Indian Army, and it was to mark this historic occasion that 15 January became the official Army Day in India.

Soon after he took over as C-in-C, Nehru told Cariappa that one of his important tasks would be to bring the army closer to the people. During British rule, the army served as an instrument of power and was deliberately kept insulated from the public. Cariappa agreed with Nehru's views and took several measures in this direction. The National Cadet Corps had already been formed in October 1948, but it was Cariappa who gave it whole-hearted support during its formative years. And it was due to his efforts that the Territorial Army was established in 1949. Cariappa also did away with the concept of martial races, and within two weeks of taking over, fixed percentages for recruitment were abolished and admission was opened to all classes. However, this was made applicable only to new raisings; older units were not disturbed. The Brigade of Guards, which was raised in August 1949, was open to all classes. It was an elite force, comprising hand-picked men and modelled on the Coldstream Guards in the UK, with whom Cariappa had been attached in 1932. Four of the seniormost battalions of the Indian Army were converted to Guards, which was made the seniormost regiment of Infantry.

At the time of Independence, India had three parachute battalions, but no parachute regiment. The year 1952 saw the emergence of the Parachute Regiment. Though Cariappa was not a paratrooper, he had a lot of admiration and respect for them. During a visit to Agra in 1950, he had witnessed a jump. On his return to Delhi, he asked Major General H.J. Wilkinson, the Director of Military Training, to draw up a programme for his pre-jump training, followed by a jump. There was consternation in Army HQ and Major General Sharma, the Director of Medical Services, was given the task of convincing the Chief that it was not advisable for him to do this. Cariappa refused to listen to his medical adviser. The next day, Wilkinson again tried, but failed to persuade him to change his mind. Finally, he told Cariappa that in case he met with an accident, it would mean the end of his career, and he would not be able to accomplish all that he wanted as C-in-C. This convinced Cariappa and he dropped the idea.

Cariappa served as Commander-in-Chief for four years, retiring on 14 January 1953. His greatest achievement was to keep the Indian Army apolitical and establish healthy traditions.

Unlike Pakistan and Burma, which achieved independence from British rule at about the same time, the Indian Army has kept out of politics even during times of crisis. Much of the credit for this must go to Cariappa. In fact, it was primarily for this reason that he refused to take back INA personnel—he was convinced that they would bring politics into the army. There was a lot of pressure on him to include them in the army, and Nehru relented only after Cariappa threatened to resign on the issue. However, he adopted INA's slogan of 'Jai Hind', which he used to end all his talks, and it soon became the Indian Army's slogan as well as a form of greeting between men and officers. He also opposed reserving vacancies for scheduled castes and tribes when, as with other government services, there was talk of implementing this in the army.

Before he retired, Cariappa paid a farewell visit to the Rajput Regimental Centre, accompanied by his son and daughter. The children were driven in a private car to the Commandant's house where they remained for the duration of the day-long visit. According to the rules, children were not permitted in the officers' mess, and being a stickler for rules, Cariappa would not violate any of them even though he was the Chief. On his way to the railway station, he was surprised and moved to find that the town's entire police force and a large number of civilians had lined up along the road to cheer him. On reaching the station, he got out of his car and went inside his saloon. Then, remembering that he had forgotten to say goodbye, he came out and found the District Magistrate, Mr Virendra Kumar, as well as the Superintendent of Police, Mr Ali Qadeer, on the platform. He thanked them and, after shaking hands with everyone present, went back into the saloon.

Though he was a staunch 'Rajput', Cariappa never did anything to favour his own regiment. In fact, just before he retired, Major (later Lieutenant Colonel) Mustasad Ahmed, the Centre Adjutant, went to Delhi to get approval for the new regimental headgear. Cariappa called him to lunch, and while they were talking, Mustasad blurted out: 'Sir, now that you are laying down the office, we feel that you have not done anything special for the regiment.'

Cariappa smiled and said: 'So that is what you all think.' Fifteen years later, in 1968, they met again in Delhi. Mustasad mentioned that since the Chief was a gunner, the Artillery was now getting the best foreign assignments. Cariappa immediately retorted: 'You remember, you once told me that I did not do anything special for the regiment. If I had, people would be saying the same about me.'

Cariappa was known for his indomitable character. He was always direct and straight-forward in his dealings, with both his superiors and subordinates. Above all, he was fair and refused to bend the rules, either for himself or anyone else. He did not have any favourites, nor did he ever nurture a grudge against anyone. When his appointment as C-in-C was announced, he wanted to take Major (later Lieutenant General) S.K. Sinha, who was his staff officer in HQ Western Command, with him to Delhi as his Military Assistant. The Military Secretary pointed out that the appointment was tenable only by a lieutenant colonel, a rank that was conferred only after a minimum service of six-and-a-half years; Sinha had only five years of service. Of course, as Chief, Cariappa could waive the rule if he wished. When Cariappa heard this, he dropped the idea; he did not want to bend the rules in anyone's favour and set a bad example. He sent for Sinha and explained the situation to him, regretting his inability to give him the coveted appointment.

Soon after taking over as Chief, he visited Madras. A general officer, who was also a close friend, tried to informally discuss his future employment with him. Cariappa curtly told him, 'Please talk to the Military Secretary.' In fact, Cariappa's reputation as a stickler for discipline and propriety made even his close friends hesitate to take liberties with him. Thimayya was related to him and had also been a colleague both during the War and later, in Kashmir. During a visit to Srinagar, when

Cariappa was the Army Commander, they were travelling in the same car. Thimayya lit a cigarette and had just taken his first puff when Cariappa reminded him that smoking was prohibited in military vehicles. Thimayya immediately snuffed it out and continued talking as if nothing had happened. After some time, out of habit, he pulled out another cigarette, but remembering Cariappa's admonishment, put it back. Cariappa noticed this, and asked the driver to stop so that Thimayya could smoke.

On the day that his appointment as C-in-C was announced, Cariappa was sitting with the British High Commissioner on the balcony of the Delhi Gymkhana Club. There was a party being held at the club and several other army officers were also present. Brigadier Sarda Nand Singh went up to Thimayya and suggested that they request the band to play 'For he's a jolly good fellow', and that as the senior officer present, Thimayya lead the chorus. The last thing one could accuse Thimayya was of timidity, but he declined, saying that the old man may consider it an act of indiscipline!

Cariappa had a quick temper, but like a tempest, it would blow over in no time at all. Even when he was angry, he was open to reason and willing to be corrected if wrong. In 1951, he visited the Rajput Regimental Centre to present the Cariappa Banner, which was awarded to the best training company of the year. There was a doubt whether the banner, like the Colours, should also be escorted on parade. The Centre Commandant, Colonel Guman Singh, did not believe in polite gestures and after looking up the orders on the subject, decided that the banner was not entitled to an escort. When Cariappa arrived and saw that the banner named after him was not being properly escorted, he went crimson with rage. The initial blast was borne by Lieutenant General Thakur Nathu Singh, who was GOC-in-C Eastern Command. He in turn gave a dressing-down to the Adjutant, Major Mustasad Ahmed, who could do little else than look at Guman Singh, who happened to be Thakur Nathu Singh's son-in-law. Without batting an eye-lid, Guman Singh told the Chief that he had read the rules carefully and the banner was not entitled to an escort. Cariappa immediately cooled down and became his charming self again.

Having donned the mantle of independent India's first Army Chief, Cariappa was faced with a very heavy responsibility. The politicians in power had no experience in defence matters, since the British rulers had kept the army insulated from public attention. It was for Cariappa to establish a sound working relationship between the armed forces and the bureaucracy, as well as the politicians in power. He had problems with both. The Defence Secretary, H.M. Patel, was always looking for opportunities to assert the supremacy of the bureaucracy over the armed forces. He once asked all three Service Chiefs to attend a conference, which he was to chair. Since the Chiefs were senior in rank to a secretary to the government, Cariappa refused to attend himself and sent his Chief of General Staff (CGS) instead. He advised the other two Chiefs to do the same.

Cariappa also had some unpleasant brushes with Nehru. Having foreseen the Chinese threat, he wanted to defend the border more effectively. In May 1951, he presented an outline plan for the defence of the North East Frontier Agency (NEFA). Nehru dismissed him saying that it was not the C-in-C's business to tell the Prime Minister how to defend the country. He advised Cariappa to worry only about Pakistan and Kashmir; as far as NEFA was concerned, the Chinese themselves would defend our frontiers! Cariappa was terribly hurt, but like a good soldier accepted the Prime Minister's rebuke. In later years, he realised his mistake. Had he persisted and countered Nehru's fantasies with more forceful arguments and facts, perhaps the debacle of 1962 would not have taken place.

One of the most well-known stories about Cariappa relates to his inadequate knowledge of Hindustani, which was one reason why many people called him a Brown Sahib. Soon after Independence, during a visit to the forward areas, he had to address the troops. He wanted to tell them that now that the country was free, so were all of them. What he said was something like this, '*Is waqt aap muft, hum muft, mulk muft, sab kuchh muft hai.*' (The word *muft* in Hindustani means free of cost or gratis. Freedom or liberty is denoted by *azad*.)

Cariappa was one of the earliest proponents of family planning. He realised that India's growing population was at least partly responsible for her backwardness, and in 1951, he wrote the foreword for a book authored by Dr Satyawati on the subject. He also stressed the need to have a small family in his speeches to the men and their families. During his 'durbars', he exhorted the men to undergo vasectomy, arrangements for which had been made in all military hospitals. Once, while visiting a hospital in Shillong, he asked a soldier what ailment he was suffering from. The soldier replied, 'From the disease you have given us.' Cariappa was puzzled until it was explained to him that the man had just undergone a vasectomy. On another occasion, while addressing a large gathering of army wives at the Family Welfare Centre in Amritsar, he said, '*Mataon aur behnon. Hum chahta hai ki aap do baccha paida karo, ek apne liye, ek mere liye.*' (Mothers and sisters, I want you to produce two children, one for yourself, and one for me.) He wanted to say that they should have two sons, one of whom would stay with the family, while the other would join the army.

Cariappa was a meticulous host and an even more meticulous guest. Even when he lived alone after retirement, Cariappa did not enter his drawing room without wearing formal dress. Once, when he was Chief, Lieutenant General Thakur Nathu Singh, then Army Commander of Eastern Command, was a house guest. Having served in the same regiment, Nathu Singh was both a colleague and a friend. Wanting to pull Cariappa's leg, Singh put on a kurta and pyjama and sat in the drawing room to wait for him. When Cariappa entered the room some time later, he immediately objected. Nathu Singh replied that what he was wearing was the national dress and that Cariappa had better get used to it. Another time, after he had retired, when he happened to visit Lucknow, he was invited to dinner by Brigadier V.D. Jayal, a retired KCIO. During dinner, the servant served him from the right side. Cariappa corrected the servant and told him to serve from the left in future. He also told Jayal that he should train his servants properly.

Cariappa was fastidious not only about his dress but about all aspects of mess etiquette. He was a moderate drinker, and insisted that dinner be served by 9 p.m. so that everyone could be home by 11 p.m. He was very particular about paying for his drinks when on tour. As Chief, he once visited the Rajput Regimental Centre at Fatehgarh. Before he left, his ADC (Aide-de-Camp) asked for a mess bill. When the mess secretary declined on the plea that as the C-in-C and Colonel of the Regiment Cariappa was an honoured guest, he was told very firmly that Cariappa had given very clear orders in this regard. If he was invited to a mess party or to some officer's home, he would graciously accept the food and drinks offered by his hosts. But any expense incurred at his place of stay would be paid by him. The Centre Commandant, Colonel Guman Singh, was well acquainted with Cariappa and his temper. He immediately had a mess bill prepared, which was promptly settled.

Cariappa laid great stress on personal integrity and did not allow any incident of moral turpitude to go unpunished. Soon after he took over as GOC-in-C Eastern Command, he ordered the dismissal of two officers who had two wives. After he became C-in-C, three senior officers were asked to retire for 'un-officer-like' behaviour. Their dismissal served to have a salutary effect on the others. He addressed two personal letters to all officers containing guidelines on how to deal with the men and other duties. The first letter had the Cadet's Prayer at West Point, and all officers had to carry copies of both in the breast pockets of their uniforms. The second letter contained advice on officers' conduct.

There can be no better illustration of Cariappa's sterling character than the incident concerning his son, Nanda Cariappa, a fighter pilot who was shot down in Pakistan during the 1965 war. Field Marshal Ayub Khan sent Cariappa a message that his son was safe and would be well looked after. He also offered to release him if Cariappa so desired. Cariappa replied, 'I will ask no favour for my son which I cannot secure for every soldier of the Indian Army. Look after all of them. They are all my sons.'*

Cariappa's love and affection for the Indian jawan was well known. He often said, 'Our jawans are absolute gems.' After his retirement, when he moved to Roshanara, his home in Mercara, he kept a statue of a jawan on his mantlepiece, placed next to a photograph of his father. Cariappa started his day by paying obeisance to both. He could not tolerate any criticism of the Indian Army or the jawan, and was quick to rise to their defence. He once filed defamation charges against a newspaper which carried derogatory remarks about the Indian Army. When the editor apologised and published a retraction, Cariappa withdrew the suit.

Though Cariappa was a strict disciplinarian, he also had a great sense of humour and could be extremely charming and full of fun. This aspect of him was described by Harjit Malik in a middle entitled 'The General Danced', published in the *Times of India* of 3 June 1993. When Cariappa was the Chief, he went on a visit to France, where the Indian ambassador H.S. Malik, invited him to stay at the embassy. When he heard that the French celebrate the Quatorze Juillet by dancing on the streets, he expressed a desire to join the celebrations. There was great consternation in the embassy as well as among his staff, but Cariappa was adamant. Accompanied by the Maliks and their daughter, Harjit, the General proceeded to the Latin Quarter, where the party luckily found an empty table at one of the pavement cafes. Cariappa sat for a while, ramrod erect, looking

---

* Nanda returned safely in due course of time, and rose to be an Air Marshal, retiring as Air Officer Commanding-in-Chief, South Western Air Command.

at the thousands of Parisiennes dancing with gay abandon or locked in embrace, oblivious to the world around. Then the music and the festive atmosphere became too much for him and he got up and asked Harjit for a dance. Soon, people saw a sedate old gentleman, impeccably dressed, dancing the foxtrot with a young girl on his arm in a crowd of long-haired and scantily dressed bohemians.

Soon after Cariappa retired, Prime Minister Nehru offered to send him to Australia as the Indian High Commissioner. After some deliberation, he accepted and sailed for Sydney in July 1953. His niece, Sagari, volunteered to go with him and keep house. When Cariappa arrived at Canberra, the Governor General, Field Marshal Slim, broke protocol and called on Cariappa at his residence even before he had presented his credentials.

His stay in Australia was fairly eventful, and soon everyone was talking about the Indian High Commissioner. During one of his trips, he saw a war memorial that had been neglected and was surrounded by bushes. Cariappa stopped the car, walked up to the memorial and began clearing the growth with his own hands. A crowd collected and the incident was widely reported in the press, leaving the Australians feeling ashamed that a foreigner had to show them how to respect their martyrs.

On another occasion, when Cariappa was on his way to attend a function organised by ex-servicemen, his car broke down. Cariappa hitched a ride on a truck. As they were driving the truck driver asked him who he was. When Cariappa replied that he was the Indian High Commissioner, the driver laughed and said, 'And I'm the King of Nepal!' When they reached their destination, Cariappa alighted, saying: 'Thank you, Your Majesty.' When the driver saw Cariappa's hosts he realised that he had indeed been travelling with the Indian High Commissioner, and quickly apologised.

Cariappa's tenure in Australia was not without controversy. Once, he made certain remarks about Australia's white migrants policy which favoured the immigration of white races only. This created a furore in the press and there were demands that he be recalled for interfering in the domestic affairs of another country. But Cariappa remained unfazed. He knew that he was right and that his view had many supporters. Eventually, public opinion on this matter forced the Australian government to review its immigration policy and make it more liberal.

Cariappa returned to India in 1956 and retired to his house, Roshanara. But he continued to take a keen interest in all matters concerning the Army. When the Chinese attacked India in 1962, he went to the local recruiting office and offered to enlist as a soldier. In 1965, after the ceasefire, he expressed a desire to visit the troops on the front. During his visit to 17 Rajput—the battalion he had raised in 1942—the troops raised their war cry after he had spoken to them. The Pakistani battalion commander on the other side became agitated and ordered his men to man the trenches. He then registered a strong protest. When he was told the reason for the war cry, he immediately came across, saluted Cariappa, and requested him to visit his men so that they too could have a glimpse of the legendary General.

Though Cariappa had been C-in-C of the Indian Army for four years, he was only 53 when he retired. Today, the Chief retires at 62. Like Cariappa, several other senior officers of that period also had very short tenures. Nathu Singh retired at the age of 51, and Thimayya and Thorat at 55. This was one of the biggest blunders of the Nehru government, which insisted on keeping on British officers after Independence on the grounds that Indian officers lacked experience. At the same time, it allowed its most experienced officers, like Cariappa, Nathu Singh, Thimayya and Thorat, to retire at a very young age, thus depriving the nation of their services when it needed them the most. When the Chinese attacked India in 1962, both Thimayya and Thorat had been out of uniform for just a year.

It is difficult to believe that Cariappa supported the proposal limiting the tenure of the Chief and Army Commanders to four years. Perhaps he acquiesced since the rule affected him directly and he may have felt that to do otherwise might appear selfish. And being the gentleman he was, this was the last thing of which he would have liked to be accused. In the event, he recommended the proposal and Nehru accepted it without going into its implications. Had he opposed it, perhaps the Indian Army would not have suffered the infamy of 1962, since Thimayya as well as Thorat would still have been around to say 'no' to Nehru and Krishna Menon, as Sam Manekshaw did to Indira Gandhi in April 1971, when she wanted to go to war with Pakistan.

The welfare of ex-servicemen always remained Cariappa's prime concern. In 1964, he founded the Indian Ex-Servicemen's League (IESL) by amalgamating the Federation and the Association, which were rival organisations often working at cross-purposes. He was also responsible for the creation of the Directorate of Resettlement. In 1957, he took up cudgels on behalf of Major General Tara Singh Bal—who had been unjustly retired by the government—and had him reinstated. Keeping the IESL free from politics was another one of his major achievements.

Cariappa also made a brief foray into politics in early 1971. Convinced that the country could not be governed by the present system of elections, he recommended that the general elections scheduled for 1971 be cancelled and President's rule be imposed for a few years, keeping the Constitution in suspended animation. Political parties were to be abolished and martial law imposed in disturbed states. Once the situation had stabilised, elections could be held with just two or three parties, as in the UK or USA. As could be expected, the political parties reacted violently and Y.B. Chavan, the Home Minister, denounced in Parliament the call for 'Army Rule by an ex C-in-C'. Cariappa wrote an angry letter to Chavan, berating him for misleading the House, and demanded an apology, which never came.

A number of his friends and admirers had been trying to persuade him to join politics and stand for elections so that he could contribute to the nation's development. After deep reflection, he agreed and decided to contest the Lok Sabha seat from north-east Bombay. Lieutenant General S.P.P. Thorat and several other retired officers came forward to assist him in his campaign, as did many well known industrialists and the erstwhile Maharaja of Mysore. Cariappa declined to join any political party and stood as an independent candidate. Unfortunately, his two opponents were V.K. Krishna Menon and Acharya J.B. Kripalani, both veterans and political heavyweights. Cariappa, though widely respected, was a novice in the rough and tumble world of politics. He refused to use money or muscle to get votes, and in his campaign speeches talked of honour, integrity and probity, all of which were unintelligible to his audiences. Most of them came to his meetings for amusement, laughing at his 'fauji Hindustani', which few in Bombay could comprehend. Not surprisingly, he lost to his two seasoned opponents, who had several decades of experience and were backed by the resources of their respective political parties. Apart from lack of experience, he also made a mistake in his choice of constituency. Had he stood from his native Coorg, he may well have won.

In 1986 the government decided to appoint him Field Marshal. Technically, a field marshal never retires and therefore retired officers cannot be given this rank. However, the decision stemmed from the deep sense of respect and esteem in which Cariappa was held by all sections of Indian society. Cariappa graciously accepted the honour. On 28 April 1986, at a special investiture ceremony held at Rashtrapati Bhawan, he was presented the Field Marshal's baton by President Zail Singh. In deference to his age— he was 86—he was offered a chair while the citation was being read out. True to his character, Cariappa declined the offer and stood ramrod straight throughout the ceremony.

After 1991, Cariappa's health began to deteriorate. He was suffering from arthritis and a weak heart, and needed constant medical attention. He was shifted to a cottage in the command hospital at Bangalore. The end came on 15 May 1994 when Cariappa died peacefully in his sleep. Two days later, his mortal remains were cremated at his ancestral home in Madikeri. The cremation took place with all the ceremony and pomp befitting a field marshal. The three Service Chiefs, along with Field Marshal Sam Manekshaw, were in attendance when his son Nanda Cariappa lit the funeral pyre and the bugles sounded the Last Post, with the Honour Guard reversing arms. Many of the mourners, including some soldiers in uniform, had tears in their eyes as they bade farewell to the man who had always treated them like his sons and whom they called the Father of the Indian Army.

Kipper is no more. But if the adage about old soldiers never dying but fading away was ever true, it was so in his case. He had become a living legend even before he rose to the highest military rank. Every man has his faults and perhaps Cariappa too had some. But they are hard to find. Even those who did not openly adore him, respected him, however grudgingly. His strong character and values represent qualities that are hard to come by today. Although a strict disciplinarian, he was always just and fair, and even those who felt the rough end of his stick will vouch for this. The Indian nation owes him an eternal debt for his contributions, which are too numerous to recount. Of course, if Cariappa were alive, he would have dismissed this saying that he only did what he felt was his duty. Though anglicised in habits and behaviour, he was a true patriot, always keeping his country's interest uppermost, followed by that of the soldier. As he takes the Final Step and passes out from the Indian Military Academy, every Indian Army officer is reminded of the immortal words of Field Marshal Lord Chetwode:

> The safety, honour and welfare of your country come first, always and every time; the honour, welfare and comfort of the men you command come next; your own ease, comfort and safety come last, always and every time.

One of the few who followed this, in letter and in spirit, was K.M. Cariappa.

2
Lieutenant General
Thakur Nathu Singh

2

Lieutenant General
Thakur Nathu Singh
A Fearless Nationalist

Thakur Nathu Singh was the second Indian officer to pass out from Sandhurst and achieve three-star rank in the Indian Army, the first being Maharaj Rajendra Sinhji. Though not very well known outside the army, he was one of the most colourful of our military leaders. He rose only to the second-highest rank and appointment in the profession, but this was more by choice than merit. He could have become the first Indian Commander-in-Chief had he só wished, but he declined in deference to Cariappa, who was senior to him. Though trained by the British, he was a true Indian and never allowed anyone to forget this. A nationalist to the core, he was frequently in trouble for his anti-British views. His brushes with authority were many, and were it not for the legendary British sense of fair play and justice, he would not have survived in uniform.

Nathu Singh was born in 1900 (although school records show his birthdate as 10 May 1902) at Gumanpura in the princely state of Dungarpur in Rajputana. He was the only child of Thakur Hamir Singhji of Gumanpura, a nobleman from the vassalage of Dungarpur. Unfortunately, he lost both his parents before he was seven years old. During a visit to his village,

Maharawal Vijay Singhji, the ruler of Dungarpur State, was impressed by his intelligence and quick wit and took the young boy under his wing. The orphaned Nathu was educated at the Maharawal's own alma mater, the prestigious Mayo College in Ajmer, along with other scions of the Rajput nobility. In school, he topped his classes and was nicknamed 'Baghi' (rebel) by his colleagues for his outspoken and forthright ways.

The Maharawal, who was a descendant of the senior branch of the Udaipur royal family—one of his ancestors, Jaimull, had died defending Chittor against Akbar—was himself a great patriot. It was the Maharawal who had planted the seed of nationalism in Nathu Singh's heart, which took root and flowered as he grew older. In 1911, he visited Delhi to attend the Grand Durbar being held for the coronation of King George V. Far from being impressed by the pomp and pageantry, he was filled with shame and revulsion at the subservience of the Indian rulers who had gathered there to pay obeisance to the Crown. This incident made a deep impression on the young boy, awakening the first stirrings of nationalism within him. While in Delhi, he also came into contact with the Nehru family. After the age of 15, he began to take an interest in national affairs and attended a few meetings of the All India Congress Committee. In 1915, he met Jawaharlal Nehru for the first time and then his father, Motilal Nehru.

Nathu Singh's background and heritage—he was from the Mairtia clan of Rathore Rajputs who were renowned for their valour—naturally inclined him towards a military profession. His guardian, the Maharawal, also wanted him to follow the martial tradition of his forbears and join the army. Unfortunately, the Maharawal died in 1918 when Nathu Singh was still in school. This left him alone in the world, without a guide or friend. Soon after he returned from school in 1920, he had the first of his many rows with the British. The Political Officer in Dungarpur was a diehard imperialist, who treated all Indians as subjects of the British Crown. He asked Nathu Singh to follow certain orders that were contrary to the wishes of the Rajmata (Queen Mother). Nathu Singh refused and there was a fearful ruckus. However, the British Political Officer later developed a liking for the young firebrand and advised the Rajmata to send him to the Royal Military College in Sandhurst, which had just been opened to Indians. Nathu Singh wanted to become a soldier, but not under the British. He would have preferred the army, or even the police, in one of the princely states of Rajputana. But this was not to be. He bowed to his guardian's wishes and applied to the Royal Military College. He had been an exceptionally bright student and this, coupled with his background, enabled him to clear the written examination and the interviews with the C-in-C and the Viceroy. He sailed for England in July 1921, along with Kumar Shri Kishensinhji and Gurbachan Singh. They were later joined by Charles Ba Thien from Burma.

Nathu Singh spent a year-and-a-half at Sandhurst. The only other cadet from Rajputana, Kunwar Sheodutt Singh, who had joined six months earlier, became his guide and close friend. Nathu Singh took the tough regimen in his stride, doing well in all activities. His British instructors and colleagues, though impressed by his intellect, were somewhat surprised at his boldness and lack of servility, which they had generally come to expect from Indians. Nathu Singh disliked the British and made no effort to conceal this. Unlike most other Indians of that time, he did not suffer from an inferiority complex and considered himself the equal, if not the better, of any Englishman. One can imagine the difficulties he must have encountered at Sandhurst because of his views. In fact, his anti-British attitude, which persisted throughout his service, frequently led him into trouble. The British saw him as a rebel, while his Indian colleagues promptly christened him Fauji Gandhi, a name which Nathu himself did not relish. By this time, Mahatma Gandhi had begun his non-cooperation movement in India and Nathu seemed to be following in his footsteps. However, much as he admired Gandhi for his patriotism, he did not share his creed of non-violence and considered his methods of achieving independence through non-cooperation as impractical. He believed that apart from causing delays, such tactics would only serve to antagonise the British and harden their attitude even further. A better strategy would be for Indians to gain a strong presence in the services, both civil and military. They could then weaken the British structure from within and take over at an opportune moment.

Addressing the cadets at Sandhurst, General Jacob of the Indian Army told them that since the British were likely to be in India for a long time, the best among them should join the Indian Army. Nathu Singh immediately sought an interview with the Commandant and told him that if the British had no intention of leaving, he was not interested in getting his commission.

While in England, he also met Subhas Chandra Bose, who was in the Indian Civil Service (ICS) at that time. They had a common meeting ground in their dislike of British rule and the desire to be rid of it. However, they differed in their views regarding the best method to achieve this goal. Both were strong personalities, and their frequent interactions helped in fuelling the fires of nationalism, which burned in the hearts of these great patriots. Their meetings also generated a feeling of mutual respect and admiration. Two decades later, when the British government ordered the trial of the Indian National Army (INA) prisoners, one of the few men in uniform who protested against the decision was Nathu Singh.

On passing out from Sandhurst, Nathu Singh was commissioned on 1 February 1923 and assigned to the 1/7 Rajput Regiment. All newly commissioned Indian officers had to do an attachment with a British battalion. Second Lieutenant Nathu Singh was attached to the 2nd Battalion, the Prince of Wales' Volunteers, which was located at Mhow in central India. His CO, Lieutenant Colonel B. Ritchie, found him a keen and energetic officer who was very popular with both officers and men. Recommending his retention in the army, he wrote: 'I certify that, in my opinion, the retention of Second Lieutenant

Thakur Nathu Singh 1/7th Rajput Regiment, attached 2nd Bn. The Prince of Wales's Volunteers, is, in every respect, desirable, and likely to be advantageous to the Service . . .' It seems that Major General L.R. Vaughan, the GOC Central Province District was also of a similar opinion. On 28 August 1924, while endorsing his remarks in the annual confidential report on Second Lieutenant Nathu Singh, he wrote: 'One of the most promising Indians I have met. He should make good if he continues trying.'

After a year with the British battalion, he was posted to his parent unit, the 1/7 Rajputs—also known as QVOLI—then located at Dardoni in the NWFP. He served with the battalion from 1923 to 1926. During these three years, he worked hard to learn the ropes. However, unlike most subalterns, he did not follow the dictum of being seen but not heard. He had strong views, which he did not hesitate to articulate. His antipathy towards the British and their ways could not remain hidden, and this soon brought him into conflict with his superiors.

Nathu Singh's first brush with authority was over the matter of dining in the officers' mess. He was a high-caste Hindu and initially refused to dine in the mess with the other officers. He made it known that in his home at Dungarpur, his parents would never have permitted him to share a table with an Englishman, regardless of his station, and he found no reason to deviate from his religious beliefs. This naturally created a huge commotion and he was hauled over the coals for it. Though finally he did agree to dine in the mess, he did so with a great deal of condescension. His CO, Lieutenant Colonel A.H. Macleverty, wrote on 1 February 1925:

> Quick and intelligent at his work, and professionally upto the standard of his rank; good at games. Must become more liberal in his views if he expects to come upto the standard of a British officer in all respects . . . I do not consider him well suited for regimental life . . . he has strong religious convictions, which

colour every question . . . He finds mess irksome, and states that he cannot dine with Europeans when at his home . . . I do not think that his heart is in his profession, as he has more than once stated that his ambition is service in his state . . . His wife is and must remain in purdah, which will seriously affect the social side of regimental life . . .

According to the custom then in vogue, for an officer to be retained in service, it was required that in addition to the CO two other senior officers of the battalion also give their recommendations. On 3 February 1925, Major B.S.A.F. Greville wrote:

I am of the opinion that the retention of 2nd Lieutenant Nathu Singh 1/7th Rajput Regiment in the Indian Army is undesirable . . . Owing to his high Hindu principles he conveys the impression that he is conferring a great concession on his brother officers by dining with them . . . He will find it difficult to come into line with British officers and, in every respect, take their place . . . On the other hand, I consider he has an excellent knowledge of his profession and has good powers of imparting it to others. He is keen on games and speaks good English.

This opinion was echoed by another officer of his battalion, Major E.M.C. Brander, who wrote:

Considering that 2/Lieut Thakur Nathu Singh has been trained at Sandhurst, he is obviously very backward in his ideas, which not only make things difficult for him but awkward for the other officers . . . He has been dining in the mess, but on account of his strict religious principles it is obviously distasteful to him . . . He appears to be completely dominated by his religion . . . I do not recommend his retention in the Indian Army. This is to be regretted as professionally he is very competent. He is intelligent, picks up things quickly and is also good at games.

The recommendations by Nathu Singh's CO and the two officers were endorsed by other senior officers in the chain. If anything, they used stronger words. Major General A.L. Jacob, GOC Waziristan District, wrote:

> This officer is entirely out of place in a regiment. The fact of his considering it a mark of condescension on his part having his meals in the mess with the other officers speaks for itself. From enquiry it appears that he himself personally had no wish to proceed to Sandhurst . . . He wishes to serve in either the army or police in a Native State, and I strongly recommend that he be allowed to do so.

Finally, General Claud W. Jacob, GOC-in-C Northern Command, wrote: 'The sooner this officer is removed from the army the better.' With this, it appeared that Nathu Singh's fate was sealed. He was called for a final interview with the Army Commander, at which his CO was also present. General Jacob was impressed by Nathu Singh's family and educational background, as well as his obvious intelligence. He decided to give him another chance, and sent Nathu Singh off after advising him to adjust to army life. He then gave the CO a dressing-down for not appreciating the impressive qualities of the young Indian officer and handling him properly. Nathu Singh who was standing outside the door, heard the entire conversation, which he often recounted in later years.

When the first report on him was written, he had been in the battalion for just three weeks. After a year, however, his CO and the other officers had begun to view him differently. Nathu Singh had obviously taken the Army Commander's advice to heart and had become moderate in his views as well as his behaviour. On 1 April 1926, Lieutenant Colonel B.S.A.F. Greville, who was now commanding the battalion, wrote:

> A keen, hard-working officer who takes great interest in his work . . . With regard to the adverse remarks in last year's

report, he has shown much improvement in all respects and appears to be much more broadminded in his views . . . His manners in the mess are now satisfactory and he finds no difficulties in the feeding arrangements . . . conveys the idea that he is very pleased and happy with army life.

Apart from his religious belief, Nathu Singh's reluctance to dine in the mess can be attributed to the fact that he was married, and since his wife was in *purdah*, as most Rajput women of station were in those days, he was hesitant to leave her alone at home while he dined in the mess. He had been married at a very young age to Surya Kumari, the daughter of Thakur Laxman Singh, a highborn Rajput chieftain from Mewar in Rajputana. He had two daughters and three sons, two of whom joined the services. The eldest daughter, Chandra Kumari, who was born in November 1927, married a police officer. The second, Anand Kumari, was born in March 1929. She married Major Guman Singh, who later commanded his father-in-law's battalion, 1/7 Rajputs, during the Jammu and Kashmir operations in 1947–48, when it performed with legendary gallantry and suffered heavy casualties. Nathu Singh's eldest son, Pratap Singh, was born in July 1931. He was commissioned into an elite cavalry regiment, but had to leave after a few years due to ill health. The second son, Ran Vijay Singh, was born in December 1932. He joined the Indian Navy and was trained at Dartmouth, from where he passed out in 1952. He retired as a Rear Admiral. The third, Amarjeet Singh, who was born in December 1935, joined a tea company.

In 1926, Nathu Singh was posted to 10/7 Rajput, which was the regiment's training battalion, at Fatehgarh in the United Provinces. He was there for three years before being posted back to his parent battalion in 1929. During his stay in Fatehgarh, he continued his association with Congress leaders, such as the Nehrus, Muhammad Ali Jinnah and Sarojini Naidu, whom he had met while giving evidence before the Skeen Committee. The committee, which had been appointed in 1926 with Sir Andrew Skeen as Chairman, was to examine the possibility of setting up an Indian Sandhurst. Pandit Motilal Nehru and M.A. Jinnah were members, along with several others. The committee examined 122 witnesses, which included commanding officers, KCIOs, their parents, and VCOs. Among the KCIOs who gave evidence were Cariappa and Nathu Singh. It was during this period that Pandit Motilal Nehru, who resigned from the committee in March 1926, heard about Singh's desire to leave the service. A nationalist to the core, Singh was unhappy serving the Indian Army—an instrument of British power. Motilal Nehru spent a couple of evenings at Nathu Singh's house in Fatehgarh, where he also met some British officers and their families. He strongly advised Singh to stick to the army instead of joining the national movement or the political department of the Government of India, or return to Dungarpur State Service, all options that Singh was considering. Nathu Singh followed this advice and continued to serve in the army, even though his heart was not in it.

While in Fatehgarh, his battalion was graced by a visit from the C-in-C, Field Marshal Sir William Birdwood. All the officers had been lined up to be introduced to him. Nathu Singh was wearing a *safa* (turban) instead of the usual regulation hat. He had been wearing the *safa* ever since he had been commissioned and, surprisingly, no one had objected to it. When the C-in-C reached Nathu, he mistook him for a VCO, who normally wore such headgear. Shaking his hand, he asked in Hindustani: *'Kaisa hai, Sahib?'* (How are you?) VCOs were usually addressed as 'Sahib', as JCOs in the Indian Army are even today. Without batting an eyelid, Nathu replied, also in Hindustani: *'Bahut accha hai, Sahib.'* (Very well, Sir.) By now, the CO had realised the confusion and introduced him to the C-in-C, as Mister Nathu Singh. The Chief quickly said: 'How do you do, Nathu Singh?' Once again, he replied: 'Very well, Sir.'

Nathu Singh returned to 1/7 Rajput, which was in Razmak, in Waziristan, in 1929. The battalion moved to Peshawar in

1930, and in the following year Nathu Singh was promoted Captain. Soon after this, the C-in-C, Field Marshal Birdwood again visited the battalion. He enquired about the number of Indian officers present in the unit. When told that Nathu Singh was the only one, he came up to him and said: 'How are you getting on? Remember, one of these days you will command this battalion. Learn how to do it now, so that you can do it well in battle.'

At that time, although Indian officers were members of the officers' mess, they were not given membership of the club, which admitted only Europeans. This created a peculiar situation, which was resolved by making them honorary members. In 1933, three Indian officers, who were honorary members of the Peshawar Club, applied for permanent membership and were blackballed. When Nathu Singh heard about it, he was furious. He had already resigned from his honorary membership, and he now advised other Indian officers to do the same. As a result, all Indians resigned en masse. This caused great consternation and the club president wrote to Nathu, on 21 November 1932:

> The Club Committee hopes that you will accept their invitation to become an Honorary Member of the Club, as they consider it would help the matter when, at a suitable time, the case for full membership is again brought up for discussion. The Committee much regretted your decision to resign from the Club the year before last.

Copies of the letter were sent by the Club to other Indian officers. Nathu Singh's anger shows in his remarks on the letter, which is marked 'strictly personal'.

> Left to me, I would have much liked to get the Bar ploughed by donkeys or better still by the breed mules, where the plot for blackballing of a few of the WOGS, who wanted to join as permanent members instead of Hon. was hatched.

Soon after this, a dinner was held at the club to celebrate the satisfactory conclusion of the Mohmand operations, for which Nathu was later mentioned in dispatches.* He decided to boycott the dinner, and the other Indian officers did the same. There was a furore. His CO, Lieutenant Colonel V.R. Munton, who was on leave at the time, wrote from England on 16 November 1933:

> Blaxland tells me he has put you in for a mention and I met Gen. Coleridge yesterday and he tells me he has forwarded it, so I hope you will get it and I add my heartiest congratulations. But about this dinner at the club question. Gen. Coleridge told me that you engineered the whole refusal. At this distance it is very difficult to visualise the show and to gauge what the atmosphere was at the time—I will look into this on my return. But I do feel it was a damned silly thing not to go to the dinner. A regiment is rather a sacred thing if you work it out, and it is hallowed by a hundred odd years of tradition & blood. To let it down merely to vent a private grievance sounds very petty. You probably didn't mean it as such but it savours of non-cooperation—and the latter in the Army is absolutely disaster. To take up the attitude of a die-hard isn't going to do much good. Quite apart from the fact that at the next show the Bn. will probably be left behind, your own military career may be affected. A successful staff officer has to show tact and sympathy, and be prepared to advance to a halfway line.

On his return from England, when Lieutenant Colonel Munton investigated the affair, he found that the mischief had been caused by some British officers and not Nathu Singh. Of course,

---

* In earlier times, before the invention of the telegraph and telephone, commanders in the field sent written reports to the King or the Commander-in-Chief. These were known as 'dispatches'. Today, deeds that do not merit a gallantry award are mentioned in dispatches. This is akin to a minor gallantry award, minus the formal presentation of a medal/cross for the recipient.

he had declined to attend the dinner, but this was in response to the blackballing of the three Indian officers. In fact, by standing up for his Indian colleagues, Nathu Singh gained the respect of several British officers, who felt that the club rules were unfair.

In 1934, 1/7 Rajputs moved to Secunderabad in the Deccan. By now, Nathu Singh and the battalion had got used to each other. At that time, as it is now, the Staff College was considered a stepping stone to higher ranks in the army, and all officers attempted to clear the entrance examination as soon as they were eligible. However, before they could do so, they had to be recommended by their COs. In Nathu Singh's case, it was not just ambition that spurred him, but a burning desire to prove to the British that he was better than they thought him to be.

For three years Nathu Singh was denied the recommendation to compete for the Staff College examination on the grounds that he lacked experience. Naturally, he was livid with rage, especially as several other officers, junior to him, were granted permission. However, he could do little but wait. Then a new CO took over, and in 1935 Nathu Singh was given the necessary recommendation. He appeared for the entrance examination and not only qualified but secured a competitive vacancy. In fact, he secured 915 marks out of 1000 in the Strategy paper, a record that still remains unequalled. The fact that he had done so without any guidance or coaching was noted, and commended by his CO. For Nathu Singh, this success was especially sweet, as his earlier CO had considered him inexperienced and not good enough to take the examination.

At Quetta, one of his instructors was B.L. Montgomery, who later achieved fame as the victor of El Alamien. 'Monty' was hugely impressed by Nathu's sharp mind and grasp of tactical problems, and predicted that he would go far in the profession. He was known for his anti-Indian bias and had a poor opinion of Indians and their intellectual capabilities. He is once said to have remarked, 'I do not like things Indian,' to which Nathu Singh promptly retorted: 'Then what are you doing here, Sir?'

After successfully completing the course at the Staff College, Quetta, in 1937, Nathu Singh was posted as Staff Captain of the Naushera Brigade. After the outbreak of World War II, he was promoted Major and appointed Brigade Major of the same brigade. He was on excellent terms with his first brigade commander, Brigadier Nye, who later became Vice Chief of Imperial General Staff. However, he was at loggerheads with Nye's successor because of his pro-Congress views. In 1942, he was packed off to Imphal as GSO 2 (Chemical Warfare) of IV British Corps. He was mainly concerned with the evacuation of refugees, who poured into India as a result of the Japanese invasion of Burma. He literally saved thousands of refugees from certain death, and his contribution was acknowledged when he was transferred to 2/7 Rajput as the second-in-command.

By now, Nathu Singh had put in almost 20 years of service and should have been promoted Lieutenant Colonel and given command of a battalion. However, his promotion was delayed by almost a year, probably due to his pro-nationalist stance, and he remained the second-in-command of 2/7 Rajput. During the Quit India movement in 1942, he was asked to suppress an agitation. Though he placed a picket on the route the rally was to follow, he persuaded the Congress leaders, with whom he was acquainted, to take another route. On the following day, the CO again asked him to stop the agitators. Nathu Singh objected, saying that it was unfair to ask him to shoot at his own countrymen, who were only asking for their freedom. He requested the CO to give the job to some other officer, but this was rejected, and he was told that if he disobeyed orders he would be courtmartialled.

Nathu Singh refused to comply and the matter was reported to the District Commander, Major General Bruce Scott. Most British officers could barely conceal their glee at the thought that the 'diehard' had finally been trapped. When he was marched up to General Scott, Nathu Singh defended himself as a 'conscientious objector', quoting similar cases in Ireland.

As luck would have it, Scott turned out to be an Irishman. He appreciated the stand taken by Nathu Singh and let him off.

On 20 October 1943, he was promoted Lieutenant Colonel and given command of 9/7 Rajput at Chhindwara. When he took over the battalion, it had been graded 'unfit for war' after having been mauled by the Japanese in Burma. Nathu Singh set to work like a man possessed, and within a few months had succeeded in turning around his battalion. He was full of energy and determination, and his hard work paid off. During the next inspection, the Brigade Commander could find little fault with the battalion, which was now graded fit for war. In fact, it was declared the best battalion in the division, and Major General 'Tiger' Curtis, GOC 14 Indian Division, congratulated them at a parade in front of the entire division. The irony that this had been achieved by Nathu Singh, who had been considered unsuitable by his CO 20 years earlier, was not lost on his British superiors or his colleagues.

The Divisional Commander, 'Tiger' Curtis, was known as a man who was difficult to please. Once, Nathu Singh was asked to conduct a demonstration for all officers of the division. Curtis was so impressed by Nathu Singh's performance that he saluted him in front of everyone—a rare honour for a subordinate officer, and that too an Indian. After this, Nathu Singh became the GOC's blue-eyed boy. This was resented by Brigadier Talbot, Commander 109 Indian Infantry Brigade, who was Nathu Singh's immediate superior. However, even he admired Nathu Singh for his professional capabilities. One day, after Nathu Singh had left the battalion, Brigadier Talbot came to visit 9/7 Rajput. While talking about Nathu Singh, he remarked: 'Your previous CO, with his electric moustaches, could get anything done.'

About a year later Singh received orders posting him as Commanding Officer, 3 Maratha Light Infantry in Italy. He was both surprised and annoyed, as he had been expecting to get command of his own battalion, 1/7 Rajput. Command of a battalion in action would entitle him to quick promotion, and he would probably get a chance to command a brigade in the field and become the first Indian to do so. But Nathu Singh wanted command of his own battalion, and nothing else. He appealed to the C-in-C, General Auchinleck, under whom he had served in the NWFP and who had become his mentor. 1/7 Rajput had been part of Brigadier Auchinleck's brigade during the Mohmand operations in 1933. Nathu Singh was the battalion's Adjutant and could be seen galloping from company to company, conveying orders and instructions under heavy fire. Auchinleck was impressed by his courage and mentioned him in dispatches. This was to mark the beginning of a long association between Nathu Singh and the 'Auk'.

The Auk promptly had his transfer orders rescinded and Nathu Singh assumed command of 1/7 Rajput on 17 September 1944. When World War II ended, he was commanding the battalion in the Andamans, and accepted the formal surrender of Japanese troops in the Andaman and Nicobar islands from Vice Admiral Teejo Hara on behalf of the Supreme Allied Commander, South East Asia. It was from the Andamans that he wrote the famous letter to Auchinleck protesting against the INA trials. Running into eight pages and couched in the strongest language, it brings out his anger and anguish at the unfairness of the trials and its repercussions.

In his letter dated 17 December 1945, Nathu enclosed a note headed 'Repercussions of the INA Trials on the Minds of an Indian in the Army.' It summarised the following main reasons which led to the formation of the INA:

1. The general treatment of Indian officers, including denial of Indian food in messes, and the freedom to wear Indian clothes, listen to Indian music, or talk in their native language.
2. Brainwashing, propaganda and torture inflicted on Indian prisoners of war by the Japanese.

3. The British government tried to satisfy the demands for Indianisation of the army by opening entry to Sandhurst and establishing the Prince of Wales Royal Military College (now called the Rashtriya Indian Military College or RIMC). With only five vacancies at Sandhurst, and only one school to prepare candidates, it was a hoax.

4. The Eight Unit Scheme, which ensured that British officers would not have to serve under Indians, effectively segregated them.

5. Restricting entry of Indians to Artillery, Navy and Air Force to negligible numbers.

6. The opening of the Indian Military Academy (IMA) was supposed to be a step towards Indianisation. However, whereas KCIOs were posted as company officers, ICOs were given command of platoons, replacing VCOs. Hence, there was no reduction in the number of British officers.

7. After the establishment of the IMA, Indians ceased to get King's commissions and were offered Indian commissions instead. This conveyed the impression that Indian officers were inferior, and were equivalent to the Provincial Civil Service, which is subordinate to the ICS, with which KCIOs were equated. As a result, the upper classes stopped sending their wards to the army and preferred the ICS.

8. Discrimination between KCIOs and ICOs in terms of pay, though they did the same job and had to maintain the same standard of living.

9. ICOs took the place of VCOs in the units, leading to reduction in vacancies for the latter.

10. As soon as World War II began, Indianisation was thrown to the winds, based on the premise that units officered by Indians could not be trusted.

Nathu Singh felt that all these factors, when put together, cast grave doubts on whether the British were really serious about Indianisation, or whether they were using it as merely window-dressing to impress the public and the outside world. Though 2.5 million Indians had fought in the two wars, not one had been able to make it to the rank of general. Important appointments dealing with operations were denied to them and only a handful were given command of units. When compared with the Soviet Union, which took shape at about the same time as Indianisation began in India, the disparities became obvious. However, his most scathing comments were reserved for the unfair treatment meted out to Indians:

> The formation of the INA was not alone the work of its leaders like Bose, or of the Jap Opportunist. The creation and growth of the INA was a direct result of the continuous unjust treatment of Indian officers in the Army. It is the natural heritage of years of dissatisfaction, disappointment and disgust of various elements in the Indian Army. The present members of the INA are to be blamed for their conduct, but equally to blame is the Imperialist Anti-Indian British element in the army who, by their talk and action, daily estranged the otherwise loyal mind of the Indian, and last but not the least to blame are the British reverses in the Far East, which left the Indian soldiers to their fate.
>
> Time is critical, and at this juncture, large issues are at stake. Momentous decisions have to be made, and on them will depend the future Indo–British relations. The previous services of those in the INA who actually fought for the British till they were captured by the enemy deserves lenient treatment. Wisdom and foresight suggest that the crimes of the members of the INA be condoned.

One can only marvel at the brashness of a lieutenant colonel addressing the C-in-C on such a sensitive political issue. No less surprising is the Auk's response. Far from taking umbrage, he understood that the feelings expressed by Nathu Singh stemmed from nationalistic fervour rather than a rebellious disposition. He not only chose to ignore the fact that Nathu Singh had violated protocol by addressing the C-in-C directly, but wrote back to him in his own hand. He could sense the anguish in Singh's heart and could empathise with him. However, he felt disturbed and hurt by the bitterness in Singh's letter and admonished him, much as a schoolmaster would his favourite pupil. The letter reveals the Auk's deep attachment to the Indian Army and his fondness for his Indian subordinate.

Marked 'Personal and Private', the Auk's handwritten letter of 19 February 1946, reads:

> I know that many of the views expressed by you are based on fact. All the same, I do feel that you are wrong to dwell so much on past mistakes and bitterness and I know that many of your opinions are exaggerated and unfair. I say *I know* this and it grieves me to think that you, whom I regard as an old friend, should deliberately rake up old errors and misunderstandings . . . You are one of the people on whom I had hoped to rely . . . I was deeply disturbed and I may say, disappointed by the general attitude of mind expressed in your note, but I still hope that it does not represent your permanent frame of mind, as this would cause me sorrow . . . Needless to say, you have my assurance that this matter is private between us. Your note will not be seen by anyone else and it will not have the slightest effect on your official standing, so far as I am concerned, because I realise that you would not have written as you did had you not had full trust in my good faith and friendship for you . . . I do value your having written to me as freely and openly as you did . . .

In May 1946 Nathu Singh was promoted Colonel and posted as Deputy Director, Personnel Services, in the Adjutant General's Branch in Army HQ, which was then located at Meerut. Very soon, differences developed between him and the Director, Brigadier Duke, which necessitated the transfer of one of them.

Under normal circumstances, Nathu Singh would have been the one to go, but the Auk decided to transfer Brigadier Duke instead, and Nathu Singh was promoted Brigadier and appointed Director in his place. Nathu Singh pleaded with the C-in-C to transfer him, rather than Brigadier Duke, but the Auk was adamant. Perhaps he felt that Nathu Singh was in the right or perhaps it was his fondness for Singh that led him to take this decision.

Nathu Singh's closeness to the Auk can be gauged from the fact that when the latter heard about his differences with Brigadier Duke, he called Singh to Delhi and invited him to stay at his own house. This house was later renamed Teen Murti Bhavan and became the Prime Minister's house in Nehru's time. The Auk even took Singh to England so that he could study the selection procedure for officers in the British Army. When the time came for Nathu Singh to return to Meerut, he asked the ADC for the bill for the drinks he had, while staying with the C-in-C. The ADC told him to take it up with the C-in-C himself, which he did. The Auk said: 'Don't be silly, Nathu. You are my guest.' To which Nathu replied: 'Sir, I wish I had known this earlier. I would have had a few more drinks.'

Soon after becoming Director, Nathu Singh submitted a paper on reorganising the army and its officer cadre, which was approved by Auchinleck. A training school was immediately set up at Yol for emergency commissioned officers (ECOs), so that they could be granted permanent regular commission (PRC). This helped about 4,000 ECOs to get absorbed in the regular army as ICOs. It was around this time that he was offered the post of C-in-C after Independence. Sardar Baldev Singh, the Defence Minister in the Interim Government, made this offer at a tea party that he was hosting, in the presence of several other leaders, including the premiers of Punjab and the NWFP. He followed it up with a letter on 22 November 1946:

Your letter of 21st November has reached me. You have been selected and earmarked to be the first C-in-C of India, with command over the three Defence Services. This decision has been arrived at after the Muslim League joined the 'Interim Government', and with the consent of all the Political Parties comprising the Government. It is on the recommendation of the present C-in-C, and with the approval of the Governor General, the Viceroy, and may be the HMG. The approval of the officers senior to you does not arise.

The letter goes on to answer several other questions raised by Nathu Singh, such as the acceleration of nationalisation, the integration of the three defence services, 'dominion status' for the country, and the appointment of an Indian as the next Governor General after Lord Wavell. Baldev Singh also made it clear that after the 'transfer of power', the C-in-C would be answerable to the Ministry of Defence. Nathu Singh is said to have declined the offer, since he felt that the appointment should rightfully go to Cariappa, who was his senior. In fact, the next letter from Nathu Singh to Baldev Singh contains no reference at all to the offer of promotion. Instead, it deals with a very important subject—the Partition of India. Dated 24 November 1946, it reads:

> In our case, unless we remain within the Commonwealth maybe for a short period of a year or two, it is clear to me that by the Cabinet Mission's latest suggestion of groupings into zones, they may have made sure of cutting the country into three pieces and controlling India, the subcontinent, as they have no doubt they will play havoc with us. To put them in their place, I know Pandit Nehru, and through him, the Congress are trying to do so. But please beware lest India is broken up by bolstering the Muslim League and other communal forces—Sikhs' demand for Khalistan, the Princes' bid for Federation and encouraging Hyderabad and Jammu and Kashmir becoming independent by joining hands with other reactionaries . . .

The Defence Minister replied, on 27 November 1946:

> Your letter of 24th has reached me, its contents are much
> appreciated by Pt Jawaharlalji, Sardar Patel, and my other
> colleagues of the Executive Council, including the members of
> the Muslim League . . . I know you are keeping yourself well
> out of the present constantly changing political developments,
> much influenced by the British Imperialists in combination
> with Mr Jinnah and other leaders, and I expect of you to keep
> a special eye on the various communities that are being tapped
> and influenced by them . . . I understand you are preparing a
> paper on acceleration of Nationalisation . . . I would much like
> to discuss this very vital matter with you before you finalise
> your proposals for the consideration of the Gopalaswamy
> Nationalisation Committee.

Nathu Singh and Sarojini Naidu had given evidence before
the Skeen Committee on the same day, and over the years had
become close friends. Sarojini insisted that Nathu call her Mah
(Mother), which is how she signed her letters to him. The two
often corresponded, and at this point Nathu wrote to her about
the problems facing the country and nationalisation of the army.
In her response on 9 January 1947, Sarojini Naidu wrote:

> Dear Nathoo Singh,
>
> Many Thanks for sending me your very illuminating Shot
> in the Dark. It gives a correct picture of the situation from
> every angle.
>   . . . As the security of the country depends entirely upon
> the army, the army should not be based on what the country
> can afford to have for its defence. It will be fatal to rely on a
> small armed force, however efficient and modernly equipped
> it may be; because our country is vulnerable, bristling with
> traitors and the fifth columnists in millions in every part of

India. We all know the character and honesty of our potential enemies and so-called friends.

Our leaders should get advice from us Indians in the army and other branches . . . and not, repeat not, from hirelings, who have their own axes to grind . . .

One thing more, probably you have noticed but have not mentioned, is how the Army is at a disadvantage because of that 'steel frame',* who wants to have the last word in everything pertaining to the Army. That steel frame must go.

Once again, many thanks for sending me the most illuminating 'Shot in the Dark'.

Yours
Mah

In February 1947, Nathu Singh was called to give evidence before the Armed Forces Nationalisation Committee. Set up in November 1946, the committee consisted of Sir Gopalaswamy Ayyangar as Chairman, Pandit Hriday Nath Kunzru, Muhammad Ismail Khan, Sardar Sampuran Singh, Major General D.A.L. Wade, Brigadier K.S. Thimayya, Wing Commander Mehr Singh and Commander H.M.S. Choudri as members, and Lieutenant Colonel B.M. Kaul as Secretary. Auchinleck had indicated that of the 22,000 officers in the Indian Army, only 8,500 were Indians. Even among them, most were ECOs, with very little service or experience. If the Indian Army were to be nationalised immediately, officers with less than nine years' service would be commanding battalions. While this might be acceptable in times of war, it would do incalculable harm during peacetime, when officers would need to exercise judgement, wisdom, patience and a knowledge of human nature, which could only be acquired with experience. He warned against the dangers of entrusting the command of the army to officers who lacked experience,

---

* The Indian Civil Service was referred to as the 'steel frame' of the British empire.

especially in the prevailing situation when disruptive forces were swaying public opinion.

Nathu Singh was in Meerut when he received a questionnaire that covered several aspects of the problem. On 8 February 1947, he wrote a personal letter to Thimayya, who was a member of the committee, in which he suggested that before Indian officers gave evidence, each issue should first be discussed 'in-house' by the army. Unless this was done, it was likely that the committee might be misled, since most officers lacked knowledge and experience, and did not have at their disposal the necessary data to arrive at valid conclusions. He recommended that:

> Each problem should be thrashed out by experienced Indian officers selected by the Nationalisation Committee, prior to the matter coming up before them. It is in this manner that the Committee will be able to get well-considered opinions for their final recommendations.

When Nathu Singh appeared before the committee, the British Prime Minister had already announced the date for transfer of power as June 1948. Nathu Singh suggested that by that date, Indians should be in full control of the army, and in order to achieve this they must begin to hold responsible positions straightaway. He strongly refuted the committee's suggestion of a military mission to continue after the transfer of power, recommending instead the appointment of advisers who would be responsible to the Indian government instead of the War Office, as would happen in the case of a military mission. He also objected to the suggestion of keeping Indian officers as apprentices or understudies for important appointments. Instead, he argued that they should be made deputies, which would give them both authority as well as responsibility. When asked about the partition of the army in case power was transferred to more than one state, Nathu Singh replied that he was vehemently opposed to it. In fact, he said that it was not possible to divide the army. He ended by saying: 'I suggest that Indians should be consulted in all future planning at AFHQ. This has not been done in the past. We are going to be holding the baby soon. We must be taken into confidence.'

The Armed Forces Nationalisation Committee submitted its report on 12 May 1947. However, by this time the date of transfer of power had been advanced to 15 August 1947, and the committee's recommendations became redundant. Nathu Singh again wrote to the Defence Minister on 31 May 1947 after reading his broadcast about partition. By this time, he had been transferred to Derajat Force in Dera Ismail Khan. In his letter to Sardar Baldev Singh he wrote:

. . . I was amazed and shocked to read your broadcast in the paper about the possibility of a division of the defence services. As an Indian I hate it. My conception is that to partition India would be equivalent of committing rape of our Motherland and to partition the defence services means nothing short of civil war within a few years['] time . . . You will play an important part in the final shape of things to come. What about your collecting a selected number of senior officers from all classes and communities from the services and forcing down the throat of uncompromising political leaders the wisdom of a united India staying within the Empire . . .

The Defence Minister replied, on 12 June 1947:

. . . I entirely agree with you that the division of India would be equivalent to committing rape of our Motherland and the division of the Defence Forces will have a serious effect on the Military. If in case there is no other solution to our political problem except the division of the country, then [the] division of the Army is inevitable, and this is what I have stated in my statement . . . I have noted your suggestion about certain officers. We have at present a number of problems facing us and we will need the help of senior Indian officers, but the final decision will have to be taken after the Provinces of Bengal and the Punjab have given their verdict about partition of the Provinces.

Nathu Singh's correspondence with Sardar Baldev clearly reveals his concern for the unity and integrity of India. He felt that the British were deliberately partitioning India to make it weak, even hoping that it would become 'ungovernable' and force the warring factions to ask them to extend their stay in the colony. He felt that the armed forces, being unaffected by the virus of religion and communalism, were capable of holding the country together and thereby avoiding Partition. He never forgave Nehru and the other leaders for their failure to consult the armed forces, or take them into confidence before deciding to accept Partition. At this time, Nathu Singh was posted on the North West Frontier, from where he could do little but write letters. Also, he was only a brigadier, and though the most voluble of the KCIOs, he was not the seniormost among them. Had this been so he may have been able to wield more influence and perhaps events might have taken a different turn. It is pertinent to note here that in January 1947, Cariappa had been sent to the Imperial Defence College in the UK, from where he was recalled only in July, and was thus absent at this very critical juncture when the fate of the Indian Army was being decided.

As mentioned earlier, when India achieved Independence, Nathu Singh was in command of the Derajat Force at Dera Ismail Khan. He not only witnessed the horrors of Partition but played an important role in the evacuation of refugees. He was shocked at the behaviour of some British officers of the civil service, who were encouraging the local Muslim population to threaten Hindus and force them to migrate to India. He tried his best to check this, and brought it to the attention of the political leaders, who pleaded helplessness. He also had a row on this matter with his Divisional Commander, Major General

W. Fleming, and the Army Commander, Sir Frank Messervy, who had him transferred as Commander, Kamptee Sub Area, on 6 September 1947. Soon after taking up his new appointment, he had a tiff with the GOC-in-C Lieutenant General Goddard. Nathu Singh had learned that the garrison at Secunderabad was being reduced, and anticipating that troops would be needed for the Hyderabad operations to be undertaken later, he promptly put a stop to it. Goddard was furious and placed Hyderabad under his direct command. He, too, got Nathu Singh transferred, this time to Kurukshetra to oversee the refugee camp that had been set up after Partition and the large-scale migration which followed. The camp had about 20,000 people, and it was not easy to keep its agitated inmates satisfied. Once, after all his efforts to convince them to keep the camp area clean failed, he collected his entire staff and, along with them, gave the refugees a demonstration of cleanliness. After this, the inmates began to cooperate and he had no more problem on this score.

While he was at the refugee camp, Edwina Mountbatten came for a visit. She was impressed and told Nathu Singh: 'You must be a genius.' She said that he should ask Mahatma Gandhi to visit the camp, which he did. When Singh met Gandhiji, they had a discussion about non-violence. He asked the Mahatma how he expected his principles of non-violence to work in the existing circumstances. He also asked: 'In 1921, you had said that we would achieve independence in one year. What happened? You had said, division of the country over my dead body. And the country has been divided.' Gandhiji had no answer.

Very soon he was promoted again, thanks to the large number of British officers who left when India became independent. He was made Major General and appointed GOC Deccan Area, where he was involved in the planning of the Hyderabad operations. While there, he was called to Delhi for a briefing, before being handed over command of the operations in Jammu and Kashmir, which had already commenced. But for some reason, he could not reach Delhi in time, and Brigadier Kalwant Singh, who was then Director of Operations at Army Headquarters and familiar with the situation, was promoted Major General and despatched as GOC JAK.

When Nathu Singh reached Delhi, he went to the Operations Room where he was apprised of this development. After studying the situation, he went to call on the Prime Minister as was customary for senior army officers at that time. He found the Prime Minister sitting on the lawn, talking to a few ministers and civilian officials. Presently, Nehru got up and went inside. The others asked Nathu Singh for his views on the best way to deal with the crisis in Kashmir. Singh replied that if he had his way, he would use the minimum troops to hold the passes, and with maximum force, attack and capture Lahore. This would compel Pakistan to withdraw and vacate all occupied territory in Jammu and Kashmir. The civilians were impressed by the logic of his argument, and when Nehru returned, they told him that the General had a good plan for getting rid of the invaders. When Nehru asked him to repeat what he had said, Nathu Singh demurred, since he knew his plan would not find any favour with the PM. But when Nehru insisted, Nathu repeated what he had said to the others. Nehru responded angrily, saying that he was amazed that a responsible senior officer like him could come up with such a foolhardy scheme which could cause an international crisis. It is interesting to recall that in 1965, a similar plan was approved by Lal Bahadur Shastri, who was then the Prime Minister, and it was the threat to Lahore which saved Kashmir from Pakistani aggression.

In December 1947, Nathu Singh was posted to Lucknow as GOC UP Area. Sarojini Naidu, who had been appointed Governor of the United Provinces after Independence, was also in Lucknow. Apart from being a well-known patriot and freedom fighter, she was a renowned poet and known as the 'Nightingale of India'. She was very close to Mahatma Gandhi and other Congress leaders, and had played a prominent part in the struggle for freedom. Nathu Singh discussed with her the problems of India's security and the armed forces. He had put down his views in a paper entitled 'Notes on National Security', of which he gave her a copy. She forwarded it to Nehru, and prevailed on him to go through the paper. Nehru's comments on it make interesting reading. In a handwritten note dated 1 January 1948, he wrote:

. . . It is axiomatic that India must be strong militarily, etc. or otherwise she will not only not progress but might break up. How best to build up strength in various sectors is a question of balancing resources . . .

. . . Strength, and even purely military strength, depends today far more than before, on our industrial growth and scientific research. It depends also on internal cohesion and peace in industry, etc. This latter is a political and economic problem of exceeding complexity and cannot be dealt with simply by military or police methods.

. . . The whole question of defence is intimately tied up with international questions as well as economic questions. The notes (of General Nathu Singh), though they refer to international matters, do not show an intimate knowledge of the international set-up or economic questions which are of vital importance today, both internally and externally.

. . . No British officer will be in operational command in the Indian Army after 31.3.1948.

. . . Some of the lines of approach in these notes are arguable. They may land us in difficulties. But generally Major General Nathu Singh's notes are helpful and it is desirable that urgent thought should be given to these matters by our senior officers and those in control of the political destinies of the nation.

(Signed)

J. Nehru

1.1.48

The divergence of views between Nehru and Nathu Singh is obvious. The ideals, so dear to Nehru's heart, and his consciousness of the international role which he saw for India, are also evident. However, one cannot help but remark that he also appears to pontificate, much as a schoolmaster would on a student's essay submitted for evaluation. His remarks about Nathu Singh's ignorance of international matters are ungracious, particularly when one recalls that having been in office for just five months, he himself had little experience—of which fact Nathu Singh was to subsequently remind him. He was also out, by almost a year, in his assertion about British officers not being in command after 31 March 1948.

Nathu Singh's tenure in Lucknow was short but eventful. He had to put down two mutinies, one in Allahabad and the other in Jhansi. By nipping them in the bud, Singh ensured that they did not affect the rest of the army. During this time, he also had an unfortunate misunderstanding with Jawaharlal Nehru over his absence at a parade held at Lucknow. Though he had known Nehru for several years, their relations soured and were never cordial after this. In January 1948, soon after taking charge, he had written a paper entitled 'An Appreciation on the Defence of India' and forwarded it to Army HQ. He was greatly perturbed by a directive issued from the office of the C-in-C that sought to reduce the size of the regular army which numbered 2.5 million during World War II, to 150,000, with an annual budget allocation of Rs 45 crore for the next three years. In the preamble, he wrote:

> We as soldiers must approach our leaders and submit our minimum requirements and make it clear that if funds are not provided for such a force, the responsibility will be upon them. A soldier is but a servant of the State. He must, however, point out any weaknesses in the defensive structure of the country with all the emphasis at his command. In order to arrive at a correct appreciation, we must consider both military and

allied factors and not be swayed by any notions of idealism or allow political considerations to affect our judgement . . .

A NEWLY CREATED NATION WHICH HAS ONLY JUST THROWN OFF HER BONDAGE OF FOREIGN RULE OF 200 YEARS AND MORE CANNOT RISK A REVERSE ALMOST AT HER REBIRTH.

. . . We must NOT decide on the size of our Defence Service on what we can financially afford but on what we need in the form of a Modern Defence based on the following considerations:

a. What is the strength and armament of the present and potential enemies of India?
b. What is the force required by India to meet this threat?
c. What will be the cost of maintaining such a force?
d. What is the maximum amount the country can afford to pay for its defence forces?
e. To arrive at a compromise between (b), (c) and (d) above, consistent with the safety of our land.

Keeping the above in view, the Land Forces which India should maintain are given in the enclosed appreciation. They are only my first thoughts.

Nathu Singh proceeded to outline the future framework of the Indian Army. By present standards, he was extremely conservative—he asked for one corps headquarters, one armoured division, two infantry divisions, one parachute brigade, one armoured brigade, and the associated complement of Artillery, Engineers and Signals. Though he restricted the number of infantry battalions to 28, he advocated a large complement of territorial army, which would provide the second line of defence and boost the resources of the regular army during war.

In April 1948, he was promoted Lieutenant General and appointed GOC-in-C, Eastern Command at Ranchi. Like many other Indian officers, he had risen from the rank of Lieutenant Colonel to Lieutenant General in less than three years. He continued his efforts to convince the political and military leadership of the need to maintain a strong army. When asked for a rundown of the army by Army HQ, he replied on 24 October 1950:

> . . . The situation facing the country from the military point of view is today virtually the same if not worse because, although Pakistan outwardly appears to be fraternising with our country, recent speeches of its leaders leave no room for doubt that they are preparing for a showdown with our country over the issue.
>
> . . . . Communist China's complete success over the KUOMINTANG and the establishment of the Peoples' Government, their recent activities, their declared policy towards liberation of TIBET, and the recent Mission from the latter country clearly indicate the writing on the wall. The Communist menace is gradually spreading towards the very borders of India.
>
> . . . To ensure the security of our borders and our State, the defence service ratio between India and Pakistan should be two to one. If this is reduced, we will be laying our country open to an ever-present danger of a major war.

Nathu Singh's remarks, especially with reference to Pakistan and China, show an insight into international affairs that very few contemporary Indians had. Even Nehru, who orchestrated India's foreign policy for almost two decades following Independence, failed to grasp the nuances that Nathu Singh had perceived. As a result, the defence forces were neglected, with disastrous consequences in 1962. Nathu Singh cried himself hoarse trying to convince the political and military leadership of the need to maintain a strong army. He did not visualise a large force—that would be a white elephant, he felt—but one that was well trained and equipped. Unfortunately, the leaders, cloistered in their ivory towers, were more worried about solving the problems of the world rather than those of their own country. Nehru was a great intellectual and a patriot. The saga of his sacrifices during the freedom struggle forms one of the most glorious chapters of the history of our nation. However, as a statesman, his achievements are more than matched by his failures. An intimate knowledge of military affairs is important for those who decide the fate of peoples and nations. Among his contemporaries, such as Churchill, Stalin, Chiang Kai Shek, Roosevelt, Eisenhower, Tito and Nasser, Nehru was one of the few who had never worn a uniform.

Soon after Independence, the Prime Minister held a meeting of senior army officers to elicit their views on retaining British officers as advisers. Nehru felt that Indian officers lacked the experience to take over responsibility for such a large army and wanted to retain British officers for a longer period, as Pakistan had done. While almost everyone agreed with Nehru, Nathu Singh objected:

> Officers sitting here have more than 25 years' service and are capable of holding senior appointments in the armed forces. As for experience, if I may ask you, Sir, what experience do you have to hold the post of Prime Minister?

There was a stunned silence, and Nehru did not reply. In the end, Nehru's proposal was accepted.

Nathu Singh had always been a stormy petrel, and neither rank nor age had dimmed his ardour. He had as many admirers as he had detractors. Most of his superiors found him a difficult subordinate. He possessed many fine qualities, but two which he lacked were modesty and reticence. Even Cariappa, who was from the same regiment, while commending his loyalty, sense of duty, concern for the welfare of troops and administrative abilities, could not help adding that he found him loquacious and arrogant. His close association with Cariappa, who became the first C-in-C, rarely deterred Singh from doing what he thought was right. Cariappa was a stickler, who never allowed regimental loyalty to affect his behaviour, and this led to several altercations between the two 'Rajputs'. But they were also close friends, and Nathu Singh was not above pulling Kipper's leg whenever he got the chance.

Once, when he was the GOC-in-C, Eastern Command, he was a house guest at White Gates in Delhi, where Cariappa lived as the C-in-C. This incident also finds mention in the chapter on Cariappa. Nathu Singh was familiar with his host's rigid dress code, but wanted to tease him. So he put on a kurta and pyjama and went and sat in the drawing room. When Cariappa entered the room some time later, he immediately noticed this and asked Singh why he was improperly dressed. Nathu Singh replied that what he was wearing was the national dress and was now permitted even at formal functions.

Cariappa had taken over as C-in-C on 15 January 1949 and retired after exactly four years, on 14 January 1953. At that time, the three Army Commanders were Maharaj Rajendra Sinhji, Thakur Nathu Singh and S.M. Shrinagesh. Rajendra Sinhji, who should have retired three months earlier, was given an extension, probably in order to enable him to succeed Cariappa. Due to a new rule promulgated in 1950, officers retired after four years in command, and when Cariappa retired, he was only 53 years old. In fact, Rajendra Sinhji, though a year junior, was six months older than Cariappa. Nathu Singh was junior to Rajendra Sinhji by a year-and-a-half, but almost three years younger in age. Eventually, Rajendra Sinhji was appointed the next C-in-C. Nathu Singh had already created a few ripples, which had effectively jeopardised his chances of being considered for the top post in the army. In March 1948, when he was GOC UP Area, he had protested at not being considered for promotion to the rank of lieutenant general merely because he had not been graded 'outstanding' by the Army Commander, Lieutenant

General Rajendra Sinhji, who promptly rectified the mistake. In 1951, he wrote to the C-in-C, General Cariappa, making certain allegations against Major General Hira Lal Atal, who was then Adjutant General (AG) at Army HQ. Nathu Singh felt that the methods adopted by the AG to screen State Forces personnel were wrong and resulted in the demobilization of several excellent officers and men, who had served with distinction during World War II. He also felt that the four-year tenure system had been proposed by Atal, primarily to ensure his own promotion as Army Commander.

Nathu Singh's letter was brought to the notice of the Prime Minister, who dismissed his allegations. This was not surprising, considering that Atal was a Kashmiri and close to Nehru. As for Nathu Singh, the Government of India's 'displeasure' was conveyed to him for trying to impugn the character and military reputation of another officer. Later, in 1952, he sent a representation regarding his extension of service directly to the Defence Minister. These letters and representations did little to endear Nathu Singh to the bureaucrats and politicians of the day. In marked contrast, the British government had taken no cognizance of the letter he had written to the C-in-C in 1946, protesting against the trial of INA prisoners. Little wonder, then that Nathu Singh, despite his dislike of the British, could not help but admire their sense of fair play. Always ready to take them on if they said anything derogatory about India, he did admit:

> If you take the best of them, we have never produced anyone quite like them. I have not known a British officer who placed his own interests before his country's and I have hardly known any Indian officers who did not.

Whatever one may say about the propriety of Nathu Singh's representation, it is difficult to refute the logic of his arguments. The four-year rule ensured that senior officers retired at a comparatively young age—Cariappa at 53, Nathu Singh at 51, and Thimayya and Thorat at 55. This was at a time when the Indian Army needed officers with experience and was even considering retaining British officers for several years. In fact, the British heads of technical arms, such as Engineers and Signals—Major General Harold Williams and Brigadier C.H.I. Akehurst—continued up to seven years after Independence, as did the C-in-C of the Navy, Vice Admiral C.T.M. Pizey. The only persons affected by the four-year rule were the Army Chief and the Army Commanders—posts that needed experience the most.

Nathu Singh retired on 1 February 1953, exactly 15 days after Cariappa retired as C-in-C of the Indian Army. He did not grudge Maharaj Rajendra Sinhji his promotion to C-in-C. But he did feel that denying an extension to him was unjust. Had he been allowed to continue, he would have automatically succeeded Rajendra Sinhji when the latter retired in March 1955. After his retirement, there were strong rumours that he was being appointed governor of a state. After all, he was just 51 years old and in the prime of his life. A known nationalist, his loyalty and integrity were beyond reproach. He had many admirers, one of whom was Sarojini Naidu. She was still the Governor of the United Provinces, and spoke to him about a gubernatorial appointment. However, by this time, his tiffs with Nehru had taken their toll. Nehru was familiar with his bold and outspoken ways and did not want to take the risk of dealing with an intractable governor who would do what he thought was right, and not what he was told.

After his retirement, Nathu Singh continued to write to Nehru and the other leaders on various issues. He was furious about the incident that resulted in Thimayya's resignation and Nehru's subsequent statement in Parliament. Nathu Singh felt that Thimayya had been shabbily treated and was concerned about the growing demoralisation in the army. He wrote to Nehru, requesting him to constitute a committee to review the current state of the army and suggest improvements. Nehru assured him that he would do so. When this did not happen, Nathu Singh wrote an angry letter to the Prime Minister, warning him of the dangers of marginalising the armed forces and lulling the nation into a false sense of security. On his own initiative, he organised a Forum of the Old Guard, which could advise the government on key issues dealing with national security. The forum had the backing of most of the retired generals, including Cariappa. Unfortunately, Nehru chose to ignore these warnings at incalculable cost.

Sometime later, he was encouraged to join politics by Maharawal Laxman Singh of Dungarpur, whom Nathu Singh respected and still regarded as his 'Chief'. He joined the Swatantra Party, which was led by Rajgopalachari (Rajaji), who had been independent India's first governor general. In 1964, he fought a bye-election from Bhilwara in Rajasthan, but lost to the Congress candidate. Being unfamiliar with the ways of politicians, he often shared the platform with his rival, during his campaign speeches. He would tell the voters that if they voted for him, he would work for the entire country and not just for his own constituency. So if they wanted something to be done for their district, they should vote for his rival rather then for him.

Even after his retirement, Nathu Singh continued to take an active interest in national affairs, especially the army. He was perturbed by the gradual deterioration in the status of army personnel and the decline of moral standards in the country. He discussed these issues with all and sundry, and kept writing letters to successive prime ministers and defence ministers, as well as presidents. In 1993, the author spent two weeks in the military hospital at Jodhpur, where General Nathu Singh was also a patient in the adjoining room. He was as mentally agile as ever, and carried a bundle of files and books with him wherever he went. He appeared to be extremely distressed by the corruption, sycophancy and decay of moral standards in the country as well as in the army. What was needed, he said, was men of character—the type missing in the current crop of leaders. Having lived all his life by the highest standards of morality, he found it difficult to stomach the ongoing state of affairs.

In strength of character, personal morality and sense of duty, Nathu Singh equalled Cariappa, though they were poles apart in other spheres. In 1947, when he was Brigadier, he visited the office of the Military Secretary at Army HQ. The Military Secretary was responsible for the postings and promotions of officers. His son-in-law, Major Guman Singh, was due for promotion and was to be posted to a battalion of the 7th Rajput regiment as CO. 1/7 Rajput, which was in Razmak, was likely to be sent to Jammu and Kashmir shortly, while the other battalion falling vacant, 4/7 Rajput, was at Ramgarh in Bihar. The Military Secretary asked Nathu Singh where he wanted his son-in-law to be posted. Nathu Singh replied that determining suitable officers for postings was the job of the Military Secretary. But when asked to indicate his views as a senior officer of the regiment, he said that he would prefer his son-in-law to be posted to 1/7 Rajput, so that he could see some active service and serve his country by fighting the enemy.

Nathu Singh was a man of simple tastes, and always drank and ate in moderation. But he was a workaholic and could rarely sit still.

He would rise at dawn and go for a long walk, a habit he continued even after retirement. He always kept a small note-pad and pencil next to him, which he used to jot down thoughts as and when they occurred to him. He kept the notepad under his pillow even when he slept, and would sometimes get up in the middle of the night or early morning to make notes. His dedication to his job or the task at hand was total, and he did not allow anything to distract him, even for a short while. His boldness and outspoken nature often antagonised his superiors, but this did not deter him from speaking out. He possessed a sharp intellect, which even his severest critics acknowledged. He was also a man of wit and his repartees are legendary.

Once, when Singh was a young officer, his British CO spat out: 'Damn the country and the people.' Nathu Singh promptly replied: 'I was in England and did not like it, so I returned. Why don't you?' Another time, a British officer asked him if he was from Rajputana. When he nodded, the officer continued: 'I believe your ancestors were bandits?' Nathu Singh retorted: 'They may have been. But at that time, yours must have been living in trees.'

Just a few days before his death, he attended a prize-giving ceremony at Mayo College. He was 94 years old, but had made the effort to attend the function, primarily to meet T.N. Seshan, who was the chief guest. He spent three days at his old school and attended every function. He spent these days continuously ticking off people and advising the boys to fight for the interests of the country. A few days later, he went to the military hospital at Nasirabad for a medical check-up. The day after he was found fit, he had a cardiac arrest and died on 5 November 1994 in the hospital itself. The following day, his body was taken to his village, near Udaipur, where he was cremated. Though he had spent his entire life in the army and retired as an Army Commander, it was a police guard of honour which reversed arms at his funeral. Charles Wolfe's famous lines, quoted below from his tribute to Sir John Moore, were never so true as in the case of Nathu Singh:

Not a drum was heard, not a funeral note,
As his corpse to the rampart we hurried;
Not a soldier discharged his farewell shot
O'er the grave where our hero we buried.

Like Cariappa and Thimayya, Nathu Singh was one of the founding fathers of the modern Indian Army. Though not as famous as the other two, he equalled them in strength of character and surpassed them in nationalistic fervour. Many called him a maverick, others a renegade or a rebel. He was highly individualistic, with scant respect for authority. He did not hesitate to express his views whether his superiors agreed with them or not. However, no one could ever fault him on professional capability, personal integrity, diligence or courage, both moral and physical. He had many faults, but these were more than compensated by his sterling qualities and his deep sense of national pride. A colourful personality, Thakur Nathu Singh was not easy to ignore and will not be easily forgotten.

3

General
K.S. Thimayya,
DSO

3

General K.S. Thimayya, DSO

Timmy Sahib, India's Most Popular General

Kodandera Subayya Thimayya is perhaps the most well known of India's military leaders. Though he was neither the first nor the most successful chief, he was definitely the most talked about and admired. The first Indian to command a brigade in battle during World War II, Timmy—as he was popularly called—had become a legend in his lifetime. After his assignment in Korea, he became known not only in India but all over the world. He is the only Indian Army Chief who had his biography written by a foreign journalist. Stories of his ready wit, fun-loving ways, quick temper and fearless nature began making the rounds soon after he donned the uniform, giving rise to the Thimayya legend. A charismatic leader, he was very popular with both officers and men, who called him 'General Timmy' or sometimes just 'Timmy Sahib'.

Timmy was born on 31 March 1906 in Mercara in Coorg, to a family of coffee planters. Like Cariappa, he belonged to the Kodandera clan. His father was Thimayya, and when he was born he was christened Subayya. According to custom, his full name should have been written as Kodandera Thimayya Subayya but this was changed when he joined school. His mother Sitamma was the daughter of Cheppudira Somayya, a leading coffee planter of the district. Sitamma was an educated and accomplished lady, who was also a social worker. In recognition of her public service, the British government had awarded her the Kaiser-e-Hind medal. The couple had three sons and three daughters. The eldest son was Ponappa, followed by Subayya (Timmy), and then Somayya. All three became officers in the Indian Army. The family lived in a large house called 'Sunnyside', which belonged to Timmy's maternal grandfather, Cheppudira Somayya.

Timmy was 6 and Ponappa 8 when they were sent to St Joseph's College, a school run by Irish brothers in Coonoor. They were the first Indians to be admitted to the school, which until then had only taken in British or Anglo–Indian students. It is perhaps for this reason that instead of Subayya, his surname was recorded as Thimayya, his father's name. The Irish brothers were strict disciplinarians and believed in using the rod freely. The school regimen was tough, the food bad and the living conditions uncomfortable. Thimayya spent six years at St Joseph's and his ordeal ended only when it was discovered that a common form of punishment in the school was to make the boys kneel on broken glass in the chapel. Thimayya never complained, but when he went home during the holidays the cuts on his knees told their own story. His shocked parents immediately decided to remove the boys from St Joseph's and send them to Bishop Cotton School in Bangalore.

Bishop Cotton was a refreshing change from St Joseph's. The living conditions were better and the food good and plentiful. Discipline was strict, but punishment was rare and inflicted in a humane manner, with a few swipes of the cane being the most severe form. The teachers were serious, but kind and pleasant. Thimayya was not very scholarly, but more than made up for this with his proficiency in games and other activities. He played hockey, football and tennis, and was a keen boy scout. He also joined the Auxiliary Force and from this was born his attraction for the army, which later turned into a passion.* He often saw khaki-clad columns of British soldiers marching smartly, and he would follow them for miles on his bicycle. By the time he left school at the age of 15, he had developed into a tall and well-built lad, who had made up his mind to be a soldier.

In 1921 Thimayya finished school and left for the Prince of Wales Royal Indian Military College (PWRIMC), which had just opened at Dehradun to train Indian cadets for Sandhurst. The first batch of five Indians had joined Sandhurst in January 1919, but only two had passed out. Though the quota for each batch, starting every six months, was 10, the number of cadets who qualified was always smaller and not all who joined passed out. In the first two years, only 15 cadets joined in four batches, and of these only eight could graduate. It was noticed that the general standard of Indian applicants was poor, primarily due to lack of education. Considering the difference in education and background between British and Indian cadets, it was decided to open a school in India, where prospective candidates for Sandhurst could be prepared and groomed. It was for this purpose that the PWRIMC was established in February 1922 at Dehradun. The first batch was carefully selected and had only 32 cadets. Only one vacancy was allotted to the Madras Area, which included Coorg. However, Thimayya had no difficulty in being selected. He spoke English fluently, had an excellent physique, was a good sportsman, and possessed the necessary social graces to move in British society.

The PWRIMC had been built in sylvan surroundings and, in keeping with the British public school tradition, its cadets

---

* After the Mutiny of 1857, a Volunteer Force was created, whose primary function was to protect British families in India. The Volunteer Force units were later absorbed into the Auxiliary Force India (AFI), which was created in 1920 for internal security duties. Its terms of service were similar to the Territorial Army of the UK. The AFI, which provided officers to the Army during World War II, was disbanded in 1947. Its units were absorbed into the Territorial Army.

were housed comfortably in dormitories. All the housemasters and teachers were British, as was the Commandant, Colonel J.L. Stoughton from the Sikh Regiment. The cadets came from diverse backgrounds, with many from royal or military families. Proficiency in sports and games was more highly regarded than scholastic achievement, and Thimayya had no problem in staying near the top of his class. Once when General Claude Jacob, the Chief of General Staff, was visiting, a cricket match was organised in his honour. Thimayya batted exceptionally well and hit a sixer, which landed almost on the General's head. Fortunately, General Claude was an avid cricketer and he not only congratulated Thimayya, but remembered him many years later.

Though the PWRIMC was meant to be a feeder institution, admission to the school did not guarantee a place at Sandhurst. And though it was called a 'college', it did not give even a school certificate to the boys who passed out after spending six to seven years there. Many Indians considered it a 'sop', which was unlikely to accelerate the pace of Indianisation of the army. During an Assembly debate on 19 February 1925, one member compared it to the Holy Roman Empire, which was neither Holy, nor Roman, nor an Empire. For some reason, the British believed that only boys with an aristocratic background or from the land-owning class were suitable for commissions, and were very careful about selecting candidates. As a result, most of those admitted to the school during the first few years possessed impeccable pedigrees, but lacked education as well as mental and physical robustness. After a year-and-a-half, there were only five cadets left in Thimayya's batch; the others had either failed the tests or had given up in between.

The next hurdle was the admission test for Sandhurst. Thimayya's academic record was not brilliant, and he knew that he would have to work very hard if he wanted to pass. Also, his parents had already spent a lot of money in sending him to the PWRIMC—the fee was Rs 5,000 for sons of military officers and Rs 10,000 for others—and it would all be wasted if he failed to qualify. Incidentally, unlike now when pre-commission training is free, in those days parents had to pay for the training at Sandhurst as well—Rs 7,000 for sons of military officers and Rs 11,000 for others. There was a stiff written examination at Simla, which required several weeks of preparation, followed by an oral test. Thimayya had some difficulty with Urdu, which he had not been able to master, but he managed to pass because he had done well in the other papers. He was then called for an interview with the CGS. General Jacob remembered Thimayya as the young lad who had hit a sixer two years earlier, and the interview was over in a few minutes. There was now only one barrier to cross—the interview with the Viceroy himself.

Sixty candidates passed the written examination and the interview with the Chief of General Staff. Most of them belonged to the nobility or the land-owning class, and had been chosen for their loyalty to the British. In the end, only six made it to Sandhurst. Thimayya and his cousin Bopayya were interviewed by the Viceroy on the same day, and both were selected. They were overjoyed, and on their return to Coorg, a huge party was held to celebrate their success. Thimayya's elder brother Ponappa as well as Cariappa who, being a Kodandera, was related to him, were present. They were both subalterns and spoke to the two successful candidates about life in Sandhurst and the sort of pitfalls they would need to guard against. The six boys sailed for England in June 1924. One of them was P.N. Thapar, who succeeded Thimayya as Army Chief in 1961.

At Sandhurst, Thimayya faced British prejudice and snobbery for the first time, and had several unpleasant brushes with the authorities. His guardian, a British colonel, had forbidden Indian cadets to dance with local girls. Thimayya met an English girl at a dance and became friendly with her. One of her letters to him was intercepted by the colonel, who berated him for dancing with an English girl against his orders. Thimayya, realising that the colonel had opened his letter, lost his temper and paid him back in the same coin. It was customary to hold a ball on the night before students passed out from Sandhurst, which Indians customarily did not attend. Thimayya not only decided to go to the ball, but also took with him two British girls, whose father had served in India and was acquainted with his own father. The next morning, as expected, he and his guardian had a fearful row. Timmy told the colonel that he was not accustomed to allowing anyone but his family to arbitrate his behaviour. When the colonel threatened to report the matter to the India Office as well as his parents, Timmy told him to go to hell.

Another incident at Sandhurst, which Thimayya remembered often, had to do with a soldier's luck. Once, during physical training at the gymnasium, he did not execute a right turn correctly. This was spotted by the Adjutant, who reported him for slackness. Thimayya was marched up to his Company Commander, but was let off with a warning, since this was his first misdemeanour. A few months later, while on parade, the Commandant pointed out a button on his uniform that had not been polished. Thimayya was once again marched up to the Company Commander, expecting the worst. Miraculously, the latter seemed to have forgotten the earlier incident and once again let him off with a warning. When they came out of the Company Commander's office, the Sergeant Major told Thimayya; 'You are lucky, Sir. And being lucky is the most important quality a soldier can have.'

Thimayya passed out from Sandhurst on 4 February 1926, along with three other Indians—Sushil Kumar Ghose, Tara Singh Bal and Pran Nath Thapar. He decided to spend a week in Paris before returning to India. He was at the Moulin Rouge when Maurice Chevalier made his debut at the famous nightclub. Introduced to the audience by the incomparable Mistinguette, Maurice Chevalier sang a song that advertised six different floral scents of a particular perfume. After the song, six girls, wearing virtually nothing except one of the scents, went around the audience, inviting the gentlemen to identify the scent they were using. When one of the girls invited Thimayya to smell her inner thigh, he went red with embarrassment. His discomfiture did not go unnoticed and was met with much sniggering and guffaws. Finally, Thimayya managed to blurt out the name of a flower, and was surprised when he was presented with a bottle of perfume for guessing correctly.

Thimayya also visited Pigalle, where the girls wore even less than at the Moulin Rouge. The place was full of prostitutes and gigolos, and seemed to represent the decadence of European society at its worst. Fortunately, he met an American family with whom he spent the evening. On the following day, before he could leave for Southampton to sail for India, he discovered that he had contracted measles. This delayed his departure by 10 days. He sailed for Bombay in early March 1926 accompanied by many of his Sandhurst colleagues who were on their way to either India, Australia or New Zealand. After disembarking at Bombay, he tried to find out where he had been posted. To his surprise, he found that his name was missing from the list. He called up Army HQ in Delhi to check what had happened. The clerk who took his call regretted the error and asked him whether he had any preferences regarding the British battalion with which he would be attached for a year. Thimayya said that he would not mind Bangalore, since that was close to his home. The clerk told him he was in luck— the 2nd Battalion, the Highland Light Infantry (HLI), had just moved to Bangalore. The next morning, Thimayya caught a train to Bangalore.

Thimayya arrived in Bangalore on 26 March 1926. He was received at the station by two officers of the HLI—Second Lieutenants Gray and Black. They greeted him politely and took him to the mess, where a number of other officers were having their pre-lunch drinks. Thimayya was introduced to them and after lunch, retired to his room for a well-earned nap. However, he was woken up several times by one or other of the officers opening the door and asking him if he was all right. Finally, he asked them what the matter was and they told him that this was the first time an Indian had joined the battalion and they wanted to make sure that he was comfortable.

Thimayya soon became acquainted with the Scots and they with him. He found that the officers had little to do and spent their time either playing games or socialising. The CO, Lieutenant Colonel Sir Robert Seagraves, was stoic but just, and ran a happy team. Thimayya was put in the company commanded by Major Sir Telfer Smolett, who soon became his mentor and guide. He was a popular figure, who exemplified the perfect officer and gentleman. His wife was equally affable and charming, and Thimayya soon became a regular visitor to their home. Before long, he got to know the men well, and his proficiency at football and hockey added to his popularity and standing in the battalion. He knew several Indian and Anglo–Indian families in Bangalore, some of whom he had met during his years at Bishop Cotton, and others whose acquaintance he had made through his parents, who used to make prolonged visits to Bangalore. He also became close friends with Gray and Black.

Soon after Thimayya joined the battalion, the Adjutant, Captain Ross-Skinner, asked him to apply for membership of the United Services Club. Thimayya told him that, as an Indian, it was not possible for him to get a membership. Ross-Skinner was surprised and spoke to the CO, who agreed to speak to the club committee when Thimayya's name was put up. However, this did not help and Thimayya was not accepted. The Scots were furious and all the officers offered to resign in protest. But Thimayya prevailed on them to desist, since he felt it would be unfair for the others to be denied entertainment facilities, because of him. In any case, Thimayya was a member of the Bowring Institute—a club for Anglo–Indians—as well as the Century Club, which was for Indians, and thus had greater opportunities for entertainment than the Scots, who could only use the United Services Club.

The British policy of excluding Indians from club membership was a sore point that galled Indians who had been granted King's commissions and were equated with British officers in all other matters. Nathu Singh had faced a similar prejudice and had made an issue of it in 1933 when he was a captain in Peshawar. This prejudice continued despite instructions to the contrary, issued by the C-in-C himself in 1919, when the decision to grant King's commission to Indians had first been promulgated. In a letter addressed to all Commandants, the C-in-C had written:

> The Commander-in-Chief feels confident that he can rely on the British officers' sense of duty, honour and fair play to secure the success of this new departure. Commanders of all grades must, while upholding the standards and ideals expected from officers . . . by advice, precept and example to assist the Indian officers in their new career and it must be remembered that these officers bear the King's commissions and the honour of that commission must be zealously safeguarded; any slight to it because it is borne by an Indian, such for instance as black-balling from a club on this ground, should be resented as a slight to the Army.

Thimayya spent a wonderful year with the Scots, and danced with the wives and daughters of the officers to his heart's content. Surprisingly, the Scots had none of the British prejudice against Indians. In a way, there were many similarities between them and the Coorgs, such as dress (the Scottish kilt was comparable to the Coorg *kupya*), the system of clans, their love for dancing, and martial traditions. The Scots took to Thimayya's family when they visited Bangalore, and some of them visited his home in Mercara as guests on social occasions and in shooting parties. By the time he left the battalion on 26 March 1927, Thimayya had become a favourite, not only of the officers, but also the men, who gave him the rare honour of 'chairing' him round the parade ground on their shoulders.

After a relatively lazy year in Bangalore, Thimayya was looking forward to some active soldiering. He asked for and was posted to 4/19 Hyderabad Regiment, then stationed in Baghdad. Being one of eight units in the Indian Army that had been 'Indianised', it already had several Indian officers. The seniormost among them was Captain Kunwar Daulat Singh from Kota. The other two were Lieutenant Har Bishen Singh Brar, who had passed out from Sandhurst in August 1923, and Lieutenant Ishfakul Majid, who had graduated in August 1924. Relations between them and their British colleagues were not very cordial and led to frequent quarrels. These occurred primarily because of Daulat Singh, who hated the British and found fault with everything they did. The CO, Lieutenant Colonel Hamilton-Britton, was a heavy drinker and suffered from gout. An unfriendly man who kept to himself, he did not inspire confidence either among the men or the officers. Thimayya's company commander, Captain Geoffrey Bull, was even worse. The atmosphere in the battalion was in marked contrast to the easy bonhomie and camaraderie of the Highland Light Infantry, and Thimayya was saddened at the prospect of having to spend the rest of his service in the 4/19 Hyderabads.

The battalion had a mixed composition, and each of the four companies had men from different regions. One had Kumaonis, the second had Rajputs, the third Jats, and the fourth, in which Thimayya was posted, had Ahirs, who were Muslim Jats from the region to the south of Delhi. They were simple village folk, who had none of the vices of the British troops that Thimayya had seen during his stay with the Scots. They were extremely honest, abjured alcohol and saved every penny they earned for their families back in their villages. Cases of indiscipline were almost non-existent and their only entertainment was to sit in groups and sing songs or tell jokes. They had full faith in Thimayya and were extremely loyal to him. Thimayya soon came to admire them and was proud of his association with them.

Thimayya spent a year in Baghdad, where his most notable achievement was a minor brush with death. One of the duties assigned to his company was to protect King Faisel I, which involved providing a guard at the gate and patrolling the perimeter of the palace. One day, while riding around the perimeter, Thimayya heard a woman's shriek from the palace and, without a second thought, rode into the grounds. He was immediately attacked by two Arabs with drawn swords and escaped only because of the agility of his horse. He later learned that he had almost entered the King's harem and was lucky to be still alive.

The CO, Lieutenant Colonel Hamilton-Britton, was originally from the Carnatic Regiment and had married a Coorg girl, who later left him. According to him, the happiest days of his life had been spent in Coorg, and when he came to know that Thimayya was from there, he became an instant favourite. Thimayya became very close to the Hamilton-Brittons and was often a guest at their house. As in Bangalore, Indians were not allowed in the Basra Club. The Colonel decided to take up the matter with the club committee. Due to his efforts, and the fact that the club was located in the cantonment, Indians were granted full membership and began to enjoy the facilities that the club offered. This also served the useful purpose of keeping the officers away from the notorious fleshpots of Baghdad. Sometime later, Colonel Hamilton-Britton recommended Thimayya's appointment as Assistant Provost Marshal, who was in charge of enforcing discipline among the troops, especially when they visited the city. It was a very responsible position and Thimayya was warned that he would have to withstand temptation, as well as pressure, to look the other way at various types of wrongdoing. Thimayya performed his task diligently and the other officers of the battalion gave him a lot of support. This also served to bring the British and Indian officers closer to each other. When the battalion left Baghdad, the CO told Thimayya: 'I am proud of you, my boy.'

In 1928, Thimayya's battalion moved to Allahabad, where he was to spend the next four years. On his way to Allahabad, Thimayya stopped for a few days in Bombay, where he met Sarojini Naidu, who introduced him to Mohammed Ali Jinnah. This was Thimayya's first contact with nationalist leaders, and he found the experience confusing. As an Indian, he sympathised with their cause. But as a soldier, he had sworn an oath of allegiance to the British sovereign. He was not sure if he could reconcile the two positions. In Allahabad, he came into close contact with the Nehrus and was a frequent guest at Anand Bhawan, where he came to know Nehru's sisters, Vijay Lakshmi Pandit and Krishna (Betty) Hutheesingh. He also met Dr Kailash Nath Katju and Sir Tej Bahadur Sapru, as well as several other prominent citizens of Allahabad. He had his first glimpse of Mahatma Gandhi when he came to Allahabad to address a public meeting. The Civil Disobedience movement had begun and there was a general upsurge of nationalist feeling among the people. Thimayya's battalion was often charged with maintaining law and order and doing flag marches. On one occasion, he almost got into trouble, when he threw his peak cap into a bonfire of British goods, at the behest of Krishna Hutheesingh.

Thimayya was deeply impressed by the nationalist fervour then sweeping the country and the sacrifices being made by the people. At one point, he and some of the other Indian officers wanted to resign their commissions and join them. Motilal Nehru advised them against it. He felt that the Indianisation of the army had been achieved after a lot of effort. When India achieved Independence, she would require trained officers for her army and Thimayya and his colleagues would then form the hardcore of the officer cadre. 'There are enough of us in the Congress; we need more people in the Army,' said Motilal. After some introspection, Thimayya was convinced that the elder Nehru was right. A few years earlier, Moti Lal had given the same advice to Nathu Singh when he was contemplating quitting the army. It is interesting to note that most leaders in those days held similar views. In 1926, Lala Lajpat Rai had given the same advice to S.P.P. Thorat, newly commissioned from Sandhurst, on board the ship that was taking them to India. In 1942, when P.S. Bhagat met Mahatma Gandhi in Poona, where he was imprisoned, and asked him how he could contribute to the nationalist cause, Gandhiji had replied in a similar vein.

For Thimayya personally, the tenure at Allahabad was rewarding. Lieutenant Colonel Hamilton-Britton had given him excellent reports and when the new CO, Lieutenant Colonel Nicholls arrived, his lack of knowledge about Indians made him rely heavily on Thimayya. In September 1930, Thimayya was appointed Adjutant—a post normally given to a senior captain or a major—while he was still a subaltern and had yet to pass the examination for promotion to captaincy. Three more Indians had joined the battalion—Naranjan Singh Gill, who had graduated before Thimayya in September 1925; Ganpat Ram Nagar, who passed out in February 1928; and Kunwar Yadunath Singh, who was commissioned in September 1928. The problem of club membership for Indians remained unresolved. The Allahabad Club refused to accept them as full members, in spite of Colonel Hamilton-Britton efforts to get this rule changed. Indians had been in the army for almost 10 years and were members of the officers' messes of their respective regiments. But the clubs at all stations in India continued to remain the preserve of Europeans right up to 1947, when the country became independent, and in some cases for several years afterwards. For many Englishmen, the club represented the last bastion of the Empire and they were reluctant to surrender it until forced to do so by events of history.

In 1931, the battalion moved to Fort Sandeman on the North West Frontier. En route, while changing trains at Quetta, Thimayya joined some friends at a party and missed the train. As a result, he reported late at Fort Sandeman, where the new CO, Lieutenant Colonel Lewis, was waiting for him impatiently. Since he was to take over as the permanent Adjutant—till now he was only officiating—his delayed arrival resulted in the postponement of a patrol on which the battalion was to leave the same day. Thimayya received a severe tongue-lashing for his tardiness, and had he not been the Adjutant, would probably have faced disciplinary action. After this inauspicious beginning, Thimayya realised that he would have to be careful if he wanted to avoid trouble in future. Also, he did not want to give British officers an opportunity to question the reliability of Indians when entrusted with important assignments.

The other two battalions in the brigade comprised the Sikhs and Gurkhas. There was considerable rivalry between the three units, especially on the sports ground. The Hyderabads were always bested by the Sikhs in hockey and by the Gurkhas in football. Being the only battalion with Indian officers, they were also treated with derision and scorn. Thimayya decided to change all this and undertook to train the battalion's hockey team himself. The Sikhs, who normally beat the Hyderabads by several dozen goals, were surprised when they had to suffer a defeat, thanks to the fighting spirit instilled by Thimayya among the Hyderabads. He also trained the battalion band till it was almost as good as the Gurkhas, who were reputed to have the best brass band in NWFP.

Lieutenant Colonel Lewis was one of the best officers Thimayya had come across, and he soon became a role model for all the officers in the battalion. Scrupulously fair in his dealings with both British and Indian officers, he was a thorough professional who set very high standards for himself, as well as the battalion. As the Adjutant, Thimayya was the closest to him and learned a lot during this tenure. Very soon, the battalion began to do well in every sphere and earned the grudging respect of the entire brigade. During this time, several other Indians—Mohinder Singh Wadalia, Mohammed Azam Khan and Kanwar Bahadur Singh—joined the battalion after passing out from Sandhurst. Captain (later General) S.M. Shrinagesh, who was senior to Thimayya, also came to the battalion from the Madras Pioneers, which had been disbanded. The presence of a large number of KCIOs enhanced the reputation of Indian officers in the eyes of the men, who found that they were as good, if not better, than the British officers.

In 1934, a new CO took over. He was the exact opposite of Colonel Lewis, and had very little interest in what went on in the battalion. He left almost everything to Thimayya, and spent very little time in the office. The battalion soon moved to Quetta, where the city's hectic social life and his attractive wife kept the CO occupied, and it was left to Thimayya to run things. Quetta was then one of the largest cantonments in India, with more than a thousand officers stationed there. There was always something or the other going on and Thimayya was kept quite busy. He was almost 28 years old and was soon due for promotion to captaincy. He thought it was now time to get married and settle down.

In January 1935, while on leave in Bangalore, Thimayya met Nina Cariappa (no relation to K.M. Cariappa), who was a distant relative. He had heard about her but never met her before, as she had spent most of her childhood in Paris. It was love at first sight and they were soon engaged. The marriage took place a month later in Bangalore. After some days at Thimayya's home in Mercara, followed by a few days in Bangalore, the couple left for Bombay, from where they sailed for Karachi. After a short voyage, which doubled as their honeymoon, Thimayya brought his bride to Quetta. They settled down to a life of domestic bliss, which was cut short by the terrible earthquake that devastated Quetta on 31 May 1935, killing 60,000 people. Fortunately, none of the troops were affected and were able to assist in the relief work, which lasted several weeks. Soon afterwards, Thimayya asked for a posting to Madras as Adjutant of the 5th Madras Battalion, of the University Training Corps where his uncle, Captain Ponappa would soon be completing his tenure. Leaving Nina at Mercara for her confinement, he left on what was known as the British Officers' Winter Tour. He spent a month visiting villages around Delhi, from where the men of his company had been recruited. Wherever he went, he was welcomed with rallies and fetes, and the tour brought him much closer to the men than he had been before. He then went on leave to be with his wife when their child was born. On 20 March 1936, Nina delivered a baby girl, who was named Mireille. A month after the birth of his daughter, Thimayya took up his new assignment in Madras.

Though Thimayya was married and almost 30 years old, he had not lost his sense of fun. In Madras, one of his duties was to act as the Master Gunner of Fort St George, which involved control of the battery of six artillery guns used for firing ceremonial salutes. One evening, during a party at his home, a young college girl was gushing about the governor, whom she had glimpsed that morning. Thimayya told her that she was more important than the governor. She was more intelligent, would make a greater contribution to society, and was also better looking. In fact, like the governor, she deserved a 31-gun salute and that was exactly what she would get when she left for college the next morning. Everyone thought that Thimayya was joking, but the following morning, the entire city heard 31 guns booming in salute. Thimayya was able to get away with it as he was authorised for a certain number of practice rounds and was thus not violating any order. However, the locals did not know this, and thought that Thimayya had defied his British superiors.

After spending four years in Madras, Thimayya was ordered to rejoin his old battalion. The 4/19 Hyderabads had been moved to Singapore when World War II began. Leaving his wife and daughter in Bangalore, Thimayya spent two years alone in Singapore. Due to a series of incompetent COs, morale in the battalion was low, and the Indian and British officers hardly spoke to each other. There was a mutiny by a company of Ahirs, who were joined the next day by the Jats. Thimayya was now commanding a mixed company and was able to keep them out of the uprising. He was instrumental in pacifying the men and the mutiny finally subsided. But by now, Thimayya was fed up and asked for a transfer. In August 1941, he was transferred to

8/19 Hyderabad Regiment in Agra, which was under raising. Two months later, he was transferred to the 10/19 Hyderabad Regiment, which was also being raised at the same station.

In July 1942, Thimayya was appointed the second-in-command of the battalion. While he was at Agra, there were violent demonstrations triggered by the Quit India resolution, adopted in Bombay by the Congress Party. Thimayya's battalion was called out on six occasions to control violent mobs. Each time, Thimayya talked to the demonstrators, who were mostly students, and avoided opening fire. After some time, posters appeared all over town, saying 'Don't be afraid of the Hyderabads—they never shoot.' Thimayya's CO, Lieutenant Colonel Charles Attfield, was annoyed and asked him why he was withholding fire. Thimayya replied that whenever he gave a warning, the mob dispersed, so where was the need to open fire?

After a short stint at Agra, Thimayya left for Quetta in February 1943, to do the Staff College course. He was one of six Indians out of a total of 140 students who attended the course. When he graduated six months later, he was placed second in the order of merit. After the course, he was given the prestigious appointment of GSO 2 (Ops) in HQ 25 Indian Division. He was the first Indian to be given the coveted 'ops' assignment, and got it only after he refused a 'staff duties' job, preferring to go back to his battalion rather than 'grow corns, sitting around Army Headquarters with the rest of these bloody overpaid, over-ranked office boys.'

Thimayya joined the 25 Indian Division at Madras, but it was soon to move to Burma. The GOC, Major General Davies, had tried to get his GSO 3, a British captain, promoted as GSO 2, but this was not permitted by Army HQ and Thimayya got the post instead. As a result, the General was not very favourably inclined towards Thimayya when he arrived. He also had a quick temper, which the others on his staff attributed to a bad liver and tolerated. But when he lost his temper with Thimayya a second time, Thimayya blew up and asked for a transfer.

General Davies called him over for a drink and a long chat. He told Thimayya that he was 'too damned sensitive' and that he should lose the chip on his shoulder. And while he could leave if he wanted, the General considered him a good officer and would be happy if he stayed on. At this, Thimayya's rage subsided and he withdrew his request for a transfer.

Soon, 25 Indian Division moved to Burma to replace 5 Indian Division, which had fought in the Arakan. Entraining at Madras, they travelled to Chittagong by rail, and from there to Maungdaw by road. In May 1944, he was promoted Lieutenant Colonel and given command of 8/19 Hyderabad, in which he had served during its raising in Agra. The battalion was in defence and was suffering casualties almost daily due to fire from a Japanese position on a hill that overlooked the Indian defences. Thimayya wanted to attack but the Divisional Commander nominated a British battalion, which suffered heavy casualties. Thimayya was blamed for an incorrect assessment of the enemy position. To vindicate his stand, Thimayya launched an attack without orders and captured the hill, killing over a hundred Japanese without a single casualty among his own troops. He was complimented by the Corps Commander. The Divisional Commander, Major General Davies, who had forbidden the attack, chose to overlook it. However, he said: 'You took a big chance, Thimayya. You had a close call. You are one of the lucky ones.' Thimayya recalled what the sergeant major at Sandhurst had told him about luck being the most important quality a soldier can have.

Thimayya's battalion, 8/19 Hyderabad, was part of the 'All-Indian' 51 Brigade, known thus because each of its battalions and all its three COs were Indian: 16/10 Baluch was commanded by L.P. Sen, and 2/2 Punjab by S.P.P. Thorat. From Maungdaw, the brigade was ordered to advance to Buthidaung in December 1944. In January 1945, it took part in the famous Battle of Kangaw, for which the Brigade Commander and three COs were all awarded DSOs. On 25 March 1945, Thimayya was given command of 36 Infantry Brigade, which was part of 26 Indian Division, and he became the first Indian to command a brigade in the field.

Thimayya's brigade was the first to enter Rangoon, which the Japanese had evacuated 10 days earlier, leaving the city in the hands of the INA. Among the captured INA officers was Thimayya's elder brother. Due to an attack of acute hepatitis, Thimayya had to be hospitalised in Calcutta and so missed the action. After he recovered, he was given a staff appointment, which he refused, threatening to resign if he was not given back the command of his brigade, which he eventually got. When the Japanese finally surrendered at Singapore, Thimayya attended the ceremony. He later visited a prison camp, where the Japanese had held the soldiers of 4/19 Hyderabad, his old battalion, which he had left just two weeks before they were captured. Thimayya was shocked at the condition of his erstwhile comrades. They were emaciated, and many had lost their reason. For Thimayya, this was the saddest moment of the war and he wept unashamedly.

After World War II ended, Thimayya was given command of 268 Brigade, which was sent to Japan as part of the British Commonwealth Force. When he reached there, Thimayya was shocked at the devastation, especially in Hiroshima, where the first atomic bomb had virtually flattened the city. His brigade was located in Matsue, a small town surrounded by many little islands. There was little to do and one of his major headaches was to keep the men occupied. The Japanese women were beautiful and due to the shortage of men after the war, quite agreeable to liaisons with the allied occupation forces. As a result, venereal disease was rampant and strict measures to control it had to be enforced. Thimayya's brigade, comprising Indian troops, did not have a single case of venereal disease, but when he reported this no one believed him. The Americans sent their own teams to carry out tests on Thimayya's men. When they too could not detect a single case, they asked the Indians whether they were using some mystic potion to control the disease! Thimayya spent a pleasant year at Matsue before being sent back to India in December 1946, to serve on the Indian Armed Forces Nationalisation Committee.

The committee had been set up on 13 November 1946 to recommend measures to accelerate the process of Indianisation of the three armed services. By now, it had been decided that the British government would hand over power to Indians by June 1948. The committee had to consider whether the Armed Forces could be completely nationalised by that time. Some Indians, such as Brigadier Nathu Singh, felt that Indians were capable of holding all appointments and that there was no need for British officers to stay on after June 1948. Others felt that this would take up to five years. Senior British officers insisted that it would take anything up to 15 years for the armed forces to be completely Indianised. The issue soon became political, with several British generals advising the Indian leaders against handing over power to Indian officers, and warning them of the danger of a coup, of the kind that had been attempted in Burma. Ultimately, Indian officers were able to convince the political leaders that they had no political ambitions, and it was decided to retain British officers as advisers for a year or two. Eventually, the transfer of power took place earlier than expected and the recommendations of the committee became redundant.

Once the decision to divide the country was taken, it was clear that there would be large-scale movement of people in the Punjab. To supervise their move and prevent violence, a Boundary Force, based on a division, was created under the command of Major General T.W. Rees with its headquarters at Lahore. Thimayya was appointed commander of 5 Brigade, located at Amritsar, which was part of this force. He was called to Delhi for a short stint on the Armed Forces Partition Subcommittee before returning to his brigade. He was also made an adviser to the Boundary Force Commander, Major General Rees. Thimayya's first meeting with Rees was not very cordial.

Rees said that he had 30 years of service to Thimayya's 20 and did not need his advice. Thimayya left, and did not meet Rees again. In fact, he found that the British officers were indifferent and not very keen to prevent disturbances. When Prime Minister Jawaharlal Nehru came to Lahore, accompanied by Defence Minister Sardar Baldev Singh, Thimayya took up the matter with them, and recommended that British officers in the Boundary Force be replaced by Indian officers. Nehru accepted the suggestion, and brought it up in the Supreme Council meeting the next day. The Pakistanis felt that they did not have enough experienced officers to replace British officers. However, the Indians decided to go ahead, and British officers began to resign from the Boundary Force. General Lockhart, the C-in-C, was furious with Thimayya for having given the suggestion to Nehru without consulting either him or his superior, General Rees. In the presence of the latter, Thimayya told Lockhart about his first and only conversation with Rees, and felt that he had acted correctly. When Lockhart did not agree, Thimayya offered to resign. Lockhart immediately cooled down and asked Thimayya to forget about the affair.

After a few months, Thimayya was transferred to 11 Brigade, located at Jullunder, which was also part of the Boundary Force. A little later, Rees was recalled to Delhi, and Thimayya was given command of the force, with the rank of Major General. He was a shocked witness to the atrocities and violence that occurred during Partition. His troops were responsible for restoring law and order, as well as for implementing relief measures, which included disposing of the dead. The senseless killings traumatised him and left a deep scar on his memory.

Soon after Independence, he was in Lahore, as a guest of his counterpart in Pakistan, Major General Iftikhar. He heard some Pakistani officers talking about locating their regiments at Gulmarg and Pahalgam. He was surprised, as Kashmir had still not acceded to either Pakistan or India. In October 1947, Pakistani raiders entered the Kashmir Valley. After Maharaja

Hari Singh had signed the Instrument of Accession, Indian troops were sent in. Srinagar was saved in the nick of time and the raiders were driven back. Gradually, the momentum of the raids increased, leading to a build-up of Indian troops, and the Jammu and Kashmir Force, comprising two brigades, was created under the command of Major General Kalwant Singh. This, in turn, was under the Delhi and East Punjab (DEP) Command, located at Delhi. In January 1948, Cariappa took over as C-in-C, DEP Command, and moved it to Jammu. In April 1948, Thimayya took over from Kalwant as GOC, Jammu and Kashmir (JAK) Force. A few days later, the force was split and two divisions were created. Sri Division was to be located at Srinagar to look after the defence of the Kashmir valley, while another division, based in Jammu, was to look after the Jammu region. Thimayya was given command of Sri Division and moved to Srinagar on 4 May 1948.

Thimayya had two brigades under his command: 161 Infantry Brigade under Brigadier L.P. 'Bogey' Sen was looking after the Uri sector, while 163 Infantry Brigade under Brigadier Harbaksh Singh was in the Handwara–Kupwara area. On 13 May 1948, Thimayya held a meeting to share his plans for the summer offensive. The main thrust, by 161 Infantry Brigade, was to advance to Domel on 20 May 1948, after being relieved by 77 Parachute Brigade under Brigadier Nair that had already arrived in the Valley. A diversionary thrust by 163 Infantry Brigade was to commence on 18 May and advance to Tithwal. By the end of June 1948, Nastachun Pass had been captured, and the area upto the Kishenganga River cleared by 163 Infantry Brigade. In the Uri sector, 161 Infantry Brigade had captured Pirkanthi and Ledi Galli. Razdhangan Pass in northern Kashmir was also captured. At this juncture, the government decided to cease offensive operations, as the matter had been referred to the United Nations. Domel had still not been captured, but over 350 square miles of territory had been liberated from enemy occupation.

The decision to suspend offensive operations came as a shock, and Cariappa protested strongly to the government, especially because Pakistan had not accepted the UN resolution and was continuing with her operations. Finally, the government approved that operations could be undertaken for the link-up with Leh and Punch, which had to be held at all costs. These were to be in the nature of defensive operations. However, the road to Leh could be opened only after the capture of Dras, Zojila and Kargil, all of which were held by the enemy. The operation for achieving this objective was code-named DUCK. Before commencement, however, some reorganisation was carried out. A new Corps HQ was created to look after all operations in the area. Major General S.M. Shrinagesh, who was Adjutant General at Army HQ, was promoted Lieutenant General and appointed GOC XV Corps in September 1948. By this time, Skardu had fallen to the enemy after a 10-month-long siege and several unsuccessful attempts to relieve the beleaguered garrison under the command of Colonel Sher Jung Thapa of the Kashmir State Forces.

At this time, Leh was held only by a weak battalion. Its defence was made possible by an audacious venture, for which the credit must go to Thimayya, at least for suggesting it. On 22 May 1948, the enemy had attacked the bridge at Khalatse and the State Forces detachment guarding it had pulled back to Leh. The next day, Major Prithi Chand, who was in Leh, sent an urgent message that the situation was critical and that if reinforcements did not reach by the following day, Leh would have to be evacuated. No aircraft had ever landed at Leh before, but if the town was to be saved, this was the only answer. Thimayya went to Air Commodore Mehar Singh, who was commanding the No 1 (Operations) Group of the IAF, and asked if he was willing to take the risk. 'Baba' Mehar, as the fiery Sikh was known, agreed to fly in a Dakota for a trial landing. Thimayya decided to accompany him and on 24 May 1948, they landed at Leh, writing their names into the history books of aviation. The local people, who had never seen an aeroplane before, thought it was a 'celestial horse' and brought grass to feed the animal! Needless to say, Leh was saved and troops were flown in regularly during the next few days. It also did wonders for the morale of the civilian population in Leh, who were spared the fate of towns like Baramulla, Mirpur and Skardu.

The capture of Zojila was another event that made Thimayya famous. He assigned the task of capturing the 16,000-foot-high pass to 77 Parachute Brigade that was being commanded by Brigadier K.L. Atal. Operation DUCK commenced on 3 September 1948, but failed due to heavy snow and the strong defences built by the enemy, who held the heights overlooking the pass. A second attempt, accompanied by heavier artillery support, was made on 14 September 1948, but this too failed, with heavy casualties. There was considerable disappointment and the troops were disheartened. Winter was fast approaching, and soon the pass would be closed, making vehicular movement impossible. Time was at a premium, and it was necessary to try different methods to achieve success.

On 23 September 1948, a meeting was held at Srinagar. Apart from Cariappa, who presided, it was attended by Thimayya, Shrinagesh and Atal. After analysing the reasons for failure, it was decided that a flat trajectory weapon was required to neutralise enemy defences, while the infantry was assaulting up the slopes. Due to heavy overhead cover air and artillery would have little effect, and the defenders could bring down withering fire on the attackers. It was then decided to use tanks during the attack on Zojila. It is not clear who came up with the idea, though Thimayya is credited with the suggestion, which Cariappa approved. Lieutenant Colonel Rajinder Singh 'Sparrow', who was commanding 7 Cavalry, was called in and consulted before the decision was finalised. Cariappa also decided to change the name of the operation from DUCK to BISON.

A squadron of Stewart tanks of 7 Cavalry was moved from Jammu to Srinagar, and then to Baltal. Many of the bridges had to be reinforced or rebuilt by the Engineers. To maintain secrecy, the turrets of the tanks were removed and carried separately. A curfew was imposed in Srinagar when the column was passing through the city. As a result, the movement of tanks was not detected and they reached Baltal, covering a distance of 260 miles, in a fortnight. The operation was to be launched on 20 October 1948. But since it began snowing on 18 October, it had to be postponed to 25 October, and then again to 1 November, the last possible day for the operation to commence, considering the time required for stocking the forward localities before the pass was blocked by snow and closed for the winter.

When the attack was launched, the presence of tanks completely surprised and unnerved the enemy. Thimayya himself was in the first tank, leading the assault. It was most unusual for a divisional commander to do this, but then Thimayya was not a run-of-the-mill commander and could literally get away with anything. The operation was a complete success and Zojila was captured by nightfall. Shortly afterwards, Dras and Kargil were secured and a link-up was established with a column pushed out from Leh on 24 November 1948. With this, the threat to Leh and the entire Ladakh region was removed. It was at this stage that winter set in and a ceasefire was ordered on 1 January 1949, after Pakistan agreed to accept the UN resolution, which she had earlier rejected. After almost 15 months of hard fighting, the war in Kashmir was officially over.

By this time, Thimayya's name had become a household word in India. He was considered a hero and the saviour of Kashmir as well as Ladakh. He was already well known in the army, and his success at Zojila added to his popularity. His nickname, Timmy, was used not only by his superiors and colleagues, but by his subordinates as well. Strangely enough, even the men used it, referring to him as 'Timmy Sahib', indicating the affection and admiration they had for him. A visit by Thimayya was regarded as the surest way to raise flagging spirits, and came to be known as 'Timmy tonic'. It became the prescribed remedy for units that were low on morale after a failure or heavy casualties.

To establish and supervise the Cease Fire Line, a United Nations Force was stationed in Kashmir, with troops from Argentina, Colombia, Czechoslovakia, Belgium and USA. Soon afterwards, there was a meeting between the Indian and Pakistani commanders under the aegis of the UN, to decide on the ceasefire line and the placement of troops on both sides. It was held at the 53rd milestone, on the road from Srinagar to Muzaffarabad. The Pakistanis provided the food and beer, while the Indians brought fresh apples. When they met, the UN officials were surprised at the warmth and absence of ill feeling between the officers of the two countries, who had been fighting each other just a few days ago. Thimayya knew most of the Pakistani officers and there was a lot of back-slapping and good-natured banter. Within half an hour, they had finished their official business and sat down to share a sumptuous lunch.

Thimayya remained in Srinagar till November 1949. He had moved his HQ from Baramulla to Srinagar, where his wife had joined him. There was considerable socialising, thanks to the presence of the UN officials, and the Thimayyas rarely had to spend an evening alone. They also made full use of the opportunity to visit the famous resorts of Kashmir and enjoy the natural beauty of the landscape, for which the region is justly famous. In November 1949, he received orders transferring him as Commandant of the National Defence Academy, then located at Dehradun. Before reporting to his new assignment, he accompanied General Cariappa, who was the C-in-C, to England, to attend the Commonwealth Conference of Chiefs of the Imperial General Staff. During the trip, Thimayya visited Sandhurst, from where he had passed out 23 years earlier. He also attended a reunion of the Kumaon Regiment, where he was touched to see that the British officers still retained a strong attachment to the regiment. However, he was surprised at the ignorance of some of them, who wondered whether the officers' mess still existed, and whether the uniform had been changed to a dhoti and kurta.

After a short stint at the National Defence Academy, in September 1951 he moved to Delhi as Quarter Master General (QMG). One of his first acts as QMG was to abolish the contractor system, which had existed in the army for centuries. The contractors, some of whom were rich and influential, tried their best to thwart him, but Thimayya stuck to his guns. He thus got rid of the ubiquitous contractor, who had fleeced the soldiers for years, and the units could employ their own tailors, barbers, etc.

One of Thimayya's most endearing qualities was his sense of humour. In February 1952, a tactical exercise was held at Lucknow. After the exercise, Thimayya, accompanied by Lieutenant General Shrinagesh and Major Generals S.P.P. Thorat, Sardanand Singh and M.S. Chopra, left for Delhi in a twin-engined Devon aircraft of the Indian Air Force. One of the engines caught fire and the aircraft had to crashland a few miles from Lucknow. Miraculously, no one was injured. The party walked to the road-head about seven miles away. By then the authorities in Lucknow had heard about the crashlanding, and when the party reached the road, they found a neat row of ambulances parked and ready to receive casualties. Waving his hand at them, Thimayya said: 'Sorry chaps, no luck today. Sorry to disappoint you.'

In January 1953, Thimayya was promoted Lieutenant General and posted as GOC-in-C Western Command. At his suggestion, the headquarters was shifted from Delhi to Simla. But he had hardly settled down when he received orders, in May 1953, appointing him Chairman of the Neutral Nations Repatriation Commission (NNRC) in Korea. After the departure of American troops from South Korea, North Korean troops crossed the 38th parallel, which had been agreed as the border between the two countries after the Korean War. The United Nations sent a large force, drawn from 16 countries, which drove back the North

Koreans and crossed the border into North Korea. At this stage, Communist China intervened, and cut off the supply lines of the UN forces in South Korea. Finally, a ceasefire was declared and negotiations began for an armistice. The UN forces had captured 170,000 Chinese and North Korean prisoners, while the North Koreans held about 100,000 prisoners from the UN forces. A large number of the communist prisoners held by UN forces refused to be repatriated, while the Chinese and North Koreans insisted on their return. It was to resolve this issue that the five-member NNRC was created. India, being a neutral country, was invited to chair the committee. The communist members were to come from Poland and Czechoslovakia, and the non-communist members from Sweden and Switzerland.

Before he left for Korea, Thimayya was briefed by Prime Minister Nehru and told that he must be strictly neutral in all his official as well as personal dealings. Thimayya soon discovered the soundness of this advice, as every decision of his was branded either communist or non-communist, depending on the side which stood to lose. It was a very difficult assignment due to the hostility between the North Koreans and the UN forces and the differences in perception regarding the rights of the prisoners. The UN officials felt that the wishes of prisoners who did not want to return should be respected, and they should not be forcibly repatriated. The Communists argued that every soldier had certain obligations to his motherland and his family, and these took precedence over his personal inclinations. They also accused the UN forces of brainwashing the communist prisoners and not allowing them to exercise their choice freely. Ultimately, about 4 per cent of the communist prisoners held by UN forces chose repatriation, while the remainder, totalling about 22,000, declined. On the other hand, 359 UN prisoners held by the Communists refused to be repatriated. Thimayya completed his assignment in April 1954, and returned to India. Both sides agreed that he had been neutral and fair, and this added not only to his, but also to India's prestige. Prime Minister

Nehru personally commended Thimayya and he was awarded the Padma Bhushan.

In May 1955 Thimayya was appointed GOC-in-C Southern Command. His tenure here was uneventful, except for an attempt by Pakistan to infiltrate the Chad Bet region of Rajasthan. This was effectively dealt with by a motorised battalion. In September 1956 he moved to Eastern Command, thus becoming the first officer to command all three field armies in India. In Eastern Command he had to deal with insurgency by the Naga tribes in North East India. At that time, General S.M. Shrinagesh was the Chief of Army Staff. He was due to retire in May 1957, and there were several contenders for the post. Lieutenant Generals Sant Singh and Kalwant Singh were from the same Sandhurst batch, having passed out on 29 January 1925. The other two were Thimayya and P.N. Thapar, who had also passed out from Sandhurst together on 4 February 1926. Thimayya had been placed 15th in order of merit, while Thapar was 18th. Technically, therefore, he was senior to Thapar. However, the most important factor was Thimayya's impressive war record—he had won the DSO and was the only Indian to have commanded a brigade in battle. The others did not have any notable achievements to their credit. Not surprisingly, Thimayya was selected for the top job and on 8 May 1957, he was promoted General and took over as Chief of Army Staff. He superseded Lieutenant General Sant Singh, who resigned, as well as Lieutenant General Kalwant Singh, who decided to continue.

Thimayya was only 51 years old when he became Army Chief. It is interesting to reflect on the turn events might have taken had the government decided to give the job to Kalwant Singh or Sant Singh, both of whom were senior to Thimayya. Perhaps Thimayya would have had to wait another two or three years before he became General. The maximum tenure for the Chief had been fixed at four years, though Maharaj Rajendra Sinhji was Chief for just two years and four months and Shrinagesh for exactly two years. Hence, Thimayya might have been Chief by

May 1961, if not earlier. If this had happened, would the 1962 conflict still have gone the way it did?

When Thimayya began his term as Army Chief, he enjoyed a close rapport with Prime Minister Nehru and was held in high esteem both within and outside the army. His assignment as Chairman of NNRC had made him an international figure. He was looking forward to a satisfying tenure at the top, when he moved into White Gates (Army House), in Delhi. But this was not to be. Not long after he took over as Army Chief a rift developed between him and Defence Minister V.K. Krishna Menon, who was a close confidant of Nehru. Menon was known for his arrogance and acerbic tongue, and thought that his intellectual brilliance equipped him with more than adequate knowledge of military matters. He soon realised that Thimayya was not as pliant as he had expected him to be. The presence of Major General B.M. Kaul, the Chief of General Staff, did little to improve matters. A brilliant officer, Kaul lacked war experience, but was powered with unbridled ambition. He became a protege of Nehru and Menon, and in order to achieve his ambition of becoming the Chief, began to poison their minds against Thimayya as well as Thorat, who was expected to succeed him.

Matters came to a head on 31 August 1959, when Thimayya resigned. The Prime Minister called him and, playing on his emotions, persuaded Thimayya to withdraw his resignation. He also promised to put things right between him and Menon. But this did not happen. News of Thimayya's resignation had somehow leaked to the press, and was given extensive coverage by all newspapers on 1 September 1959. The issue was also raised in Parliament, and several members demanded a statement from the Defence Minister. Since Field Marshal Ayub Khan, the President of Pakistan, was arriving that day, the Prime Minister had gone to the airport to receive him and was therefore not present in the House. However, it was conveyed by the Minister for Parliamentary Affairs that the Prime Minister would himself give a statement the next day.

On 2 September 1959, Nehru gave his statement in Parliament. He underplayed the importance of the issues raised by Thimayya, calling them trivial and of no consequence. He added that the difficulty seemed to be temperamental and went on to say that he had advised General Thimayya to have a talk with the Defence Minister, which he had done. He defended the actions of the Defence Minister in the matter of promotions, which appeared to be the real irritant, and insisted that correct procedures had been followed. In the end, he paid a tribute to Krishna Menon, praising him for his energy and enthusiasm.

Nehru's statement did not satisfy the House. Several prominent members, such as Acharya Kripalani, N.G. Ranga, Frank Anthony and Ashok Mehta, were not happy and felt that Nehru had belittled Thimayya, and that in praising Krishna Menon had congratulated the wrong man. But Nehru did not budge from his stand, and the Speaker finally closed the discussion when Nehru assured the House that the issue had been resolved. It was widely felt that Nehru had not been fair. He had humiliated Thimayya and defended Krishna Menon. The top brass in the army was aghast and expected Thimayya to insist on being relieved. Surprisingly, he did not do this. As a result, his prestige and authority suffered, and he was never the same man again. On the other hand, Menon became more powerful than ever. Thimayya spent his last days in office a broken man, a shadow of the ebullient 'Timmy', loved and respected by the officers and men of the Indian Army.

A year later, there was another controversy in which Thimayya was embroiled. In 1954, soon after his return from Korea, he had met Humphrey Evans, an American writer who was visiting India. Thimayya had mentioned to Evans that he was thinking of writing a book about his experiences in the army. Evans had taken notes during their conversation, and had sent a gist of them to his agent in New York, who promptly cabled back asking him to write a book about Thimayya's experiences in Korea. Evans and Thimayya had worked on the manuscript for the next four months, but when permission was sought from the Government of India, it was refused. Since he was still a serving officer, Thimayya could not publish a book without obtaining permission. However, Evans was not subject to any such restriction. He went back to the USA and published a book, entitled *Thimayya of India—A Soldier's Life.*

The book was published in 1960. Several Indian newspapers published reviews, and the issue of its publication was raised in Parliament. Some communist members felt that it was improper for Thimayya to write such a book. The Defence Minister clarified that the book had not been written or published by Thimayya, but was based on notes taken by Humphrey Evans when they were working together on the book that the General had intended to write. One member felt that he had revealed Indian tactics while describing the operations in Kashmir, notably the attack on Zojila, where tanks were used. When asked about it, Thimayya confirmed that he had not authorised the publication of the book and had learned about it only after it was reviewed in the newspapers. After this, the issue was closed, though it did creep up again on several occasions.

Thimayya retired on 8 May 1961. Though he recommended Lieutenant General S.P.P. Thorat as his successor because of his distinguished service record, the government ignored his advice and appointed P.N. Thapar, who was from the same Sandhurst batch as Thimayya. It was an unfortunate choice, as Thapar could neither stand up to Krishna Menon, nor control the unbridled ambition of Kaul, who had begun to run the army like his fief. After the 1962 Indo–Chinese conflict, Thapar was made a scapegoat and had to resign. On the eve of his retirement, Thimayya spoke to the men in words that proved prophetic. He said: 'I hope I am not leaving you as cannon fodder for the Chinese . . . God bless you all.'

No story about Thimayya can be complete without mention of his orderly, Ram Singh, who became a legend in the Kumaon Regiment, just as Timmy became one in the Army. When

Thimayya took over command of 8/19 Hyderabad in Burma, he asked the Subedar Major to detail the 'biggest bonehead you can find' as his orderly. What he got was Ram Singh, a tall and hefty Jat from Sonepat in Haryana. Ram Singh stayed with Thimayya for the next 20 years, until he retired in 1961. Many are the tales told of Ram Singh and his boss, each of whom thought that he was indispensable to the other. Ram Singh always followed Thimayya like a shadow, and considered himself his protector. During a sudden artillery bombardment, when Thimayya took cover in a trench, Ram Singh jumped in on top of him, almost crushing him in the process. When asked the reason for his behaviour, Ram Singh innocently replied that as the CO, Thimayya's life was more precious than his own.

When Thimayya was awarded the DSO in Burma, the whole battalion was overjoyed. The only person who seemed to be unhappy was Ram Singh. When Thimayya asked him the reason for his long face, Ram Singh told him that he was disappointed, as he felt that he too deserved the medal. 'After all, I have been to every place you have', he told Thimayya. When Thimayya became Chief, Ram Singh moved with him to White Gates, the Army House in Delhi. Once, Lieutenant Colonel (later Brigadier) Teg Bahadur Kapur, who was then commanding 4 Kumaon, called on Thimayya. Ram Singh greeted him warmly and went in to inform the Chief of his arrival. However, before he ushered him in, he said, *'Dekhiye Sahib, Thimayya Sahib to Jernal ban gaya, aur Chief bhi ban gaya, par usne manne Subedar tik banaya konni.'* (You see, Sir, Thimayya Sahib has become a General and also the Chief, but he has not made me even a Subedar.)

Another anecdote about Ram Singh concerns Thimayya and his bath. Very often, Ram Singh would run the water in the bath, but by the time Thimayya entered it, it would invariably be cold and the hapless orderly would get a tongue-lashing. One day, Ram Singh made sure that the water was almost boiling before telling Thimayya that it was ready. When Thimayya stepped into it, he was almost scalded. He yelled for Ram Singh, who entered with a grin. After Thimayya had finished with his tirade, Ram Singh said innocently: 'Look, Sahib, sometimes you say the water is cold, and today when I made sure it was hot, you say it is too hot. Why can't you test the water with your hand before jumping in?'

Thimayya was very attached to the Kumaon Regiment, of which he was the Colonel. In fact, he chose to spend his last day in uniform with his beloved 'Kumaonis' at the regimental centre in Ranikhet. He had initiated a number of welfare measures for the ex-servicemen and war widows of the regiment. He had persuaded Govind Ballabh Pant, who was also from Kumaon and then Chief Minister of Uttar Pradesh, to give 550 acres of land at Kamola, near Nainital, for a regimental farm. (Jim Corbett lived close by, at Kala Dhungi.) The farm was later named Thimayya Bagh and the income from it was used to start the Kumaon Regiment School and War Memorial Hostel, and provide assistance to war widows and the children of Kumaonis who died in action. When he was in Delhi, he often brought his friends, including diplomats, to the farm for a quiet weekend or some shooting. Lieutenant Colonel Ram Singh, who was then Commandant of the Kumaon Regimental Centre, recalls that Timmy always paid for the hospitality extended to him and his guests.

After retirement, Thimayya moved to Sunny Side, his home in Mercara, with Nina and Mireille. After the 1962 debacle, the government decided to form a Defence Council to take stock of the situation and advise the government on matters relating to defence and security. The council had 31 members, and Thimayya was one of the few from the military. At the first meeting, the council relied on his knowledge and experience and requested him to brief them. Thimayya did so, using maps and diagrams, and his presentation proved invaluable in helping the council to understand the problems faced by troops in extremely harsh terrain, with little or no communications. However, he soon realized that the government was not serious about implementing the suggestions of the council, which soon became defunct.

Soon after his retirement, Thimayya was invited to be the Deputy President of the United Planters Association of South India (UPASI) in Coonoor. In June 1964, the UN Secretary General, U. Thant, invited him to become Commander of the UN forces in Cyprus. Cyprus is a small island, about 60 km from the Turkish coast, with a mixed population of Greeks and Turks. It was under Turkish control until 1878, when British rule began. It became independent in 1960, and soon afterwards, fighting broke out between the two factions. Archbishop Makarios, the President of Cyprus, appealed to the United Nations, which sent a peacekeeping force to the island. Major General P.S. Gyani from India was commanding the force, but he did not want to continue and asked to be relieved. Thimayya had already served in Korea, and was one of the most experienced commanders available. He was familiar with the United Nations, and was well known and widely respected. He decided to accept the appointment and left for New York, en route to Cyprus, on 30 June 1964.

The UN Peacekeeping Force in Cyprus comprised about 6,000 soldiers drawn from Canada, Denmark, Ireland, Sweden, Britain and Australia. The political atmosphere was vitiated, and every action was seen as either pro-West or pro-Muslim. The composition of the UN force made Thimayya's task difficult and he had to tread very carefully. In spite of his reputation for impartiality, there were allegations from Pakistan that he was acting against the interests of the Turks, who were Muslims. Many thought that being an Indian, he would follow the policies of the Indian government. However, Thimayya was not perturbed by the criticism, having experienced it earlier in Korea, and continued to act boldly but impartially. Each time his term of office, which was for three months, was about to expire, it was extended. He was held in high esteem by Archbishop Makarios and gradually, even the Turks, who initially doubted his bona fides, grudgingly admitted that he was fair.

On 18 December 1965, Thimayya died of a heart attack in Nicosia. Ironically, the UN mandate in Cyprus, which was to expire on 26 December 1965, had been extended by three months just a few hours before he died. His death came as a shock to everyone in Cyprus, as well as in India. For a day, his body lay in state at the HQ of the United Nations Force at Nicosia, where wreaths were placed by Archbishop Makarios and his cabinet colleagues, as well as representatives of many nations. His body, along with a 10-man guard of honour drawn from the UN troops, was flown in a special UN aircraft from Nicosia to Beirut, where the Indian ambassador formally took charge of it. From Beirut, the body was flown to Bombay in an Air India plane, where it was received with due ceremony before being transferred to an Indian Air Force aircraft for its final journey to Bangalore. It was received at Bangalore by Thimayya's wife and daughter, together with a large crowd of mourners, which included General Cariappa. It was buried at the Lal Bagh gardens with full military honours, accompanied by a 17-gun salute.

Over six feet tall, Thimayya had a magnetic personality and, as one writer said: 'Moved as gracefully as a cheetah, despite his 200 pounds'. Tough and flamboyant, he reminded Americans of the Wild West, and his career could well have been the subject of a Hollywood film. Full of fun and humour, he was always the soul of every party. But he was also strict and straightforward, and never hesitated to take a stand. Above all, he was a soldier who always did what he thought was right. It is a pity that he had to suffer underserved humiliation just when he was at the pinnacle of his profession. There were aspersions cast on Thimayya's loyalty, and some said that he was planning a coup. Soon after the resignation incident, when Nehru spoke to Mountbatten about Thimayya, the latter told him that he could count on Thimayya's complete loyalty. He assured Nehru that Thimayya would never abuse his position or even consider anything like a coup. In fact, Mountbatten told Nehru that he could not possibly get a better man than Thimayya, not only as Chief of Army Staff but later on, as Chief of Defence Staff, a position which he thought Nehru should create.

Timmy is no more, but he has not been forgotten by his countrymen. Along with Cariappa and Manekshaw, he remains one of the most popular military leaders of India. His no-nonsense approach, sense of humour and moral courage had earned him the love and respect of the Indian jawan. To them, he was always 'Timmy Sahib', whom they loved and respected like an elder brother. With him in charge, they knew that success was ensured, and that he would never expose them to risks or hardship which he would not undergo himself. Thimayya's visits to units raised their flagging spirits as nothing else could. This was no mean accomplishment and one which few generals have achieved, in India or abroad. A 'soldiers' general', he was a true son of his motherland, who fought and died for her honour.

4

Lieutenant General
S.P.P. Thorat,
KC, DSO

4

Lieutenant General
S.P.P. Thorat, KC, DSO

A Professional to the Core

Shankarrao Pandurang Patil Thorat was a name well known
in military circles during and after World War II. One of the
seniormost King's commissioned Indian officers, he was known
and respected for his professional acumen, impeccable conduct
and forthright views. After a brilliant career, during which he held
some of the most coveted appointments in India and abroad, he
retired as an Army Commander in 1961. Along with Cariappa
and Thimayya, he was one of the chief architects of the Indian
Army. Like Thimayya, he too fell out with the irascible Krishna
Menon and his counsel was ignored, leading to the debacle and
ignominy of 1962. In 1947, when India gained independence,
Thorat had a ringside seat and witnessed the momentous events
at close quarters. He had the unique opportunity to rub shoulders
with great men like Nehru and Patel, the founding fathers of
modern India. It is a tribute to his reputation that in spite of his
close association with political leaders, there was never a whiff
or whisper tainting his conduct as an officer and a gentleman.

Thorat was born on 12 August 1906 in Vadgaon village in
the erstwhile princely state of Kolhapur. His father, Rao Bahadur
Dr Pandurang Chimnaji Patil Thorat, was the village headman,

who later became the principal of the Agricultural College in Poona and, after retirement, the Minister for Agriculture and Education in Kolhapur State. Thorat was the eldest of four children, including one sister. He received his early education at the village school, and then at various other places depending on where his father was posted. In 1914, Dr Thorat was transferred to Poona, where he moved with his entire family. Young Thorat was initially admitted to the Poona High School, and later shifted to Nutan Marathi Vidyalaya, from where he matriculated in 1923. Thorat then joined the New Poona College, which was later renamed Sir Parshuram Bhau College.

The Thorat family had not thought of a military career for the young lad. However, just three years earlier, the first batch of Indian cadets had gone to Sandhurst and this had opened up a new avenue for aspiring young men. Thorat decided to try his luck and applied, after having deposited the requisite fee of Rs 20,000 to cover the cost of his education and leave expenses. The selection procedure was very stringent and after an initial screening by the provincial governors, only 10 candidates from the whole of India and Burma were allowed to take the written examination held in Simla. This was followed by a series of interviews, beginning with a selection board. After being cleared by it, Thorat was interviewed by the C-in-C, Field Marshal Sir William Birdwood. His final interview was with Lord Reading, the Viceroy of India, and Thorat was so overawed that he addressed him as 'Your Majesty'. Lord Reading rarely smiled, but this time he did. At the end of the interview, he shook hands with Thorat, saying that he hoped Thorat would make a good officer.

Thorat was one of five boys selected for admission to the Royal Military College, Sandhurst, the others being Digamber Singh Brar, Gurbachan Singh Bhagowal, Agha Mahmood Raza and H.A. Francis. All five sailed from Bombay in December 1924, aboard the P&O liner Caledonia, and reached England after a voyage lasting 14 days. They joined Sandhurst in January

1925, to commence the first of their three terms of training. Thimayya and Thapar were already there, having joined six months earlier. Rajendra Sinhji and Thakur Nathu Singh had passed out earlier, in 1921 and 1923 respectively, while Cariappa had been commissioned after passing out from the Cadet College at Indore in December 1919. Thorat found himself in the same company as Thimayya, and this was the beginning of a lifelong friendship and close association between the two.

Unlike Thimayya, who had been educated in a public school, Thorat had never mixed with Europeans before, and initially suffered from an inferiority complex. But thanks to his prowess with the rifle and in the saddle, he soon overcame his diffidence. He did well in musketry and was one of the 12 cadets graded as 'marksmen', which entitled him to wear the coveted 'marksman' badge on the sleeve of his uniform. He also excelled in equitation and was awarded his 'spurs' during the first term itself, a rare feat in those days. These awards earned him the respect of his British colleagues, who began to treat him as an equal. He also did well in studies and other games. Soon, he had a large circle of friends.

By the end of his first term, Thorat had gained enough confidence to go on a long holiday. He toured Scotland, Ireland and England extensively, rounding off his tour with a couple of weeks in London. This was in the summer of 1925, and the London season was in full swing. As a Sandhurst cadet, Thorat had no difficulty in being a part of the many social events which took place almost everyday. Though Britain was then at the height of her power, and prejudice against coloured people was quite common, Thorat found that his being Indian actually helped in opening doors. In those days, only wealthy Indians, mostly from the princely class, could afford to visit England, and they were treated with courtesy, not only in hotels and shops, but also by Englishmen of the upper classes. Of course, to pass as a gentleman, one always had to be suitably attired in a suit, along with a bowler or a top hat, spats and a cane.

At the end of his second term, an incident occurred which left a deep impression on Thorat. After a regatta, some boisterous cadets drowned all the canoes in the college lake. The same evening, the Commandant, Major General Cochran, asked the cadets who had played the prank to own up. Without hesitation, every hand, including Thorat's, went up. 'Good', said the Commandant. 'Now will you please run along and fish them out?' It was very cold, a thin crust of ice had settled on the lake. The guilty cadets spent the better part of the night fishing out the canoes, their teeth chattering. Next morning, the Commandant told them that he had known the name of every cadet responsible for the incident. Had any of them not owned up, he would have been rusticated not for drowning the boats, but for not having the courage to admit that he had done so. He added: 'Remember that when you are commissioned. You will be known not only as officers, but as officers and gentlemen, and never you forget the gentleman part of it. Remember also that a person who is afraid of telling the truth is a moral coward, and no coward can become a successful officer.' Thorat never forgot these words. As a young officer, whenever he was tempted to hide the truth in order to get himself out of a spot, it was Cochran's advice that prevented him from doing so.

During his third and final term, a subcommittee of the Skeen Committtee appointed by the Government of India visited Sandhurst, to determine the possibility of starting a similar college in India. It consisted of Mohammed Ali Jinnah, Sir Pheroze Sethna, and Major Zorawar Singh, MC. Based on the recommendations of the Skeen Committee, the Indian Military Academy (IMA) was later established at Dehradun. On 30 August 1926, Thorat passed out from Sandhurst with an above-average grading and 'exemplary' character. Among the 32 cadets who were commissioned, there were only three Indians, with Thorat being placed 15th, Brar 17th, and Gurbachan Singh 32nd, in the order of merit. Thorat and his two Indian colleagues sailed for India in September 1926 on the P&O liner 'Kaiser-i-

Hind'. Among the passengers were two well-known Indians—Lala Lajpat Rai and Mohammed Ali Jinnah. As Thorat recalls in his memoirs, both of them took a paternal interest in the newly commissioned Indian officers. Lajpat Rai asked Thorat to check the proofs of his latest book, *Unhappy India*. One day Thorat asked him: 'Sir, do you think that we have done wrong in joining the Indian Army on the strength of which the British are ruling us?' Lalaji thought for a while and then replied: 'No, I don't think so at all. How long will the British continue to rule us? One day, India shall become a free country, and then we will need trained men like you. So work hard and qualify yourself for that moment.'

As was customary, Thorat had to be attached to a British battalion for a year before being posted to one of the eight Indianised units. He did his attachment with the 2nd Battalion of the Middlesex Regiment, then stationed at Ahmednagar. He was the first Indian officer to serve in the unit but since, like the other British officers, he held a King's commission, he was readily accepted by both the officers and the men. Thorat was given command of a platoon and he soon got to know his men well. He and his company commander, Lieutenant Phil Wray, shared a common passion for shikar, and spent many a Sunday afternoon shooting partridge, quail and sand grouse. Once in a while, they also bagged a black buck or a chinkara. Wray taught Thorat the rules and etiquette of hunting, such as not shooting a sitting bird or a female with young. Thorat also learned about closed seasons for various types of game, and the art of stalking, which helped him in later years when he took to hunting big game.

In October 1927 his attachment with the Middlesex Regiment ended, and he was posted to the 1/14 Punjab Regiment, also known as 'Sher-e-Dil Ki Paltan', then stationed at Manzai in the NWFP. He was given command of a Pathan company and had his first taste of life on the frontier. The Pathans were a recalcitrant race, with their several tribes continually fighting each other or the British. Blood feuds were common and were rarely settled, being handed down from one generation to the next. However, Thorat found that the Pathan could also be a staunch friend. Once, the Political Officer arrested Malik Abdul Rehman, the headman of a small tribe, and handed him over to Thorat's battalion for safe custody. One day, Rehman requested Thorat for permission to visit his wife, who was expecting their first child. Thorat obtained the necessary parole and Rehman went off, swearing to return the day his wife delivered. He was back in three days, with the news that his wife had delivered a son. He told Thorat that his wife had asked him to convey to the Sahib that henceforth, she would regard Thorat as her brother. Almost eight years later, when Thorat was again posted to NWFP, Rehman came to meet him, with his son, whom he introduced as 'your nephew'. He also carried a large basket, which he said was from 'your sister'. It contained dozens of hard-boiled eggs, about 50 quail, and a whole *barra* (the meat of an unborn lamb), which was considered a great delicacy. Thorat was touched by another gift—a *tawiz* (charm to ward off evil)— which his 'sister' had obtained from a holy man to protect him from harm.

After a year, in December 1928, the battalion was ordered to move to Aurangabad, having completed its two-year tour of duty on the frontier. On reaching Aurangabad, some more Indian officers joined the battalion. Among them was Second Lieutenant Mohd Ayub Khan, who rose to be C-in-C of Pakistan and also its President. Thorat remembers him as a strikingly handsome officer with average professional abilities. He was able to indulge in his passion for shikar, and shot his first panther, followed by a tigress. He also bought his first car, a second-hand Ford, which cost him all of Rs 450.

Thorat spent about three years on regimental duties before being posted to Delhi in October 1931 as Adjutant of the Territorial Army Battalion of the 14th Punjab Regiment. Thorat decided to travel by road in his now third-hand Ford.

Accompanied only by his bearer, he left for Delhi in December 1931. The roads were metalled but not tarred, and full of potholes. There were no facilities for getting punctures repaired, and petrol was sold in four-gallon drums, that too only during certain hours. The fords were often deep and frequently cars had to be pulled across by bullock carts. No wonder it took him 11 days to cover the distance of 1,100 kilometres between Aurangabad and Delhi.

Thorat spent about three years with the Territorial Battalion before being reverted in 1934, to 1/14 Punjab, which was then located at Jhelum. In 1935 it was ordered to move to Peshawar, to take part in the Ghalanai operations on the Khyber front. By now, several more KCIOs, such as Khan Ata Mohd Khan, Rajinder Singh Kalha, Mahabir Singh Dhillon and Rajendra Nath Nehra, had joined the battalion. In addition, some Indian officers had also joined after passing out from the recently set up IMA at Dehradun. Among them were Mohan Singh and Shah Nawaz, who later joined the Indian National Army formed by Subhas Chandra Bose with the help of the Japanese.

It was in the Ghalanai operations on the frontier that Thorat first saw real action and was 'blooded'. The operations lasted two months and involved a force of two brigades, under the command of Brigadier (later Field Marshal) Sir Claude Auchinleck. Thorat was once given the task of laying a large ambush, with the aim of destroying a party of Pathan tribesmen who had been harassing the Force HQ. Accompanied by about a hundred men, Thorat set a night ambush on a route that was frequently used by the tribesmen. After a long wait, the tribesmen walked into the ambush and there was a bitter hand-to-hand fight in which Thorat wounded several of the enemy with his kukri. The Pathans lost 17 men, while Thorat's company suffered eight casualties. The ambush was successful, and Auchinleck himself summoned Thorat and his CO to congratulate them.

During his stay in Delhi, Thorat had met Leela, who was studying medicine at Lady Hardinge Medical College. She was a brilliant student, good at sports and dramatics, and an ardent admirer of Mahatma Gandhi. Her father, Bakshi Bhagatram Anand, was a leading advocate in Amritsar. The young couple fell in love and decided to get married. By now, Leela had passed her final examinations and was doing her internship at the Lady Hardinge Hospital. Thorat had also been promoted Captain in August 1935. But there was a small hitch. Thorat came from a traditional Maharashtrian family, while Leela was a Punjabi. Finally, he and Leela were able to wear down their parents' opposition and were married on 29 January 1936. Thorat's father, Dr P.C. Patil, attended the wedding, which was held at Amritsar with great fanfare. Leela had obtained a scholarship to go abroad, but she gave it up, in favour of marriage.

Soon after his wedding in 1936 Thorat was posted to the Training Battalion at Ferozepur, where he remained for two years before returning to his battalion as Adjutant in 1938. By then, 1/14 Punjab was in Bannu in Waziristan. Though it was a frontier post, families were permitted in Bannu and Leela not only joined him there, but soon began doing medical work in the villages around the camp, which was surrounded by barbed wire and heavily protected. One day, when Thorat came home for lunch, he was told that his wife had still not returned from a delivery case she had gone to attend to in the morning. By the time she returned, late in the evening, Thorat was anxious for her safety and scolded the two Pathans who had accompanied her, saying: 'I thought that you people had murdered her.' One of them laughed and replied: 'Why should we kill her who saves the lives of our women and children? We would gladly cut off your head, but why hers?'

The year 1939 saw the commencement of World War II. In September 1940, 1/14 Punjab was moved to Secunderabad to join the newly raised 11 Indian Brigade, which was to proceed to Malaya. However, Thorat was not destined to go with the battalion. He was selected to do the staff course and left for Quetta. On completing the course in 1941, he was posted to the Staff Duties Directorate in Army HQ, then located in Simla. His section, SD 2b, was responsible for weapons and equipment. The Indian Army was then on low priority, and there was an acute shortage of weapons and ammunition. Most units had less than half their quota of rifles, and even less of mortars and other service weapons. The workload was heavy, but routine and boring. Thorat began to agitate for a transfer to regimental duty, but since there were very few staff-trained officers, his request was turned down. Then his luck changed, with the decision to convert some Indian State Forces into regular units. One of these was the Rajaram Rifles of Kolhapur State, and Thorat found himself posted to this unit since he happened to be a native of Kolhapur.

He served for about a year with the Rajaram Rifles, but he was not very happy. He wanted to serve in an active unit and not in one that seemed to have no chance of ever going to war. Since his own battalion, 1/14 Punjab, had been captured by the Japanese, he asked for a transfer to any battalion of the 14th Punjab Regiment. Finally, after a great deal of badgering, he was able to get a posting to 4/14 Punjab, that was part of 114 Brigade of the 7th Indian Division, then involved in pushing back the Japanese from the Naga hills. Thorat was in the reinforcement camp at Dimapur when the famous battle of Kohima took place, but he was able to take part in the subsequent operation of clearing the Japanese from Kohima. Shortly thereafter he was posted to 9/14 Punjab at Imphal as second-in-command. The battalion was part of 20 Indian Division.

At this time, 20 Indian Division, along with two other divisions, was trapped in Imphal, having been surrounded by the Japanese from all sides. The divisions had to rely on IAF for their supplies as well as for the evacuation of casualties. Thorat got a lift in a cargo plane carrying live goats—also called 'meat on hoof'—for troops. He requested his CO to give him command of a company for a few days, so that he could get the feel of the ground and the troops. The CO agreed, and he was given charge of a company. However, after a few days, the CO had to be evacuated and Thorat assumed command of the battalion.

Thorat recalls an interesting anecdote concerning his orderly Nandu, who was utterly fearless. During an attack, Thorat and the Artillery Forward Observation Officer (FOO) started moving towards a vantage point, followed by Nandu, who was carrying a bedroll on his head. They suddenly found themselves under fire from the Japanese artillery, and a salvo of five or six shells landed close by. Thorat and the FOO dived for cover, but Nandu kept walking. Thorat shouted: 'Nandu, you idiot, why don't you throw away that bedding and take cover?' 'Throw the bedding down?' Nandu shouted back. 'And what will happen to the thermos which is inside? How will you get your tea at the other end?'

In November 1944, 20 Indian Division was ordered to concentrate west of the Chindwin river for the final push into Burma. Thorat marched with his men through terrain that had been heavily mined by Indian troops during the retreat from Burma. In spite of extensive mine clearance, there were many casualties by the time they reached the Chindwin. Just then Thorat received a signal posting him, on promotion, as CO of 2/2 Punjab, also called the 69th Punjabis, in the Arakan.

In Maungdaw at the time, 2/2 Punjab was recuperating after being badly mauled in the famous Battle of Buthidaung. The CO, Lieutenant Colonel Middleton-Stewart, along with several other men, had been killed in an unfortunate accident while debriefing a patrol. This, coupled with the casualties suffered during the Buthidaung battle, had considerably lowered the morale of the unit. Thorat was the first Indian officer to command the battalion, which was almost 200 years old, and he knew that he would have to gain the confidence of the men as well as the officers before they would accept him. The best way to do this was to lead them in a successful action, and the opportunity to do this soon arose.

The battalion was part of 51 Indian Infantry Brigade, under the command of Brigadier R.A. Hutton. It was also known as the 'All Indian Brigade', since all the battalions were Indian, unlike other brigades which had at least one British or Gurkha battalion. What is more, all three battalion commanders were Indians. Apart from 2/2 Punjab commanded by Thorat, 8/19 Hyderabad was commanded by Lieutenant Colonel K.S. Thimayya and 16/10 Baluch by Lieutenant Colonel L.P. Sen. In January 1945, the brigade took part in the famous Battle of Kangaw, which lasted three weeks and cost 2,000 lives, but succeeded in bloodying the nose of the Japanese. Mountbatten called it the 'bloodiest battle of the Arakan'. When it ended, the Brigade Commander and the three Indian COs were all awarded DSOs.

In the Battle of Kangaw, 51 Indian Brigade suffered about 800 casualties, while about 2,000 Japanese were killed or wounded. It was decided to send the brigade back to India for rest and recuperation, and in February 1945 Thorat moved with his battalion to Pollachi in South India. Soon afterwards, the Allied plan for the invasion of Malaya was finalised. The invasion force was to comprise two corps, XV and XXXIV, and seven divisions were to land at Port Swettenham in September 1945. The operations commenced, but before the landings could take place the Japanese surrendered and the war ended on 5 August 1945. The invasion force, which included 51 Indian Brigade under 25 Indian Division, became an occupation force after landing in Malaya. After spending a few months in Kuala Lumpur, Thorat's battalion was moved to Quantan on the east coast of Malaya. He visited the battlefield where his parent battalion, 1/14 Punjab, had been overrun and captured by the Japanese in 1941. A large number of its men had joined the Indian National Army as part of the Japanese force, and had fought against the Indian troops.

Shortly after this, Thorat was called to the Divisional HQ, as the AA & QMG. A large number of Japanese were being held as prisoners of war (POW) and it was part of Thorat's job to look after the POW camps. A Japanese battalion had been detailed to clear and repair an airfield that had been damaged during the war. Once, when Thorat was visiting the camp, an elderly Japanese officer wearing the rank badges of a brigadier, came running and saluted him smartly. When Thorat asked him why he was running, he was told that the Supreme Commander had issued orders that the prisoners were to do all work on the double. Thorat spoke to the GOC and got the order rescinded. The next time he visited the camp, the same brigadier marched up to him, and said: 'Colonel, allow me to thank you for what you have done. Neither I nor my country will ever forget it.' And he was true to his word. Ten years later, when Thorat went to Korea as Commander of the Custodian Force, he and his wife visited Tokyo and stayed at the Imperial Hotel. When he drove out of the hotel in his car, the entire traffic outside was held up to let his car pass. Thorat was surprised. On enquiry, he found that the same brigadier had persuaded the Tokyo police to accord him this courtesy.

While Thorat was busy fighting in Burma, Leela had not been idle. Though she had a young child to look after, she joined the Indian Medical Service as a commissioned officer, and did excellent work in the military hospital at Lahore. After the war, when Thorat came to Delhi, Leela set up a free clinic in the stable of their house in Dupleix Lane, together with Lady Monica Smith, the wife of Lieutenant General Sir Arthur Smith, CGS. The clinic became very popular, and when the number of patients became unmanageable, several other ladies pitched in to help. Auchinleck gave them a large stock of captured Japanese medicines and medical equipment. Leela also began to educate her patients about family planning, for which she came into conflict with Rajkumari Amrit Kaur, the Minister for Health. Kaur felt that this was the prerogative of her department, and asked Leela to stop her activities in this area. Leela told her to mind her own business and carried on. The only person who encouraged her was General Cariappa, who understood the importance of family planning and stressed the need for it in all his talks.

The Thorats had three children, two daughters and a son. The eldest daughter, Kusum, was born on 16 June 1937 at Amritsar. She later married a Punjabi, C.N. Kapur, who was in the Indian Railways. The second daughter, Kumud, was born on 30 September 1942, in Delhi. She married a Bengali, R.K. Bose, who worked with Dunlop. Their son, Yashwant, was born on 11 November 1947 at Ranchi. He married Usha, a South Indian girl whose father, M. Ramachandran, was a civil servant. Yashwant, who is affectionately called 'Bhaiyya' (brother), joined the Reserve Bank of India, and is based in Bombay. Incidentally, he and the author were in school together at St Francis Convent in Jhansi, where Yashwant was three years junior. The author vividly remembers a birthday party at the Flag Staff House in November 1954, when Yashwant had turned seven, and the author was a little over 10 years old. Yashwant's father had just returned from Korea and brought back a lot of toys and a huge balloon, the likes of which had never been seen before.

Thorat was promoted Brigadier in 1946, and appointed Secretary of the National War Memorial Committee, which had been formed to establish a military academy on the lines of the United States Military Academy at West Point. At this time, various proposals were being discussed regarding the construction of a suitable war memorial to commemorate the services of Indian soldiers during World War II. Funds were readily available, as the Government of Sudan had donated £100,000 to the Viceroy of India in 1941, as its contribution to the war effort. The credit for suggesting that the memorial take the form of a training institution, rather than a building or archway, like the War Memorial built after World War I (now called India Gate), goes to Brigadier A.A. Rudra, who was then Director for Morale at the General Headquarters (GHQ) in Delhi. This suggestion was accepted by the C-in-C, Field

Marshal Auchinleck, who wrote to Lord Wavell, the Viceroy, recommending the establishment of a military academy on the lines of the United States Military Academy at West Point, where basic training would be imparted not only to the army, but also to the naval and air force cadets. He felt that this would make an excellent national memorial, and his advice was accepted.

The National War Memorial Committee was set up on 2 May 1945 with Auchinleck as Chairman and Dr Amar Nath Jha, the Vice Chancellor of Allahabad University, as the Vice Chairman. The other members were the Chief of General Staff; Flag Officer Commanding Indian Navy; Secretary of the Government of India War Department; Educational Adviser to the Government; Sir Mirza Ismail, Prime Minister of Jaipur State; Rao Raja Narpat Singh of Jodhpur; Mian Afzal Husain of Punjab; Mr William Xavier Mascarenhas of the College of Engineering, Poona; and Mr A.E. Foot, Principal of the Doon School. The Secretary's post was initially occupied by Lieutenant Colonel P.C. Gupta, but he was later replaced by Brigadier S.P.P. Thorat.

While the committee held formal meetings every two months, informal discussions were held more frequently. The Prime Minister, Pandit Jawaharlal Nehru, took keen interest in the project and usually attended the meetings. One of the most important decisions taken by the committee was that cadets of all three services were to be trained together, which was not being done anywhere else. Even at West Point, the academy trained only army and air force cadets, while naval cadets had to go to Annapolis for training. Another important decision concerned the location of the proposed academy. Almost every important leader wanted it to be located in his own region or state. Malik Khizr Hayat Khan, the Chief Minister of Punjab, recommended Punjab; Dr Rajendra Prasad suggested Patna; and Sardar Baldev Singh felt that Ranchi was the most suitable. Auchinleck personally visited Bangalore, Bhopal, Belgaum, Deolali, Dehradun, Jabalpur, Vishakhapatnam, Secunderabad,

Karachi and Khadakvasla. Eventually, the Committee chose Khadakvasla, which was located close to Poona, had adequate land and also a lake, which could be used for training naval cadets.

The committee finalised its recommendations in 1946. The name of the proposed academy was changed from National War Academy to National Defence Academy (NDA). The period of training was set for four years, and the age of entry between 16 and 19. The minimum educational qualification would be matriculation, and admission would be granted after an entrance examination, followed by a test conducted by the selection board and a medical check-up. Cadets would be admitted purely on merit and there would be no reservation of any kind, including for sons of ex-servicemen. The entire expense, including tuition, accommodation, messing and clothing, would be borne by the government. At the end of their training, cadets would join the respective service training institutions for specialised training. They would pass out with a diploma, which the universities would be persuaded to recognise as equivalent to a degree. (This did not happen, and to enable cadets to get a degree, the educational qualification was later revised to Class 12, and the age of entry correspondingly raised by two years.) Though this would be the main route of entry into commissioned ranks in the three services, it was decided that other entry channels would also be kept open. Entry through universities under the UOTC scheme, and through the ranks, would continue, though on a much smaller scale.

There was a hitch when the question of transferring the 12,000 acres of land that had been identified in Khadakvasla came up. The Chief Minister of Bombay State (now Maharashtra), Balasaheb Kher, wanted the academy to purchase the land, while Thorat felt that the Government of Bombay should gift it. Thorat met Sardar Patel, who was a member of the Viceroy's Executive Council, and explained the case to him, including the benefits that would accrue to Bombay State. Patel listened patiently, but gave no assurances. Within a few days, however, Thorat got a phone call from Bombay to inform him that the 'Government of Bombay would be happy to make a free gift of the required land to the Academy'.

Thorat recalls several other incidents involving Sardar Patel. In early 1947, Thorat was given command of 161 Brigade located at Ranchi. Shortly thereafter, the brigade was rushed to Calcutta to quell the communal riots that had erupted there. During the unrest, a patrol led by a lance-naik (a naik is equivalent to a corporal, and lance appointments rank below the ranks which they prefix) encountered a gang of armed hooligans. The police sub-inspector accompanying the patrol asked the lance-naik to open fire, which he did. As a result, one gang member died. Later, however, the lance-naik was charged with murder. Thorat tried to get the charge dropped, but the West Bengal government insisted that the lance-naik stand trial, though promising that he would be exonerated. Thorat was not satisfied. He felt that the indignity of being tried for murder, when all that the lance-naik had done was his duty, would affect the morale of troops. During a visit to Delhi, he called on Sardar Patel, who was the States Minister. When Thorat explained the case to him, Patel had the charges dropped.

India became independent of British rule on 15 August 1947, and soon after this Thorat was posted to Delhi as Director, Staff Duties & Weapons and Equipment (SD-&-WE), at Army HQ. One of his jobs was to divide the assets of the army between India and Pakistan, in the ratio of 3:1. He was also responsible for sending Pakistan its share of weapons and equipment. He soon realised that most of them were being used against Indian troops in Kashmir. Thorat tried to stop, or at least slow down, the flow of arms and ammunition into Pakistan but the C-in-C, General Bucher, insisted that it continue. Thorat sought an appointment with Sardar Patel, who was also the Deputy Prime Minister. After hearing him out, the Sardar smiled and said: 'Why have you come to me? You should have gone to the Prime

Minister.' Then, without waiting for a reply, he added: 'All right. Don't be too prompt in doing your duty.' Thorat was puzzled and said: 'Sir, these are the orders of the Commander-in-Chief. What will I tell him when he finds out?' Patel smiled, and said: 'Surely you can tell a plausible lie for the delay? I am with you.' After this there was a sharp decline in the quantity of arms and ammunition, but a corresponding increase in innocuous items to make up the tonnage that was being sent to Pakistan.

On 31 January 1948, a day after Mahatma Gandhi's assassination, Thorat was promoted Major General and appointed GOC Delhi Area. Conditions in Delhi were disturbed, and refugees from Pakistan were still pouring in. Thorat also had to provide protection to the Muslims in Delhi, as well as in the surrounding areas of Punjab, and several princely states in Rajasthan. In addition, he had to assist the establishment of civil administration in Alwar, where the Maharaja had been taken into 'protective custody'. This was also done in Bharatpur, where the ruler accepted his arrival with grace, inviting Thorat to the annual duck shoot, for which Bharatpur was famous. During winter, millions of migratory birds from Siberia arrive at the lake in Bharatpur. No shooting was permitted till the annual duck shoot, when the Viceroy and hundreds of other guests were invited. Thorat had heard about these shoots, but never seen one. After a few months, he accompanied Lieutenant General Rajendra Sinhji and several other guests, including a few maharajas, to Bharatpur. Thorat shot almost a hundred ducks, with the total bag running into several thousand. Fortunately for the birds, this was one of the last of the 'royal shoots', and conservationists soon prevailed upon Parliament to make laws banning them altogether. The lake has now been converted into a sanctuary, and visitors can shoot birds only with a camera.

During this period, a large number of refugees were housed in refugee camps around Delhi. Colonel A.B. Jadhav has an interesting anecdote to relate about Thorat in this regard. To cater to their needs, a large number of DTLs (deep trench latrines), such as those used by troops in the field, had been set up in the camps. During one of his morning walks, Thorat found that the refugees were not using the DTLs, but defecating in the open. Diseases such as cholera and hepatitis were already on the rise, and Thorat was alarmed. He tried to persuade the refugees, through his staff, to use the DTLs, but they continued to go to the fields. As a result, conditions in the camps soon became unhygienic, and Thorat knew that he would have to do something quickly. One day, he collected all the children in the camp and told them that if they found anyone answering the call of nature in the field instead of the DTL, they should surround him, raise their hands above their heads and chant: 'Oye, Oye, Oye'. He promised them each a four-anna (a rupee had 16 annas) coin everyday for this chore. The children agreed and set to work the following morning. Within a few days, the DTLs began to be used.

After just six months in Delhi Area, Thorat was asked to take over the East Punjab Area from Thimayya, who was being sent to Kashmir. He moved to his new HQ in Jullunder, where the problems of refugees, evacuee property and border defences kept him quite busy, and he had to visit Lahore several times. The C-in-C of the Pakistani Army, General Gracy, had been Thorat's guardian at Sandhurst, and the CGS, Major General Hutton, his brigade commander in Burma. As a result, Thorat was always treated as a VIP in Pakistan and was received at the Wagah check-post with a ceremonial guard of honour. On every visit, he made it a point to visit the men of his parent battalion, 1/14 Punjab, which was fighting in Kashmir but had its rear party in Lahore.

In March 1950, Thorat was asked to take over as CGS at Army HQ in Delhi. Thorat was surprised by the appointment, which was normally held by a senior lieutenant general. He was only a major general, and that too one of the junior ones. However, the C-in-C, General Cariappa, had selected him and he had to go. During this time, the strength of the army was about 500,000, which the bureaucrats in the Ministry of Defence wanted to reduce to 300,000. In spite of vehement opposition from Army HQ, the Defence Secretary and Financial Adviser succeeded in persuading the Cabinet to accept this measure. As soon as the process started, Pakistan started virulent propaganda against India. Army HQ wanted the Armoured Division to be moved to Amritsar as a precautionary measure, but Prime Minister Nehru did not agree. Finally, General Cariappa went to meet the President, Dr Rajendra Prasad, accompanied by Thorat. Dr Prasad listened to them and asked Nehru to re-examine the proposal. A meeting was called to discuss the issue, but Nehru was not in a good mood. At the end, he said: 'I refuse to believe that Pakistan will go to war. How can I take a warlike stance, when I am myself trying to maintain peace in the world?'

Thorat requested the Prime Minister for a hearing. He showed him a map of Punjab and explained the strategic importance of the river Beas. If Pakistan decided to capture Amritsar, it would not be possible to reinforce it since there was only one bridge on the Beas, and that too of limited capacity. Nehru grasped the situation and rescinded his earlier decision. The concentration of troops in Amritsar was completed and Pakistani propaganda died down.

In February 1952, Thorat had what one can only describe as a providential escape from death. A tactical exercise was being held in Lucknow and Thorat, accompanied by several other senior officers, including Shrinagesh and Thimayya, left Delhi in a twin-engined Devon aircraft belonging to the IAF. On the return flight, one of the engines caught fire, which soon began to spread towards the fuselage. There was every likelihood that the petrol tanks would explode, and the cabin soon be engulfed in flames. The pilot put the plane into a nosedive, hoping to land before this happened. Just then, the burning engine fell out, its frame having been melted by the intense heat. The fire subsided, but the plane now seemed to be out of control. Finally, after many anxious moments, they landed in a field close to Lucknow.

Miraculously, no one was hurt, and after picking up their hats and canes, they got out of the aircraft in strict order of seniority! They were soon rescued by the villagers and by early next morning, were back in Lucknow, much to the relief of everyone, including their families, who had only heard that the plane was missing and had been waiting for news throughout the night. When Dr Rajendra Prasad was told of their miraculous escape, he sent his own aeroplane to fly them back to Delhi.

At this time, Thorat and his family were staying at 16 Akbar Road in New Delhi. Leela was fond of gardening, and the house had a garden full of flowers in front, and a large vegetable patch at the back. Once, they had a bumper crop of pumpkins and ladies fingers, and one of the two vegetables would be served at lunch, and the other at dinner. One evening, Thorat said to his wife: 'Leela, there's a new restaurant called Kwality that has been opened in Connaught Place. Why don't we take the children out, and have dinner there?' Kusum, Kumud and Yashwant were thrilled, and when the family arrived at the restaurant, Leela and the children lost no time in ordering delicacies like *chana bhatura* and pizza. But Thorat, after a lot of deliberation, asked for pumpkin and ladies' fingers. The family looked at him in surprise, till he explained that he did not want to break a good habit. Leela got the hint, and the family soon got a respite from the ubiquitous pumpkins and ladies' fingers.

In 1953 Thorat was sent to Korea as Commander of the Custodian Force of India (CFI). Thimayya had been appointed Chairman of the five-nation Neutral Nation Repatriation Commission (NNRC). The CFI was a military force, responsible for the security of prisoners of both sides. It functioned under the directions of the NNRC. The CFI comprised 190 Infantry Brigade, under the command of Brigadier R.S. Paintal. It had three infantry battalions and an engineer company. Later, two more battalions, and a company of Mahar machine-gunners were also added. Thorat selected Brigadier Gurbaksh Singh, DSO, to be his deputy commander. In July 1953, when the Armistice was signed, about 30,000 North Korean and Chinese prisoners were captured by the United Nations Command. The Korean Peoples Army (KPVA) and the Chinese People's Volunteers (CPV) Command held several hundred British, American and South Koreans as prisoners. All these were transferred to the custody of CFI, under Thorat, having refused repatriation after the cease-fire. It was hoped that after some time in custody of the neutral CFI, the effects of propaganda and brainwashing would wear off, and the prisoners would agree to be repatriated.

The first contingent of the CFI left Madras on 18 August 1953 by sea, reaching Inchon on 14 September. The fifth contingent, which was also the last, left on 5 September and reached on 28 September.

They were divided into three groups and housed in canvas tents at a place known earlier as Tong-Jong-Ni. Thorat gave it the name Hindnagar, which soon became well known. The prisoners were housed in compounds, each accommodating about 500. The compounds had separate tents for living, kitchen, dining hall, and latrines. They were surrounded by a double wire fence, with the space between them used for patrolling. A number of compounds were grouped together into an enclosure, which also had a double wire fence around it. Initially, prisoners from both sides were quite friendly with the Indian troops guarding them. However, this changed as soon as some of them began to ask for repatriation. The others resented this and beat up the prisoners who wanted to surrender to the guards, sometimes even killing them. The Indian troops tried to prevent such incidents, and this brought them into conflict with the prisoners who were against repatriation.

On 25 September 1953, there was an anti-India demonstration in one of the camps. Thorat entered the compound accompanied by a few officers and left after talking to the prisoners. As they were leaving, the prisoners caught hold of the interpreter, Major H.S. Grewal, and bodily carried him back into the compound. Thorat turned back and rushed in followed by about a dozen

Indian soldiers. The prisoners closed the gates and attacked the Indians held captive inside with wooden poles and stones, causing injuries to some of them. Thorat gave his men strict orders not to retaliate, realising that they were heavily outnumbered. He also ordered the brigade commander, who was outside, not to fire, since this would lead to a massacre and India's position would become untenable.

Thorat found a POW who spoke English and started talking to the prisoners through him. He asked them to release Major Grewal, but they refused. Thorat then took out his cigarette case, but it was empty. He said: 'What sort of Chinese are you? I and my men have been your guests for about an hour but you have not offered us a cup of tea or even a cigarette. Where is your traditional hospitality and the good manners for which your race is renowned?' The prisoner was bewildered by this remark, but turned around and barked some orders. Soon mugs of tea and packets of cigarettes appeared.

The situation changed as if by magic. The Chinese apologised and brought Grewal to Thorat. He accepted their representation and promised to forward it to the NNRC. They formed a guard of honour, and cheered lustily as Thorat left the compound followed by the Indian troops. This incident received wide publicity in the world press. After his return to India, Thorat was awarded the Ashoka Chakra Class II (now called the Kirti Chakra) and the Padma Shri for his courage, composure and presence of mind in preventing an ugly situation which could have caused several deaths.

On 15 October 1953, 'explanations' started. A large number of North Korean and Chinese prisoners captured by the UN Command had refused to be repatriated. The KPVA–CPV Command contended that this was because the prisoners had been fed false information about the conditions prevailing in their homelands. They argued that if they were given a chance to explain things to them, the prisoners would change their minds. This was to be done by teams from parent nations, who would be allowed to talk to each prisoner, in camera. Every prisoner had to undergo the process of 'explanation', but was free to choose whether or not he wished to be repatriated.

When the explanations started, the prisoners refused to come out of their compounds. Thorat and his troops had a difficult time persuading them to meet the teams. Sometimes they even had to use force to bring the prisoners to the explanation tent. The prisoners often spat on the members of the explanation team or beat them up. Occasionally, they even tried to rough up the guards. If the troops used force, they would be denounced by the Swiss and Swedish members of the NNRC, who viewed it as a violation of human rights. If they did not, the Czech and Polish members would accuse them of not giving adequate protection to the explanation teams. Ultimately, on the insistence of the Czech and Polish members, who threatened to withdraw if force was not used, the matter was referred to the Government of India. It was decided that no force should be used, and that prisoners were to be given explanations only on request. After the 90-day period for explanations had expired, the prisoners were handed over by the CFI to the side which had captured them. The UN Command released its prisoners in January 1954. The KPVA–CPV Command initially refused to take back the prisoners, but eventually did so. Their fate was never known.

The CFI returned to India in early 1954. They were seen off by General Maxwell Taylor and given a guard of honour by the 8th US Army. On their arrival in Madras, they received a tumultuous welcome. Chief Minister C. Rajagopalachari and his entire cabinet were at the quay to receive Thorat and his men when their ship berthed. They left for Delhi by special trains, which were greeted at every station en route and showered with sweets and garlands. At Nagpur, the Chief Minister of the state was present with his ministers. When their train steamed into Delhi they were greeted by a huge crowd, which included Prime Minister Nehru, at the railway station.

In May 1954, the Custodian Force of India was disbanded and Thorat was given command of 5 Infantry Division at Jhansi. In 1955, the division was ordered to move to Ferozepore. The move up to Rohtak was made on foot, and Thorat marched with the division. They entrained at Rohtak and proceeded to Ferozepore to join the newly raised 11 Corps. Soon thereafter, he was promoted Lieutenant General and given command of 11 Corps, which had its HQ at Jullunder. At the time, 11 Corps was the only strike force in the Indian Army and Thorat had under his command two infantry divisions, an armoured brigade and an independent infantry brigade.

During his tenure at Jullunder, Thorat met with two accidents. General Maxwell Taylor was visiting Delhi and wanted to meet him. Thorat left for Delhi in his staff car. He had dozed off after lunch when the accident occurred. He suffered a temporary loss of memory and later it was discovered that he had also injured his spine. He was in hospital for a month, and had to wear a plaster for even longer. He was lucky to have survived—one side of the car had been completely smashed. The second accident occurred when, during an exercise, Thorat, Major General Bahadur Singh, GOC 4 Infantry Division, and Brigadier M.S. Pathania, his senior staff officer, were crossing the Yamuna river in an assault boat. All three had fishing tackle with them and were casting for fish. The boat dashed against a rope that had been slung across the river and capsized. Bahadur Singh and Pathania abandoned their fishing rods and began to swim towards the bank. Thorat, however, held on to his fishing rod with one hand, using the other to swim. To everyone's surprise and amusement, he reached the bank still clutching his precious rod.

An upright and meticulous soldier, Thorat was always correct in his dealings with his seniors and subordinates. He rarely fell foul of his seniors. But once, in 1956, while he was commanding 11 Corps, he did manage to offend the army commander. Torrential rains had flooded Jullunder and Amritsar districts and the Grand Trunk Road was submerged under 5 feet of water. An artillery unit at Kasu Begu near Ferozepore was also threatened by a breach in a canal. Thorat rang up Air HQ in Delhi and requested an aerial reconnaissance to determine if there were any other breaches. The Army Commander, Lieutenant General Kalwant Singh, was very annoyed and threatened to take disciplinary action against Thorat for failing to follow the proper procedures. Thorat stood firm and, when asked to explain, replied that since the safety of his men and installations was in danger and he could not contact the Command HQ in Simla, he had no other option but to approach Air HQ. He also told the Army Commander that in case he decided to take action, he himself was more likely to land in trouble than Thorat. The matter was dropped.

When General S.M. Shrinagesh retired in May 1957, Thimayya was nominated to succeed him as Chief of Army Staff, superseding Lieutenant General Sant Singh, who was commanding the Eastern Army, and Lieutenant General Kalwant Singh, in Western Command. Kalwant decided to continue, but Sant preferred to take retirement. Thorat was appointed GOC-in-C Eastern Command, which at that time had its HQ at Lucknow and comprised the area of the present Central and Eastern Commands. Thorat soon fell in love with Lucknow, which was called the city of nawabs, and its people, who still spoke flawless Urdu of their forbears. Lucknow was famous for its *tehzib* (good manners), courtesy and leisurely lifestyle. It was also a centre for classical dance and music, and Thorat soon became a connoisseur of the *thumri, dadra* and *kathak.*

But Thorat did not get much time to savour the delights of Lucknow, as he was kept fairly busy with operational and administrative matters. The Eastern Command was very large—it covered almost the whole of eastern and central India.

---

* The thumri and dadra are forms of vocal music, and kathak is a style of classical dance.

The Naga tribes were in rebellion, and the border problems with the Chinese in the North East had begun. Thimayya and Thorat were both perturbed at the state of defences in the North East Frontier Agency (NEFA), and tried their best to improve them. However, this was not to be. At about the time when Thimayya took over as Chief of Army Staff, V.K. Krishna Menon had become the Defence Minister. Differences soon developed between Menon and Thimayya, leading to the latter's resignation, which was later withdrawn. Thorat, too, fell out with Menon due to a sharp difference of opinion over the question of how the defence of the Sino–Indian border was to be organised. At this time, the defence of NEFA was the responsibility of the Assam Rifles, a paramilitary force which functioned under the Central Government. Technically, the army had no responsibility or authority in the matter. But Thorat realised that if there was trouble, the army would have to step in since it was responsible for the defence of the entire nation. He therefore requested that the defence of NEFA be included in the operational tasks of the Eastern Command. When Thorat saw that Nehru and Menon were not taking the problem seriously, he decided to put it in writing. On 8 October 1959 Thorat produced a paper on the defence of NEFA and sent it to the COAS. It was forwarded to the Ministry of Defence, but Krishna Menon did not show it to Nehru, accusing Thorat of being an alarmist and a warmonger. Subsequently, an exercise code-named LAL QUILA was held in Lucknow in March 1960, which was attended by the Chief and all Principal Staff Officers in Army HQ. The exercise clearly showed that with the troops, weapons and equipment available at that time, a Chinese attack could not be contained or defeated, and that the 'forward policy' being advocated by Menon and Kaul was not practicable. Thorat also came up with a timetable to show how the defences would fall day by day in case the Chinese attacked. Kaul, who attended the exercise as QMG, had different views. By that time, Thimayya's position had already been undermined and he had lost all authority. In May 1961, both Thimayya and Thorat retired and Kaul was appointed CGS. With Thapar as Army Chief, Kaul had a free hand to implement his ideas.

When Thimayya retired in May 1961, it was expected that Thorat would succeed him as Army Chief. He was highly decorated, had combat experience, and was held in high regard by the service. Most important, he was GOC-in-C Eastern Command and was familiar with the situation on the border with China. But the government nominated Thapar, who was senior but had little else to commend him. Many factors were cited for bypassing Thorat. One was a laudatory speech that Thorat made during the farewell dinner for General Thimayya at the Kumaon Regimental Centre. Another was the fact that he was not recommended by B.N. Mullick, the all-powerful Director of the Intelligence Bureau (IB). In fact, Mullick had suggested to the government that Thimayya was planning a coup, and Thorat was an active participant in the plot. Whatever the reason, both Thimayya and Thorat could not see eye to eye with Krishna Menon, who quite naturally preferred the more pliant Thapar as Chief.

When Thorat retired in May 1961, he was still three months short of his 55th birthday. Similarly, Cariappa had retired at the age of 53, Nathu Singh at 51, and Thimayya at 55. This was because soon after Independence, a rule had been promulgated to limit the tenures of the Chief and Army Commanders to four years. The decision was unfortunate, as it removed the top leadership of the Indian Army at an age when they had several years of useful life still left, and the nation could have benefited from their experience. The rule did not apply to the civil bureaucracy, or to the navy or the air force. Even in the army, it was applicable only to the Chief and Army Commanders, not the heads of technical arms and services. If Thimayya and Thorat had not retired in May 1961, the events which took place after a year may well have taken a different turn.

On 8 May 1961, Thorat was given a ceremonial farewell at Lucknow. Donning his uniform for the last time, he inspected the guard of honour and then mounted an open jeep, which was pulled by the officers of Eastern Command to the tune of 'Auld Lang Syne'. When he entered his railway saloon after bidding farewell to the large number of military and civil officials who had come to see him off, his eyes were moist. When he saw the Eastern Command flag being lowered and heard the buglers sounding the 'Retreat' he sprang to attention and saluted the flag. He then unbuckled his sword from his Sam Browne belt, and handed it over to his son Yashwant.

Leela, who was reclining on a couch in the saloon, looked askance at him, and asked him why he had given the sword to Bhaiyya. 'I thought a soldier never retires. Isn't that what you always said?' she asked. Thorat laughed and replied: 'Don't worry. If I am recalled for duty, I will again wear the sword.'

After retirement, the Thorats settled down in Kolhapur. Before he retired, Thorat had been offered the appointment of Vice Chancellor of Lucknow University, which he had declined, since he felt that he did not have the credentials for a job which should be held by an outstanding academic. A little later, the Chairman of Hindustan Steel requested him to join the company as a director. Thorat agreed, and the proposal was cleared by Sardar Swaran Singh, the Minister for Steel. However, as Thorat later learned, it was turned down by the Prime Minister, on the advice of Krishna Menon.

Soon after his arrival in Kolhapur, Thorat was informed that Yeshwantrao Chavan, Chief Minister of Maharashtra, wanted to meet him. Thorat went to the Circuit House, where Chavan was staying, and after greeting him, asked why he had been called. Chavan handed Thorat a sealed envelope and said: 'General Sahib, this contains a formal letter requesting you to accept the post of the Chairman of the Maharashtra State Public Service Commission for five years. If the proposal is to your liking, kindly open the envelope. Otherwise, just tear it up.'

Thorat replied: 'Mr Chavan, you know I am not in the good books of Panditji.' Chavan said, 'General Sahib, don't worry about that. Maharashtra is far from Delhi.' Thorat then said that he and his wife had got used to living in bungalows and would feel cooped up in a flat in Bombay. Chavan told him that he would not have to live in a flat, but would be provided a large bungalow. Thorat then came to his most important condition: he would accept the job only if he was allowed to function independently. The day he felt that he was under pressure from any minister or politician, he would resign. Chavan readily agreed to this condition as well. Thorat then said that they had just moved from Lucknow and his wife was still unpacking and setting up the house. He would like to discuss the matter with her before giving a final reply. Chavan again agreed and Thorat left with the envelope still unopened. After discussing the offer with Leela, he decided to accept and sent his confirmation to Chavan. Along with his appointment letter, Chavan issued a directive that no minister, secretary or party functionary would exert any pressure, or interfere in any manner with the functioning of the commission. These orders remained in force even after Chavan left for Delhi to replace Krishna Menon as Defence Minister, and Vasantrao Naik became the Chief Minister of Maharashtra.

Soon after Thorat was appointed Chairman of the Maharashtra State Public Service Commission, Chavan met Krishna Menon during the annual session of the Congress Party at Trivandrum. Menon casually remarked that Chavan had made a mistake by giving Thorat such an important appointment and advised him to reconsider his decision. Chavan smiled and replied: 'Mr Menon, I have never interfered or expressed any views about your handling of defence matters. I would request you to show the same courtesy to me as far as affairs of my state are concerned.'

After the Chinese overran the defences in NEFA in 1962, there was a lull in the battle, which took place almost exactly as Thorat had predicted. Nehru sent for him and asked: 'Thorat, how could this have happened? You were in Eastern Command. Did you have any inkling of this disaster?' Thorat replied: 'Yes sir. The possibility had occurred to us and the ministry was warned.' When he saw the paper that Thorat had sent him in October 1959, Nehru was stunned. 'Why was this not shown to me?' he asked. Thorat suggested that perhaps the Defence Minister could answer this question. At this Nehru exploded: 'Menon, Menon! Why have you got your knife into him? You people do not realise what an intellectual giant he is.'

Thorat said: 'If he is, Sir, I have seen no evidence of it in the case under consideration.' Nehru glared at him angrily for a few seconds. Then he smiled and said: 'You know, Thorat, you Maharashtrians are like mules. Normally you are good and docile, but once you dig your toes in, it is impossible to dislodge you.' The tension broke, and Nehru rang for some tea. He once again became the affable Nehru that Thorat knew so well from the days of the partition riots and after his return from Korea.

Nehru went on to discuss the possibility of the Chinese, who had declared a ceasefire unilaterally, advancing into the Brahmaputra valley. Thorat told him that they were unlikely to do so, since Chinese lines of communication were already stretched, and they could not get their artillery and tanks across the Himalayas. At this, Nehru perked up and invited Thorat to be a member of the National Defence Council, which he was thinking of forming.

Thorat was appointed a member of the council, which was chaired by the Prime Minister himself. It also included some senior cabinet members and the chief ministers of different states. Surprisingly, neither Krishna Menon nor Kaul, the two defence experts on whom Nehru had relied the most, were nominated as members. In the event, the Council did not achieve much, but Thorat felt that his honour had been vindicated. He had been accused by Krishna Menon and Kaul of not implementing the forward policy, which they had been advocating, and which had proved to be a miserable failure.

In 1967, Thorat was persuaded by Chavan to stand for election to Parliament as a Congress Party candidate. Soon after he had filed his nomination, the Maharani of Kolhapur also announced that she would contest from the same constituency. Chavan advised him to change his constituency and offered him the ticket for the Satara seat, but Thorat refused. Since he had filed his papers earlier, he felt that it was up to the Maharani to change her constituency. In the event, he lost the election and decided not to contest again.

Thorat was liberal and cosmopolitan in his views and this was mirrored in his family life. He was a Maharashtrian, while his wife was a Punjabi. His son Yashwant married a South Indian Aiyyar girl. His two daughters, Kusum and Kumud, also married outside the state: one chose her life partner from Punjab, and the other from Bengal. The Thorats' home in Kolhapur, called 'Indu Niketan', soon came to epitomise gracious living and was always humming with tongues from every part of India. Although Thorat had always been a good sportsman, he had never played golf, which he took up at the age of 73. For the next 12 years, he was a regular on the golf course. While he went round his nine holes, Leela sat in the clubhouse, reading a book or knitting, or sometimes strolling in the lawns.

Thorat's strong character and sterling qualities were inherited by the entire family. In 1986, his granddaughter Kanchan got married. The ceremony was held in Kolhapur and there were about 300 guests at the function which was held on the lawns of Indu Niketan. Leela was running a high fever, with her temperature touching 105 degrees. But she insisted on receiving the guests as they entered the porch of the house. Her daughters then took her inside and put her to bed. Soon after this, she went into a coma. Not wanting to mar the occasion, the entire family put up a smiling front throughout the evening, till the last guest had departed. At midnight, Thorat drove his wife to the mission hospital at Miraj. She had meningitis, and it was two weeks before she was declared to be out of danger. None of the guests who had attended the wedding had any inkling of how serious her condition had been while the party was going on.

A similar incident occurred when Thorat tragically lost his younger daughter, Kumud. Thorat was in Bombay when Kumud took ill and had to be taken to the Hinduja Hospital. After struggling for two days, she expired. At that time, Leela was alone in Kolhapur and her recent sickness had sapped her both physically and mentally. Realising that she would not be able to bear the shock alone, Thorat did not tell her the sad news on the telephone. Immediately after cremating his daughter, he left for Kolhapur with his son. When their car reached the porch of the house, Leela rushed out, surprised by their unexpected arrival. She asked her husband why he had come back and whether there was any problem. Thorat took her inside, and seating her on a chair, gently told her that Kumud was no more. Leela began to cry; it was only after she had calmed down that he told her about Kumud's hospitalisation and death.

In 1987, Yashwant was seconded to the Bank of England. Before he left, he told Thorat that he would like to visit Sandhurst, about which his father often spoke with nostalgia. Thorat laughed and said: 'Bhaiyya, I left Sandhurst 61 years ago. I wonder if they will even remember me. Anyway, I will write to them.' He wrote and received a prompt reply from the Commandant, saying that they would be pleased to show his son around the college. Yashwant left for England with the letter, and a copy of his father's autobiography, *From Reveille to Retreat*.

In London, Yashwant became engrossed in his work and almost forgot about Sandhurst, until the end of his visit. He telephoned the Royal Military College to inform them of his arrival. When he reached Camberley, he was received by a British colonel, who conducted him to a staff car bearing the Indian flag along with that of the Royal Military College. They were piloted by a motorcycle escort. Yashwant was overwhelmed by this reception, which clearly reflected the high esteem in which his father was held by his alma mater. After being shown around the college, he was taken to the India Museum, where he found his father's name inscribed among the heroes of World War II, along with a description of his gallantry in action in Burma, for which he was awarded the DSO. Later, the officers hosted a lunch in his honour, during which the Commandant made a speech, giving a vivid account of Thorat's career. Yashwant came away feeling that they knew more about his father than he himself did. He remembers his visit to Sandhurst as one of the most memorable experiences of his life.

One quality for which Thorat was admired, both by officers and men, was his concern for the welfare of the troops, and his humane and compassionate attitude towards them. He was able to empathise with his subordinates and always treated them with warmth and consideration. One of his aides, Captain Har Mander Singh, who later joined the Civil Service recalls how the Thorats made him feel at home on his very first visit to them. Not only Singh, but his family too came to be accepted as part of the Thorat household. Thorat's behaviour towards young officers was like that of a father with his son, and his daughters behaved with his aides as they would with their brother. When being driven in his car, if he saw a young officer walking, he always stopped and asked the youngster if he wanted a lift. He never asked his aides to perform menial tasks, like carrying bags, opening doors or pouring drinks. Irrespective of rank, he treated every soldier with respect, and never made him feel small.

Thorat was a good orator and a voracious reader. He had a scholastic bent of mind and was well versed in Sanskrit. Though he always addressed troops in simple Hindustani, he often used Sanskrit *slokas* (verses) to drive home a point. Thorat's behaviour with the ladies was impeccable, and other than smoking, he had no vices. He rolled his own cigarettes, which he carried in a slim cigarette case. He had a habit of tapping a cigarette three times before putting it between his lips and lighting it. This idiosyncracy was often mimicked by younger officers, who felt that it would make them look suave and debonair.

Thorat died on 10 August 1992, in Kolhapur at the age of 86. His death was widely mourned not only in Maharashtra, but in the entire country, by soldiers as well as civilians. Due to his tenure in Korea, he was well known outside India as well, and almost all national dailies carried an obituary. He had many friends and admirers, and it was difficult to find a single instance in his long and distinguished career when he acted in a manner that was not expected of an officer and a gentleman.

It was indeed unfortunate that both Thimayya and Thorat had retired when the Chinese attacked in 1962. Had they still been active, the nation might perhaps have been spared the ignominy and humiliation it had to suffer, resulting mainly from the lack of courage, experience and decisiveness in the top military leadership at that critical juncture. Though he did not rise to the highest rank, Thorat's place in Indian military history is assured. A highly respected soldier, known for his upright behaviour and gentlemanly ways, he epitomised the highest standards of professionalism in the army.

5

Brigadier Mohd Usman, MVC

5

Brigadier Mohd Usman, MVC
The Epitome of Valour

It is said: 'Those whom the Gods love, die young.' The brave rarely have long lives and so it was with Mohammed Usman. When he laid down his life for his motherland, he was 12 days short of his 36th birthday. But in his short lifetime he achieved more than most mortals who live twice as long or more. A grateful nation awarded him the Maha Vir Chakra (MVC) and he was given a state funeral, a rarity for a military leader. Usman's valour, courage and tenacity against fearful odds played a crucial role in 1948, when a newborn nation faced its first test in battle. His deeds are now part of the legends of Naushera and Jhangar. A true patriot and war hero, his name will always be enshrined in the annals of the Indian Army.

Usman was born on 15 July 1912 in Bibipur village of Azamgarh district in the United Provinces. His father, Kazi Mohammed Farook, was a police officer, who later became the Kotwal (the officer in charge of the main police station in a city) of Banaras (now Varanasi) and was given the title of 'Khan Bahadur' by the British government. Though he was named Sheikh Mohammed Usman, the prefix 'Sheikh' was later dropped. He had three elder sisters and two brothers, one of whom, Gufran, joined the army and rose to the rank of brigadier, while the other, Subhan, became a journalist. Usman was sent to the Harish Chandra High School in Banaras. Even as a young lad, he showed signs of the courage that later brought him fame as a war hero. When he was 12 years old, he was passing through a village where he saw several people gathered around a well. When he learned that a child had fallen in the well, Usman unhesitatingly jumped in and saved the child's life.

Usman suffered from a speech impediment which made him stammer. His father felt that this would make it difficult for him to enter the civil service, and decided that he should join the police force. He took Usman to meet his superior, an Englishman who also stammered. He asked Usman a few questions, and when the latter replied the Englishman thought that the young boy was mocking him and was visibly annoyed. This put paid to his chances of joining the police. His father was disappointed, but not Usman. He had always wanted to join the army, about which he had spoken to his friends in school.

Indians had been joining the army as commissioned officers since 1920, though the competition was very tough and preference was given to men of aristocratic or upper class backgrounds. Usman decided to try his luck and applied for Sandhurst. He was selected and sailed for England in July 1932. In fact, this was the last course at Sandhurst to which Indians were admitted, and subsequent batches had to join the Indian Military Academy which had opened in Dehradun in the same year. Usman passed out from Sandhurst on 1 February 1934, along with 10 other Indians, including Apji Randhir Singh and R.N. Nehra. Incidentally, among 45 cadets who passed out, Apji was first in order of merit, while Usman was 30th and Nehra 34th. The first batch of ICOs had joined the Indian Military Academy (IMA) at about the same time that Usman's batch went to Sandhurst, and included Sam Manekshaw, Smith Dun and Mohammed Musa, who rose to become Army Chiefs in India, Burma and Pakistan. This batch of ICOs was commissioned on 1 February 1935, with their seniority antedated by a year to account for the difference in duration of training between the

Royal Military College and Indian Military Academy. However, to ensure that they remained junior to the KCIOs, the ICOs were given seniority from 4 February 1934. Thus, Manekshaw's batch was three days junior to Usman's.

As was customary after commissioning Usman was sent to a British battalion for a year's attachment. On 19 March 1935, he joined the 5th Battalion (King George's Own) 10th Baluch Regiment, also known as Jacob's Rifles. After a stint of regimental duties, he qualified on a wartime staff course and did a staff tenure. Towards the end of World War II, he was posted to 16/10 Baluch as second-in-command. The battalion was then in the Arakan in Burma, and part of 51 Infantry Brigade under 25 Indian Division. The CO, Lieutenant Colonel John Fairlay, was one of the few Britishers who liked Indian officers and had a high opinion of their capabilities. This was probably because he had served at the IMA, Dehradun, as an instructor, and had seen them at close quarters. Z.C. 'Zoru' Bakshi, who later became a Lieutenant General and one of the most highly decorated soldiers of the Indian Army, was in the same battalion as a young officer.

Soon after he joined the battalion, Zoru Bakshi was sent on a patrol with some men of his company, which comprised Pathans. On his return, Zoru reported that he had come across a hill feature, which was held by the Japanese. Despite the fact that he was being transferred the next day, the CO promptly gave orders for its capture. The task was assigned to Zoru, who was told to take the Dogra company with him instead of the Pathan company. Colonel Fairlay had started his career with the Dogras and therefore had more faith in their prowess. Zoru was not very happy about this, but there was nothing he could do. In order to strengthen the platoons, even the men employed in the mess were rounded up. One of these was Sepoy Bhandari Ram.

The following night, Zoru went ahead with the Dogra company and launched an attack on the feature from three sides, using a platoon from each direction. After a bitter fight, the feature was captured. This was the first time Bhandari Ram had been in action, but he showed conspicuous gallantry. Apart from sustaining several bullets he was seriously wounded by a grenade which burst right in front of him. After the operation, Zoru described Bhandari Ram's bravery to Usman, who was officiating as CO, since the new incumbent, Lieutenant Colonel L.P. 'Bogey' Sen who was to replace Fairlay, had yet to report for duty. Usman decided that Bhandari Ram deserved a VC, and when the new CO joined the next day, Usman requested him to forward his name for the award.

The VC was the highest award for gallantry and given only for exceptional acts of valour. Since Bogey Sen had just taken command, he was unsure about sending a recommendation for the VC so soon. He felt that the Brigade Commander may be more inclined to consider a recommendation for the Indian Order of Merit (IOM). Usman was very upset, and felt that this would be unfair to Bhandari Ram.

He argued that since he was in command on the day the action took place, his opinion must be given due weightage. But Sen did not relent and refused to change his recommendation.

Usman was not one to take things lying down. He walked up to the Brigade Commander and apprised him of the situation. The Commander, Brigadier R.A. Hutton, agreed with Usman. He sent back the recommendation to the Battalion HQ, with the remark that on going through the citation, he felt that the action merited a VC rather than an IOM. After this, Sen had no hesitation in sending a fresh recommendation and Bhandari Ram was awarded the VC, which he deserved. But had it not been for the stand taken by Usman, this would not have come about.

Incidentally, 51 Infantry Brigade later became famous as the 'All Indian Brigade', since all three battalions of the brigade were being commanded by Indians. Lieutenant Colonel S.P.P. Thorat was commanding 2/2 Punjab, Lieutenant Colonel K.S. Thimayya was in command of 8/19 Hyderabad, and Lieutenant Colonel L.P. Sen was the CO of 16/10 Baluch. In the battle of

Kangaw in January 1945, all three were awarded DSOs. After World War II, 25 Indian Division was disbanded, and had not been re-raised when Usman fought and died in Jhangar many years later. Today, the same division is responsible for the defence of the sector.

Soon after Zoru had captured the hill, another attack was launched on a different objective. This one was carried out by a senior subaltern, who had never led an attack before and Usman felt that he needed the experience. But the officer went to pieces during the action and made a sorry spectacle of himself in front of the men. Usman was extremely angry and wanted the officer to be courtmartialled, but the CO did not agree. Usman then vowed to get rid of him as soon as possible.

After operations ceased in Burma, the battalion was sent back to India for rest and refit, and was located at Pollachi near Madras. Most of the officers and men were sent on leave. Usman, Zoru and the senior subaltern were the only three officers left. One day, they received a message asking for volunteers for parachute duty. Usman told Zoru to advise the officer to volunteer, but the latter refused. Usman told him that if he did not sign on the dotted line, he would have him courtmartialled for cowardice in the face of the enemy. The officer signed and was soon packed off for parachute training. Usman sighed with relief, thinking he had seen the last of the officer. Little did he know that very soon he would himself join the paratroopers.

The battalion did not stay in India for long; it was soon moved to Malaysia with the rest of the division. However, as soon as they landed, the Japanese surrendered after the bombing of Hiroshima and Nagasaki. Usman was promoted Lieutenant Colonel, and given command of 14/10 Baluch, which was in the same division. Since the war was over, there was little to do, though the troops remained in Malaysia for almost a year before being repatriated to India. Towards the end of 1946, Usman was posted as GSO 1 to the 2nd Airborne Division, which was being Indianised. When World War II ended, pressure on the British to accelerate the pace of Indianisation increased. After the Eight Unit Scheme had been introduced in 1922, only one division (4th Indian Division) and one cavalry brigade had been Indianised. It was now decided to also Indianise 2nd Airborne Division, which was then located at Karachi. Earlier known as the 44th Airborne, the division had three parachute brigades—the 50th, located at Quetta; and the 77th and 14th, both located at Malir. Each brigade had one British, one Gurkha and one Indian para battalion. After reorganisation, all British and Gurkha troops were withdrawn and replaced by Indians. The Indian Parachute Regiment, raised in December 1944, was disbanded and the para battalions were to become regular units, from certain nominated regiments of the Indian Army.

Major General S.C. Sinha, who was then serving in 3 Para Battalion of the Mahratta (now Maratha) Light Infantry as a captain, recalls that Usman's posting came as a surprise to everyone. A few months earlier, when Major General Downes, a British officer serving as GOC 2nd Airborne Division, was being posted out, he gave a farewell speech to the officers of his division. Most of the officers were British, and he tried to reassure them that they need not worry about losing their jobs to Indians, since it would take the latter many years to come up to the required standards. To reinforce his point, he mentioned that he had interviewed several Indian officers for the appointment of GSO 1, and found only one who could fit the bill. And this officer, he gloated, was not a volunteer for parachute duties. General Downes had obviously not heard about Usman, who was subsequently selected for the job. Fortunately, the new GOC, Major General C.H. Boucher, was from the Gurkhas, and did not have any bias against Indian officers. He himself had not been a paratrooper, and underwent the basic para course and jumps at Chaklala before assuming command of the division on 31 March 1946.

The process of reorganisation continued for several months. The British and Gurkha battalions were replaced by

Indian units. By January 1947, 14 Para Brigade comprised 4 Para Battalion of the 6 Rajputana Rifles (Outram's), 1 Para Battalion of the Frontier Force Regiment, and 3 Para Battalion of 16 Punjab Regiment; 50 Para Brigade had 3 Para Battalion of 1 Punjab Regiment, 3 Para Battalion of the Baluch Regiment, and 2 Para Battalion of the Madras Regiment; while 77 Para Brigade had 1 Para Battalion of 2 Punjab Regiment, 3 Para Battalion of the Mahratta Light Infantry, and 3 Para Battalion of the Rajput Regiment. These units were spread out all over the country, and it was a colossal job to bring them together. They belonged to some of the oldest regiments of the Indian Army, and continued to wear their regimental insignia and embellishments. However, to distinguish themselves as paratroopers, they began wearing maroon berets or turbans, and the coveted 'wings' on the right arm.

In February 1947, the British government announced that India would become independent by June 1948. The announcement was followed by large-scale communal violence in the Punjab and NWFP. Since the riots could not be controlled by the civil administration, the army had to be called in, and 2nd Airborne Division played a major part in quelling the disturbances. Usman had his hands full, rushing troops to areas where the situation had become critical—to Multan, Jacobabad, Lahore, Ambala, Rawalpindi and several places in Punjab. The operation became one of the biggest air-transported deployments of troops in India after World War II. Para units carried out their assigned tasks in an exemplary manner, and their conduct was appreciated by political leaders like Nehru, who toured the affected areas to reassure the people. Edwina Mountbatten, the Vicereine, also visited the refugee camps and hospitals, and praised the work done by the troops. Gradually, the situation improved and the riots ceased. However, the scale and ferocity of the violence convinced Mountbatten that the communal divide was too deep-rooted to remain dormant for long, and he took the momentous decision to advance the date for the transfer of power to 15 August 1947. He also persuaded the Indian National Congress to accept partition of the country.

As part of the partition settlement, 2nd Airborne Division was also divided. The divisional HQ and 50 and 77 Para Brigades were allotted to India, while 14 Para Brigade went to Pakistan. The para battalions did not go with their respective brigade HQ, but with their parent regiments. Thus, para battalions of the 1st and 15th Punjab, the Baluch and the Frontier Force regiments went to Pakistan, while the rest came to India. Along with the units, all officers, VCOs and other ranks were also given the option to choose between the Indian and Pakistani Army. Usman was then in England and had been posted as Commander 77 Parachute Brigade, which had been moved from Quetta to Multan for internal security duties. Since he was a senior Muslim officer, it was expected that he would opt for Pakistan. But he surprised everyone by opting for India. A large number of officers from the Baluch Regiment, to which he belonged, questioned his decision and asked him to reconsider on the grounds of regimental loyalty. Both Mohd Ali Jinnah and Liaqat Ali Khan tried to make him change his mind, promising him quick promotions, but Usman stood firm. He returned to his homeland and moved with 77 Parachute Brigade to Amritsar.

After Partition, HQ 2nd Airborne Division had moved to Dehradun, where it was placed in suspended animation. The two para brigades were placed under a joint Boundary Force commanded by Major General T.W. Rees, and employed for the evacuation of refugees. After the Boundary Force was wound up on 1 September 1947, responsibility for the security of refugees was taken over by the respective governments of the two countries. Major General K.S. Thimayya who, had been an adviser to Rees as a brigadier, was promoted and appointed GOC 4 Indian Division. As the force commander, he became responsible for the evacuation of refugees, in place of Rees. At that time 50 Para Brigade was in Gurdaspur under the command of Brigadier Y.S. Paranjpe, while 77 Para Brigade, under Usman, was in Amritsar, which was directly on the route taken by the refugees during their mass exodus in both directions. Though a Muslim, Usman was free of religious prejudice, and with his impartiality, fairness and secular outlook, set a fine example for the troops under his command. In those days, communal passions rose to unprecedented heights, and even seasoned soldiers sometimes found it difficult to avoid falling prey to the hysteria. Not very far from Amritsar, there had been an incident involving 3 Para Baluch, which fired 3-inch mortars on a refugee camp of Hindus and Sikhs.

October 1947 saw the start of the troubles in Kashmir. The 4th Battalion, Jammu and Kashmir Infantry, was located at Muzaffarabad. It had two companies of Muslims and two of Dogras. On 22 October the Muslims fell on the Dogras and murdered them, opening the way for raiders from Pakistan to enter Kashmir. By 26 October, the tribesmen had reached the outskirts of Srinagar, and on the next day, Indian troops were flown into Kashmir. The first battalion to be flown to Srinagar on 27 October was 1 Sikh, followed by 1 Para Kumaon (now 3 Para) on 29 October. At the same time, 50 Para Brigade, which was in Gurdaspur, was ordered to move to Jammu. The brigade had only two battalions, 1 Para Punjab (now 1 Para) and 3 Para Rajput. Both units had recently shed their Muslim companies and were deployed on internal security duties. Thimayya had foreseen the need for deployment of the brigade, and had sent Brigadier Paranjpe to carry out a reconnaissance of the area as soon as he was apprised of the situation in Kashmir. On 28 October, 50 Para Brigade began to move to Kashmir and by 4 November had concentrated in Jammu. It was charged with protecting the road from Jammu to Srinagar, and also to assist in the maintenance of law and order. Soon after it reached Jammu, 1 Para Punjab was flown to Srinagar, where the situation had become critical. By mid-November, after the battle at Shalateng had restored the situation in the valley, the battalion returned to Jammu.

At this time, the borders of the erstwhile Jammu and Kashmir State were manned by elements of the State Forces. There was a brigade each at Mirpur, Jammu and Punch. The HQ of the Mirpur Brigade was at Jhangar, with a battalion at Kotli, two companies at Naushera, and a company at Mirpur. These troops had no artillery, and the battalion had 400 men, while the company had 100. By the beginning of November, Pakistan had invaded the sector in strength. Mirpur, being very close to the border, had been encircled, Jhangar was besieged, and Kotli was threatened. On 7 November, Rajauri was captured and 30,000 Hindus were killed, wounded or abducted. Over 1,500 refugees were slaughtered at Chingas. There were fervent appeals from the Military Adviser of Jammu and Kashmir to the Defence Minister, and from Mehr Chand Mahajan, the State's Prime Minister, to Jawaharlal Nehru, to relieve Kotli and Mirpur and save the State troops, as well as thousands of civilians from being massacred. Due to a paucity of troops and the operations in progress in Kashmir, little help could be given, until after the capture of Uri by Indian forces on 13 November 1947.

At that time, Major General Kalwant Singh was GOC JAK Division. When 50 Para Brigade reached Akhnur on 13 November, Kalwant issued orders for the relief of Naushera, Jhangar, Mirpur, Kotli and Punch on 16 November. According to his plan, 50 Para Brigade was to relieve Naushera by 16 November, Jhangar by 17 November, Kotli by 18 November and Mirpur by 20 November. Another column from Uri, comprising two battalions of 161 Infantry Brigade under Brigadier L.P. 'Bogey' Sen, was to move on the Uri–Punch axis on 16 November, reaching Punch the same day. The task of protection of the line of communication was to be taken over by 268 Infantry Brigade.

Kalwant's plan was ambitious and had several flaws. This was pointed out by the officiating C-in-C, Lieutenant General F.R.R. Bucher, who felt that the advance of two columns was 'positively dangerous', and the despatch of a column from Uri to Punch, with the enemy still in position, was 'almost foolhardy'.

Brigadier Y.S. Paranjpe, who was commanding 50 Para Brigade, also had several objections. Apart from the dates being unrealistic, he felt that after establishing a firm base at Jhangar, Mirpur should be relieved first so that the advance to Kotli could not be threatened by the enemy. Both his battalions, 1 Para Punjab and 3 Para Rajput, were below strength, with 350 to 400 men in each. However, he was overruled by Kalwant, who got his plan approved by Lieutenant General Dudley Russell, GOC-in-C DEP Command, and the operations commenced on 16 November 1947.

After a brief engagement, Naushera was occupied on 18 November. Paranjpe had just three companies with him, and wanted to wait until the rest of the column fetched up before proceeding. However, Kalwant seemed to be in a tearing hurry to reach Kotli and ordered him to continue. Much against his will, Paranjpe resumed advance on 19 November and occupied Jhangar the same day. Two roads forked out from Jhangar, one leading to Mirpur and the other to Kotli. Paranjpe was in favour of relieving Mirpur before going for Kotli, so that his flank was secure. However, Kalwant did not agree and ordered him to head for Kotli. Paranjpe set out from Jhangar on 20 November, but after about 15 miles the advance was held up due to enemy snipers and the roadblocks set up by the raiders. At some places, armoured cars and field guns had to be brought up to clear the blocks. It was only on 26 November, after negotiating 47 roadblocks that they succeeded in relieving Kotli, where they found two companies of demoralised Kashmir State troops and about 9,000 civilians. However, by this time the fate of Mirpur had been sealed. It could not be relieved, and was torched by the enemy after being evacuated. About 400 soldiers and 10,000 refugees managed to escape to Jhangar. The Pathans killed several hundred soldiers and civilians, and captured hundreds of women, who were taken away to the frontier as war booty. En route, many of them were sold for Rs 150 after being paraded naked through the streets of Jhelum by the exultant tribesmen.

On 27 November, the day after it had been relieved, Kalwant decided that holding Kotli was not tenable owing to the vulnerability of the long line of communication, and ordered the troops to return to Jhangar. This was accomplished on 28 November. If Kalwant's decision to rush to Kotli without securing his open flank by taking Mirpur was surprising, his decision to fall back to Jhangar immediately after capturing Kotli was even more so. In the event, Mirpur was lost. And thereby hangs a tale. The wife of one of the Maharaja's ADCs—she was also reportedly one of his many mistresses—lived in Kotli. It was rumoured that a large treasure belonging to the State was kept in Kotli. Kalwant Singh's haste to relieve Kotli was probably due to these two factors rather than for tactical reasons. And though the lady and the treasure might well have been saved, the lives of several hundred men and the honour of several thousand women, were lost. Of course, Kalwant Singh blamed the delay in capturing Kotli for the misfortune which befell Mirpur, saying that a more energetic commander than Paranjpe would have succeeded in saving both.

After falling back from Kotli, 50 Para Brigade occupied the townships of Jhangar and Naushera: 1 Para Punjab was asked to hold Jhangar, while the Brigade HQ and the second battalion were at Naushera. Soon after returning to Naushera, Brigadier Paranjpe was hospitalised and had to be replaced. He had been keeping indifferent health for some time due to an injury he had sustained while in Gurdaspur. Brigadier Mohammed Usman, who was then commanding 77 Para Brigade, was transferred to relieve Paranjpe as Commander 50 Para Brigade.

Though 50 Para Brigade was holding Naushera, the enemy was occupying several positions around it, particularly in the north. Usman realised the inherent danger of enemy presence in the close vicinity of Naushera, and made several attempts to remove them and clear the road towards Chingas. But the troops available to him were inadequate for the task, and he did not succeed. The situation in Jhangar was also causing concern.

Besides 1 Para Punjab, which had just 450 men, the garrison comprised a troop of 7 Cavalry and a platoon of Mahar medium machine-gunners. There were also some personnel from Signals and the Field Ambulance.

The enemy could advance to Jhangar from Kotli as well as Mirpur, and 50 Para Brigade had not only to cover both these approaches, but also the road to Naushera. A line of hills ran along the route from Kotli to Jhangar and continued to Naushera. The road towards Mirpur was dominated by the Pir Matalsi ridge, and its occupation was essential for the defence of Jhangar. Lieutenant Colonel G.I.S. Kullar, who was commanding 1 Para Punjab, had sited his battalion to defend the two approaches from Mirpur and Kotli, with the Battalion HQ at the crossroads in the middle. Due to the distance between the companies, the positions did not have mutual support, a factor which proved critical during the enemy attack on Jhangar.

Since the beginning of December, the enemy had been harassing the garrison at Jhangar with fire from mortars and small arms, but it was difficult to gauge their strength. To get a clearer picture, Kullar sent a company down the Mirpur road on 9 December, and ordered the company occupying Pir Matalsi to cover their move. It had barely advanced about 750 metres when it came under effective fire and one man was killed. The company was ordered to return and soon afterwards, the enemy launched an attack. The attacking troops reached within 50 metres of the defences on Pir Matalsi before they were beaten back, leaving 40 dead. During the attack, Kullar was at Pir Matalsi with Lieutenant Colonel Rawind Singh Grewal, MC, standing beside him. Grewal was commanding 3 Para Mahratta Light Infantry (MLI), which was part of 77 Para Brigade. As soon as Usman was moved from 77 to 50 Para Brigade, Grewal warned his officers that they should be prepared to join 50 Para Brigade, as he had a hunch that their erstwhile Commander would ask for them. He had gone over to Jhangar to directly assess the situation, and what he saw there was not very encouraging.

On his return, he ran into Major General Kalwant Singh in the officers' mess at Jammu. Kalwant was in a happy frame of mind, and asked Grewal about the chances of 1 Para Punjab holding out at Jhangar. Kalwant was visibly annoyed when Grewal told him that considering their depleted strength the chances were very slim.

Besides a lack of troops, the brigade was severely handicapped by lack of intelligence about the enemy. Their main source of information were refugees, who were prone to exaggeration and therefore unreliable. The local Muslim population had been alienated due to years of neglect by the Dogra rulers, and their loyalties had been subverted by Pakistani propaganda, which made them believe that the raiders would liberate them. Apart from the Kashmir valley, Hyderabad was also proving to be a trouble spot and required troops. This meant that there were hardly any that could be spared for the defence of the Jammu sector. It was not surprising, therefore, that repeated requests for reinforcements by local commanders kept being turned down by Delhi. The fate of Jhangar was sealed even before it came under attack.

The enemy strength at this time was about 1,500. They attacked at dawn on 24 December, a day before Christmas, which was also Jinnah's birthday. Jhangar was planned as a birthday present for the Qaid-e-Azam (supreme leader), the title Jinnah had assumed after becoming President of Pakistan. A day before the attack, Usman had decided to reinforce Jhangar with a company of 1 Rajput, which had joined the brigade. As predicted by Grewal, he had asked for 3 Para MLI but this battalion had still not reached Naushera. A column of the 1 Rajput company left Naushera on the morning of 23 December, escorted by two armoured cars of 7 Cavalry. Four miles outside Naushera, the column was ambushed and had to stop. Two armoured cars that had set out from Jhangar to meet the column halfway met with the same fate—they were ambushed just a kilometre away from the point where the first ambush had taken place. To ensure that the columns could neither advance nor retreat, the enemy blew up bridges on both sides of the ambush site.

To extricate the ambushed company, Usman sent the remainder of 1 Rajput, which succeeded in its mission but at the cost of seven casualties. However, when the enemy attacked Jhangar, the 1 Rajput company was not there. The first objective to be assaulted was Pir Matalsi, which was overrun in an hour, despite the gallant efforts of the company that was holding it. The second company guarding the Mirpur approach fell soon afterwards, and Kullar readjusted his defences by occupying small features around the road junction. After a few hours, the enemy launched another attack, this time from the north-west. With the road to Naushera blocked, reinforcement was not possible, and due to bad weather, even the air force could not provide any succour to the beleaguered troops defending Jhangar. Wisely, Kullar decided to withdraw to Naushera and sent back all available transport. He did not know that the road was blocked, since wireless communications with Naushera had broken down after the second assault, at 7.30 a.m.

As soon as Usman learnt of the attack on Jhangar, he decided to send reinforcements, in spite of roadblocks. He despatched 1 Rajput, less a company, with a section each of mountain artillery and medium machine-guns, to Naushera via a diversion. It was too late, however. The defences of Jhangar had been already overrun, and the enemy was knocking at the gates of Naushera itself. The relief column came up against a roadblock after advancing just 3 kilometres, and had to halt. Attempts by the Rajputs to force their way in were foiled by the enemy, who had occupied Kothi Dhar, which overlooked the roadblocks. By the afternoon, the troops who had withdrawn from Jhangar reached the roadblocks and fought their way to Naushera with the help of the relief column. Stragglers continued to stream into Naushera for the next two or three days.

The loss of Jhangar was a big blow to the Indian Army. It was the first major reverse of the operations in Jammu and

Kashmir—1 Para Punjab suffered 101 casualties: 55 killed and 46 wounded. Enemy casualties were estimated to be around 1,000, but that was little consolation. However, the debacle did have some positive fallout. It brought home to the top leadership the dangers of neglecting the defence of strategic positions. Soon afterwards, JAK Division was allotted an additional brigade; the administrative set-up was improved; steps were taken to establish an intelligence organisation; and it was decided to institute gallantry awards.

After the capture of Jhangar, it was obvious that the enemy's next objective would be Naushera, since it would provide them a firm base to progress operations towards Jammu. As a prelude to its capture, the enemy began to encircle the town. By the first week of January, it was dominating all four roads leading out of Naushera. On 27 December, 3 Para MLI had started arriving, and by 3 January the entire battalion had moved in. It was still in the process of settling down when it suffered a setback. On 4 January 1948, Usman had ordered the battalion to clear the enemy from Bhajnoa on the Jhangar road. The enemy was well entrenched, and the attack was launched without artillery support. Not surprisingly, the attack was beaten back. The battalion suffered seven casualties, including the CO, Lieutenant Colonel Rawind Singh Grewal, who was wounded and had to be evacuated. He was replaced by Lieutenant Colonel Harbans Singh Virk, DSO, who took over on 7 January 1948.

The failure of the attack by 3 Para MLI on 4 January had raised the enemy's spirits and he mounted an assault on Naushera the same evening, this time from the south-west. However, with the help of artillery and mortars, the Indians were able to fend off the attackers. Two days later, another daylight attack came from the north-west. This too was repulsed. The enemy then launched a force of about 5,000, supported by artillery, the same afternoon. After a bitter fight, which drained all the resources of the garrison, the Indians were able to repel this attack as well.

With many places around Naushera in enemy hands and the threat of a major assault ever present, 50 Para Brigade was in a precarious situation. The morale of the garrison was at rock bottom. After the bitter communal frenzy of Partition, some of the troops were unsure of the loyalty of a Muslim commander. The situation was not improved by the exaggerated accounts of the enemy given by men of 1 Para Punjab, which made them seem invincible. Usman was faced with a daunting task. He not only had to frustrate the designs of the enemy, but also win the confidence of his own troops. He set about it in real earnest, and his forceful personality, good personnel management and professional acumen soon changed the situation. He introduced the greeting 'Jai Hind' in the brigade and directed that all orders and briefings be in Hindi at all levels of command. So that the other units in Naushera were not demoralised by their tall tales, 1 Para Punjab was sent to Beripattan. It also did the unit good to be trusted with an independent task after its defeat at the hands of the enemy.

The defence of Naushera was given due attention. Apart from the perimeter, troops were deployed to man pickets on all important features overlooking and dominating the approaches to the town. The line of communication to Beripattan was often cut by the enemy, and this interfered with the movement of supplies and reinforcements. To clear the way, road-opening parties had to be sent from both directions. Usman was not one to passively sit and wait for the enemy. He started 'reconnaissance in force', which entailed hitting the enemy whenever he could. To free the infantry for such limited offensive actions, he used administrative elements, such as drivers, to man the perimeter by day. It was with one such offensive that he captured Kot and Pathradi, thus clearing the enemy from the immediate vicinity of Naushera defences and reducing the threat to the line of communication back to Beripattan. The story of how or why Kot was captured is interesting.

In January 1948 Lieutenant General K.M. Cariappa had taken over DEP Command (later Western Command) from Lieutenant

General Sir Dudley Russell. Soon after assuming command, he visited Naushera. Accompanied by Major (later Lieutenant General) S.K. Sinha, he landed at the airstrip in Naushera in a two-seater Auster. Usman received the Army Commander and took him around the brigade. Before he left, Cariappa turned to Usman and said that he wanted a present: he wanted Usman to capture Kot, which was the highest feature in the range of hills overlooking the Naushera valley. The enemy was building up for an attack on Naushera, and it was vital to wrest Kot from them before this happened. Usman assured Cariappa that he would capture the feature within the next few days.

Kot lay about 9 kilometres north-east of Naushera and overlooked the Naushera Tawi valley to the north, south and south-west for about 10 kilometres. It served as a transit camp for the enemy, since it lay on their route from Rajauri to Siot. The strength of the enemy battalion was estimated to be about 500 men, most of whom were deserters from the State Forces and ex-servicemen of the Indian Army. They were reported to have two or three 3-inch mortars and one or two medium machine-guns, in addition to four light machine-guns and about 400 rifles. The defences at Kot had mutual support with the enemy position at Pathradi.

The operation for the capture of Kot was code-named KIPPER, the name by which Cariappa was affectionately known in the army. Usman planned the operation meticulously. He decided to attack both features simultaneously, with one battalion for each feature. While 3 Para MLI was to advance on the right and capture Pathradi and Uparla Dandesar, 2/2 Punjab, which had been given to him for the operation, was to attack from the left and capture Kot. The attack was to be supported by a squadron of 7 Cavalry, a company less a platoon of Mahar machine-gunners, and two batteries of field artillery. The IAF was asked to provide some air support, if required, from their base at Jammu. A deception plan was also made to give the enemy the impression that an advance to Jhangar was in the offing. Mules and ponies were hired, and it was given out that they would be required to go to Jhangar.

To ensure the element of surprise, Usman had decided on a silent attack. Having moved off at last light on 31 January, the troops of 3 Para MLI were almost on the objective before first light next morning when a dog in the village of Pathradi began to bark and alerted the enemy, who opened up with everything he had. The assaulting troops rushed forward to charge the enemy, with the famous war cry of the Marathas—*Bol Shri Chhatrapati Shivaji Maharaj ki Jai*. There was hand-to-hand fighting, and the bayonet was used with effect. The enemy withdrew, leaving several dead and wounded. After consolidating the defences at Pathradi, a company was sent to Uparla Dandesar, which was captured by midday.

The attack on Kot was launched at 0630 hrs on 1 February 1948. By 0700 hrs, it appeared that the feature had been captured, and 2/2 Punjab sent a success signal at 0710 hrs. However, it was later learnt that the battalion had gone through the village without searching it thoroughly and had missed some of the enemy who were sleeping. They soon launched a fierce counter-attack, and by 0715 hrs had recaptured the feature. Usman was prepared for this contingency, having kept back two companies in reserve. These were now ordered to move up, and after heavy artillery and air bombardment, the feature was recaptured at 1010 hrs. The enemy losses numbered 156 dead and 200 wounded; 2/2 Punjab suffered 11 casualties—seven dead and four wounded. In the attack on Pathradi and Uparla Dandesar, 3 Para MLI had 13 casualties—three dead and 10 wounded—after killing 50 of the enemy. This was the first major reverse inflicted on the enemy in prepared defences, and a costly one at that. Since it cut off the supply route to Naushera, its loss was a critical factor during the battle which took place six days later.

On 6 February 1948, one of the most important battles of the Jammu and Kashmir operations was fought at Naushera.

Intoxicated by his success at Jhangar, the enemy tried to capture Naushera several times, but failed, due mainly to the strength of the garrison and the clever positioning of troops by Usman. The loss of Kot and Pathradi was a big blow for the enemy and, infuriated by the defeat, he put everything he had into the battle at Naushera. At that time, there were five battalions under Usman: 3 Para Rajput, 3 Para MLI, 1 Rajput, 2/2 Punjab and 1 Patiala. In addition, he had a squadron of 7 Cavalry, and a battery each of field and mountain guns. The strength at his disposal was thus considerably more than what he had at Jhangar.

Usman had planned to attack Kalal at 0600 hrs. However, from intelligence reports he learned that the enemy was also planning to attack Naushera on the same day. Usman immediately alerted all the pickets, and his timely warning played a crucial role in preventing a major catastrophe. On 6 February at 0640 hrs the enemy launched a determined attack, in which about 11,000 troops were used. After a mortar bombardment lasting 20 minutes, about 3,000 Pathans attacked Tain Dhar and an equal number hurled themselves at Kot. In addition, about 5,000 tribesmen were used to attack surrounding pickets, including Kangota and Redian.

The Tain Dhar feature, which overlooked Naushera and was the key to the defence of Naushera valley, was held by 1 Rajput under the command of Lieutenant Colonel Guman Singh. Though Usman had anticipated the enemy attack, its timing and quantum of force used surprised him. He had foreseen the possibility of an attack on Tain Dhar and had catered for reinforcements. The Gujar company of 3 Para Rajput under Major Gurdial Singh had been pre-positioned halfway up the Tain Dhar slopes, with the task of reinforcing the main position on orders from him. Starting at first light, wave after wave of hostiles hurled themselves against the defences. The brunt of the attack was borne by picket number 2, of 1 Rajput. The picket comprised 27 men, of whom 24 lost their lives or were severely wounded. The three surviving soldiers continued to fight gallantly hand-to-hand, till another two were fatally wounded, and there was only one survivor left. It was at this critical moment that reinforcements arrived and the situation was saved.

At about 0715 hrs, Usman ordered Gurdial to move forward and reinforce the picket. The company reached the Tain Dhar picket just as it was about to be annihilated. Its timely arrival proved to be the turning point of the battle. Had the company reached even a few minutes later, Tain Dhar would have been lost, rendering the defence of Naushera untenable. While the attacks on Tain Dhar and Kot were still underway, a horde of about 5,000 Pathans attacked the positions from the west and south-west. The tribesmen were engaged by artillery, mortars and machine-guns, all of which combined to bring down deadly fire on the attackers. However, their numbers appeared to be inexhaustible and they continued the attack for almost four hours before calling it a day.

In the event, the attacks failed and the enemy was beaten back, leaving 2,000 dead. Most of the casualties inflicted on the Indian side—33 dead and 102 wounded—were suffered by the dauntless Rajputs, whose valour in battle was in keeping with the highest traditions of the regiment. It was in this battle that Naik Jadunath Singh was posthumously awarded the Param Vir Chakra (PVC). In addition, the battalion won two MVCs, one of which was awarded to the company commander, Lieutenant Kishen Singh Rathore, and four Vir Chakras (VrCs). Apart from the heroic Rajputs, it was the artillery that played a decisive role in the action, and Naushera is often referred to as the 'gunners battle'. After this failure, the enemy withdrew, and the tide turned. The tribesmen lost the will to fight and were replaced by regular troops.

However, it was not only combatant soldiers who displayed gallantry in the action. A non-combatant sweeper of 1 Rajput also showed tremendous courage during the attack on Tain Dhar. Seeing the never-ending swarms of tribesmen attacking the pickets and the depleted strength of the Indian troops, he picked up a rifle from a wounded comrade and began firing at the enemy. When he ran out of ammunition, he snatched a sword from a tribesman and killed three enemy soldiers. Another unique feature of the operation was the role played by the *Balak Sena* (Boys' Army), which had been raised by Usman and comprised the orphaned children of Naushera. Between 6 and 12 years old, these children could be found thronging the men's kitchen for leftovers. Usman formed them into a boys' company, and arranged for their education and training. They were given regular meals and a place to live. Some of them were employed as apprentices in workshops. During the battle of Naushera, they served as couriers carrying messages, often under fire. After the operation, three of these boys were honoured for their bravery during battle and presented with gold watches by the Prime Minister.

The Battle of Naushera brought Usman into the limelight. Overnight, his name was on everyone's lips and he became a national hero. The Pakistanis announced a prize of 50,000 rupees for his head. However, Usman remained unaffected by his sudden fame. Soon after the operation, Major General Kalwant Singh, GOC JAK Division, held a press conference, giving full credit for the success at Naushera to Brigadier Mohd Usman, Commander 50 Para Brigade. When Usman heard about it, he wrote to Kalwant, protesting that the credit should go to the soldiers who fought so valiantly and laid down their lives for the country and not to him as the brigade commander.

After Naushera, it was decided to recapture Jhangar. This was planned to be done in three stages. Initially, the focus would be on assessing the enemy's strength. This exercise was to last till the end of February, and was to be followed by the capture of Ambli Dhar and Kaman Gosha Gala from 1–4 March. The third phase, code-named Operation VIJAY, involved the recapture of Jhangar, between 5 and 18 March. As a prelude to the recapture of Jhangar, 19 Infantry Brigade was inducted into the area. Commanded by Brigadier (later Major General) Yadunath

Singh, the brigade comprised 4 Dogra, 1 Rajputana Rifles and 1 Kumaon Rifles. In addition, 2 Jat was moved from Beripattan to reinforce 50 Para Brigade. Major General Kalwant Singh moved his tactical HQ to Naushera to direct the operations.

By the end of February, the first phase of the operation had been completed. In the second phase, which commenced on 1 March, 50 Para was given the task of capturing Ambli Dhar. Ever since he had heard about the plans for recapturing Jhangar, Usman had been in high spirits. He wanted to avenge the loss of Jhangar by his brigade—the defeat continued to rankle. His battalion commanders were soon infected by his enthusiasm, and the operation for the capture of Ambli Dhar was completed without any hitch by 2 Jat, assisted by 1 Rajput. By 5 March, 19 Infantry Brigade had dislodged the enemy from Kaman Gosha Gala, and by 9 March was firmly established astride the Handan ridge, after capturing Orange Hill and Kataria Choti. By this time 50 Para Brigade had also taken Point 3030, west of Shan da Mohra. Both brigades were now poised for the final thrust, and on 10 March, Major General Kalwant Singh ordered the recapture of Jhangar.

It was at this time that Usman issued his famous order of the day, in which he quoted Lord Macaulay's famous poem, 'Horatius'.

Comrades of 50 Parachute Brigade Group,

Time has come when our planning and preparation for the recapture of Jhangar has to be put to test. It is not an easy task but I am confident of success—because our plan is sound and our preparations have been good. More so, because I have complete confidence in you all to do your best to recapture the ground we lost on 24 December and to retrieve the honour of our arms.

The eyes of the world are on us. The hopes and aspirations of our countrymen are based upon our efforts. We must not falter—we must not fail them.

> To every man upon this Earth
> Death cometh soon or late
> And how can man die better
> Than facing fearful odds
> For the ashes of his fathers
> And the temples of his Gods.

So forward friends, fearless we go to Jhangar. India expects everyone to do his duty.

Operation VIJAY was to commence on 12 March; however, it had to be delayed by two days due to heavy rain. It began with 50 Para Brigade advancing in the south of the valley and 19 Infantry Brigade in the north, while a squadron of 7 Cavalry moved along the road in the middle. Under the command of 50 Para Brigade were 3 Para MLI, 3 Para Rajput, 1 Patiala and a company of 3/1 Punjab. 19 Infantry Brigade had 1 Rajput less a company, 4 Dogra and 1 Kumaon Rifles. The heavy rain and slush had turned the roads into a quagmire, making movement difficult and slow. Field artillery could not move, but Kalwant decided to go ahead with the operation. It was nightfall by the time 3 Para MLI, which was in the van of the advance of 50 Para Brigade, reached Kothi Dhar and bivouacked there for the night.

Ahead of Kothi Dhar lay the formidable obstacle of Phir Thal Naka, where the enemy had his main line of defences. From Kothi Dhar, the route followed by the Indian troops had to pass through a deep saddle before going on to Phir Thal Naka, which had a sharp cliff on its north-eastern face, but a more gradual slope towards the south-west. The peak in the north-east dominated the rest of the ridge, while the entire ridge overlooked the saddle in the south-east, through which the advance of 50 Para Brigade had to pass. The saddle which ran north to south was narrow at the northern end, where it was blocked by a col joining Kothi Dhar to Phir Thal Naka. Towards the south, it widened to about 2,500 metres, which is where the advancing troops were planning to cross. About a third of the way across was a hillock, with a village named Kea on its northern edge. It was surrounded by open, terraced fields, strewn with boulders.

Soon after reaching Kothi Dhar, the battalion commander despatched patrols to Chahi village and towards Phir Thal Naka. The patrol to the village did see an enemy patrol of platoon strength on the move, but the patrol that had gone towards Phir Thal Naka only saw what they thought was a group of peasants carrying baskets on their heads. The following morning, 3 Para MLI commenced their advance at 0830 hrs, and had started climbing the hillock at Kea by 1000 hrs. As soon as the leading company had gone over the top and were beginning to go down the slope on the opposite side, the enemy suddenly opened fire with automatic weapons from Phir Thal Naka. Among the first casualties was the company commander, Major S.P. Chopra, who was shot through the head even as he was trying to pass on a message to the battalion HQ. The stalled advance and breakdown in wireless communications added to the general confusion. Lieutenant Colonel Virk sent Captain (later Major General) S.C. Sinha, the battalion signal officer, to find out what had happened. Within a few hours, 3 Para MLI had suffered 18 casualties, including two officers who were killed. Three lives were lost trying to recover the body of Major Chopra under heavy enemy fire, but the task was accomplished.

Usman wanted to pull back 3 Para MLI and make another attempt after some additional preparation, including getting artillery support, which they did not have. But Virk insisted that he would be able to hold on and Usman gave his consent. However, it was obvious that the advance would have little chance of success unless they had some artillery support, and by the end of the day, some field guns were brought up. The company of 3 Para MLI, which had been pinned down, was extricated after last light and its command given to Sinha. Usman spent the next day preparing for the attack on Phir Thal Naka. He decided to attack with two battalions, with both artillery and air support. 3 Para MLI was to attack from the right, while 1 Patiala was to go in from the left. A company of 3/1 Punjab was to divert the enemy's attention by engaging the feature from the south, while 3 Para Rajput was to be kept in reserve. The IAF was requested to soften up the objective before the assault went in, and light tanks were to operate along the road to Jhangar. The route to the objective was reconnoitred by junior officers, both during the day and by moonlight at night.

The attack on Phir Thal Naka commenced at 0730 hrs on 17 March 1948. For this operation, Usman had managed to muster a considerable amount of artillery—24 field guns and the mortars of all three battalions that had been brigaded. He had arranged for an intense 15-minute barrage to cover the move of the assaulting troops. The fire lifted just as the troops reached the forward trenches of the enemy who, taken by surprise, fled without offering any resistance. When the assaulting troops reached the enemy bunkers, they found food being cooked and kettles on the boil. 3 Para MLI did not suffer a single casualty in this attack. A major factor in the success of this operation was the intelligent use of artillery. Usman had concentrated all his artillery on a very limited front, covering the highest point of the feature, which was attacked first. He had also brigaded all mortars of the infantry battalions, and placed them under the CO of his artillery regiment. As a result, the fire could be concentrated and used effectively. Lieutenant Colonel Virk and Major Chopra were awarded the MVC for this operation, while Captain Sucha Singh, who led the final successful assault, was given the VrC.

3 Para MLI did not rest after capturing Phir Thal Naka. Taking a company of 3 Para Rajput along, the battalion set off towards Susloti Dhar, which they captured at 1300 hrs. Meanwhile, the advance of 19 Infantry Brigade was well under way and, by 17 March, they had cleared Gaikot forest. The way was now clear for the attack on Jhangar, and both brigades prepared for the final assault on the next day. At 0830 hrs on

18 March, 3 Para Rajput took Uparli Karhali, and by 1000 hrs, Usman had reached there with his HQ. The brigade now advanced on a two-battalion front, with 1 Patiala on the right, and 3 Para MLI on the left. At 1300 hrs, when 3 Para MLI reached Point 3399, word came through that 19 Infantry Brigade had already entered Jhangar. Operation VIJAY was over.

After the loss of Jhangar in December 1947, Usman had taken a vow, like Rana Pratap, that he would not sleep on a bed, until he had avenged its loss. True to his vow, he had spent the last three months on the floor, even though it was bitterly cold. Now that he had redeemed his pledge, he asked for a cot to be brought in. Since none was available in the brigade HQ, one was borrowed from the village and that night, Usman slept on a bed.

After the capture of Jhangar, 50 Para Brigade stayed on to defend the town, while 19 Infantry Brigade was withdrawn to Naushera. The next three months were spent consolidating the defences and beating back enemy attacks, which continued to be launched. There were two major ones against Jhangar, on 16 April and 10 May 1948. Both were beaten back, with heavy casualties to the enemy. After this, Usman decided to clear the enemy from the area of Sabzkot, an advance base that was being used to protect the line of communication from Mirpur. The enemy strength was estimated to be about two companies. One of its forward positions, called MG Hill, was just 1,800 metres from the Indian positions. Usman gave the task of clearing MG Hill, which was expected to be held by a company, to 3 Para MLI, while 2 Rajputana Rifles, which had been loaned to 50 Para Brigade from 19 Infantry Brigade, was asked to put in a flanking attack behind the feature along Keri, and take Point 3150. Thereafter, 3 Para MLI was to capture Point 3900, with the other battalion mopping up the area. After completing this task, both battalions were to encircle SabzKot and destroy it. It was a well-conceived plan; unfortunately, it was based on imprecise intelligence.

The attack on MG Hill by 3 Para MLI was launched at first light on 21 May 1948, and progressed well till the assaulting troops were about 150 metres from the enemy's forward defences. Then the enemy opened up with automatics and men began to fall. Some managed to reach the top of the hill, but were pushed back by enemy counter-attacks. It soon became clear that the enemy strength was almost a battalion, and not a company, as Usman had estimated based on the intelligence available to him when he planned the operation. In a clever move, the enemy had kept the major portion of their force on the reverse slopes, sitting only a few bunkers on the forward slope. Usman ordered the battalion to break contact and withdraw with the support of tanks and artillery. This was achieved shortly after midday. 3 Para MLI suffered 37 casualties, including eight dead; 2 Rajputana Rifles also ran into rough weather in their attack and had to fall back after suffering casualties. It was decided to postpone the capture of MG Hill, until additional troops were available.

By now, 50 Para Brigade had been in Jhangar for three months. Except for the forward troops, who lived in properly fortified bunkers, those in the Brigade HQ and administrative units in the rear lived as in cantonments, with open trenches dug around the camp for perimeter defence. This was because the enemy had no artillery in the sector and the fire from their small arms could reach only the forward troops. In the middle of June, an Indian aircraft flying over the enemy positions to the south of Jhangar saw some gun pits. A few days later, another sortie reported that the guns were now manned. Some air attacks were mounted with limited effect. At the same time, orders were passed that the HQ and units in the rear should improve their defences and construct bunkers with proper overhead protection. Very few people took these orders seriously, especially in the Brigade HQ, which had its office and mess in the two-roomed inspection bungalow at the crossroads in Jhangar. One person who did follow the instructions was Captain Brij Lall, who was in command of the signal section in Brigade HQ. He made sure that his bunkers were strong enough to withstand enemy shells.

At this time, Captain S.C. Sinha of 3 Para MLI had been moved by Usman to Brigade HQ as the Brigade Intelligence Officer (BIO). When Usman took over 50 Para Brigade after the fall of Kotli, its morale was low, and it had fallen even further after the loss of Jhangar. In a few months, Usman had managed to motivate the men under his command, and the battles of Naushera and Phir Thal Naka bear testimony to his leadership. He was a charismatic commander, who was very popular with both officers and men. He had a delightful sense of humour, and could remain cheerful even in the most trying circumstances. Sinha was deeply impressed by Usman's devotion to duty, sense of humour, and boundless energy. His courage and selflessness were obvious, and did wonders for the morale of the troops. He inspired confidence in his subordinates, whom he led by personal example. Above all, he was fair. While he was quick to reward the deserving and give credit where it was due, he rarely condemned anyone without first giving him a fair hearing. But he was also a hard taskmaster who demanded the best from everyone and did not hesitate to reprimand those who did not pull their weight. He believed that loyalty was a two-way street, and always stood up for his subordinates.

One day, a very strongly worded signal was received from HQ JAK Force. It demanded an explanation from the BIO for sending in clear a six-figure map reference of one of our pickets that had been shelled by the enemy. This had been included in the Situation Report (SITREP), which is sent every day to higher HQ. Since the BIO was responsible for this error, the Divisional HQ wanted his head served to them on a platter. A very scared Sinha took the signal to Usman, expecting to receive a blasting which he admittedly deserved. Usman looked at the signal and, without raising an eyebrow, asked for a message pad. He drafted a reply: 'A six-figure map reference of our own position in question may have been news to the JAK Force HQ, but I assure you it was no news to the enemy.' This was the last that was heard of it.

Usman lost his life on 3 July 1948; the circumstances surrounding his tragic death have been described by S.C. Sinha, who was present. Every evening at 5.30 p.m., Usman held a meeting in the sand model room, which was nothing more than a couple of tents rigged together. That day, the time of the meeting had been advanced by half an hour and it finished earlier than usual. At 5.45 p.m., the enemy started shelling the Brigade HQ. But for the change in timing, Usman and his staff would have been inside the tents when four 25-pounder shells landed about 500 metres north of the crossroads. These were ranging shots, since the next salvo fell nearer. Everyone scrambled for cover, with the medical officer diving under his *charpai* (string-bed used in Indian villages) and the cooks clinging to the tent walls in the mistaken belief that this would give them adequate protection.

Usman and a few of his staff officers had been walking around the HQ after the meeting ended. When the shelling began, they found shelter under a large overhanging rock in a terraced field, just above the signallers' bunker. With Usman were his artillery battery commander, Major Bhagwan Singh, and the BIO, Captain S.C. Sinha. In an effort to silence the enemy guns, our own field battery began to return fire. Realising the futility of firing at the enemy guns, which were well entrenched, Usman ordered Bhagwan Singh to turn his guns to the west and engage Point 3150. Bhagwan was surprised, since the enemy was firing from the south. But when Usman insisted, Bhagwan realised that Point 3150 was the obvious place for the enemy to site its artillery observation post (OP). He ordered his eight guns to engage the target indicated by Usman. This achieved the desired result, and the enemy guns ceased firing.

The shelling had damaged the wireless aerials on top of the command post, which was located a few metres away. Once the shelling stopped, a few signallers, led by Lieutenant Ram Singh of the brigade signal company, came out and started repairing the aerials. Usman, too, decided to move to the brigade command post. He started off ahead, leaving Major Bhagwan Singh and Captain S.C. Sinha to follow. They had barely taken a few steps when Bhagwan Singh heard a sound, which he immediately recognised as artillery gunfire. Instinctively, he caught Sinha by the arm and pulled him back. By now, Usman had reached the entrance to the command post, where he had stopped to have a few encouraging words with the signallers. Just then, a 25-pounder shell landed on the rock nearby. The flying splinters killed Usman on the spot, wounding Lieutenant Ram Singh and two of the signallers working outside. The shelling continued throughout the night, and about 800 shells were dropped on Jhangar. Fortunately, except for two abortive attempts at infiltration by a company, it was not followed by an infantry attack. Besides Brigadier Usman, four men lost their lives during the shelling, while eight were wounded, including three officers.

Usman's untimely death cast a pall on the entire garrison. For his last journey, they used the brand new caravan, which had just arrived and which Usman had not yet had the chance to use. When the troops lined up on the road to bid him farewell, there was not a single one among them whose eyes were not wet. Veteran soldiers cried unashamedly for the man who had endeared himself to all of them in so short a time. From Jammu, his body was flown to Delhi, where a large crowd had gathered to pay homage to a brave son who had laid down his life for his motherland. The government decided to honour him with a state funeral, which was held at Mehrauli, and was attended by Governor General Lord Mountbatten and Prime Minister Jawaharlal Nehru. Shortly thereafter, the government announced that Usman had been posthumously awarded the MVC, the second highest award for gallantry in India.

When Usman died, he was still 12 days short of his 36th birthday. If he had lived, there is no doubt that he would have risen to the top of his profession. Kind, humane and totally impartial, he had all the qualities of a military leader. After the fall of Jhangar, a large number of civilians had sought refuge in Naushera. There was a shortage of food, and many of them did not have enough to eat. Usman had ordered his troops to observe a fast on Tuesdays, so that the saved rations could be given to civilians. A man of simple tastes, he was a teetotaller, and after serving with Dogras, had become a vegetarian. He remained a bachelor, and a large part of his salary went to support poor children and pay for their education. After his death, many of them felt orphaned and wrote to the Brigade HQ mourning the loss of their benefactor.

Though a devout Muslim, Usman was a staunch nationalist and apparently had no problem remaining loyal to his religion as well as his country. During the attack on Naushera, he was told that some of the enemy were hiding behind a mosque and that the Indian gunners were reluctant to open fire on a place of worship. Usman said that the mosque was no longer holy if it was being used to shelter the enemy, and ordered that it be blown up. Little wonder then, that the enemy hated him and had announced a reward of Rs 50,000 for his head. Pakistan also spread false reports about his death to demoralise the Indian troops, for whom Usman had already become a hero. In late June 1948, when one such report was published by a Pakistani newspaper, Usman's brother wrote anxiously to the army authorities. Brigadier Sarda Nand Singh, who was in charge of administration at HQ Western Command, sent a signal to Usman, enquiring about his welfare. Usman replied: 'I am fit and flourishing—still in the world of the living.' Ironically, he was killed just a few hours after this message reached HQ Western Command.

Mohammed Usman was the seniormost Indian officer to have lost his life during the Jammu and Kashmir operations of 1947–48. Even today, he is venerated by the people of Jammu and the surrounding region. Memorials have been built at Naushera and Jhangar, where veterans gather on the anniversary of his death to honour his memory. The memorial at Jhangar is built on the same rock where the shell which took his life had landed. Usman was a true soldier and a patriot, unflinching in the face of adversity. Though a bit of a showman, he was not immodest and gave credit where it was due. As a war hero, his place in the Roll of Honour of the Indian Army is secure. As he had exhorted his men to do before going into battle at Jhangar, he died 'for the ashes of his fathers, and the temples of his Gods'.

6

Field Marshal
S.H.F.J. Manekshaw, MC

6

Field Marshal
S.H.F.J. Manekshaw, MC

The Architect of India's Victory Over Pakistan

Field Marshal Sam Hormusji Framji Jamshedji Manekshaw is, without a doubt, the most popular and colourful of military leaders in India. Having led the nation to its first decisive victory in 1971, 'Sam Bahadur', as he is popularly known, became a household word. He was India's first Field Marshal, and remains, even today, the most admired and idolised of our Army Chiefs. He has a charismatic personality, and it is impossible not to feel overawed in his presence. Vigour, dash and elan—he has them all, the typical signs of a great soldier. However, if there is one attribute which can be called his hallmark, it is his ready wit, and sense of humour. Anecdotes about Sam abound, and one keeps hearing new ones even now, more than 30 years after he has quit active service. A Field Marshal never retires, and Sam epitomises the spirit, as no one else can. His admirers are legion, and not a few of them are of the fairer sex. Though now over 90, he can still make girls in their teens swoon when he walks into a room.

Sam is a Parsi, and was born on 3 April 1914 in Amritsar. The Parsis are a very small community, found mostly on the western coast of India, especially Bombay and certain areas in Gujarat. Though small in number, the Parsis are a very progressive community, with 100 per cent literacy. Though their main occupation is business, they have produced some of the most eminent politicians, lawyers, industrialists, artists, doctors and engineers in the country. Sam's grandfather, Framroze, was a teacher, who lived in Valsad and had taught Morarji Desai, who later became Prime Minister of India. Sam's father, Hormusji, was born in Valsad and became a doctor. He was married to Hilla, a Parsi girl from Bombay whom he had met while studying medicine at the Grant Medical College. Hormusji began practising in Bombay but later moved to Amritsar, where there were fewer doctors and better prospects for setting up a medical practice. During World War I, he served in Mesopotamia and Egypt and was given the rank of a Captain in the Medical Services.

Hormusji and Hilla had six children, who were all born in Amritsar. The eldest, Fali, joined Stewarts and Lloyds in Calcutta after getting his engineering degree from England. Cilla, the second child, was a lovable girl with a zest for life and sense of humour, qualities that endeared her to everyone in the family, especially her nephews and nieces. Jan, the second son, followed his elder brother and studied engineering in England. He joined Calender Cables (later Indian Cables), from where he retired as Director. The next was Sehroo, who was considered the beauty of the family. She got married and settled in Bombay. Sam was the fifth child, followed by Jemi, the only one who followed his father and became a doctor. He joined the Air Force and was the first Indian to get his air surgeon's wings from Pensacola, USA.

Sam was initially given the name Cyrus, but one of his aunts changed it to Sam, because she had heard that a Parsi called Cyrus had been sent to jail, and she thought the name would prove unlucky for her nephew. Sam's eldest brother Fali did his schooling in Bombay, but the others boys—Jan, Sam and Jemi—

were all sent to Sherwood College, Nainital for their education. His two sisters went to the Convent in Murree.

The family was together only for three months of the year when the children came home during their holidays, from December to February. By all accounts, they had a lot of fun, with the three youngest siblings always up to some mischief. Hormusji was fond of music and gardening and all his children inherited these interests in some measure. Hilla was known for her cooking, and spent a lot of time in the kitchen, especially when their ravenous brood was at home. She was an expert at Parsi dishes, and her speciality was *chokha ni rotli* (rice chapati). Her son Jemi's wife Bhicoo Manekshaw recalls that a pile of a hundred rotlis cooked by her mother-in-law would be no higher than two inches, and if a silver rupee coin was placed on top, it would sink to the bottom. She confesses that none of Hilla's daughters-in-law could match her culinary skills.

Sam passed his Senior Cambridge with distinction and returned to Amritsar. He was then 15 years old and reminded his father about his promise to send him to England to study medicine. Hormusji felt that Sam was too young to go abroad, and asked him to wait till he was 18. Sam was very angry and did not speak to his father for 18 months. He joined the Hindu Sabha College, to study for his F.Sc., as the Intermediate (Science) was then known.

The Skeen Committee, set up in 1925, had recommended the establishment of an Indian Sandhurst by 1933. To work out details of the proposed military training college, the Government had appointed the Indian Military College Committee in early 1931. The committee was chaired by Sir Philip Chetwode, and had a large number of service and civilian members. After detailed deliberation, the Committee submitted its report on 15 July 1931. It recommended establishment of a college to train Indians for commissions in the Indian Army, after an examination to be conducted by the Public Service Commission. The course was to be of three years' duration, with the age of entry between 18 and 20 years. On graduation, officers would be granted Indian Commissions, which would be signed by the Viceroy. (The Commissions of officers graduating from Sandhurst were signed by the King.) The total fee would be Rs 4,600, which would cover tuition, board, lodging, uniforms, books and pocket money. Indian Army cadets would be exempted from the fees, and given a stipend of 60 rupees per month. After getting their commissions, the officers would be given the rank of Second Lieutenants, with a monthly salary of 300 rupees.

One of the important points which the Committee considered was the location of the proposed college. It had to be centrally located, easily accessible, with a temperate climate all year round, and adequate accommodation as well as space for future expansion. The presence of a military garrison in the vicinity was also desirable. After considering over a dozen locations, the Committee shortlisted three—Dehradun, Mhow and Satara. Finally Dehradun was selected, because of its central location, climate, proximity to the PWRIMC, and the fact that the Railway Staff College was closing down, and its accommodation was readily available.

Early in 1932, it was announced that an examination for entrance to the Indian Military Academy (IMA) would be conducted in June or July. Sam took some money from his mother, went to Delhi and appeared for the entrance examination on 14 July 1932. There were a total of 40 vacancies—15 to be selected through open competition, 15 from the Army and 10 from the Indian State Forces. Only 15 cadets were selected and Sam was sixth in order of merit. The first Commandant was Brigadier L.P. Collins, DSO, and the staff was carefully selected to ensure that the standards were kept at par with those at Sandhurst. Training commenced on 1 October 1932, though the Academy was formally inaugurated on 10 December 1932 by the C-in-C, Field Marshal Sir Philip Chetwode, Bart, GCB, GCSI, KCMG, DSO. The first batch, called 'The Pioneers', had three future Chiefs—Manekshaw rose to head the Army in India, Smith Dun in Burma and Mohd Musa in Pakistan.

Sam enjoyed his stay at the IMA, though he was often in trouble. Gentleman Cadets (GCs) were permitted to go on 'liberty', on weekends. The IMA records credit Sam with the distinction of being the first Gentleman Cadet to ask for weekend leave to go to Mussoorie, which was just an hour's drive from the Academy. He also holds the record for being awarded the first extra drill at the IMA. He was destined to have many more firsts to his credit, such as the first of the Academy's alumni to join the Gurkhas, to become a General and later a Field Marshal.

One weekend, Sam and two of his buddies, Maharaj Kumar Jit Singh of Kapurthala and Haji Iftikhar Ahmed went up to Mussoorie. Since the hill road could take only one-way traffic, there was a 'gate' system between Mussoorie and Dehradun. On Sunday evening Sam and his cronies were watching the floor show in Hakman's Hotel and lost track of the time. When they came out, they found that the last bus going down had already left and they had to go back to the hotel and spend the night there. When they arrived at the Academy on Monday morning, they were promptly 'put on charge'. All three were 'gated' (confined to lines) for 15 days. In addition, Sam, who was a Corporal, lost his stripes, which were ceremoniously peeled off his sleeve by the Adjutant, Captain McLaren of the Black Watch Regiment.

One of Sam's attributes that came to the fore at the IMA itself was his sense of humour. Gentleman Cadet S. Manekshaw wrote an article entitled 'A Letter from "Maneksam"', which was published in the June 1933 issue of the IMA journal. In the guise of a letter to an imaginary friend called Rustom, the letter advises a prospective Gentleman Cadet on various facets of life at the Academy and gives tips on the behaviour and conduct that would get him the best results. The letter runs as follows:

My dear Rustom,

I was delighted to see in the paper that you were successful at the recent examination for the IMA and I hasten to congratulate you. A few hints on your deportment on first arrival at the IMA may not come amiss, and in view of our old friendship, I send them to you. When you arrive at Dehra Dun Station you will be met by various representatives from the IMA, the Company Commander, Adjutant, Quartermaster, etc. They are sent to carry your luggage for you, so give them yours at once. I was lucky enough to be met by the Adjutant, a big man who wears funny trousers and belongs to that barbarous English sect called the Scots—I believe they are regarded as 'untouchables' in England. I had thought of going up to Mussourie, but the Adjutant and I were having such an interesting conversation that I decided to defer the visit and drive to the Academy with him. As exploration is encouraged, I advise you on arrival to inform the Adjutant that you are going up to Mussourie and won't be back till the evening. Tell him to have your bath ready on your return.

Now a few words about "The Life". You will be delighted to hear that you have both Drill and PT daily. We love all these things. Our enthusiasm is such that we all apply for "Extra Drills" and are given plenty of them. I advise you to do the same, the staff are very obliging in this respect.

People like myself are termed Seniors—the best way for you to show your independence, a characteristic which is admired, is to ignore seniors, especially those with stripes on their sleeves. When the latter talk to you just put your hands in your pockets and turn your back on them; they will appreciate you all the more.

You feed in a large room called the Mess. To show that you are a strong man, eat as much as you can at each meal. For breakfast, the average number of eggs you should consume is six, in addition to the other courses. You will make a friend of the Mess caterer, if you show that you appreciate his food, and he is worth cultivating.

There is a small man with three stripes on his sleeve, who is sure to have a good deal to say for himself. As soon as he starts on you, call him "Foo-Choo". After this friendly greeting on your part, all will be well between you and him and you will find he will take a fatherly interest in your future welfare.

Then, as I said, there are some people called Company Commanders. Whenever one of these individuals dines in Mess, always make a point of sitting next to him at dinner. He will appreciate your efforts to get to know him really well.

You used to be keen on music so apply for the appointment of "Announcer" at our Wednesday Night Concerts, and offer to play a Solo on your mouth organ. There is a cadet here who will accompany you on his violin and he has an extensive repertoire. Be sure to bring your gramophone and the three records with it. You will have plenty of opportunity to play it after what is called 'Lights Out', and when you are dressing in the mornings. By bringing a gramophone you will be considered original and make many friends.

Only one more piece of advice: let everyone know how good you are at everything. Propaganda of this sort will make you the favourite of your professors.

Consider yourself very lucky to have passed into the IMA. We all look back to our first few weeks here with joy, and I envy you the glorious time before you on the Square (The Adjutant's El Dorado). Oh, I nearly forgot to tell you—Be well turned out on arrival at Dehra Dun, wear your cap and your Oxford tights.

Yours ever,
Maneksam

Only 22 cadets from Sam's batch were able to complete the course, and passed out from the Indian Military Academy on

22 December 1934. However, they were commissioned on 1 February 1935, with the date of seniority fixed as 4 February 1934. This was done in order to make them junior to officers commissioned from Sandhurst, a year earlier, after giving them one year's ante-dated seniority, to account for the difference in duration of training at the two institutions. A batch had passed out from Sandhurst on 1 February 1934, which was also the last to include Indians. A unique feature which differentiated the newly commissioned ICOs from the KCIOs was that while the latter were employed as company officers, and had powers of command over British officers who were serving under them, the ICOs were to replace VCOs as platoon commanders. They had no powers of command over British officers, even if serving in the same unit.

The first Sword of Honour was awarded to Under Officer Smith Dun, and the first Gold Medal to Sergeant N.S. Bhagat. Smith was a Karen from the 2/20 Burma Rifles, then part of the Indian Army. He became the C-in-C in Burma, after Independence. There is an interesting story about how he got his name. The Karens were mostly Christians and had adopted European names, but did not use surnames. When Smith arrived at Dehradun (sometimes also written as Dehra Dun), and was asked his name, he gave it as Smith. His company commander insisted that he must have a surname, so Smith decided to adopt one on the spot. The first name that came to his mind was Dehra Dun, where the Academy was located, so he chose Dun as his surname and became Smith Dun.

After commissioning, ICOs selected for the Cavalry and Infantry were attached to a British unit in India, as in the case of KCIOs commissioned from Sandhurst. Sam was attached to the Royal Scots at Lahore. The Scots found it difficult to pronounce his name and being more familiar with the prefix 'Mac', began to call him Makenshaw. After a year with the Scots, in February 1936 he was posted to 4/12 Frontier Force Regiment (FFR), also known as the 54th Sikhs, which became his parent unit.

Unlike the KCIOs, personal numbers were allotted to ICOs on completion of their attachment based on the seniority of the regiments which they eventually joined and not on merit, as at present. In the first batch, Bhagwati Singh, who was third in order of merit, was given IC-1, while Sam was allotted IC-14. The battalion was then in Ferozepore, but soon moved to Fort Sallop, in the North West Frontier Province. Sam learned to speak Pushto fluently, and because of his complexion was often mistaken by the tribesmen for a Pathan.

On 22 April 1939, Sam was married to Silloo Bode in Bombay. The couple's first child, a girl whom they named Sherry, was born on 11 January 1940. The second child, also a girl, was born on 24 September 1945. She was named Maya, though she later changed it to Maja. According to her, 'at thirteen, I thought it was hellishly impressive to spell my name as Maja but Sam insists on spelling it as Maya.' Sherry Manekshaw later became Mrs Batliwala and her daughter was named Brandy. Maja Manekshaw became a stewardess with British Airways and married Dhun Daruwala, who was a pilot. She later became a lawyer and joined the chambers of Salman Khurshid in Delhi before setting up her own practice. She has two sons, named Raoul Sam and Jehan Sam after their illustrious grandfather.

In 1942, Sam's battalion was ordered to move to Burma. Soon after their arrival in Burma, the Japanese attacked. Sam was given command of a Sikh company. Having been born in Amritsar, he could speak Punjabi fluently, and got along famously with the Sikhs. This was the first time he had been in action, and he soon had the chance to prove his mettle. There were a large number of casualties among non-commissioned officers, and a conference was held by the CO to select suitable men for promotion as corporals and sergeants. There was a soldier called Surat Singh in Sam's company, who was considered a 'bad hat'. When his name came up, and Sam was asked for his recommendation, he said that it was no use promoting him, since he would lose his stripes within a few days as had happened many times in the past. Surat Singh was then passed over and some others, who were junior, were cleared.

When Sam returned to his company in the evening, he found an eerie silence, which was most unusual, since the Sikhs are noisy and boisterous by nature. Soon, his senior JCO, Subedar Balwant Singh, came to his tent and told him the reason. Surat Singh had come to know that he had been overlooked for promotion and had declared that he would kill his company commander for not recommending him. He had been disarmed and bound, awaiting Sam's return. On hearing the story, Sam immediately ordered that the company should fall in and Surat Singh be marched up to him. Within a few minutes, the company was formed up in a hollow square, facing a table and a chair. After Sam had taken his seat, the offender was marched up before him. During war, mutiny and cowardice are punishable by death and the men knew this. After the charge had been read out, Sam took out a pistol and walked up to Surat Singh. Handing over the pistol to the burly Sikh, he told him to do what he had threatened to do. Surat Singh immediately broke down and started begging for mercy. Sam gave him a sound slap and told him that if he lacked the guts to kill, he should not make such statements in future. He dismissed the case and ordered that Surat Singh's weapon should be returned to him.

Sam thought that this was the end of the episode and retired to his tent. However, after some time Subedar Balwant Singh again came in and told Sam that he had made a mistake by letting off Surat Singh, who would certainly kill him during the night, since his weapon had been returned to him. Sam sent for Surat Singh and in front of the JCO, told him that tonight, he would work as his orderly and should sleep outside his tent. He dismissed him, after ordering him to wake him up at 5.30 in the morning with a cup of tea and hot water for his shave. That night, Sam could not sleep a wink out of fear. But he knew that if the men came to know that he was afraid, he would never be able to command them. Next morning, at 5.30, Surat Singh entered his tent with a mug of tea and hot water for his shave. For the rest of the war, Surat Singh followed Sam like a puppy and became one of the most disciplined soldiers in his company.

Sam was a captain, but was made acting major since there was an acute shortage of officers during the war. Soon afterwards, his battalion took part in the battle of Sittang Bridge, during which he was severely wounded. He took nine bullets in the lungs, liver and kidneys, and no one thought he would survive. It was here that he was awarded the Military Cross for gallantry. The medal was given to him on the spot by Major General Cowan, who was then the Deputy Commander of the British Forces. Cowan, who later commanded 17 Indian Division during the retreat through Burma, probably thought that Sam's chances of survival were slim, and since the MC cannot be given posthumously, decided to award it on the spot. Sam was evacuated from the front line in a serious condition.

Sam would have died had not his faithful Sikh orderly, Sepoy Sher Singh, carried him in his arms and, collaring a doctor, forced him to attend to his wounds. The Australian surgeon initially declined to operate on Sam, since he saw little chance of his surviving. However, Sher Singh would not take no for an answer. By now Sam had regained consciousness. When the surgeon asked what had happened to him, Sam replied: 'A bloody mule kicked me.' The surgeon laughed, and said: 'By Jove, you have a sense of humour. I think you are worth saving.' He removed much of Sam's intestines and stitched him up. Later, his father wrote to him at the hospital: 'Son, if you smoke or drink now, you are finished.' According to Sam, he did exactly that and that is why he lived!

In 1943 Sam went to Quetta to attend the Staff Course, after which he was posted as Brigade Major of the Razmak Brigade. Soon afterwards, he was selected to be an instructor at the Staff College. But before he could go, Sam was asked to join 9/12 FFR in Burma. He was given the task of supervising the disarming of about 60,000 captured Japanese soldiers and the setting up of a prisoner of war camp. According to Sam, this was one of the easiest jobs he had ever done. All he had to do was to call the senior Japanese officer and tell him what he wanted done. The job would invariably be completed well before time. Cases of indiscipline were unheard of, and the Japanese never tried to escape.

After his return to India, Sam was selected by Field Marshal Claude Auchinleck, the C-in-C, to go to Australia. His job was to educate Australians about India. The Auk felt that Australia, though a member of the Commonwealth, had little contact with India and most Australians were ignorant about the country and her armed forces. Sam spent three months in Australia, giving lectures and holding meetings. On his return, at the end of 1945, the Auk had another surprise for him. He was posted to the Military Operations Directorate as GSO 1. The MO was the holiest of holies and no Indian had ever set foot in its hallowed precincts. This was indeed a rare honour and Sam not only became the first Indian to join MO, but rose to head the organisation in the years to come.

In 1947, when India achieved independence, Sam was a Lieutenant Colonel, posted as GSO 1 in MO-3, the section that dealt with future operations and planning. Yahya Khan, who later became President of Pakistan, and S.K. Sinha, who later became Vice Chief of Army Staff in India and is presently the Governor of Jammu and Kashmir, were also posted in MO as majors. Major General W.D.A. Lentaigne was the Director of Military Operations (DMO). A few days before Partition, they were asked to divide the records between Pakistan and India. This was accomplished by adopting a rough and ready method. Files concerning geographical areas which were to go to Pakistan were earmarked for that country, and those pertaining to areas which would remain in India were to be left behind. Those that did not fall in any category were destroyed. Sam took the precaution of making copies of all documents that were going to Pakistan. Surprisingly, as both Sam and Sinha recall, there was no animosity or disagreement between the Muslim and Indian officers during this period.

Shortly afterwards, Sam received orders posting him as CO 3/5 Gorkha Rifles. Before he could move, fighting broke out in Kashmir and his posting orders were cancelled. On 22 October 1947, Pakistani raiders entered the Kashmir valley. On 23 October, they captured Domel and Muzaffarabad and reached Uri. On 24 October, Maharaja Hari Singh made an urgent appeal to the Government of India for troops. On Mountbatten's advice, the Indian Government agreed to send troops only if the Maharaja was willing to accede to India. On 25 October, V.P. Menon was sent to Srinagar, with the Instrument of Accession. Sam was also sent along, to assess the situation and carry out an aerial survey of the Srinagar–Baramulla–Uri road. They flew back the same night, reaching Delhi at 4 a.m., after having obtained the signatures of Maharaja Hari Singh on the document. A cabinet meeting was held, which was attended by Mountbatten, Nehru, Patel, Baldev Singh, and several others. After V.P. Menon had handed over the Instrument of Accession, Mountbatten asked Sam to explain the military situation. Sam gave the Cabinet a rundown on the latest developments, pointing out that the Pakistani tribesmen were just 9 kilometres from Srinagar. If the airfield was taken, Kashmir would be lost, since it would not be possible to fly in troops.

Sardar Patel was in favour of sending troops to Kashmir immediately, but Nehru had his reservations. He gave a long exposition about the history of the state, the circumstances of its accession and the role of the United Nations. The last thing he wanted was for India to be accused of taking the state by force of arms. Finally, Patel lost his patience and asked: 'Jawahar, do you want to save Kashmir or not?' 'Of course I do,' thundered Nehru. Patel turned to Sam and the other military officers present and said, 'You have your orders. Now go and carry them out.' The very next day, on 27 October 1947, Indian troops were flown into Kashmir. By this time, the raiders were closing in on

Srinagar. Kashmir, whose fate had hung by a slender thread, was saved.

After Sam's posting as CO 3/5 Gorkha Rifles was cancelled, he could not get out of MO, thanks to the crisis in Kashmir followed by the one in Hyderabad. In fact, he never commanded a battalion and was promoted to the rank of Colonel and then Brigadier in the same office. In September 1948, when the Hyderabad operations took place, he was the DMO. Sardar Patel, the Home Minister, often called Sam to find out the latest situation and also sent him to Kashmir on several occasions. During those turbulent days, Sam met Sardar Patel almost daily and he has many reminiscences about the 'iron man'.

One day, Sam was called by the C-in-C and told to fly down to Calcutta, where fierce riots had caused thousands of deaths. Sam flew to Calcutta in a special aircraft and went to the Chief Minister's office. Sardar Patel was already there, discussing the situation with B.C. Roy, the Chief Minister of Bengal. Patel asked Sam: 'If the situation is handed over to the Army, how many people will be killed, and how long will it take to control the situation?' Sam was a newly promoted Brigadier and took a few seconds to answer. 'About a hundred men will be killed and it will take about a month,' he said.

Patel told B.C. Roy: 'Thousands are being killed now. A hundred is nothing.' He turned to Sam and said: 'Let the Army take over.' Troops were immediately deployed and the situation was soon under control. Not a single person was killed. When things had returned to normal, Patel called Sam and, speaking in Gujarati, asked him; 'Why didn't you tell me the truth?' Sam was nonplussed, till Patel smiled and said: 'You said you would kill one hundred Bengalis, but you did not kill even one.' He patted Sam on the back and congratulated the Army for doing a good job.

There is an interesting anecdote regarding Sam, which was related by Colonel Teja Singh Aulakh, who had joined MO as a Captain in May 1947. Teja's village, Narowal, went to Pakistan after Partition and he had therefore opted for the Pakistani

Army. Sam had also been asked for his choice, and though Jinnah had asked him to opt for Pakistan, he had opted for India. He had been born and brought up in Punjab, but his wife and the rest of the family were in Bombay. Acceding to Jinnah's request may have resulted in faster promotions, but he preferred to remain in India. When the records were being divided, Sam had asked Teja to collect all the files he wanted to take with him to Pakistan. However, just before he moved, Teja came to know that his family had crossed over at Dera Baba Nanak and come to India. He promptly changed his choice, and opted to remain in India. His family later joined him in Delhi and they were living in Chattarpur, a village near the Qutb Minar, about 10 kilometres from his office in South Block. Teja used a bicycle to commute between his home and office and was often late. He was subsequently promoted Major and Sam had by then become a Brigadier. One day, there was a lot of work and they broke off at about 8 p.m. Silloo brought around the car to pick up Sam. When she saw Teja getting on his bicycle, which had no lights, she asked, 'Why don't you use the Brigadier's motorcycle that is rotting in our verandah?'

Next day, Teja took one of his colleagues, Jimmy Dorabjee, to fetch the motorcycle and also teach him how to ride it. He began using it regularly to commute to his office. After a few months, Teja was nominated to attend the staff course at Wellington and he decided to buy the motorcycle. He had found out that Sam had purchased it from a British officer for 400 rupees. He went up to Sam and offered to buy it. 'Why do you want to buy it?' asked Sam. 'If you don't need it, throw it into a *khud* (ditch).' When Teja insisted that he would like to pay for it, Sam agreed to accept 300 rupees. But Teja wanted to pay 400, so Sam asked him to toss a coin to decide the issue. Teja lost, and Sam walked away, saying, 'OK. You bloody well pay 400 as you wanted.'

At Teja's farewell party, Silloo was sitting next to Teja's wife and learnt that they owned a buffalo, which gave five seers (a seer is about two pounds, in weight) of milk each day. On the way home, she told Sam about it and expressed a desire to buy a buffalo so that they could save on the expenses on milk. Sam was very fond of his garden and knew what a buffalo would do to it. Next morning, he came to the office in a foul mood. He walked straight to Teja's room, hopped on to his table, and looking him straight in the eye, said, 'Teja, if you don't want to pay for the motorcycle, don't pay. But don't put that buffalo of yours on my head.'

In April 1952, Sam was given command of 167 Infantry Brigade at Ferozepur and got some respite after his hectic schedule at Delhi, where Partition, integration of the Indian States and the operations in Jammu and Kashmir had kept him fully occupied. He could now devote some time to his family and indulge in his hobby of gardening. He grew vegetables, flowers, even cotton. They had a huge house with a large garden and Sam kept himself busy outside, while Silloo looked after the inside. Their children remember them as a popular couple with a hectic social life, full of parties and visits to the club. They were also a sporting family and played badminton, tennis and table tennis. Sam was an indulgent father and doted on his two daughters who remember, wistfully, the games and stories of which Sam seemed to have an inexhaustible repertoire.

After finishing his tenure as a brigade commander, Sam was posted as the Director of Military Training at Army HQ in April 1954. After a short tenure at Delhi, he was transferred to Mhow as Commandant, Infantry School, in January 1955. At that time, the training manuals were little more than reproductions of British manuals. Sam believed in realistic and practical training and began having free-for-all discussions, where tactical concepts laid down in training manuals were questioned. Based on these discussions, he had his staff revise the training pamphlets on various operations of war. This was a significant contribution to the indigenisation of tactical concepts in the Indian Army.

In 1957 Sam was sent to London to attend the Imperial Defence College course. He spent about a year in England with his wife and two daughters. The family enjoyed their sojourn and went for picnics on weekends, where Sam did the cooking. Though not an expert, Sam had picked up the rudiments of the art from his mother and practised them whenever he got a chance. He is especially proud of his *koru na murumba* (white pumpkin preserve) and *eeda pakh* (a sweet made with eggs, cream etc.).

On his return from the UK in December 1957, Sam was promoted Major General and posted as GOC 26 Infantry Division. At that time Thimayya was the Chief of Army Staff and Krishna Menon the Defence Minister. During a visit to his division, Menon asked Sam what he thought of Thimayya. Sam said that he was not permitted to 'think' about his Chief. Menon was annoyed, and said, 'Stop your British way of thinking. I can get rid of Thimayya, if I want.' Sam replied, 'You can get rid of him. But then I will get another Chief, and I won't be allowed to think about him too. You know, it is very wrong to ask a Major General what he thinks of the Chief. Tomorrow, you will be asking a Brigadier what he thinks of me. This is not done in the Army.' This put Menon in his place, and he fell silent.

In September 1959, Sam was posted as the Commandant of the Defence Services Staff College, at Wellington. Very soon, he was involved in an unsavoury incident, which almost ended his career. In May 1961, Thimayya retired and was succeeded by General P.N. Thapar as Chief of Army Staff. A year earlier, B.M. Kaul had been promoted Lieutenant General and appointed Quarter Master General against the recommendations of Thimayya, who had been overruled by Krishna Menon, leading to Thimayya's resignation. As soon as Thimayya retired, Kaul was appointed Chief of General Staff (CGS) to replace Bogey Sen, who went to Eastern Command as GOC-in-C. The CGS was then the most important appointment in Army HQ next to the COAS, and Kaul, because of his proximity to Nehru and Menon, in fact, became more powerful than the Chief himself.

Sam often made disparaging remarks about Indian politicians, which led some people to brand him as anti-national. Based on information gained by informers who were sent by Kaul for this purpose, Army HQ ordered a Court of Inquiry to investigate his behaviour. Normally, the Adjutant General's Branch handles such cases but in this case, it was the General Staff Branch under Kaul, which dealt with the inquiry. The members of the Inquiry were Lieutenant General Daulet Singh, GOC-in-C Western Command, and Lieutenant General Bikram Singh, GOC 15 Corps.

There were three charges against Sam. The first charge was that he was disloyal to the country. This was based on the fact that he had hung in his office pictures of British Viceroys, Governors General and Commanders-in-Chief, instead of Indian leaders. Actually, Sam had found these old pictures of Clive, Hastings, Kitchener and Birdwood dumped in a store, and had decided to put them up in a suitable place in his office. The second charge concerned Sam's failure to take action against an instructor, who had during a lecture remarked that Indians lacked a sense of perspective and tended to build up personalities out of proportion. The instructor, who was a naval officer, mentioned that Shivaji's statue in Bombay showed him riding an Australian Waler when in actual fact, the terrain in the Western Ghats was suitable only for ponies. Sam had later told the instructor to be more tactful, but it was felt that he should have taken more drastic action.

The third charge was even more interesting. An officer on his staff deposed that the Commandant had said that he did not want any instructor at the College whose wife looked like an *ayah* (maidservant). When questioned by the Court of Inquiry, this officer agreed that he had not heard Sam say these words and neither could he remember who had told him. Kaul had also managed to get a report from the Intelligence Bureau about Sam's anti-Indian views but when called to give evidence, its Director, B.N. Mullick, refused to appear.

It appears strange that a Court of Inquiry was ordered by Army HQ on such insubstantial grounds, and that too against a senior officer. Apart from the charges being flimsy and downright ludicrous, the fact that Kaul was able to rope in two lieutenant generals— including an Army Commander—to conduct the proceedings, is a measure of the authority and power that he wielded at that time. It is rare for a lieutenant general to conduct an inquiry, and almost unthinkable for an Army Commander to do so. In contrast, the inquiry to investigate the reasons for the debacle during the Sino– Indian War of 1962 was headed by Major General Henderson Brooks, with Brigadier P.S. Bhagat as a member. Fortunately for Sam, Lieutenant General Daulet Singh, who headed the Court of Inquiry, was known for his integrity. Sam was exonerated of all charges and the Court also recommended disciplinary action against the officers who had made the false allegations. When the inquiry had been ordered, Sam's career appeared certain to be ruined and there was a strong likelihood of his being dismissed, or even worse. He escaped by the skin of his teeth, but the incident left a taint on his career. Harbaksh Singh and Moti Sagar, both his juniors, were made Corps Commanders before him.

According to Sam, it was the Chinese who came to his rescue. The Sino–Indian conflict in 1962 ended in a debacle for the Indian Army. The two men who had tried to ruin Sam's career were also largely responsible for the ignominy suffered by the Indian Army at the hands of the Chinese. Much against his wishes, Nehru had to sack Krishna Menon as Defence Minister. Kaul was removed from command of 4 Corps and later resigned. In November 1962 Nehru summoned Sam to Delhi and asked him to assume command of 4 Corps. When Sam told the Prime Minister that he had been waiting for almost 18 months for his promotion, Nehru told him that what had happened was a mistake.

When Sam assumed command, he found that he had a first-class team of officers on his staff and the reason for the poor performance of the Corps was only bad leadership. In fact, after assuming command, he asked Lieutenant General Bogey Sen, the Army Commander, as to why he did not sack Kaul and take over himself. Sen replied, 'It is all very well for you to say this, Sam; but do you know what his stature was then? He never talked to me; he would just pick up the phone and talk to the Prime Minister. He never even consulted the COAS. I would have got no support from anyone. Krishna Menon and Bijjy Kaul were running the Armed Forces of the country.' Sam did not agree, and told Sen that had he been in office, he would have said, 'Sorry, out you go. I am taking over.' He felt that even if the government had sacked him, at least the country would not have been disgraced.

Sam's first task was to restore his team's morale, which had sunk to the boots, as soldiers often say. On the day he took over, after he had been briefed about the general situation, he called his Chief of Staff and told him that he wanted to issue orders. Sam recalls that the Chief of Staff took out his cap, threw it on the ground and jumped on it, saying, 'Thank God there is somebody giving orders. We have never had any orders till now.' After his staff had assembled, Sam issued his famous order; 'Gentlemen, there shall be no more withdrawals.' He knew that nothing else could restore confidence as quickly as advancing to the positions they had lost.

Sam had been in command for just five days when the Prime Minister visited his headquarters in Tezpur, accompanied by his daughter, Indira Gandhi and the Chief of Army Staff, General J.N. Chaudhuri. When Sam informed them that his troops were advancing, Nehru reacted strongly, saying that he did not want any more people killed. The Army Chief tried to pacify the Prime Minister, telling him that he would talk to the Corps Commander and get the orders reversed. Sam was incensed and asked the Chief to either let him command his Corps the way he liked or send him back to Staff College.

Indira Gandhi had no official position in the government but wielded enormous influence. She remonstrated that it was shameful that they had a commander who wanted to fight but was not being allowed to do so. The country and the Army had already earned a bad name and she felt that it was time someone did something about it. Nehru tried to interrupt her but she would have none of it. Turning to Sam, she told him to go ahead and do what he liked. Sam could do little more than thank her.

Sam's next task was to reorganise the defences of the North East Frontier Agency (NEFA). He went around the area, visiting the units and talking to the commanders and troops. Morale was low and the men had many complaints. Sam tried to do his best to improve things and took corrective action to overcome the shortages of clothing, equipment and accommodation. He felt that NEFA could have been defended and often gave the example of the North West Frontier, where a handful of tribesmen on hilltops could hold up entire brigades comprising trained British and Indian troops, supported with artillery and air. In his view, the only reason for the failure was low morale and lack of higher direction—from Delhi as well as from Army and Corps Commanders.

In December 1963, Sam was appointed GOC-in-C Western Command. He remained there for only a year, before moving to Eastern Command as Army Commander in November 1964. During one of his visits to the Mizo hills, he found that the communications were very bad. When he asked the reason, he was told that the Post and Telegraph Department had been asked to provide the telephone line, but it was likely to take at least 4–5 years since the distance was over 200 kilometres. 'That is too much,' said Sam. 'Can't we do it ourselves?' He was told that according to the Telegraph Act, only the Post and Telegraph Department could own telephone and telegraph lines and that the Army had to hire them from it. This conversation was taking place over a glass of beer in the brigade officers' mess. Brigadier R.Z. Kabraji was the brigade commander. He called his Signals officer and Sam asked him how long it would take to lay the line.

'Two months,' replied the officer, 'provided I have the stores.'

'Where can we get the stores?' asked Sam.

'The P&T has a big dump at Silchar,' replied the officer.

'Then go and get it,' said Sam. 'But don't get caught.'

Sam had said this as a joke, but the Signals officer, who was young, immature and impetuous, took it seriously. He took a fleet of lorries to Silchar and went straight to the P&T Department stores. When the official in charge protested, he brought him along with the stores and released him only after a week. The P&T Department raised a hue and cry and reported the 'theft' and kidnapping of their officer to the Ministry. Soon the matter reached Army HQ. The COAS ordered disciplinary action to be taken against the officer, as well as the brigade commander. By now the line was almost complete and the Army Commander was informed of the case. Though Sam had forgotten about the incident, he immediately wrote to the Chief assuming full responsibility for the officer's actions, saying that he had acted on his specific orders.

While in Eastern Command, Sam went to Jorhat. During his visit to the hospital, he found a soldier who had sustained a bullet injury in the stomach. He was moaning with pain. When Sam asked him how many bullets he had got, the soldier replied 'One'. Sam pulled up his own shirt and, showing the scar running all the way down his abdomen, asked, 'How many do you think I got?' The soldier grinned sheepishly and stopped moaning, as Sam tucked in his shirt and moved on.

On another occasion, he went to Sikkim to visit a battalion of 8th Gorkha Rifles. The battalion was at a high altitude, holding picquets on the border with China. The CO, in a bid to please the Army Commander, had laid on a lavish reception. A lot of silver had been brought up from the base, as well as sofa sets and carpets. When Sam saw all this, he was very angry, knowing the ordeal the men must have undergone carrying all this up on their backs. The battalion had finished its tenure and was due to go to a peace station. 'I had thought you chaps are having a hard time and deserve a good peace station,' said Sam. 'But seeing how comfortable you are, I think another year will not do you any harm.' When the CO protested, Sam gave him a tongue-lashing that he never forgot.

The Chief of Army Staff, General P.P. Kumaramangalam, was due to retire in June 1969. Sam and Harbaksh Singh were the two contenders for his post. Sam was senior, but Sardar Swaran Singh, the Defence Minister, favoured Harbaksh, who had commanded the Western Army during the 1965 Indo–Pak War. However, Prime Minister Indira Gandhi decided in favour of Sam and he became the Chief on 8 June 1969. He had reached the pinnacle of his career, which had almost been cut short a few years earlier when he was at Wellington. He was destined to write his name into history books, as India's first Field Marshal and the victor of the 1971 War.

As Chief, Sam cut a dashing figure, with his side cap and pleated shirts. He was full of beans and his enthusiasm and energy were contagious. This, coupled with his ready wit and sense of humour, made him a popular figure and his visits to formations and units were looked forward to. After each visit, there were always a few stories, which became the favourite topic of conversation in messes and drawing rooms. On one such visit to Mhow, he was asked to inaugurate a new wing of the Club of Central India, which has now become the Defence Services Officers Institute. Sam noticed that the new wing had still not been properly furnished, and when he remarked so, he was promptly asked for some funds. He agreed to a generous grant from the Chief's Welfare Fund, and then said, 'I just don't know how to say no. Sometimes, I thank God for making me a man, and not a woman. Can you imagine my condition if it had been otherwise? I would have been always pregnant!'

Sam was once invited to Bombay to inaugurate the HQ of the newly formed Western Naval Command. When he landed at Santa Cruz airport, the Area Commander and several other senior officers of the Army and the Navy were present to receive him. Sam was escorted to the Mercedes Benz that had been hired for the Chief. The trouble began when it was found that the Chief's flag could not be fixed on the car, as the flag post was the wrong size. Sam's suitcase had to be put in another car because the boot of the Benz would not open. To top it all, the car came to a spluttering halt just outside the airport. While everyone was on tenterhooks at such an inauspicious beginning, Sam transferred calmly to another car and the cavalcade resumed its journey without further problems. When driving along the Marine Drive, Sam was impressed by the upkeep of the buildings, some of which were very old. These stately mansions looked as if they had been built only recently. When he reached Colaba and saw the newly constructed MES buildings, he remarked that they looked much older than the ones on Marine Drive.

The same evening, there was a party in the officers' mess. Knowing the Chief's preference, the Area Commander had told his ADC to keep an adequate supply of Dimple scotch whisky. The ADC, a young Captain from 18 Cavalry, had given the barman a sealed bottle along with one that was more than half full with instructions that the sealed bottle was to be opened only with his permission. Due to a mix up, the open bottle was used to serve the first drink not only to Sam but also to several others. When the barman reported that only two pegs were left in the bottle, the ADC was aghast. The GOC's wife had told him to make sure that Dimple was served only to the Chief, and if he opened the new bottle so early in the evening, he was sure to be taken to task. So he asked the barman to get some Indian whisky and poured two pegs into the bottle of Dimple. Sam was not a heavy drinker and the four pegs should suffice for the evening, he reasoned.

When the next drink was served, Sam took one sip and grimaced. 'This is not Dimple,' he said. The bottle was promptly brought for his inspection and he sniffed it. He had another sip, then shook his head. When he asked where it had come from, he was told that it was from the canteen. 'Don't tell me the canteen is giving you spurious Scotch. You must report the matter,' he said. The new bottle was then brought and opened. When Sam sipped his new drink, he proclaimed that this was indeed Dimple. After this, the party got underway and ended without further mishap.

After the party, the GOC and his wife grilled the ADC and the mess staff. The ADC confessed his crime and was lambasted. He was asked to go to the Chief next morning and make a clean breast of the whole affair. The next day, a very sheepish Captain went to the Chief of Army Staff and said that he wanted to say something. When he was given the necessary permission, he blurted out the whole episode. Sam had a hearty laugh and said, 'You have been naughty, young man.'

During this period, India was going through a difficult time and the problems facing her seemed insurmountable. In neighbouring Pakistan, the Army had seized power and there was speculation that India may go the same way. Once, a visiting American diplomat asked Sam when he was going to take over. Sam retorted, 'As soon as General Westmoreland takes over in your country.' The American Ambassador, Kenneth Keating, was present and he had a good laugh.

One day, Sam was summoned by the Prime Minister to her office in Parliament House. When he entered, he found Indira Gandhi in very low spirits. She was sitting at her table, with her head in her hands. On being asked what was troubling her, she replied that she had problems. Sam asked her what the problem was and was surprised when she told him that he was the problem. When Sam asked her to elaborate, the Prime Minister said that she had heard that he was going to take over. Sam was shocked. He assured her that he did not harbour any political ambitions. He knew that military coups had not succeeded in any country in the world. India was a democratic country and would always remain so. He was quite happy commanding the Indian Army, and as long as he was allowed to do that, she could run the country the way she wanted. Indira Gandhi seemed to be relieved and thanked Sam profusely.

The most well-known anecdote about Sam is the one he often relates himself. In 1971, when refugees from East Pakistan began to cross over into India, Sam was the Army Chief, Indira Gandhi the Prime Minister and Babu Jagjiwan Ram the Minister for Defence or Raksha Mantri. There was a meeting of the Cabinet on 27 April 1971, to which Sam was invited as the Chairman of the Chiefs of Staff Committee. The Prime Minister appeared to be distraught and angry. Refugees from East Pakistan were pouring into West Bengal, Assam and other parts of Eastern India. Waving a telegram from the Chief Minister of one of the eastern states, she asked Sam, 'Can't you do something?'

'What do you want me to do?' asked Sam.

'Go into East Pakistan.'

'This would mean war,' said Sam.

'I know,' said Indira Gandhi. 'We don't mind a war.'

'Have you read the Bible' asked Sam.

'What has the Bible to do with this?' asked Swaran Singh, the Minister for External Affairs.

'In the Bible, it is written that God said, "Let there be light, and there was light." You think that by saying "Let there be war," there can be a war? Are you ready for a war? I am not.'

The Prime Minister did not seem to be very pleased and there was a scowl on her face. Sam went on to explain the reasons for his reluctance to go to war with Pakistan immediately. In a few weeks, the monsoon would set in, making the ground unsuitable for operations as East Pakistan had a number of rivers, which were prone to flooding. All movement would have to be on roads, which could be blocked. The Air Force would not be able to support the ground troops due to bad weather. The armoured division was in Jhansi and one of the infantry divisions in Secunderabad. Moving them to the East would require time as well as all available road and rail space. The wheat crop was being harvested and movement of foodgrains would be adversely affected. Turning towards the Agriculture Minister, Fakhruddin Ali Ahmed, Sam said, 'If there is a famine, people will blame you, not me.'

The Agriculture Minister squirmed in his seat. Sam then turned to the Finance Minister, Y.B. Chavan, and said, 'My armoured division has only 12 tanks which are operational. You know why? Because whenever we asked you for funds, you said you had no money.'

Sam advised postponement of the operations till the winter months. This would give him enough time to build up the infrastructure required for large-scale operations in the East. The government would also get enough time to garner international support through diplomatic channels, so that other countries did not interfere or extend military assistance to Pakistan. During winter the northern passes would be blocked with snow, eliminating the threat of intervention by the Chinese. Most members of the Cabinet seemed to see the logic of his arguments and nodded their heads, though Indira Gandhi seemed to be somewhat unhappy.

Finally, Sam addressed the Prime Minister herself. 'As your Army Chief, it is my duty to put the facts before you. If your father had me as the Army Chief in 1962 instead of General Thapar, and he had told me to throw the Chinese out, I would have said the same thing and he would not have been shamed the way he was. If you still want me to go ahead, I will. But I guarantee you a one hundred per cent defeat. Now tell me what you want me to do.'

There was a stunned silence. Then the Defence Minister, Babu Jagjiwan Ram, said, 'Shyam,'—he always pronounced Sam as Shyam, a popular Indian name—'maan jao na' (please agree).

Sam said, 'I have given my professional assessment. It is now for the Government to take a decision.'

The Prime Minister did not say anything. She appeared to be visibly angry. She closed the meeting, asking everyone to come back at 4 p.m. As everybody rose and started leaving, the Prime

Minister asked Sam to stay back. When they were alone, he offered to resign, either on physical or mental grounds.

'Sit down, Sam,' she said. 'I don't want your resignation. Just tell me, is everything you said earlier true?'

Sam replied, 'Yes, it is. Look, it is my job to fight, and fight to win. Today, if you go to war, you will lose. Give me another six months and I guarantee you a hundred per cent success. But I want to make one thing quite clear. There must be one commander. I don't mind working under the BSF, the CRPF, or anybody you like. But I will not have a Soviet telling me what to do. I must have one political master giving me directions. I don't want the refugee ministry, home ministry, defence ministry, all telling me what to do. Now, you make up your mind.'

'All right, Sam, nobody will interfere,' said the Prime Minister. 'You will be in command.'

'Thank you,' said Sam. 'I guarantee you a victory.' And so it was. Later, Sam was to recall that there is a very thin line between becoming a Field Marshal and being dismissed.

Once the decision to undertake operations was taken by the government, and Sam was given the go-ahead, he set about it in earnest. The government also decided to extend support to the freedom movement in East Pakistan, led by Sheikh Mujibur Rehman. The task of training and equipping the *Mukti Bahini*, as the freedom fighters were known, was entrusted to the Indian Army. Sam decided to train and equip three brigade groups of regular Bangladesh troops. They would be based mainly on the personnel of the East Bengal Regiment, the shortfall being made up from the East Pakistan Rifles. In addition, about 75,000 guerrillas were to be trained and equipped with weapons and ammunition. From the middle of 1971 till the end of the war, they operated in small bands, harassing the regular troops of the Pakistan Army. The Government of Bangladesh, as the new nation was intended to be named once it became independent, had started functioning in Calcutta and Colonel M.A.G. Osmani was appointed the Military Advisor and C-in-C of its Army. As the atrocities committed by Tikka Khan's troops in East Pakistan grew in intensity, so did the flood of refugees streaming towards India. The international media, which initially viewed India's action in providing help to the *Mukti Bahini* as interference in the internal affairs of a neighbouring country, slowly began to veer around and articles documenting the horrible atrocities committed by Pakistani troops began to appear in the press.

On the diplomatic front, the government went all out to convince the world of the righteousness of India's stand. Indira Gandhi visited several foreign countries and personally briefed the heads of government. Except the Soviet Union, none of the major powers supported India's stand. In fact, some were critical of her actions and the USA as well as China came out openly in support of Pakistan. Indira Gandhi, realising the threat of intervention by China as well as Pakistan, sent D.P. Dhar to Moscow with feelers regarding obtaining support from the Soviet Union. The Russians responded favourably and the Indo–Soviet Treaty of Peace, Friendship and Co-operation was signed on 9 August 1971. This was a major achievement and effectively neutralised the threat from USA and Pakistan, giving India considerable freedom in deciding her course of action.

The strategy for the operations in East Pakistan, as decided by Sam, was to mount a multi-pronged attack, bypassing strongly held areas, with the aim of capturing maximum territory in the shortest possible time. This was essential because of the possibility of a UN sponsored ceasefire after a few weeks. It was intended to liberate a large enough area to facilitate the establishment of a Bangladesh government. The capture of Dacca or the fall of the whole of East Pakistan was neither planned nor visualised at this stage. The task of executing the strategy formulated by the Army HQ was given to Eastern Command, then headed by Lieutenant General Jagjit Singh Aurora, who had Major General J.F.R. Jacob as his Chief of Staff. Three Army corps were to be used for the operation—2 Corps, under Lieutenant General T.N. 'Tappy' Raina, (later General, and Army Chief) was to advance from the west; 4 Corps, under Lieutenant General Sagat Singh, was to enter from the east; 33 Corps, under Lieutenant General M.L. Thapan, was to come down from the north; and 101 Communication Zone Area, under Major General Gurbax Singh Gill, was to mount a subsidiary thrust from the north-east. The Indo–Pak War of 1971 started on 3 December 1971, after Pakistani aircraft bombed Indian airfields in the western sector. Indira Gandhi was then in Calcutta. Sam Manekshaw telephoned Jacob at 6 p.m. and asked him to inform the Prime Minister that the war had begun and he was issuing orders to Eastern Command to go ahead immediately. Characteristically, Sam 'informed' the Prime Minister rather than seeking permission. Jacob informed the Army Commander, who left at once to brief the Prime Minister, who was staying with the Governor at Raj Bhawan (Government House). The Navy and Air Force were also informed and full-scale operations commenced the next day.

As the operations progressed, Pakistani resistance broke down. The Indians bypassed all strongly held positions and the isolated Pakistani troops, taken by surprise, began to withdraw or surrender. American proposals to get the United Nations to effect a ceasefire were frustrated by the Soviets, who vetoed the resolutions. An interesting feature of the war were the three broadcasts made by Sam, calling on Pakistani troops to surrender and assuring them of honourable treatment. The first message was broadcast on the radio and dropped in the form of leaflets after the fall of Jessore on 9 December. Addressed to the 'officers and jawans of the Pakistan Army', it exhorted them to lay down their arms before it was too late. It went on to say:

> Indian forces have surrounded you. Your Air Force is destroyed. You have no hope of any help from them. Chittagong, Chalna and Mangla ports are blocked. Nobody can reach you from the sea. Your fate is sealed. The *Mukti Bahini* and the people are all prepared to take revenge for the atrocities and cruelties you have committed . . . Why waste lives? Don't you want to

go home and be with your children? Do not lose time; there is no disgrace in laying down your arms to a soldier. We will give you the treatment befitting a soldier.

Two other messages, on the same lines, were broadcast on December 11 and 15, in reply to messages from Major General Rao Farman Ali and Lieutenant General A.K. Niazi. These messages were a severe blow to the morale of the Pakistani troops and convinced them of the futility of further resistance. Accounts of Pakistani officers and men captured subsequently revealed that these messages had played a significant part in degrading Pakistani resolve to fight and it is estimated that they had shortened the war by at least two weeks.

In the early hours of 11 December, Lieutenant Iftikhar of the Pakistan Army came up on the wireless set, indicating his willingness to surrender. He came out with a white flag near the Mirpur bridge and surrendered to Indian troops. The same day, Major General Rao Farman Ali, the Military Adviser to the Governor of East Pakistan, sent a message to the United Nations asking for a ceasefire. The Security Council was about to begin discussing the message when another message was received from President Yayha Khan countermanding Farman Ali's message, which it described as 'unauthorised'.

As early as 9 December, the Governor of East Pakistan, Dr A.M. Malik, had sent a message to Yahya Khan advocating a ceasefire. Yahya Khan had replied that he was leaving the decision to Malik and had instructed General Niazi, the Army Commander, accordingly. Malik could not make up his mind and continued to wait for instructions from Rawalpindi. On 13 December, Niazi spoke to the Army Chief, General Hamid, requesting him to arrange a ceasefire. On 14 December Yahya Khan sent instructions to Niazi to take action as he deemed fit to stop the fighting and preserve the lives of his men. Before this message reached Niazi, another development had taken place. Malik convened a meeting at midday, on 14 December at

Government House in Dacca, to discuss the issue. The wireless message giving the time and venue of the meeting was intercepted by an Indian Signals interception unit. The Indian Air Force bombed the Government House, causing a lot of damage. Malik was badly shaken and his concern for the safety of his Austrian wife and daughter, who were with him, finally pushed him towards a decision. He immediately wrote out his resignation and, accompanied by his cabinet and other civil servants, moved to the Hotel Intercontinental, which had been occupied by the International Red Cross and was treated as a neutral zone.

The decision to surrender was actually taken by Niazi, who addressed a message to Sam Manekshaw on 15 December and requested the United States Consul General in Dacca, Herbert Spivack, to convey it to him. Instead of sending the message to India, Spivack had it sent to Washington, from where it was relayed to India. Sam had already made two broadcasts asking the Pakistani forces in East Pakistan to surrender. Leaflets containing his call to surrender had been translated into Urdu, Pushtu and Bengali and dropped over the area held by Pakistani troops. When he received Niazi's message, Sam broadcast a reply, indicating that a ceasefire would be acceptable only if the Pakistani troops surrendered to the Indian Army by 9 a.m. on 16 December 1971. He gave the radio frequencies on which Niazi could contact Aurora's headquarters. As a token of good faith, Sam also informed Niazi that he was ordering cessation of air action over Dacca. Niazi later requested an extension of the deadline for surrender, from 9 a.m. to 3 p.m., which Sam accepted. Around midnight, on December 15, Niazi sent a message to all his formation commanders to contact their Indian counterparts and negotiate a ceasefire. The war was over.

The formal surrender ceremony took place at Dacca on 16 December. In front of a large crowd, General Niazi handed over his pistol to Lieutenant General Aurora, the Army Commander, and signed the Instrument of Surrender at 1655 Hours. Along with Niazi, about 93,000 Pakistani soldiers became prisoners of war. On 10 January 1972, Sheikh Mujib returned to Dacca in triumph and took over the reins of the Government of Bangladesh. In March 1972, Indian troops began to withdraw along with civil servants who handed over charge to their counterparts in Bangladesh.

Before the Indian troops went into East Pakistan, Sam had wanted to make sure that they did not resort to the traditional occupations of a victorious Army—loot and rape. He therefore gave strict orders that anyone found looting was to be courtmartialled. As regards the second problem, he thought he should talk to the men directly. Wherever he went, he stressed on the need for Indian troops to be on their best behaviour and stay away from women. Finally, he broadcast a message to the troops just before they went into action. 'When you see a Begum, keep your hands in your pockets, and think of Sam,' he said. As a result, cases of loot and rape were negligible and the Indian Army came out with flying colours, not only for its feat of arms but the behaviour of its soldiers.

As the war progressed, battle casualties began trickling in. Sam's wife, Silloo, made it a point to receive all casualties personally and went to the Military Hospital everyday to visit them. During one of her visits, she was told that a wounded Pakistani officer had also arrived. He had been kept under guard in a separate room. Mrs Manekshaw went to visit him. The officer did not reply when she asked him how he was feeling. This was repeated on the next two days. After she left, on the third day, the Pakistani officer asked one of the nurses about the lady in slacks who came to visit him daily. When he was told that she was the Chief's wife, he was aghast. The next day, when Mrs Manekshaw went to visit him, the officer apologised profusely for his rude behaviour. He could not stop his tears, saying that he had not been able to recognise her as this sort of thing did not happen in his own country.

During the 1971 war, India took a very large number of prisoners. They were lodged in several camps all over the country. When the first train carrying the prisoners reached Delhi en route to one of these camps, Sam went straight to the railway station to meet them, without informing anyone in Army HQ. The POWs had just arrived and were waiting on platforms when Sam reached the station, the first Indian officer to meet them. The POWs and their escort were surprised to see the Chief walking around, with just his ADC for company. After chatting with them for some time and sharing a cup of tea, he left, as several other senior officers began to arrive. The POWs were seen shaking their heads, saying that they wished they had generals like this in Pakistan.

Sam insisted that the POWs were well looked after. At several places, Indian troops were asked to vacate their barracks and live in tents so that the POWs could be properly accommodated. They were allowed to celebrate their festivals and given copies of the Koran. The Red Cross and other international agencies were given free access to the POW camps, and they were permitted to receive letters and gift parcels.

During the 1971 war, India won a decisive victory over Pakistan. A new nation had come into being and Sam, as the prime architect of the victory, became a hero. Apart from capturing almost a hundred thousand prisoners, the Indian Army had occupied several hundred square kilometres of Pakistani soil in Ladakh. After a year, when talks were held in Simla between the Prime Ministers of India and Pakistan, it was expected that India would be able to wrest some major concessions from Pakistan and negotiate a permanent solution to the Kashmir problem. Unfortunately, Sam was kept out of the summit and had no part to play in the negotiations. Though Bhutto and Indira Gandhi had informally agreed to accept the ceasefire line in Kashmir as the international border, this was not reduced to writing. As a result, the military gains, achieved at great cost in human lives, were frittered away by politicians and bureaucrats. When Indira returned from Simla, she told Sam about the meeting. Bhutto had told her that he had recently taken over and was not in a position to take major decisions. He needed more time and promised that in six months everything would be done as she desired. Sam reportedly told the Prime Minister: 'Bhutto has made a monkey out of you.'

The prisoners taken by India and Pakistan were exchanged on 1 December 1972. Withdrawal of troops of both sides had still not taken place due to disagreement on the alignment of the Line of Control. Talks had been going on between both countries for over four months, to delineate the Line of Control in Jammu and Kashmir. There was a deadlock due to conflicting claims of both sides over certain key areas, including the village of Thako Chak near Jammu and certain features in Kaiyan, across the Tutmari Gali in Kashmir. The enclave of Thako Chak in the Chicken's Neck had been occupied by Pakistan during the war. In the Kaiyan Bowl, a large area had been captured by an overenthusiastic company of 9 Sikhs, which was part of 19 Infantry Division. However, a small hillock that had been reported as captured was discovered to be still held by the enemy when ceasefire was declared. The anomaly was discovered several months later, during the delineation talks being held at Wagah. To retrieve the situation, the divisional commander decided to capture the feature. The strength of the feature was not correctly assessed, and the attack launched in May 1972 failed, with heavy casualties.

To resolve the issue, Sam flew down to Lahore, and had two meetings with his counterpart General Tikka Khan, on 28 November and 7 December. Though Indira Gandhi had authorised him to give up Thako Chak to break the deadlock, Sam was not one to give up so easily. Finally, he managed to get back Thako Chak, in return for some territory in Kaiyan that was not as valuable. The withdrawal of troops commenced soon afterwards, and was completed by 20 December 1972.

Like Thimayya, Sam was very popular with the troops, who literally adored him. When visiting the messes of JCOs and OR, he always drank rum instead of whisky or beer, which are normally served in officers' messes. His behaviour and conduct with his orderlies and domestic staff was particularly informal. One day, just as he was about to leave Army House for his office, he was told that an old woman wanted to meet him. Coming out, he found it was the widow of Sher Singh, his old Sikh orderly from 4/12 FFR who had saved his life. Sam made her sit in his car and took her along to South Block. Taking her to his office, he made her sit down, and asked for some tea. He chatted with her for an hour, keeping several senior officers waiting outside. Finally, he asked his ADC to take her in his car and drop her at the railway station where she had to catch a train. As the old lady left, she said, '*Main dua karti thi ki Rab tujhe Jangi Laat bana de. Ab main chain se marungi.*' (I used to pray to God to make you the Commander-in-Chief. Now I can die in peace.)

Sam is known for his quick wit, and the ability to say the right thing at the right time. When President de Gaulle died, Mrs Indira Gandhi went to attend his funeral. On her return, the three service Chiefs had gone to the airport to receive her as was customary, along with other dignitaries. When Indira Gandhi came to Sam, he complimented her on her hairdo. She smiled, and said 'You are the only one who has noticed it.'

Another of Sam's endearing qualities is his sense of humour. In September 1970, Sam and Silloo went to the USSR. After being received with due ceremony by several Soviet Marshals, they were taken to their hotel suite. Silloo asked one of the Marshals, 'Where is my room?' The Russians were nonplussed, till Sam explained that he and his wife slept in separate bedrooms, because he snored. Then taking the Marshal aside, he whispered, 'You know, she is the only woman who has ever complained.' The Russian laughed, and slapped Sam on the back.

During his visit to Lahore, for the delineation talks after the war, he was invited to an officers' mess where he recognised a silver trophy, which looked like one from his old regiment. On enquiry, it was found that the trophy had indeed once belonged to 4/12 FFR. Sam had recognised it after more than 30 years. During the same visit, Sam asked General Tikka Khan why he always wore dark glasses. 'You don't smoke, you don't drink, and neither do you like pretty faces. I do all these things, and still I don't hide my face.'

There is an intriguing anecdote about Sam's distaste for dark glasses. He had bought an expensive pair of sunglasses when he was a young officer. Sam did not know that his Commanding Officer had an aversion to glasses. One day he saw Sam wearing them and in a fit of rage, literally ground them into pieces. Sam was flabbergasted and stood glued to the ground as the old man rode away. He never wore sunglasses again.

Though Sam had an excellent rapport with Indira Gandhi, his relations with Jagjiwan Ram were somewhat strained. When Jagjiwan Ram tried to raise the issue of reservations for scheduled castes and tribes in the Army, Sam put his foot down. A note was sent from the Defence Ministry to Army HQ wanting to know why action should not be taken against those responsible for failing to implement the government policy on recruitment, formulated at the time of Independence. Sam sent a reply, saying that action should first be taken against him as the Chief since he had not only failed to implement the policy, but was in full agreement with the actions of his predecessors. No more was heard from the Ministry on the subject. When Lieutenant General N.C. Rawlley's name was proposed to take over as GOC-in-C Eastern Command, the file came back from the Ministry, asking Army HQ to propose another name. Sam sent the file back, with the remarks that there was no officer more suitable for the appointment. Ultimately he had his way, and Navin Rawlley became an Army Commander.

Another of Sam's habits that others considered odd was his practice of addressing Indira Gandhi as 'Prime Minister' instead of 'Madam'. Some bureaucrats were shocked and complained to the Cabinet Secretary about the disrespect being shown to the Prime Minister. When the Cabinet Secretary mentioned this in

Sam's presence at a meeting of the Committee of Secretaries, he got a reply that left him speechless. 'I hope you know that the term is reserved for certain ladies who are in charge of houses of ill fame.'

Soon after the end of the war, Indira Gandhi decided to promote him to Field Marshal and also appoint him the Chief of Defence Staff (CDS). However, the bureaucracy was not in favour of this. The CDS would become part of the Ministry of Defence and perform most of the tasks presently being done by bureaucrats from the Indian Administrative Service (IAS). However, since the decision was personally taken by the Prime Minister, no one opposed it openly. His promotion had to be cleared by the Appointments Committee of the Cabinet, but once it was known what Indira Gandhi wanted, this was a formality. There was a hitch when Y.B. Chavan, the Defence Minister, recorded his opinion that he felt that the effect of Sam's promotion on the other two services should also be considered. This delayed his promotion but could not stop it since Indira Gandhi had already made up her mind.

Though his promotion to the rank of Field Marshal was cleared, the proposal to appoint Sam the Chief of Defence Staff was torpedoed, by the time-honoured strategy of 'divide and rule'. Since the CDS was to exercise control over the Army, Navy and the Air Force, the views of all the three were solicited. As expected, the Air Force strongly objected. Air Chief Marshal P.C. Lal, who was the Chief of Air Staff, had been unhappy with the manner in which Sam had functioned during the war. In his book, *My Years With the IAF*, he writes:

From the way Manekshaw carried on in 1971 and in the publicity that was showered on him both during the war and after, the impression was created that he was, in fact, operating as a de facto Chief of Defence Staff even though he was at the time Chairman of the COSC (Chiefs of Staff Committee), in which capacity he was one of three equal partners.

Lal was at Chabua, near Dibrugarh, on 24 March 1972, when he received a telephone call from P.N. Haksar, the Principal Private Secretary to the Prime Minister. Haksar told him that the government was considering the creation of the post of CDS and appointing Sam Manekshaw to it in recognition of the manner in which he had directed the Bangladesh War. Lal was asked for his views before a final decision was taken. The Air Chief sent his comments to Haksar the same evening, in which he raised serious objections to the proposal. In fact, he asserted: 'I saw in the proposed arrangement a positive danger to frank and free discussions particularly if the CDS happened to be excessively assertive and intolerant of the ideas of others.'

In view of the strong opposition from the Air Force, or rather, the Air Chief—Lal could not possibly have consulted others in the few hours before he sent his reply—the proposal to create the post of CDS was dropped. In subsequent years, the Services came to realise the need for the appointment and clamoured for its creation. There was some talk of creating the appointment in 1987, when Rajiv Gandhi was the Prime Minister and Arun Singh the Defence Minister, but Exercise 'Brass Tacks' and the Bofors affair put paid to the proposal. The opportunity was allowed to pass, and may not come again.

Sam was due to retire in June 1972, but was given an extension of six months. He was not keen to continue and had made known his desire to the Prime Minister. However, she wanted him to stay on and told Sam that he would not be allowed to proceed with retirement. When Sam told her that he had no intention of staying on and there was no law under which he could be forced to do so, there was some consternation. Finally, someone found a way out. It was reasoned that if Sam received a direct order from the President who was also the Supreme Commander of the Armed Forces, he would have to obey. The President's consent was obtained and his directions published in the Gazette of India, indicating that Sam would continue to hold the office of Chief of Army Staff till the President was pleased to dispense with his services.

The rank of Field Marshal was formally conferred on Sam at a special investiture ceremony held at Rashtrapati Bhawan on 3 January 1973. Since no Indian had held the rank earlier, neither the insignia nor the baton were available. The Encyclopedia Britannica was consulted and the insignia fabricated overnight in the Army workshop in Delhi. For the baton, a stick orderly's cane was used after suitable modification. An interesting sidelight of the investiture concerns the baton, which is traditionally used by a Field Marshal for paying or accepting compliments. After the ceremony, some politicians were heard remarking that Sam had become swollen-headed and did not salute the President properly, as Army officers normally do. There was much amusement among the Service officers present, who had to explain that a Field Marshal traditionally uses his baton to salute, instead of his hand.

After the 1971 war, Sam commanded immense prestige not only in India but also abroad. He was literally mobbed wherever he went, and everyone wanted to shake his hand or touch his feet. Soon after the war, he was invited to Bombay as the Chief Guest at the Filmfare awards function. As usual, there was a huge crowd of onlookers at the entrance. But this time, the throng wanted to see Sam and not the film stars. When Sam arrived, they surrounded his car and cheered lustily. In stark contrast, the film stars were virtually ignored, which was a novel experience for most of them. Everyone wanted to shake hands with the Chief and take his autograph, including several well-known celebrities.

Sam's popularity was not confined to India. During one of his visits to Lahore after the war, the Governor of Punjab invited him for lunch. When the lunch was over, the Governor told him that some members of his staff wanted to shake hands with the Indian Chief. When Sam went outside, he found the entire staff lined up. As he went down the line shaking their hands, one of them took off his *pagree* (turban) and kept it at his feet. When Sam asked him why he was doing this he replied: 'Sir, it is because of you that we were saved. I have five sons who are your prisoners. They write letters to me. You have given them the Koran. They are living in barracks while your men are in tents. They sleep on cots while your men sleep on the ground. Now I will never believe anyone who tells me that Hindus are bad.'

Sam's popularity came at a price. Many people, especially in politics and the bureaucracy, began to perceive him as a threat. Indira Gandhi also found it difficult to allay her fears on this score, and soon found a chance to cut him to size. A young lady reporter asked him for an interview and he agreed. She came to his house and during their conversation, Sam mentioned that during Partition he had been asked to opt for Pakistan, but he had chosen to remain in India. When the reporter asked Sam what would have happened if he had opted for Pakistan, and been commanding the Pakistani Army, instead of the Indian, he replied, 'They would have won.' Sam undoubtedly made the witty remark without considering the consequences, which were immense. Soon afterwards, he had to go to the UK and while he was away, there was a question in Parliament based on the story which the reporter had written giving prominence to his remark. The Prime Minister was in the House but chose to remain silent. Sam was branded an egotist, and soon became *persona non grata*. Though the government could not take away his rank, it did take away every thing else and treated him shabbily. He was given a salary which was much lower than what he was entitled to, after handing over as Army Chief. None of the other facilities that a Field Marshal gets, such as secretarial staff, a house or a car, were given to him.

A few years later, the author had a chance to witness the tremendous popularity which Sam still enjoyed. It was in 1975, and he had come to Indore, where the citizens had organised a civic reception in a large auditorium. When Sam arrived he was almost mobbed and reached the stage with great difficulty. The crowds kept on shouting *'Manekshaw ki jai'*, till they were hoarse and no amount of entreaties by the organisers could silence them. After sometime, when they were quiet, someone started the welcome speech in Hindi. What he said went something like this: 'We have in our midst today, a soldier whose very name is synonymous with valour. He makes us remember Rana Pratap, Jhansi ki Rani and the gallant Shivaji, whose deeds form our national heritage. When we hear him talk, the blood courses through our veins with greater speed.'

And so it went on for a good half hour. After this, Sam was asked to speak. He too spoke in Hindi: 'I only want to make one request. Can I have an English translation of the speech I just heard? I want to give it to my wife. Whenever I tell her that I am a great man, she doesn't even listen. Now she will believe me.' Needless to say, this brought the house down and the ovation went on and on.

Sam's ability to communicate with people of any age group, especially the younger generation, is one of the reasons for his immense popularity. The author was doing the staff course at Wellington in 1977 along with Behram Panthaki, who had been Sam's ADC when he was COAS. It was a Saturday and there was a party at Behram's house at the 'Rosery' in Upper Coonoor, very close to 'Stavka', where Sam lives. Hearing the loud music, Sam came over and asked Behram, 'You chaps are having a party, and did not invite me?' When he came to know that it was a pound party, where everyone brings their own food and drinks, he promptly sent his Gorkha orderly home to fetch a bottle of Scotch. He stayed there till midnight, surrounded by a bevy of starry-eyed women, who would rather listen to his stories than dance with their husbands, much to the chagrin of the latter.

In 1989, Sam went to visit the Military Hospital in Secunderabad. Along with the medical officers, the nurses were also lined up to meet him. He stopped near the youngest one and asked her why she was improperly dressed. The poor girl blushed a deep scarlet, and began to stammer. The matron, who was an old battleaxe, came to her rescue, and asked Sam what he meant.

'Matron, as far as I remember, skirts are to end three inches above the knee. Your girls have skirts going right down to the knee.' And holding the hapless girl's skirt with both hands, he lifted it until it came to the correct height.

There were giggles galore, but the matron was not to be silenced. 'Sir, I have asked the girls to wear longer skirts, because the men stare at them in the wards,' she said.

'Matron, have you ever asked the girls whether they mind the men staring at them?' asked Sam, moving on. This silenced the matron, while the girls grinned from ear to ear.

Sam's sense of humour is unmatched and cannot be curbed, even on the most serious of occasions. In 1995, while delivering a lecture on leadership in New Delhi, he began to reflect on how times had changed. Even the English Language had changed, he lamented, and went on to cite several examples. In his younger days he said, the word 'gay' was used to describe someone full of the joys of spring; a 'queer' was a chap who'd rather spend his evenings in his room reading Milton than playing games; and only generals had 'aides'.

Sam's views on leadership, and the so-called good things of life, are interesting. In April 1993, he was invited to deliver the inaugural address of the Holiday Programme for Youth by the Bombay Parsi Punchayet. Talking about leadership, he said, 'By and large, men and women like their leaders to have all the manly qualities. The man who says he doesn't smoke, he doesn't drink, he doesn't . . . that man doesn't make a good leader. He may make a mahatma, he may make a saint, and he may make a priest, but he doesn't really make a leader.' He went on to add, 'Julius Caesar was a great leader. He had his Calpurnia, and he had his Cleopatra. And when he came to Rome and walked down the streets, senators used to lock up their wives. Take Napoleon Bonaparte. He had his Josephine, he had his Marie Valesca, Georgette, Ninette and every other vette. And you will agree that he was a great leader. Take the Duke of Wellington. Do you know, before the Battle of Waterloo, there were more countesses and marquesses with luscious proportions in his ante chamber than staff officers and commanders?'

Sam has a very prominent nose, and he often draws attention to it, in his own inimitable way. After talking about Caesar, Napoleon, and the Duke of Wellington, he would close with the remarks: 'All these great leaders had one special characteristic in common; they all had long noses.' He would then turn sideways, presenting the famous Manekshaw profile in a theatrical pose. This would invariably bring down the house.

Sam's aversion for the new breed of Indian politicians is well known and was largely responsible for landing him in trouble when he was the Commandant of the Staff College. However, this has done little to change his attitude and he continues to hold the tribe in contempt. During the same talk, he said,

> I wonder whether those of our political masters who have been put in charge of defence of the country can distinguish a mortar from a motor; a gun from a howitzer; a guerrilla from a gorilla—although a great many in the past have resembled the latter.

Not surprisingly, there was little love lost between Sam and the political bosses, who ultimately had their revenge.

After his retirement from active service, Sam settled down in Coonoor in the Nilgiris, very close to Wellington. In 1962, when he had been sent to NEFA as Corps Commander, he had left his family at Wellington. Silloo bought half an acre of land for 18,500 rupees, and designed 'Stavka', the house in which he now lives. The name of the house was suggested by Sherry, who had recently read Tolstoy's famous novel, *War and Peace*. In the book, 'Stavka' was the headquarters of the highest military commander in the land.

Until about 15 years ago, when he gave up driving, student officers in Wellington often ran into him, filling his car at the college pump and he would linger on to chat with them. He still has several Gorkhas working for him and when the wife of one of them was admitted in the military hospital, Sam made it a point to drive the *kancha* to the hospital daily, so that he could look her up. No wonder the Gorkhas worship him. It is such qualities that made Sam a legend, and one of the most popular military leaders of the Indian Army. He is still active, both physically and mentally, and takes an avid interest in every thing, however mundane. It is a pity that the political leadership chose to sideline him, and thus deprived the nation, and the armed forces, of the benefit of his rich experience and undoubted talents. Any other person, so treated, would have sunk into oblivion, but not Sam. Quite sensibly, he shunned politics, and refused gubernatorial and ambassadorial assignments. But he keeps himself busy with other pursuits. He is on the board of several large companies, and takes an active interest in their affairs.

Sam is a born leader, and practises the techniques of the battle field in the boardroom as well. During the 1971 war, a decision had to be taken to launch a pre-emptive air strike against the Pakistani defences in Karachi. The Air Chief agreed to do it, but suggested that they get it cleared by the Defence Minister. 'Why should we?' asked Sam. 'Once the political decision to wage war has been taken by the Government, we must take responsibility for all military decisions ourselves.' It was this type of leadership and the excellent cooperation between the three services, which won the war. A similar style of leadership, if displayed in 1962, might have produced different results and saved the nation from the ignominy it suffered.

Silloo, Sam's companion for over 60 years, passed away recently. Her departure left a void in his life, and though he does not show it, Sam has lost some of the spring in his step. Sherry and Maja visit Stavka whenever they can, and so do Sam's grandchildren. Everyone, including his grandchildren, calls him Sam. Like he used to do with his daughters, Sam tells droll stories and jokes to his grandchildren too, including some risque ones in Gujarati. Sam had never regretted not having a son, till very recently. 'I have so many rifles, pistols, fishing tackle and clothes—he could have them all,' he says.

In the twilight of his years, Sam Manekshaw remains a much loved and respected figure. A Field Marshal never retires and Sam is a living example. Though he has quit active service, he continues to take an active interest in the Army. His lectures on 'Leadership', at military as well as civilian institutions are very popular and draw large audiences. He remains a colourful personality, full of fun and good cheer, and it is difficult to believe that Sam is already 90 years old. He is a household name in India, where he will always be remembered as an outstanding military leader, who gave us our first decisive victory against a foreign power in 1971. A living legend, his place is assured in the hall of fame of the Indian Army.

7

Lieutenant General
R.N. Batra,
PVSM, OBE

7

Lieutenant General
R.N. Batra, PVSM, OBE
Communicator par Excellence

Rajinder Nath Batra was one among the pioneers who helped
lay the foundations of the present-day Indian Army. Unlike most
well-known military leaders who commanded armies, corps and
divisions, he was not a commander in the strict sense of the term.
He was, rather a team captain and an achiever. Though he had
all the qualities and qualifications for making it to the top in
the 'general cadre', he was destined to make his mark not as a
generalist, but as a technocrat. He is widely regarded as one of
the founding fathers of the Indian Signal Corps, and is credited
with having conceived and initiated the process of modernisation
of military communications in India. His contribution to the
Indian Army has been prodigious, and in terms of enhancing
operational capability, ranks on par with the achievements of
some of our best-known field commanders.

Rajinder (his family and a few close friends called him Inder)
was born on 27 December 1916 at Jhang Maghiana in the
Punjab province of undivided India, where his father, Ram Lal
Batra— an irrigation engineer in the Punjab Civil Service—was
then posted as the sub-divisional officer. His mother, Puran Devi
(Vidya), was an outstanding sportswoman who could outswim

and outride her husband. The couple had nine children, six boys and three girls. Raj was the fourth child, having been born after a brother and two sisters. After retirement, Ram Lal settled down in Montgomery, though he also had a house in Lahore.

Rajinder began his education in 1922 at Modern School in Delhi. The school had been established in Daryaganj in 1920, and his elder brother, Rajeshwar, was among the first batch of the school's 20 students. In 1923, Rajinder's younger brother Rabinder (Robin), who was then just 4 years old, also joined Modern School as a boarder, as their parents were going abroad. However, the brothers were not destined to study in Delhi for long. Since Ram Lal's service in the Irrigation Department entailed frequent transfers, often to small stations, it was decided to send the two younger boys to a boarding school. Bishop Cotton School in Simla was the most highly regarded school at that time, and since Ram Lal wanted his sons to have the best education, that is where he decided to send them. When the two brothers were admitted to Bishop Cotton School in March 1927, Rajinder was just 10 years old and Robin only seven. In the years to follow two of their cousins, Jagan and Mohinder, and Rameshwar, another one of Raj's younger brothers, also joined the same school. As it happened, four of the five Batras who were at Bishop Cotton eventually joined the defence services, with two going to the army and two to the navy. Of these four, three were to attain three-star rank. Rajinder and Mohinder became Lieutenant Generals, Robin rose to be Vice Admiral, while Rameshwar retired as a Commander. Raj's two youngest brothers, Gopal Krishen (Guppi) and Ram Krishen (Kaka), were educated at St Joseph's College, Nainital. They too, joined the services, with Gopal retiring as Major General, and Ram Krishen as Group Captain.

Rajinder's eldest brother, Rajeshwar, lovingly called Raj, had a short but eventful life. As a schoolboy, he had seen Sir Alam Cobham land his seaplane on the Yamuna during his historic flight from England to Australia, and had set his heart on becoming a pilot. After passing out from Modern School in 1928, he joined the Government College, Lyallpur. He also became a member of the flying club at Lahore, from where he got his 'A' licence. After graduating from college, he applied and was selected for a commission in the Royal Air Force. He was sent to Cranwell, but a row with one of his instructors led to his withdrawal. However, he stayed on in England to obtain a commercial pilot's licence and on returning to India in 1931, became the youngest pilot in the country. He joined a private airline, where his job was to ferry mail between Lahore and Karachi. During one of his sorties, his plane crashed near Jacobabad and he was killed in 1937 at the age of 25.

Soon after he had started flying, Rajeshwar had bought a life insurance policy from his maternal uncle, Vidhyadar Chawla, saying, half in jest, that it would provide for his mother after his death. He must have been prescient, for his parents built their home, named Raj Smriti in his memory, with the insurance money. Rajinder was at Dehradun when Rajeshwar died. When he reached home, he hugged his mother and promised her: 'I am no longer Inder. From today, I will be your Raj.' After that day, he began to be called Raj.

At Bishop Cotton School, Raj did well, both academically as well as in sports. Particularly good at mathematics and science, he always stood first in his class. He played all games, excelling at boxing, in which he represented the school for three years. He had a flair for languages, and began to learn Latin, French and Urdu. At that time, Bishop Cotton had almost 200 boys, of whom only around 30 were Indians. The Britishers tended to look down on Indians, whom they dismissed as lacking in physical and mental abilities. Raj Batra's performance put paid to this theory, and he became a shining example for the other Indian boys.

In 1932, Raj and his cousin Jagan passed the Senior Cambridge examination, with Raj getting a first and three distinctions. Back then, the school had a college wing attached to it, which he joined the next year. Summer classes were held in Simla and the winter ones at the Government College, Lahore. In May 1934, Raj took his Intermediate examination at Simla, and once again passed in the first division. He then joined Government College, Lahore, the premier college in Punjab.

Raj's father wanted him to join the ICS, which was then the most sought-after government service for Indians. Entry to Sandhurst had been stopped after the Indian Military Academy (IMA) was established at Dehradun in 1932. However, ICS trainees still had to go to England, which added to the glamour surrounding the service. The ICS was regarded as the 'steel frame' which held India together for the British Empire, and therefore enjoyed a lot of prestige and authority. Though his father had arranged for him to go to Cambridge, Raj had made up his mind to join the army. He took the Public Service Commission entrance examination for the IMA in 1935 without any preparation. He not only qualified, but stood first, and his father reluctantly agreed to his joining the IMA.

Raj Batra entered the IMA at Dehradun on 19 August 1935. At that time, there were three types of entries—Open, Army and State families. Each batch had 40 cadets, with 15 each from the 'O' and 'A' categories, and 10 from the 'S' category. Batra's batch was the seventh one to join the academy, and had 16 'O' cadets, 20 'A' cadets, and only two 'S' cadets, making a total of 38. Raj was allotted to A Company, where he met B.S. 'Tutu' Bhagat, who had joined six months earlier. Tutu soon became a role model for Raj, as well as his guide and mentor. He was responsible, in some measure, for Raj's brilliant performance at the Academy. Tutu Bhagat was an outstanding cadet, and both Raj and Tutu's younger brother, Prem Bhagat, who later won the VC, had to strive to emulate him. Raj tried to follow in his footsteps and made his mark in the first term itself, by getting a place in the Academy's football team. He continued to excel in the subsequent terms, and by the time he passed out his performance had surpassed Tutu's. He had represented the

Academy in almost every game, had won his spurs, as well as a prize in the fourth term camp for 'showing the most initiative and power of leadership'. A brief on the cadets who were passing out was prepared by the Indian Military Academy, and contains the following description of Raj: 'Batra is a fine combination of brain and brawn. He is equally at home in the ring or the examination hall. Undoubtedly one of the finest boxers the IMA has had.'

Raj's natural leadership qualities had become apparent at the Academy itself. His batch was one of the best to pass out from the IMA, and produced no less than nine generals (R.N. Batra, K.N. Dubey, D. Premchand, Virendra Singh, D.G.R. Rajwade, D.B. Chopra, Niranjan Prasad, Kamta Prasad and R.S. Shergill 'Sparrow') in India alone. All the cadets in the batch called themselves the 'Zunts', which was Punjabi slang for 'smart ones'. Raj emerged as the leader of the group and galvanised them into a team which developed a distinctive sense of esprit de corps and camaraderie. The nine or 10 who settled down in Delhi after retirement continued to meet regularly, and even their spouses, who called themselves the 'Zuntinas', as well as their children and grandchildren, who were called Zuntlings, became part of the unique fellowship. The Zunts held regular meetings in each other's homes, and whenever the Zuntlings got married, the Zunts would give them a collective present—a silver salver—a practice that they follow to this day. Raj, the unelected president of the Zunts, was the moving force behind the association, holding them together as their numbers dwindled. The surviving Zunts and Zuntinas bear testimony to his stellar role, and the moral and physical support that the group provides to each one of them, particularly in their twilight years.

The Punjabis are a robust and fun-loving people, and Raj was no exception. Major General Niranjan Prasad, one of his batchmates at the Academy, recalls that Raj's zest and exuberance often landed them in very difficult situations. But when in trouble, there was no better friend than Raj. Some of the cadets often spent their summer holidays with Prasad in Kashmir, and they have many anecdotes about their adventures there.

Once, Raj Batra, Masood Ali Baig, Kartar Dubey, Mark Ranganathan, Dewan Prem Chand and Manohar Lal were in Srinagar during their holidays. At that time, swimming boats on the Dal and Nagin lakes carried noticeboards with the warning: 'Indians Not Allowed', or 'Europeans Only'. One day, when the cadets attempted to go for a swim, they were shooed away by the boatmen. On the following day, they decided to forcibly board the boats. Led by Raj, the gang donned swimming trunks and got into shikaras (a shikara is a narrow boat, similar to the gondola, which seats two people and is manned by a boatman). Like in a military operation, they approached the swimming boat from both sides in order to distract the three boatmen. When the latter tried to push them away, the cadets dived into the lake and clambered aboard. As the boatmen tried to hit them with their oars, the cadets knocked them down and threw them into the lake. Within a few minutes, there was complete pandemonium. The boatmen shouted for help, and dozens of other boats converged on the scene. Hundreds of Hanjis surrounded them, and a free-for-all ensued, with the cadets giving as good as they got. Finally, an elderly gentleman intervened and brought the situation under control. The cadets left only after removing the offending notice-boards, and an undertaking that they would be allowed to swim.

Another interesting incident occurred in December 1936, when Raj was in Lahore during the winter vacation. His elder brother, Rajeshwar had just turned 25 and a tea dance was being held to celebrate the occasion. In those days, two attributes were prized by Indians, especially in the north—fluency in speaking the English language and skill in ballroom dancing. Having been to one of the best schools, Raj was quite proficient in both. The 18 months he had spent at Dehradun had added to his dexterity and boosted his confidence. So when he saw an attractive English lady at his brother's party, he went up to her and asked her for a dance.

The lady gave him a sweet smile, but instead of rising from her chair, said; 'I am sorry, I cannot dance with a child.' Raj was shattered. The thought that he could be considered a child had never entered his mind, and was a big blow to his vanity. He retreated like a defeated warrior. A few minutes later, when he related the incident to his elder brother, Rajeshwar burst out laughing. It was only after Rajeshwar explained that the lady was in an advanced stage of pregnancy and therefore in no condition to dance, that Raj was mollified and regained his composure and confidence.

The Commandant's Parade, during which the awards were announced, was held on 22 December 1937, with Raj as the Parade Commander. He made a clean sweep of the honours, and was awarded the Birdwood Sword of Honour for the best all-round performance. He was also given the Gold Medal for standing first in the overall order of merit, and the Baluch Regiment Prize for mountain warfare. His performance was truly awesome and has rarely been surpassed. Raj's company commander, Major Cadogan Rawlinson, wrote in his report:

> An outstanding cadet, who possesses both initiative and drive, and whose work in the company both on and off parade has been of a very high order. He is professionally and intellectually well above the average, is well read and has wide interests. He is the right type with the right ideas and is eminently suited to his profession.

Rawlinson went on to add that Batra possessed a strong character and a definite personality with an above-average power of command. The Commandant, Brigadier H.E.W.B. Kingsley, DSO, endorsed the remarks, and wrote:

> GC under officer Batra has entered whole-heartedly into all the activities of the Academy and has made himself the

outstanding figure of his term. He is obviously a leader and men will follow him. If he continues as he has begun he should become a first-rate officer. I hope he will do so. He will be welcome in any social circle.

As was then the practice, though the batch had actually passed out earlier, Raj and his batchmates were only granted commissions from 1 February 1938, in order to bring them on par with the batch commissioned from Sandhurst. Raj had topped his batch, and could have got the regiment of his choice. He chose Signals because it had for long been the exclusive preserve of British officers, and once Indians began to be taken, only the very best were selected. A desire to strike at this 'last bastion of the British', as Signals was regarded at that time, might also have influenced his choice. Raj left Dehradun on 15 January 1938, and after spending his leave in Lahore, reported to the Signal Training Centre at Jubbulpore (now called Jabalpur) on 10 February 1938. According to the procedure then in vogue, he had been formally posted to 3rd Cavalry, but sent on attachment to the Indian Signal Corps. While officers commissioned into Infantry and Cavalry had to do a year's attachment with a British battalion before joining their parent units, Artillery and Engineers officers went directly to their regimental centres. In the case of Signals, the procedure was slightly different. Because of the sensitive nature of its role, Indian officers were not taken into Signals directly, but were posted, on paper, to a Cavalry or Infantry unit. They were accepted into Signals only after completing an 18-month course at the Signal Training Centre, Jubbulpore, followed by a three-month course at the Army Signal School Poona, and a six-month attachment to a non-Indianised Signal unit (Waziristan District Signals). They were seconded for duty with the Signal Corps, and formally posted to an Indianised Signal unit (4 Indian Divisional Signals), only after they could meet the required standard. Those found unsuitable were reverted to the regiments to which they had been formally posted. Before Raj, only five Indians from Dehradun had been commissioned into Signals, starting with A.C. Iyappa in August 1935, and followed at six-monthly intervals by G.K. Mehta, Joe D'Souza, B.D. Kapur and B.S. Bhagat. Mehta did not make the grade, and was reverted to 19 Hyderabad Regiment. The only KCIO to have been sent to Signals, Sangram Keshav 'Sunshine' Ray, who had passed out from Woolwich in September 1932, had also been similarly reverted to the Cavalry.

Raj's first day at Jubbulpore was inauspicious. He was received at the railway station by B.D. Kapur, who took him to his quarters. The next morning, at breakfast, when he was telling Kapur about the achievements of his company—which had won the Commandant's Banner—as well as his own in winning the Sword of Honour and the Gold Medal, a senior British officer, Major 'Father' Williams, who was sitting across the table, suddenly shouted: 'Shut up, Batra. Breakfast is a quiet meal.' This put an end to the conversation, and Raj's exuberance subsided like a burst bubble under the cold stare of Charles Ommaney, the Senior Subaltern. Later in the day, Raj was taken to the Adjutant, Captain Donald Burridge, and then formally presented to the Commandant, Colonel George Pollard, who was also known as 'The Terror'. It was only several months later, when Raj let himself be beaten by the Commandant at squash, that Pollard began to approve of the young Indian. However, he still had to contend with Ommaney, who had not forgiven him for his behaviour at breakfast on his first day in the mess.

Raj's stay at Jubbulpore was eventful, and he always remembered it with nostalgia. One of his favourite stories relate to Ronald Frankau's famous poem: 'I am terribly British'. After the Signal Training Centre had beaten the Scottish battalion at squash, they were invited by the Scots to their mess. Supper was followed by cockfights and billiard fours, interspersed with jokes and skits. Finally, the Scots challenged them to a 'rugger scrum', which resulted in many torn dinner jackets. All this was forgiven but not Raj's misbehaviour in reciting 'I am terribly

British', much to the Scots' delight. In Ommaney's eyes, this was an unforgivable sin, and Raj got a severe tongue-lashing from the Senior Subaltern the next morning. At that time, neither of them knew that they would become close friends, and meet each other in England and in India, long after they both retired. And whenever they did, Raj would again recite his favourite poem, to the delight of everyone present.

In September 1938, Raj was sent to Poona to attend the three-month All Arms Signals Course at the Army Signals School. Poona was a large city, with many distractions for a young officer. There were horse races, late-night dances at the club, and weekend visits to Bombay. Raj did not miss out on any of them, and made the most of his stay at Poona. In December 1938 he returned to Jubbulpore after receiving a 'Distinguished Certificate' for the course. More than the certificate, what pleased Raj was the qualification pay of Rs 40, that he now started getting, in addition to his salary of Rs 300 a month. In April 1939, he was detailed to attend the four-month 'S' course for British Other Ranks for promotion to sergeant. His earlier training had been confined to technical aspects of signalling, such as Morse, flag wagging, heliograph and radio theory. In this course, he learnt brigade-level signal tactics, detachment drills, organisation of higher formation signal units and general administration.

In November 1939, after completing 18 months of training at Jubbulpore, Raj was posted to Waziristan District Signals at Dera Ismail Khan in the NWFP. Life on the frontier was tough, and Raj gained a lot of experience, especially during the Ahmedzai operations. He spent some time at Razmak and Wana, where he learned the finer points of signalling. After six months, he asked for three months' leave—which was permitted for service on the frontier—and went to Lahore. He also visited Mussoorie, a hill resort in northern India, which was especially popular with bachelors. However, his holiday had to be cut short when he received a telegram cancelling his leave and ordering him to join 10 Indian Infantry Brigade Signal Section, which was to proceed to the Middle East as part of 5 Indian Division. After this posting, he was struck off the strength of 3rd Cavalry and transferred to the Indian Signal Corps, which now became his parent arm.

Raj reached Jhansi, where 10 Infantry Brigade was located in early May 1940. He reported to the Commander, Brigadier (later Field Marshal and Chief of Imperial General Staff) 'Bill' Slim. Raj's first impression of the great soldier was of a man with a strong, determined jaw, but with kind eyes above a closely clipped moustache. Slim gave Raj the welcome news that Army HQ had approved his promotion to Captain, and he could take over the brigade signal section from the reservist British officer who was then in command. Slim also told him that they would be sailing for the Middle East in about two months. When Raj assumed command of the brigade signal section, it comprised one-third British and two-thirds Indian Other Ranks (IORs). He soon discovered that the section was to be Indianised, and only three British non-commissioned officers (NCOs)—one sergeant, one lance sergeant and one corporal—were to remain. In addition, their equipment was to be 'modernised'. The No. 1 wireless sets were to be replaced with No. 5 sets, the D-3 telephones with D-5, and the old magneto exchange with one with lights. Raj had to train his men, now almost all Indians, on the new equipment, in just 60 days. It was a daunting task, but Raj was young and brimming with confidence. He had a good second-in-command, and with the help of the British NCOs, they were able to finish up in good shape, after working day and night for two months.

When the brigade entrained for Bombay, Raj's parents were there to see him off. Having lost four children, his mother was inconsolable at the thought of her now eldest son going to war. Bill Slim spoke to his parents and reassured them that Raj would be safe. (After his father's death, when Raj was sorting out his papers, he found that Slim had written to his parents regularly, informing them of his progress and well-being.) In early July 1940, they embarked at Bombay and set sail for the Middle East. They disembarked at Port Sudan, having suffered a few air raids by enemy aircraft during the voyage. From Port Sudan, the brigade went by train to Gedaref, where HQ 5 Indian Division had already arrived. Raj met the CO of the divisional signal regiment, Lieutenant Colonel Leslie Morgan, and then proceeded with his brigade to a place about 11 miles away, just short of Gallabat which was held by the Italians. Shortly afterwards, the brigade launched an attack on Gallabat. Preceded by a heavy bombardment, the attack took place in the early hours of the morning, and the Italians were driven out of Gallabat after an operation lasting about 72 hours. This was the first time Raj had been in actual combat, and he had his hands full, maintaining communications with the forward troops and the Divisional HQ, which had moved up. Fortunately, the wireless and lines functioned without a break, but Raj did not get any sleep for almost 72 hours. He was able to get some rest only after Slim sent for him and ordered him to bed, saying: 'I would rather have my communications fail, than my signal officer collapse.'

After the capture of Gallabat, 5 Indian Division was ordered to assist 4 Indian Division, which was then engaged in pushing the Italians back into Eritrea, but was held up at the Keren Pass. By this time, Raj had been promoted acting Major and given command of No. 3 Company of the divisional signal regiment. A coordinated attack by the two divisions succeeded in driving back the Italians, and 5 Indian Division entered Asmara, the capital of Eritrea. The division continued to follow the retreating Italians towards Abyssinia, till they made a stand at Amba Alagi with the help of the Duke of Aosta. The Italians were again beaten and forced to surrender. The division then turned towards the port city of Massawa, which also was held by the Italians. The city was captured with help from the Navy, which foiled an attempt by the Italians to scuttle their ships in the harbour. The Eritrean campaign being over, the division was moved to Mena Camp near Cairo for rest and refit.

Raj and his section had been in Mena Camp for about three weeks when the division was ordered to move to Kirkuk in Iraq, to suppress a revolt fomented by a German agent. It took them five days to reach Kirkuk via Baghdad. The situation soon stabilised, and after a month in Iraq the division returned to Cairo. Meanwhile, Crete had fallen, and it was expected that the Germans would now turn their attention to the island of Cyprus. 5 Indian Division was ordered to replace the British Territorial Division in Cyprus, and prepare for an airborne attack by the Germans. The Divisional HQ was established at Famagusta, while the brigades were located at Kyrenea, Limassol and Morphu. After establishing communication on line, wireless and helio, Raj found ample time to do some sight-seeing. Cyprus was full of vineyards but, due to the war, none of the wine could be exported. As a result, excellent wine was available for almost nothing, and Raj probably drank more of it than was good for him. In April 1942, Raj received a cable, sent about two months earlier, informing him of his father's death in Lahore and asking him to return home. He applied for leave, but it was refused. Instead, he was posted to the Signal Training Centre. It was felt that his war experience would be useful in improving the training of recruits and preparing them for the war theatres. Raj returned to Cairo, and after picking up his heavy baggage, left by train for Damascus, en route to Baghdad. From Basra, he went by sea to Bombay, and then by train to Jubbulpore. After reporting for duty, he proceeded on two-months' leave, leaving his baggage at Jubbulpore. Shortly afterwards, 5 Indian Division also returned to India, from where it proceeded to Burma to fight the Japanese.

Raj did not stay at Jubbulpore for long. He was posted to Army HQ as a GSO 3 in the Signals Directorate. Raj's posting surprised everyone, since appointments in Signals Directorate were the exclusive preserve of British officers and Raj was the

first Indian to break this monopoly. His service in the Signals
Directorate proved to be extremely useful to Raj, as it broadened
his horizons and acquainted him with the functioning of the
higher echelons of the military and the government. After a
short spell in Delhi, Raj was posted as second-in-command of
Landikotal District Signals at Peshawar. Again, his stay here was
very short, since he was nominated to attend the Staff College at
Quetta in February, 1943.

Before he left for Quetta, a confidential report was initiated
by his CO, Lieutenant Colonel I.St.Q. Severin, who wrote:

> This officer has a quick brain, plenty of drive and initiative
> and plenty of self-confidence. He is smart and soldier-like in
> his appearance and has good power of command. At present
> he is too interested in his own welfare and inclined to be self-
> assertive. His keenness also tends to make him too impulsive,
> otherwise he has a pleasant personality and gets on well with
> officers and men. Very good at games.

During those days, career advancement was frowned upon, and
many senior officers of the old school did not take kindly to
young officers who wanted to go to Staff College. Staff officers
were derided as 'pen-pushers', and regimental service was held
in higher esteem than a staff job.

When he completed the staff course in October 1943, Raj
was again posted to the Signals Directorate as GSO 2. World
War II had been going on for four years, and focus had shifted
from the European and North African theatre to the East, where
Indian troops were now facing a different enemy. The Japanese
onslaught had been stopped just on the borders of India, and the
Allied troops had started pushing them back into Burma. Raj
had a hectic schedule in Delhi, and could spare little time for his
young wife, whom he had married during this period. This was
to have unfortunate consequences in the years to come. In March

1945, he was promoted Lieutenant Colonel, but remained in Signals Directorate as GSO 1.

In January 1946, Raj took over command of 15 Indian Corps Signal Regiment in Jakarta from Lieutenant Colonel George Dutton. The Corps was occupying Java, Sumatra, Borneo and Bali, and its main task was to look after the Japanese prisoners of war. It also had to protect the thousands of Dutch—who had been under Japanese custody and were awaiting repatriation to Holland—from being butchered by the Indonesians. After finishing the task of providing communications to the subordinate formations and headquarters of the South East Asia Command, Raj and his officers had little to do. He now had a new problem on his hands—how to keep his officers occupied. Raj discussed the problem with his Adjutant, Captain Gordon Nation, a very smart and handsome British officer. They soon came up with a solution. With his good looks and skill at ballroom dancing, Gordon had little difficulty in persuading young women working with the Red Cross, nurses from the military hospital, and a few eligible Dutch ladies, to join them for parties and dances in the officers mess. Of course, the officers had to collect the ladies from their homes and drop them back under armed escort.

Raj had been in command of 15 Indian Corps Signal Regiment for barely three months when he was recalled to India towards the end of April 1946. He had been selected to lead the Signals contingent for the Victory Parade, which was to be held in London. After several enforced halts due to engine trouble and bad weather, he landed in Rangoon, from where he hitched a ride on Mountbatten's plane to reach Calcutta. He took another plane to Delhi and then went on to Bareilly, where Brigadier (later General) J.N. Choudhury was getting together the Indian contingent. He took charge of the Signals contingent, which comprised 12 IORs. They sailed from Bombay to England, where they were put up in a tented camp in Southampton.

Raj marched in the Victory Parades in London, Manchester, Edinburgh and Glasgow. After the parade in London on 8 June

1946, he read in the newspapers that he and eight others had been awarded the Order of the British Empire (OBE). He was surprised and naturally very pleased, since the OBE was quite a rare and prestigious award. The awards were to be presented by the King, at a formal ceremony to be held in Buckingham Palace a few days later, but Raj was in a hurry to join his unit, and decided to fly back to India. As it happened, he had to wait for several years to receive the award, which was presented to him after Independence by General K.M. Cariappa, the C-in-C of the Indian Army.

After returning to India in early July and making his report to Major General R.F.H. Nalder, the Signals Officer-in-Chief (SO-in-C) in Delhi, Raj requested that he be sent back to command his unit in Java. He was told that 15 Corps Signal Regiment was on the high seas, on its way to India, and that he could have a month's leave before joining the unit in Quetta. Raj was recalled from leave and ordered to proceed to Poona to raise Force 401 Signal Regiment. Force 401 had three infantry brigades, two Indian and one British, and was to proceed to Basra to protect the British oil interests in Iran.

Once again, Raj had to prepare his unit for overseas duty in a matter of two months. This time, his task was even more difficult, since the unit was a new raising and included a number of 'bad hats', who had been sent to Force 401 by other units wanting to be rid of them. Raj needed some good officers in his team, and he specifically requested for Captain Gordon Nation who, apart from being socially accomplished, was also an outstanding officer. Gordon had just returned from overseas service and was entitled to a period of rest, but he immediately agreed. He left his unit even before reaching Quetta and joined Raj in Poona. Raj was also lucky to have a good second-in-command in Major (later Brigadier) Apar Singh MBE, who had passed out from the IMA exactly a year after him. Apar Singh still recalls the hard work they had to put in to get the unit ready in time. Raj was thorough and meticulous, and no details, however small, escaped his attention. By mid-September, they were ready to sail from Bombay.

They disembarked at Basra, where they put up in a tented camp. It was bitterly cold, and the frequent rains had drowned the entire area knee-deep in slush. It was worse in summer, when flies and mosquitoes added to their woes, and the men started to grumble. The British troops had been away from their homes for far too long, and since the war was over, wanted to return to 'Blighty' as soon as possible. Some of them wrote to their Members of Parliament, complaining about the terrible living conditions. Raj had a difficult time keeping things under control, but he managed with the help of his team of officers, especially Major F.P. Stewart, who had replaced Apar Singh as his second-in-command, and his Adjutant, Gordon Nation. Force 401 was entrusted with the task of protecting the British oil fields in Iran from a communist take-over. Fighting an imaginary enemy did not appeal to the battle-hardened troops and their resentment was understandable.

The Force Commander, Major General F.J. Loftus Tottenham, was impressed by Raj. After only three months of observation, he wrote in his confidential report, on 3 January 1947:

> Exceptionally strong character. Knows his job inside out and has plenty of energy, determination and resourcefulness. A bit impulsive, but thinks things out and certainly knows what he wants. Leadership and drive to a marked degree. He inspires confidence and would carry heavy responsibility well. Among Indian officers I know I consider him outstanding and he should be marked for further advancement.

General Tottenham's belief was not misplaced. Raj did rise to high ranks and more than justified his commander's assessment. The remarks about his strength of character and impulsive nature echoed earlier assessments of him, and continued to appear in future reports throughout his service.

In May 1947, Raj returned to India on a month's leave. But before he could return to Basra, he was informed that Force 401 was on its way to India for demobilisation, and that he had been posted to take over command of 7 Infantry Divisional Signal Regiment at Rawalpindi. In July 1947, he relieved Lieutenant Colonel Crichton, who was going back to England. By now, the exodus of British officers and men—barring a few who had volunteered to stay on after Partition—had begun. Up until then, very few Indians had been taken into Signals owing to the sensitive nature of the job and the sudden departure of the British created a vacuum that was difficult to fill. The task before the few Indian officers in Signals was thus a very difficult one, and it is to their credit that they performed magnificently.

Shortly after he took over, Raj's cousin Mohinder, or Major (later Lieutenant General) M.N. Batra, joined him as his second-in-command. The day he joined, Raj told him:

> Mini, you have come as my 2ic, but I am not going to show you any favours just because you happen to be a close relation of mine. In my office we will have a very professional relationship. After office hours it is a different matter.

There were several British Other Ranks in the regiment at that time, and Raj always referred to them as 'my BORs'. Some of them still recall the affection with which he treated them, and the respect and regard they all had for their first Indian CO.

On 15 August 1947, the day India became independent, a function was held to enable officers who were going to India or Pakistan to bid farewell to each other. As one of the senior-most officers in Rawalpindi, Raj organised the show, which was a grand success. There were several emotional scenes as officers who had served and fought together said goodbye to one another. As a result of Partition, several units had to move across the newly created border between the two nations. 7 Infantry Divisional Signal Regiment in Rawalpindi and 4

Infantry Divisional Signal Regiment in Jullunder had to change places. The killings had already begun, and it was quite a job to get everyone across, especially the families. Raj moved his mother and the rest of his family to Lucknow. He had given them strict instructions that they, like any other refugee family, should carry only the minimum essential baggage. As a result, they had to leave a large part of their valuables and jewellery behind. Such was his authority that even his mother did not dare ask if she could carry an extra trunk.

By October 1947, the Kashmir operations had begun. Raj had been ordered to send all BORs to Delhi immediately after Partition, but he was very reluctant to part with them. He kept making excuses, saying that he needed them for the erection of an aerial park which was required for the Kashmir operation, to delay their departure. Finally, when he realised that he could not hold on to them any longer, he agreed to let them go. The day before they left, he came to their mess and told them that he had a surplus of Rs 500 in the regimental funds. He had decided to spend the money on a farewell dinner for the BORs, and he would be happy to preside if that was what they wanted. The BORs were overjoyed, and it turned out to be an emotional evening, with old comrades sitting down together for the last time. When RQMS Booth, the seniormost BOR present, proposed a toast to 'Lieutenant Colonel Batra and his BORs' there were many moist eyes.

In November 1947, Raj was promoted Colonel and posted to Army HQ as Deputy Director, Signals (DD Sigs). He handed over his unit to M.N. Batra, who was promoted Lieutenant Colonel, and left for Delhi. The Director of Signals and SO-in-C at that time was Brigadier C.H.I. Akehurst, OBE. This was the third time Raj was being posted to Signals Directorate, having served there earlier in 1941–42 and 1943–45. In fact, Raj had the unique record of serving in the Signals Directorate in every rank, from Captain to Colonel, and later as Major General. He also had the distinction of commanding three types of major signal units as a Lieutenant Colonel. It must be remembered that though Indians were being commissioned in the army since 1920, they always served in units which had Indian troops, and very few Indian officers got the chance to command British troops. Raj was one of the lucky few who got this opportunity, and he came out with flying colours.

Raj remained in Delhi until July 1949, when he was promoted Brigadier and posted as Chief Signal Officer, HQ Eastern Command, replacing Brigadier A.C. Iyappa, MBE. Eastern Command was then located at Ranchi with Lieutenant General Thakur Nathu Singh as the Army Commander. Ranchi was a small station, known only for a mental asylum and for serving as the summer capital of the Government of Bihar State. Soon after his father's death in 1942, Raj had married a Christian lady from Allahabad. His commitment to his work, and the long periods of absence due to overseas assignments, did not allow Raj to devote enough time to his young wife, and they had begun to drift apart. When he went to Ranchi, Raj's wife did not accompany him and he went through a difficult period of separation, which finally ended in divorce by mutual consent in November 1952.

One of his close friends from college days, Brigadier (later Major General) M.G. Dewan was also posted at Ranchi. Raj found solace in the company of Madan, his wife Guddo, and their young son, and their house became a second home for him. Guddo recalls that Raj did a lot to enliven the social life of Ranchi, organising regular parties and dances in the club, as well as other forms of entertainment, like plays and skits. A very good dancer himself Raj was also a fantastic organiser, and word about the exciting parties of Ranchi soon spread to as far away as Calcutta, from where people began to come over during weekends. Invariably, Raj took the lead in all such gatherings, readily joining in the singing and dancing. His recitation of Ronald Frankau's poem, 'I am terribly British, you see', and the joke about 'Andre, the flea', were perennial favourites. At a party hosted by Brigadier Umrao Singh, the Brigadier General Staff, Raj, played the 'tabla' with such vigour that the drumskin broke. He was promptly christened 'Tees Mar Khan' (a Hindustani term, literally meaning one who had killed 30 birds; used to refer to anyone who does something extraordinary).

In December 1953, Raj was on leave in Delhi, visiting his cousin Pran Nath Luthra. Pran had just got engaged to Indira Seth, who invited her friends to meet her fiance. Among them was Priyo Singh, her classmate from Kinnaird College, Lahore. She was from a deeply patriotic and socially active Sikh family of Abbottabad, where they owned a hotel. The family also owned extensive property in the Chitral Valley. Her father had been a follower of Mahatma Gandhi and Khan Abdul Gaffar Khan, and she had been trained as a teacher by Madam Montessori herself. Priyo was taking part in one of Sheila Bhatia's Punjabi plays, and Raj would wait patiently to take her home after rehearsals. After a few months of courtship, they decided to tie the knot. They were engaged in a simple ceremony held at Priyo's home where her mother read some verses from the Granth Sahib (the holy book of the Sikhs) and blessed them both. They were married on 14 March 1954 in Delhi, just after Raj was posted to Simla as Chief Signal Officer, Western Command.

Raj and Priyo enjoyed their stay at Simla. In January 1955, Priyo gave birth to their daughter Preminda and later, in November 1956, to a son, Ranjit. Raj became a frequent visitor to his old school Bishop Cotton, and attended all the functions and meetings of the Old Cottonians Association while he was in Simla. In mid-1956, Raj was informed that he had been selected for the appointment of Military Attaché at the Indian Embassy in Washington. Raj and Priyo were thrilled with the news and began to prepare for their departure. Once again, Raj handed over to his cousin, Brigadier M.N. Batra. After a few months' attachment in Delhi, he left for Washington in December 1956 with Priyo and the children. En route, they spent some time with the Dewans in London, where Madan was posted as the Military Attaché.

Raj and Priyo were a gregarious couple and soon became popular members of the Corps of Attachés in Washington. Captain (later Major General) Bir Paintal, an Indian signal officer, was doing a course at Fort Monmouth, New Jersey, in 1959. He and his wife Mira still recall their first meeting with the Batras, when they went to call on them at their gracious home in Maryland. Mira was a very nervous bride, and even now remembers how quickly Raj and Priyo had disarmed her, so that in just a few minutes she had begun to feel as if she had known them all her life. Both Bir and Mira were literally bowled over by the famous Batra charm, and became their ardent admirers. Little did they realise that they were destined to become close relatives—25 years later, Ranjit Batra was to marry their daughter Lalita, who was yet to be born.

Raj was affable and hospitable by nature, and soon his neighbours were walking in and out of his house. He was sandwiched between two blue-blooded American families. After he moved in, he invited them over for dinner, only to discover that this was the first time the two families were sitting down together! The Paintals often met visiting American generals from Washington in Fort Monmouth. All of them had the highest regard for 'that fantastic Indian General from Signals in Washington'. (In most armies, brigadiers are called 'Brigadier Generals'.) As for the ladies, most of them cooed: 'Oh, that darling General of yours.' Given his charm and excellent dancing skills, it is not surprising that he got more than his share of 'passes' from many of them, all of which he adroitly parried.

The four years that Raj spent in Washington provided him with an extremely privileged world-view and enriched his personality. He had been brought up and educated in a British colonial setting, and the environment in America made for a refreshing change. He took his job seriously, closely studying the organisation, functioning and latest developments in the US Army and Navy, as well as those in other developed countries. Because of his signals background, he paid special attention to developments in the communications field. He did a two-week course at the US Army Signal Corps School at Fort Monmouth. The excellent personal relationship he shared with Major General Nelson, the American Chief of Signals, also made it possible for him to visit several signal units and establishments. This was to prove fortuitous when Raj returned to India, and took over the reins of the Corps of Signals. There is little doubt that without the advantage of this exposure in Washington for over four years, Plan AREN would not have materalised when it did.

After four years and three months in Washington, Raj returned to India in May 1961. At about the same time, Thimayya retired and Thapar took over as COAS. While he was in Washington, Thimayya had indicated that Raj would be given command of a brigade when he returned. At that time, there were no separate promotion boards for induction into the 'general cadre', and officers of Artillery, Engineers and Signals were given command of infantry brigades based on their reports. Raj had been recommended for command of a brigade by Lieutenant General Kalwant Singh, GOC-in-C Western Command, in his confidential report initiated on 7 July 1956. However, fate willed otherwise. Major General A.C. Iyappa, SO-in-C, had completed his term, and there was no one to replace him. Starting with Iyappa, who was from the second batch, one officer had been commissioned into Signals every six months. However, none of them was available. Mehta from the third batch had been reverted to the 19th Hyderabad Regiment; D'Souza from the fourth batch had been boarded out on medical grounds; B.D. Kapur from the fifth batch had gone to Bharat Electronics; and 'Tutu' Bhagat from the sixth batch had quit the army and joined Rallis (India), a private sector company. That left Raj, who was from the seventh batch and next in line after Iyappa.

In May 1961, Raj was promoted Major General and appointed Director Signals and SO-in-C. The suffix 'in-Chief' is used by the heads of Engineers and Signals, since they also have certain responsibilities towards the air force and navy, in addition to their own service. Raj was pleased at his promotion, but also a little disappointed at being denied command of a brigade. 'Tutu' Bhagat had been given command of an infantry brigade in March 1956, about nine months before Raj proceeded to Washington. Even Prem Bhagat from Engineers, who was junior to him, had commanded a brigade from March 1957 to August 1959, and there was little doubt that he would soon get command of a division. If Raj had not been sent to Washington, it is quite likely that he too would have been given command of a brigade. Who knows, he might have become an army commander or even the Chief, as Prem almost did. On 4 August 1961, General Thimayya, who had just retired, wrote to him from Bangalore to congratulate him on his promotion and appointment. He went on to add: '. . . I am, however, sorry that I could not get you through a Brigade first. I have no doubt you would have shone, but there were too many difficulties in my way.' As is well known, Thimayya's authority had been severely eroded after the episode of his resignation. In the event, his inability to give Raj the command of a brigade was propitious. The Indian Army probably derived much greater benefit with Raj heading the Signal Corps, than it would have if he had joined the general cadre.

When Raj took over as the Director Signals, Krishna Menon was the Defence Minister, P.N. Thapar the Army Chief, and B.M. Kaul the CGS. As is well known, the army was ill-equipped in every department, as was amply proved in the conflict with China in 1962. Although his predecessors, Brigadier C.H.I. Akehurst and Major General A.C. Iyappa, had set in motion plans for the modernisation of signals equipment, Raj found that except for the C-42 VHF wireless sets newly installed in tanks, and a small start in the production of radio relay sets, all other equipment was still of World War II vintage. In peacetime, the army had to depend entirely on the Posts and Telegraphs (P&T) Department for its communications, backed by its own high-frequency radio. Field formations did have wireless and line facilities for their internal communications, but still had to rely on the P&T Department for long-distance speech and teleprinter circuits.

Soon after Raj took over as SO-in-C, the Goa operations took place. A few days before the operations began, Raj went to visit HQ 17 Infantry Division at Belgaum. He then visited 50 Para Brigade in its concentration area at Savantvadi. Brigadier (later Lieutenant General) Sagat Singh, who was commanding the Para Brigade, was a good friend of Raj. He had learned that 17 Division had been given some radio relay sets for their rearward communications to Belgaum. He asked Raj to also give a radio relay detachment to his brigade, as the existing arrangements were unreliable. Raj told Sagat that the C41/R222 radio relay sets had been introduced in the army very recently, and had still to be blooded. Only one section had been raised, which was directly under the control of Army HQ. Four sets had been supplied to 17 Infantry Division for trials while four were kept for training purpose at the Signal Training Centre at Jabalpur. These also comprised the GS reserve, and he could not give them to Sagat.

Sagat was not to be shaken off so easily. He asked Raj what sort of a friend he was, if he could not do this small favour. Raj thought for a moment, and then agreed to give the sets. But he told Sagat that he would have to arrange to pick them up from Jabalpur, and return them after the operation in one piece. Within minutes of assuring Raj that this would be done, Sagat got through to the Parachute Training Centre at Agra and got them to send an aircraft to Jabalpur the same day to pick up the sets. They reached Sagat just a day before he moved to the assembly area at Dodamarg. By a stroke of good luck, his signal officer, Major (later Colonel) R.R. Chatterjee, found that there was a permanent line route of the P&T Department running past Dodamarg. This was patched to the rear terminal of the radio relay link, and enabled the brigade exchange to get through to Belgaum. Thanks to the new sets, Sagat was never out of touch with Command HQ. The orders for his brigade to capture Panjim were conveyed to him on the radio relay link, because 17 Infantry Division's communications had broken down. According to Sagat, Raj would do anything for a friend, as this incident amply proves.

The Indian Army faced its greatest challenge in October 1962, when the Chinese attacked India. Though the number of troops involved was very small, we suffered a humiliating defeat, which many consider to be a blessing in disguise. The situation is best described in Raj Batra's own words:

But then, and if I can say fortunately, came the Chinese intrusion in the month of October 1962, and like the rest of the army, our Corps too was caught completely off balance. At that time, I was already a member of the P&T Board, and to supplement our single and totally unreliable speech and teleprinter circuits rented from the P&T Department to our newly formed Corps Headquarters at Tezpur, the P&T Department kindly gave me a full-time liaison officer based in Guwahati, and under his supervision our line construction sections built an open 4-wire copper carrier route from Guwahati to Tezpur in record time. In addition, P&T Department put up a carrier centre for the exclusive use of our Corps Headquarters at Tezpur in army accommodation.

They also strengthened their existing carrier centre at Guwahati and with these we were then able to obtain reliable speech and teleprinter circuits from Army HQ and Command HQ to the Corps HQ. Forward of Corps HQ, of course, all Signal communications were provided and maintained by our Corps.

However, when the withdrawal (shall I say the disorganised retreat) started, my CSO Corps (Brigadier P.S.

Gill) telephoned me to say that he had orders to blow up this specially installed carrier centre at Tezpur. I had to use all my powers to persuade the Chief, General P.N. Thapar, to prevent this from happening. He very kindly issued direct orders to both Army Commander and Corps Commander regarding this. This non-destruction of the carrier centre paid off really well in later days after the Chinese withdrawal.

Because of the Chinese intrusion, not only we did get considerable American help in terms of equipment, but also our Government realised the necessity of modernising Signal equipment and considerably loosened their purse-strings. Therefore, after years of stagnation, we were able to get considerable types and quantities of new Signal equipments. It also gave tremendous incentive to LRDE, BEL and ITI to develop a new generation of the much needed new signal equipments for our army. If I may, in all humility, say that I was lucky to get this circumstantial golden opportunity, and I grabbed it to the maximum advantage of the army.

Raj Batra's major achievement during his tenure as the SO-in-C was the formulation of the new communication philosophy for the Indian Army, which also earned him the sobriquet 'Father of Plan AREN'. His stint in the USA had already exposed him to the new concepts being propagated in the advanced countries. In 1962 and 1964, he attended the Commonwealth SOs-in-C conferences in UK. On both these occasions the British SOs-in-C were his old friends from pre-World War II days in India. When attending one of these conferences, he spent a few days at the British Corps HQ in the British Army on the Rhine (BAOR) to study signal communications within their Corps. A briefing from the Commandant of the British Army's Signals School at Catterick Camp on their future thinking with regard to signal communications in the field made it apparent that, both in the USA and UK, they were not only depending on secure radio relay, but also going in for digital techniques. He made a detailed study of the HOBART and BRUIN systems, that were being planned in the UK, as well as the area grid system being followed by the USA.

In the event of a war, Raj realised that our armed forces would either remain within our own territory, or at best exploit success to about 100 miles or so in enemy territory. He concluded that future signal communications within each corps should use secure radio relay systems on an interconnected grid of communication nodes, covering an area of 100 × 100 miles. Divisional and brigade HQ could then hook on to the nearest such node, based on a computer-controlled digital automatic electronic switch. During mobile operations, the grid would roll forwards or backwards, with nodes leap-frogging ahead or behind, without any disruption in communications. The system would provide each crucial appointment with a fixed number, and no matter where he moved within the corps area, he would be able to receive speech, teleprinter, fax and data communication automatically.

The new communication system conceived by Raj was named AREN, an acronym for Army Radio Engineered Network. It sounded like 'RN', which were the two initials of his name. Major General J. Mayadas, who was then a major, vividly recalls that in 1964, when Raj returned from the UK after the SOs-in-C conference, his enthusiasm was boundless. He quickly assembled a team of officers to give concrete shape to his ideas. Apart from Brigadier I.D. Verma, who was his deputy, the team included Colonel K.S. Garewal; Lieutenant Colonels M.S. Sodhi, J. Mayadas, M.B. Hart and S.L. Juneja; and Majors R.K. Gupte, B.S. Paintal, M.K. Ghosh, M.C. Rawat and Sushil Nath. (Four of them—Verma, Garewal, Sodhi and Ghosh— rose to the rank of Lieutenant General and became SOs-in-C, while the others— except for Dick Hart who retired prematurely—became Major Generals.) There were long sessions running late into the night, but everyone was so enthused by Raj's passion that there were no complaints, except from the wives.

The process was frenzied, and was interrupted only by the Indo–Pak War of 1965. After the dust had settled, they began where they had left off. There were monthly presentations, and Raj's ardour and conviction began to rub off on everyone, including General J.N. Chaudhury, the Army Chief. In late 1965, Raj made the first formal presentation of Plan AREN to General Choudhary, the Army Commanders and the Principal Staff Officers. Their response was heartening, and Raj knew that he had won the first round. His grasp of the fundamentals and their application in the field of combat communications, coupled with his forceful personality, convinced those who mattered in the South and North Blocks of the desirability of Plan AREN, provided the cost was not unreasonable. Once this was achieved, it was easy to justify the associated raisings and funding for the project.

Though Plan AREN was his best-known achievement—his magnum opus in a sense—Raj was responsible for scores of other changes and developments during his tenure as Director Signals and SO-in-C. These cover a wide canvas and encompass every field and facet of signals, including organisation, training, equipment, policy, procedures, security, ciphers, personnel and administration. He was a visionary, who could look 10 or 20 years into the future and visualise requirements, which at the time, appeared to be in the realm of science fiction. Plan AREN is a classic example of a revolutionary concept in military communications, which was conceived 20 years ahead of its time, even before the general staff felt a need for it.

Shortly after the Chinese invasion in October 1962, the government decided to raise 10 mountain divisions for the defence of the northern borders. With his wide experience, Raj immediately realised that forward deployment of these formations would require setting up communication zones behind them, comprising road, rail, air and telecommunication networks, in addition to numerous administrative installations. Higher formations and the forward divisions would also need reliable communications *between* them. Raj and his team immediately set to work, planning the deployment of these communication zones and spelling out the scale and extent of the forecast signals requirements. A clear need for 12 communication zone signal regiments was established, cases prepared, presented to the government, and sanctioned in record time. This was an extraordinary achievement, and a direct result of Raj's foresight, intuition and enthusiasm.

It was at his behest that the Tactical Communications Committee was formed in 1964, with Raj as Chairman, to examine all requirements of military communications for field formations. During his tenure, the communication requirements of mountain divisions were finalised and the signal units reorganised accordingly. In 1965, the committee studied the special communications requirements for armoured and infantry divisions, air defence, offensive air support and counter bombardment. As a result, two important decisions were taken: switching from HF (high frequency) to VHF (very high frequency), and introducing radio relay in divisions.

In addition, there were a large number of organisational changes that Raj pushed through. When he took over as SO-in-C, his cousin, Brigadier M.N. Batra had assumed the office of Director of Military Intelligence after attending the first course at the National Defence College. The appointment was later upgraded to Major General, and M.N. Batra continued to hold it after promotion. As signal officers, both were convinced of the immense potential of signals intelligence and the need to upgrade Indian capability in this field. As a result of their deliberations, in 1963 Raj put forward a case for the establishment of a Directorate of Signals Intelligence (DSI) to function under the Director of Military Intelligence (DMI), which was accepted. The new set-up was an interservices organisation which covered intercept units of the army, navy and the air force. Its establishment paid handsome dividends, as was amply demonstrated during the 1965 and 1971 wars with Pakistan, the operations in Sri

Lanka, as well as the counter-insurgency operations in Jammu and Kashmir and the north-east.

Raj was also responsible for the raising of several new units, such as the Special Signal Regiment which carries out trials of new equipment, air support signal regiments, radio monitoring companies, and air defence brigade signal companies. He also reorganised the Army HQ Signal Regiment into two regiments, one in Delhi to man communications, and the other in Meerut to look after the transmitters and receivers. The conversion of command and area signal regiments from brick to tailor-made establishments, and of corps signal regiment into brick-type establishments, was also Raj's brainchild.

It would be incorrect to assume that Raj always met with success in his ventures. A number of his proposals did not materialise, mainly because of opposition from other arms and services, or bureaucratic resistance to change. One of the changes he proposed was for Signals to take over from the Corps of Electrical and Mechanical Engineers the responsibility for field repairs of signal equipment in field formations, in addition to static establishments. Another proposal that he mooted was that field signal units be rotated between formations, as was being done for the Armoured Corps and Artillery. This would not only facilitate continuity of service of the individuals in these units, but also the implementation of the 'parent unit' system that was being followed in several other arms. Unfortunately, neither proposal was accepted.

One of the most important areas on which Raj concentrated was electronic data processing systems. His tenure in the USA had convinced him of the tremendous power of computers, and he decided that the Indian Army must begin using them as soon as possible. A steering committee, with Raj as Chairman, was appointed to go into the question of its feasibility. Captain (later Major General) Bir Paintal, who had joined the team when he returned from his course in the US, remembers that none of them ever walked—they ran. There were frequent brainstorming sessions, and everyone was encouraged to come up with new ideas, however bizarre or absurd. The committee's first report was approved by the Army Chief and submitted to the government, which constituted another high-powered committee to review it. Meanwhile, Raj convinced the Chief that they should go ahead with the mechanisation of procedures in order to save time, beginning with the Central Ordnance Depot in Delhi and the Signals Records in Jabalpur.

As a result of the expansion of the army after the 1962 operations, there was a spurt in the intake of officers as well as other ranks. To cater to the increased training load, two additional centres for training of recruits were established at Jabalpur and Goa. Raj realised that it would be impossible to open another school for training officers or increase the size of the School of Signals in the immediate future. He decided to run a number of short courses to train officers on specific systems or equipment till the situation stabilised. These courses, of four to six weeks duration, were run at the School of Signals and focused on wireless equipment, line equipment, line construction and radio relay. In addition, vacancies were obtained in the USA and the UK to train officers in techniques and equipment that was being imported in large quantities. Graduate engineers began to be inducted, and a three-year engineering degree course was put in place for the others, to ensure that every signal officer would be capable of handling the sophisticated communication systems that were to be introduced in the near future.

At that time, satellites had been launched only by the USA and the USSR, and their relevance in the sphere of military communications was yet to be understood. Raj was one of the few who could appreciate the tremendous potential of satellites, and though he could not achieve much in the field, his concepts proved to be of great help to his successors. Similarly, except for the rudimentary aspects of jamming, electronic warfare was relatively unknown. Raj constituted a sub-committee of the

Joint Communication Electronics Committee, of which he was Chairman, to study the subject. He submitted a report to the Chiefs of Staff Committee. After it was approved, he initiated the process of acquiring capability in this field. Another area in which he made a significant contribution was in the automation of handling of messages in the army's signal centres, a task that was hitherto being done manually. Apart from reducing errors, this resulted in considerable saving of time and effort.

During his five-year tenure as the SO-in-C, Raj literally transformed the Corps of Signals and made an extraordinary contribution to the Indian Army in terms of enhancing its capability. A number of factors were responsible for facilitating his task. The first was his tenure in Washington, which exposed him to modern communication systems and the future trends in this and related fields. The second was the 1962 war with China, after which it was realised that the army was ill-equipped and the government was forced to increase its budgetary allocation for the defence forces. The third was the close rapport which Raj was able to forge with General J.N. Chaudhury, as well as officials in the Ministry of Defence. The fourth factor was the excellent team of officers which Raj was able to assemble to give concrete shape to his ideas. He had an excellent eye for talent, and was able to discern between the brilliant and the pedestrian, which is not very easy, especially among soldiers. The last, and probably most important factor was his own personality and strength of character. He was a determined man, who rarely gave up until he had achieved what he had set out to do. His powers of persuasion, coupled with his passion and vitality, affected everyone who came into contact with him, and he almost invariably got what he wanted.

In recognition of his immense contribution, Raj was awarded the Param Vishisht Seva Medal (PVSM), the highest non-gallantry award for the armed forces. He was presented with the award at a formal investiture ceremony held in the Durbar Hall of Rashtrapati Bhawan on 21 April 1966. After the ceremony, President Dr S. Radhakrishnan met the awardees informally at tea. When he was introduced to Raj's mother, who was present, he said: 'You must be very proud of your son today.' The dignified lady drew herself up to her full height and told Dr Radhakrishnan with obvious pride: 'I have four more, just like him.'

In July 1966, after having held the appointment of SO-in-C for over five years, Raj was appointed Director General of Civil Defence on deputation to the Ministry of Home Affairs. He handed over to Major General I.D. Verma, who had been his deputy and was familiar with the various ongoing projects that Raj had initiated. Soon after assuming this new office, he was promoted to the rank of Lieutenant General. As Director General Civil Defence, Raj was responsible for the recruitment, training and employment of the home guards, who functioned as a second line of defence, and were designed to relieve the army and assist the police in carrying out routine tasks, especially during war, natural calamities and civil unrest. He served in this appointment for about four years, making several organisational changes to enhance the effectiveness of the force.

Raj was to retire on 30 September 1970, but he took premature retirement on 28 February 1970 to become the General Manager of Somaiya Organics Limited, a chemical manufacturing concern which was setting up with French collaboration a modern plant at Barabanki, near Lucknow. It was to produce alcohol-based products for the industry, including pharmaceuticals. Raj had virtually no experience in the field, but had spent several decades successfully getting things done. The fact that he remained with the company for almost 25 years, at first as its General Manager and later its Director, bears testimony to the success he achieved. According to Mr G.H. Keswani, who was also a Company Director, Raj 'lent his deft and adept hand in the establishment and subsequent expansion of the plant. He himself brought colour, vivacity, intelligence and understanding to his work, particularly in his dealing with other people.'

After spending about five years as General Manager of Somaiya Organics, Raj decided to settle down in Delhi. He had built a house in Defence Colony, where most of his brothers, as well as a large number of his friends, were living. To keep himself occupied, he joined Danfoss (India) Limited as General Manager (Administration) though he continued to be a director in Somaiya Organics. He joined the Delhi Golf Club and began to play golf regularly. He had also bought a small farm on the Delhi–Haryana border and tried his hand at being a farmer for some time. He built a small house on the farm, where he and Priyo lived for a couple of years.

. After about five years with Danfoss (India), Raj decided to retire completely. He was now the head of the Batra clan, and continued to nurture his family. His brothers, nephews and nieces often went to him for advice and assistance. He kept in touch with every member of the family, and did his best to keep them together by making sure that everyone attended all family functions. Their eldest daughter, Preminda, had been married in August 1981 to Sanjiv Langer, an Armoured Corps officer, and the couple had a daughter and a son. Ranjit Batra had married Lalita, the daughter of Bir and Mira Paintal, in April 1984, and they too had a son. The youngest daughter, Preeti, born in 1958, while they were in Washington, had become a teacher like her mother. She married Gurdeep Singh Ahluwalia in 1989, and they had a daughter and a son. Raj and Priyo tried to spend as much time with their children and grandchildren as they could, sometimes going abroad to visit them.

Raj and Priyo now decided to travel to places they had been unable to visit earlier, and they went on a number of holidays. They both loved to travel, and visiting Raj's army associates was a source of great pleasure. In December 1980, they decided to tour southern India, a trip on which they had lunch with General K.M. Cariappa at his house, Roshanara, in Madikeri. They also met Nina Thimayya and Lieutenant General A.C. Iyappa in Bangalore. During his pre-Independence service Raj had developed close ties with many British officers. In Washington too, he had made numerous friends, not only with Americans but also with diplomats from several other countries. Over the years, he had kept in touch with all his friends, especially his comrades from the British Army. The Indian Signals Association of Great Britain, which comprised British veterans who had served in Indian Signals during World War II or earlier, played an important role in helping him maintain these links.

In 1986 Raj and Priyo spent two months holidaying in the United Kingdom, Spain and Kenya. In England, Raj was able to meet scores of his old comrades, some after almost 40 years. In Almeria, Spain, they were house guests of Major Dougan Elliot— who had been one of his company commanders in Force 401 Signal Regiment in 1946—and his wife Betty. They went abroad again in 1991 to visit Ranjit, Lalita and their son Rajbir, who were based in Germany, and to attend the Royal Signals reunion, in England. The President of the Indian Signals Association in Great Britain, Major General David Horsfield, OBE, was an old friend of Raj's. Horsfield, 10 days older than Raj, referred to him as 'my Indian twin'. He put together a three-week programme for the Batras, with the help of what came to be known as 'Horsfield Instant Tours', that took them on a whirlwind tour of London, Blandford, Catterick, Aldershot and Southill House in Somerset, which is where the Horsfields lived, and had been hosting the annual dinner for Colonels Commandant for the past 18 years. The Batras were hosted and fêted wherever they went. Describing their visit in the association's newsletter, under the heading 'The Fabulous Links With India—1991', General Horsfield wrote:

> This was a very happy visit and Raj did so much to show to all concerned what a marvellous institution the old Indian Army was, for all of us. As 'the Commander in the Field', I gave Raj an immediate award of Honorary Membership. Raj is unequalled in showing all around him the depth of his interest

and the warmth of his heart. I borrow one of his favourite expressions in saying '"God Bless you", Raj'.

A few months after he returned from the trip to Germany and UK in 1991, Raj had to consult a urologist, who recommended surgery of the prostate gland. This was quite normal for a person of his age and after the operation he returned from the hospital in seemingly good health. In June 1995, they went to New York en route to England. In New York, the couple spent some time with their daughter and son-in-law. Raj spent a lot of time with his grandchildren—Mayanti and Avalok—who cooked for him and accompanied him on long walks. They then went on to England in June 1995, where they were part of a delegation of eight retired signal officers from India and one from Pakistan, who had been invited to attend the 75th anniversary celebrations of the Royal Signals in the United Kingdom. They were all treated 'royally' for a fortnight, and Raj was always there to give an inspiring and humorous 'thank you' speech after every function. Raj was the senior member of the delegation, and in spite of his age—he was almost 79—endeared himself to everyone with his good humour and joie de vivre.

On their way home, Raj and Priyo spent a week in Moscow with Major General Gopal Batra's daughter and son-in-law, Vanita and Lieutenant Colonel Arun Sahni, who was the Assistant Military Attaché at the Indian Embassy. They attended every show and visited all the art galleries possible in seven days. They returned to India in July 1995. On 29 September 1995, Raj went to Bombay to attend a board meeting of the Somaiya Group, spending a weekend in Poona with Priyo's brother, Brigadier Pritam Pal Singh, before returning to Delhi. This was his last trip.

Slowly, Raj began spending more and more time in bed, getting up only to watch television if a golf tournament or a cricket match was on. All visitors were still greeted with a smile, and the jokes and leg-pulling continued as before. His in-laws, siblings, children, young nieces and nephews would take turns to sit with him every evening, talking to him or playing the music that he loved best—songs from 'My Fair Lady' or 'South Pacific'—surrounding him with the sense of family he so loved.

The marriage of his nephew, Kapil (son of Group Captain Ram Batra) was scheduled to take place on 19 November 1995. He told Priyo that no matter what happened, the wedding was not to be put off. By 16 November, the entire Batra family had arrived for the wedding. Raj met each one of them that day, and in the evening, while listening to his favourite music, closed his eyes and peacefully passed away. It was almost as though he had been waiting for this day, when all his loved ones would be around him. In deference to his wishes, the wedding was celebrated on 19 November, with solemnity and grace.

Raj was cremated at the military cremation ground at Brar Square in Delhi, very close to the famous War Cemetery. The mourners included almost the entire top brass of the Corps of Signals, retired officers, soldiers, as well as a large number of his civilian friends and admirers. The large turnout was but an indication of the tremendous popularity, esteem and affection, which Raj enjoyed. For several months after his demise, tributes kept pouring in, not only from his own, but also his children's friends, who had always looked upon Raj as a favourite uncle. Letters reached Priyo from almost every corner of the globe, often bringing tears to her eyes.

From England, David Horsfield wrote:

Raj deserved to the full the respect, admiration and affection that came his way, but he achieved something more and something very rare. People loved him unreservedly and it is this which makes his loss so painful. We believe that—as in everything he did—Raj got it right. It was time to go.

From Singapore, Glenda Singh, a friend of Preminda's wrote:

I'm sure everyone has a lot of fine things to say about him and his many outstanding achievements, but we will always remember him for his endearing sense of humour and larger-than-life personality.

From Germany, Herta Schemdl wrote: 'Raj always wanted people to be happy and he invariably succeeded.' For Anne Wright, who had once been a tenant at the Batras' farmhouse, Raj was . . . 'one of the world's great gentlemen, and there are so few of them'.

G.D. Gokarn, who had been Engineer-in-Chief of the Overseas Communications Service, felt that:

So wide was General Batra's vision and scientific temper, that in those days, in my humble opinion, he was in the same class as Dr Homi Bhabha, Dr Vikram Sarabhai and Dr Satish Dhawan Raj 'Bahadur' was indeed the Field Marshal of Indian Telecommunications.

Captain Martin Howard of the Royal Navy and his wife Anne had first met Raj and Priyo on the lawns of Rashtrapati Bhawan, when they were among the extras used in the shooting of the film, 'Mountbatten, the Last Viceroy'. Martin was the British Naval Adviser in New Delhi at that time, and what was a chance meeting later turned into a lifelong friendship. In his opinion:

It was either very deft appointing or the hand of God that turned him into a communications or signals officer, giving him thereby the very best career possible in the army, and one in which his rise to the top of his branch was unstoppable.

There were a large number of letters from the 'Zunts', both from India and Pakistan, recalling the wonderful association they had with Raj. There were letters from people who had served with him in the army, as well as in industry, in a similar vein. Perhaps

the most wonderful letter came to Priyo from David Horsfield's
wife, Sheelah, who wrote:

> What a joy Raj was. So full of life, bubbling over . . . But what
> a sparkling memory. What a jewel to keep in one's room of
> happy times.

Rajinder Nath Batra was among the top-notch soldiers produced
by the Indian Army. After a brilliant record in school, college
and at the IMA, he had an outstanding career in the army. A
human dynamo, he was always full of energy and enthusiasm.
He was also blessed with a contagious sense of humour and
joie de vivre. He had a magnetic personality, with the ability
to develop and sustain human bonding. It was providential
that he became a communicator, and was thus able to achieve
what he did. Though his contributions in the sphere of military
communications are stupendous, he is equally well known
for his skill at communicating with people. He had a deep
understanding of human nature, which enabled him to change
his 'frequency' to suit the wavelength of the person with whom
he was interacting. As a result, he never faced a breakdown
of communications and was always able to get 'through'. For
a signaller, that is the ultimate accolade. And Raj was a true
Signaller, if there ever was one.

8

Lieutenant General
P.S. Bhagat,
PVSM, VC

8

Lieutenant General
P.S. Bhagat, PVSM, VC

The Soldiers' General

Premindra Singh Bhagat was one of the rare breed of generals who excelled in war, as well as in peace. He was, perhaps, the only Indian general whose hallmark was courage. Physical and moral courage are seldom found together in the same person, yet Bhagat had this distinction. For the first, he won a Victoria Cross (VC), during World War II. Of the second, the instances are too numerous to recount. Though he never attained the highest rank and retired as an Army Commander, there is no doubt that if anyone deserved to become the Army Chief, it was Bhagat. If he had, the history of the Indian Army might well have been very different. And perhaps that is why he was denied the post. Due to his immense popularity, even Indira Gandhi did not dare to supersede him, and had to resort to subterfuge to get him out of the way.

Prem Bhagat was born on 13 October 1918. His father, Surendra Singh Bhagat, was an executive engineer in the United Provinces. He had two brothers, Nripendra (Tony) and Brijendra (Tutu), both of whom were older than him. Prem's mother died when he was just 9 years old. At that time, his father was posted in Gorakhpur, and his two elder brothers were in school at the Prince of Wales Royal Indian Military College (PWRIMC), in Dehradun. The PWRIMC had been established in 1922, following the recommendations of the Esher Committee, appointed in 1919 with Lord Esher as Chairman, and of the Select Committee of the Legislative Assembly, set up in March 1921, under the chairmanship of Sir Tej Bahadur Sapru. The Select Committee had recommended that 'adequate facilities should be provided in India for the preliminary training of Indians to make them fit to enter the Royal Military College, Sandhurst'. Soon afterwards, the C-in-C announced that the military college would be established in Dehradun. It was inaugurated on 13 March 1922 by the Prince of Wales, therefore its name, which was later shortened to Royal Indian Military College.

Within a year of his mother's death, his father remarried. Prem's stepmother, Sheila, was only 18 years old, less than half his father's age. Prem and his brothers treated her more like a friend than a mother, and called her Aunty. In 1930, at the age of 12, he was sent to the RIMC to join his two brothers. Prem's course, or batch, was the tenth to join the RIMC, which was run like a military school, with the students being called cadets, instead of boys as in public schools. Instead of Houses, there were Sections, named after Rawlinson, Roberts and Kitchener. Though it was called a college, it was only a school whose primary purpose was to train prospective candidates for entry into Sandhurst. As a youngster, Prem was not very robust. He played all the games, but was good only at tennis and swimming. He was reasonably good at studies, but did not excel in any subject. On the other hand, Tony was exceptionally bright, while Tutu was an outstanding sportsman. As a result, nobody thought that Prem would do as well as his brothers. Many years later, when the award of the VC was announced, everyone thought that it must be going to one of his brothers, and were quite surprised when they discovered that it was Prem who had won the decoration.

Prem joined the tenth course at the IMA in June 1937. His elder brother, Tony, had joined the first course in 1932, which came to be known as 'the Pioneers' and included three future Chiefs—Sam Manekshaw, Smith Dun and Mohammed Musa. Tony passed out on 22 December 1934 with a gold medal, having stood first in the order of merit, and was commissioned into the Engineers. Tutu passed out two years later and was commissioned into Signals. Prem performed creditably in all spheres, but did not excel in any. He was awarded colours for tennis and squash, and captained both teams. He also won his spurs in equitation, as well as his physical training (PT) badge. But according to Prem, his most important achievement had been to pass the 'drill square' test in three months on his first attempt. Passing this test, which consisted of a series of drill movements carried out on the drill square, or parade ground, entitled Prem to an 'outpass', and he could visit Mussoorie on weekends. His father was building the family home, called Bhagat Kot, at Mussoorie, and Prem often joined him at the Savoy, where he was staying. Prem's father died in Banaras (now Varanasi) in January 1938 due to an unfortunate riding accident. Prem was on vacation with him at the time. Despite losing both parents, he remained very close to his stepmother and her four children.

Prem's performance in the first term was not very encouraging. His company commander, Captain Jebens, wrote on 19 May 1937:

> Intelligent, capable and good all round performer at games. He has, however, much too high an opinion of himself and suffers from a quick temper . . . His instructors at academic subjects report that he is careless. Unless he eradicates this fault he will not pass examinations.

Endorsing the report on 3 June 1937, the Commandant, Brigadier H.E.W.B. Kingsley, DSO, wrote:

> I have noted his failings with regret . . . they show that he thinks far too much of himself and not enough of others . . .

I hope it is just the fault of youth and the result of an athletic
success at school . . .

At the end of the second term, there was only marginal
improvement in Prem's performance. His company commander
again commented on his 'high opinion of himself', and felt that
he was a bad influence on the rest of his batch in the company.
After a stern warning that an officer who sets a bad example
does not deserve a commission, Prem showed some signs of
improvement. Brigadier Kingsley wrote on 3 January 1938:
'After these two clear warnings, I hope he will change his
outlook. It will be a great pity if a boy of his ability were to fail
through a foolish fault of this nature . . .'

After the first year, Prem mellowed down, and there was
visible improvement in his performance at the Academy. It is
quite likely that his father's death in January 1938 had a sobering
effect on him, and he realised that he was now virtually on his
own, and could not afford to fail. At the time of his father's
death, both his brothers were away, and Prem was the only male
member of the family present. He therefore had to shoulder all
the responsibilities connected with the funeral. When he returned
to the Academy, he was depressed for some time and seemed to
have lost interest in everything. Fortunately, he soon came out of
it and applied himself with new vigour.

At the end of the fourth term, his company commander,
Major Jebens, wrote on 10 December 1938:

> He has this term justified my confidence in him. He has worked
> hard and played hard. As senior GC of his term he has shown
> leadership and set a good example . . . I have recommended
> him as Under Officer for his company next term.

Major Jebens' assessment was endorsed by the Commandant,
who seemed genuinely happy to see that Prem was able and
willing to take good advice. Apart from the report by his

company commander, Brigadier Kingsley had another reason to revise his opinion about Bhagat. About six months earlier, in the third term, selections were being made for the technical arms—Artillery, Engineers and Signals. Those selected were to be transferred to Woolwich Wing, which laid greater stress on mathematics and science subjects. There were only three vacancies in Engineers, and four GCs had applied—Shiv Dayal Singh, Y.C. Tiwari, Arjan Singh and P.S. Bhagat. The Commandant called Prem and Arjan to his office and after explaining the situation, suggested that Arjan Singh withdraw. Even before Arjan could respond, Prem offered to withdraw his own name. The Commandant was surprised and impressed. He rang up Army HQ and requested them to allot an additional vacancy, making it possible for both of them to get Engineers. Arjan Singh and Shiv Dayal were assigned to Bengal Sappers; Tewari to Madras Sappers; and Prem to Bombay Sappers.

Prem's individualistic streak and propensity to stand out in a crowd were evident in the Academy itself. For some reason, he always wore his peak cap at a rakish angle and was frequently ticked off on the drill square for being improperly dressed. Once, he was marched up to the Adjutant, Captain A.G. Bennet, who was regarded as a veritable terror.

'What do you have to say for yourself?' roared the Adjutant.

'Nothing, Sir,' replied Prem. 'I just like to wear my cap that way.'

'Don't you know,' thundered the Adjutant, 'that only the Prince of Wales has the privilege of wearing his cap at an angle?'

Prem's reply left even the formidable Captain Bennet dumbfounded. 'Sir,' he said, 'I am no less than the Prince of Wales.'

Prem was commissioned on 15 July 1939 and proceeded to the Bombay Engineer Group located at Poona, where his elder brother Tony was also posted. Soon after World War II began in September 1939, he was posted to 21 Field Company, also located at Poona. As a young officer, he enjoyed the social life of the city, and was a frequent visitor to the Poona Club, also known as the New Club (the Poona Gymkhana was still not admitting Indians), and the races. He soon became acquainted with some married officers and began visiting their homes frequently. Prominent among them were Colonel R.K. Dhawan and Colonel M.G. Bhandari of the Army Medical Corps. Both had grown-up daughters and their wives were good friends. Prem's first attempt at getting to know Mohini Bhandari— considered the most beautiful girl in Poona—ended in a fiasco. He then sought a proper introduction through S.N. 'Bimbo' Bhatia from Signals. Bimbo, who was a close friend of Prem's, was related to the Bhandaris. After this, Prem was tolerated but still not welcomed in the Bhandari household. Colonel M.G. Bhandari was a protective father and he did not take kindly to Prem's boisterous nature and scant regard for etiquette and formality. Stories about his exploits in Mussoorie were well known and his wild ways in Poona did little to enhance his reputation. Mohini was then only 16 years old, and studying English at Wadia College.

As all his friends and colleagues recall, Prem was a warm and generous person. He was kind not only to those he knew, but even to total strangers. Once, while filling up his car at the petrol pump near Koregaon Park, he saw that the attendant, a Pathan, was shivering with cold. Prem was wearing his sports kit and a white pullover. Without a moment's hesitation, he took off the pullover and offered it to the surprised Pathan, who remonstrated with him, saying that Prem would catch a cold. But Prem would have none of it. He told the Pathan that he was in a car and was in any case going to his room in the mess, which was quite warm. He then drove off. No one had witnessed the incident, nor did Prem ever talk about it. Many years later, when a Sapper officer stopped at the petrol pump and asked the attendant how he had come by the pullover—it had the regimental colours—the Pathan proudly told him that it had been given to him by 'Bhagat Sahib'. The pullover was faded and in tatters, but the Pathan seemed to glow with pride as he recounted the story.

Prem's kindness was not confined to people. An interesting anecdote about Prem and his pet dog was related by Mrs Bhandari and reproduced in the Commemorative Issue of the *Bombay Sappers Newsletter* dated 23 May 1976. After losing consistently at the races for several weeks, Prem decided to take a break. It was Sunday, and he was sitting on the mess lawns drinking beer when a mongrel crept in through the hedge and stood near him, whining with fear. It was an ugly creature, dirty and unwashed, with a wound on its hind leg. Soon afterwards, there was a crunch of boots on the gravel and the dog slunk under his chair. A corporal entered, saluted, and after informing him that he was from the dog-killing squad, enquired if he had seen the nasty-looking dog which had just entered.

By now, the corporal had spied the dog under Prem's chair and started to move towards the animal. Prem peremptorily asked him to get lost, since the dog belonged to him. The corporal was surprised, but had little choice except to back off. After this, the dog followed Prem wherever he went, and it lost him a few friends in the bargain. One day, it trailed him to the swimming pool. Prem was practising underwater swimming and when he did not surface for some time, the dog began to bark and then jumped in. The pool had to be drained out and then refilled, remaining closed for a week. Prem, of course, got an imperial rocket from the Commandant.

Prem's proclivity for treading on people's toes and his scant regard for age or seniority were other black marks against him, especially among the genteel society of Poona. However, there were some who had a high opinion of Prem and could see the firm resolve and strength of character that lay below the surface of the seemingly casual and carefree demeanour. One of these was MacLachan, the Commissioner of Poona Division. One day, MacLachan was playing golf with Mohini's father, Colonel Bhandari. MacLachan had taken his stance and was about to tee off when his concentration was broken by a loud rattling noise. He paused and stepped back with irritation. Soon afterwards, a Model T Ford, with Prem at the wheel, stopped in front of them. Prem waved to them and called out: 'Sorry, I took the wrong turn.' The Commissioner waved back, while Colonel Bhandari only frowned. Prem engaged the reverse gear with a metallic screech and released the clutch. The car shot backwards like an arrow released from a bow, cleared a two-foot ditch, and came to rest with a jarring thump.

Prem stepped out to see what had happened. The golfers, too, had little chance but to watch. Prem grinned, and said: 'Didn't see the ditch.' Climbing back into the driver's seat, he noisily engaged the first gear and released the clutch. The car shot forward and once again the rear wheels cleared the ditch, landing with a thump. Prem waved at the golfers and drove off. 'That chap', said MacLachan. 'He's off to the wars. You mark my words. He will either get shot or get a VC.'

Obviously, Colonel Bhandari did not share MacLachan's views about the young subaltern, who seemed to be getting too friendly with his daughter. He tried to discourage their friendship, but without any success. Prem had an ally in Mrs Bhandari, who did not share her husband's opinion of him and stood up for her daughter's right to make her own choice. Whenever Prem tried to be alone with Mohini, or asked her out for a dance, her father refused permission. After Prem was ordered to proceed to Africa for the War, he made one last attempt. It was his last night in Poona and Prem had gone to the club. He was with some British officers and had been drinking rather heavily. When he saw Mohini and her mother, he walked over to their table and requested Mrs Bhandari's permission to dance with her daughter. Before she could reply, Colonel Bhandari appeared on the scene and Prem beat a hasty retreat. However, before he left India, he did manage to obtain permission to write to Mohini, arguing that the morale of soldiers on the battlefront depended to a large extent on letters from home and those not directly involved had a duty in this respect, like rolling bandages and visiting the sick and wounded. Colonel Bhandari could not refute this argument and reluctantly gave his consent.

In September 1940, 21 Field Company was sent to East Africa with 5 Indian Division. Prem sailed from Bombay on 23 September 1940 on the SS 'Devonshire'. His brother Tutu and 'Bimbo' Bhatia were posted in 7 Infantry Brigade Signal Section, and sailed in the same convoy. After a long voyage lasting almost a month, they arrived at Port Suez. 7 Infantry Brigade disembarked and was sent to Egypt, while 10 and 11 Infantry Brigades carried on, disembarking at Port Sudan. They became part of the Sudan Defence Forces under the command of Lieutenant General W. Platt. 21 Field Company was part of 10 Infantry Brigade, then being commanded by Brigadier W. J. Slim. It was located near Gallabat, which was held by the Italians. Captain (later Lieutenant General) R.N. Batra was commanding 10 Infantry Brigade Signal Section, and this was the beginning of a long association between Raj and Prem.

On 6 November 1940, Slim's brigade launched an attack on Gallabat. The assault was spearheaded by 3 Royal Garhwal Rifles, commanded by Lieutenant Colonel S.E. Taylor. No. 2 Section of Prem's company was placed to support the battalion launching the attack. Prem himself was travelling in one of the bren carriers with the section. After a spirited attack, Gallabat fort was captured, but had to be relinquished because of a fierce counter-attack. A withdrawal was ordered, and the Sappers were given the task of road denial, to prevent the enemy from following too closely. During this operation, two derelict tanks were filled with explosives and jammed on a narrow culvert to cause a bottleneck. The charges were fired, but one of the tanks failed to blow up and the culvert did not break. The situation was critical, since the enemy was following closely. At that moment, Prem dashed out from under cover and crawled beneath the tank. He adjusted the charges and after lighting the fuse, ran back in a hail of bullets. The tank exploded, and the culvert collapsed in the face of the enemy.

Prem's act of heroism was witnessed by his CO, who later recommended him for the MC. Despite it being his first exposure to the battlefield, he had shown exceptional courage. However, in his letter to Mohini, he dismissed what he had done as a 'small thing'. But while Prem was overly modest about his own achievements, he did not fail to commend those of others. During the same battle, he witnessed an act of courage which he often recounted later. The enemy had occupied a hill, and repeated attacks by 3 Royal Garhwal Rifles had failed. Finally, a foothold was gained, halfway up the hill. The slope was steep and the going slow. The enemy opened up with artillery and mortars, and men started to fall. There was a wave of panic and the brigade began to retreat. Only a company of Garhwalis and Bhagat's section of Sappers stood firm.

Seeing the men turn rearward, Lieutenant Colonel Taylor, the CO of the Garhwalis, leaped onto a prominent rock. While this made him vulnerable to enemy fire, it also ensured that he was visible to his troops. Soon, Prem also joined him. Colonel Taylor began to shout at his men, exhorting them to turn around and face the enemy. He stood there for 20 minutes, exposed to enemy fire. Encouraged by their CO's fearlessness, the men began to rally, and slowly, the rout was stemmed. The men turned about, overcome by shame and a determination to win. They attacked with renewed vigour and the hill was soon captured. At some point during the attack, Prem noticed that Colonel Taylor was swaying, and that one of his arms was hanging loose. He was shocked to see that the CO had been wounded, his arm reduced to a mass of mangled bone and flesh. Prem reached out to help him, but Taylor barked: 'Stay where you are. Don't let the men know I have been wounded.' And he stood there till the tide had turned and the retreat averted. Only then did he ask for medical aid and collapsed. Prem was stunned. Never before had he witnessed such cool courage and dedication.

In mid-November 1940, 10 Infantry Brigade was relieved by 9 Infantry Brigade in the Gallabat area. In January 1941, the general offensive for the battle of Keren commenced. On 31 January, a mobile column of 3/12 Royal Frontier Force Rifles under the command of Lieutenant Colonel J.A. Blood was sent to probe towards Metemma. It included a detachment of 21 Field Company under the command of Second Lieutenant P.S. Bhagat. He was in one of the leading bren carriers, with the recce party. The road was heavily mined and very soon his carrier blew up. Fortunately, there were no casualties. Then it went over another mine and this time, the sapper sitting next to him as well as the driver were both killed. Prem got into another carrier and continued. Whenever they encountered a minefield, he would get down and painstakingly defuse the mines by hand. He worked for three days straight, without rest or food. On the fourth day, they ran into an ambush.

The third time his carrier was blown up, on 2 February 1941, Prem's eardrum was punctured. He continued with his task, under close enemy fire, and refused to be relieved on the grounds that having learnt how to defuse the mines, he was better qualified to do the job, and would be able to do it faster than anyone else. Finally, on 3 February 1941, he was ordered by Colonel Blood, CO 3/12 Frontier Force Rifles, to relinquish his post. With blood oozing from his ears and utterly exhausted, he was evacuated to safety, and then to a hospital in Khartoum. By this time he had been working for 96 hours and had cleared 15 minefields, covering a distance of 55 miles.

In February 1941, Prem Bhagat became the first ICO to be awarded the VC, the highest gallantry award then in existence. The coveted cross was awarded not for an isolated act of valour, but for the longest recorded feat of sheer courage. With characteristic modesty, Prem did not mention the award in any of his letters to Mohini. In fact, he never talked of the incident even when asked about it in later years. His association with the Royal Frontier Force continued even after the regiment was redesignated as the Sikh Light Infantry after Independence. He remained Colonel of the Regiment even after his retirement, a rare honour.

In June 1941, after the Eritrean Campaign had ended, a victory parade was held at Asmara. General Wavell took the salute at the parade, which was held in the forecourt of the palace of the Duke of Aosta. During an investiture ceremony at the parade, Wavell presented the VC ribbon to Lieutenant P.S. Bhagat and the DSO ribbon to Second Lieutenant Cochrane. Prem wore khakhi shorts, hose-tops, ankle puttees, a fore and aft khakhi cap with the Sapper grenade, and the blue lanyard of the Royal Bombay Sappers on his right shoulder. He had completely recovered from the wounds he had sustained, except for a slight loss of hearing in his right ear.

In July 1941, Prem returned to India. He was now a war hero, and was fêted and lionised by everyone. Datelined Bombay, 28 July 1941, *The Times of India* wrote:

> To all who met him on his landing in Bombay on Saturday afternoon he was a picture of a dashing but a modest soldier. He was characteristically ill at ease with the press and reluctant to discuss his daring exploit which won for him the highest award for valour . . . Were it not for the small purple ribbon on his tunic, it would be impossible to guess from his self-effacing conduct that he has displayed a bravery that makes the imagination reel . . . Indeed he might have been playing golf instead of exploding land mines.

The Victoria Cross was presented to Prem at a formal investiture ceremony held in the forecourt of the Viceroy's House in Delhi on 10 November 1941. The VC is traditionally presented by the King at Buckingham Palace in London, and this was the first time it was awarded by the Viceroy. Watched by thousands of spectators, Lord Linlithgow pinned the coveted bronze cross on the chest of Acting Captain Premindra Singh Bhagat, the first Indian officer to win the award. Prem was wearing a gaberdine service dress, with a Sam Browne cross-belt and peak cap. Photographs taken at the ceremony show his cap at the characteristic tilt which was to become his hallmark.

Prem now began to concentrate on the next battle—wearing down the resistance of Mohini's father. Their long separation had brought Prem and Mohini closer and they were convinced that they were in love. Mrs Bhandari had always liked Prem and felt that he would be a loving and caring husband to her daughter. Even Colonel Bhandari agreed that Prem seemed to have changed. The VC also helped in changing his opinion about the young man. These signals were conveyed to Prem, and he decided to meet Colonel Bhandari and formally ask him for his daughter's hand. Taking a deep breath, he walked in. Mohini was waiting outside the door. He emerged a few minutes later, wiping the sweat from his brow but with a smile on his face. 'My God!' he exclaimed. 'I shouldn't have got the VC then. I should have got it now.'

Prem and Mohini were married on 24 February 1942 in Poona. Prem was then 23 years old, and had just three years of service behind him. They spent about 15 months together, in Poona. During this period, he had to undertake a number of tours in rural Maharashtra to encourage young men to join the Bombay Sappers. His VC ensured that he was treated like a VIP wherever he went, and his tours were very successful. During the Quit India movement in 1942, Mahatma Gandhi was interned at the Aga Khan Palace in Poona, under the direct care of Prem's father-in-law. Accompanied by his colleague, Arjan Singh, Prem went to meet the great man, and asked him how they could help in the freedom movement. Gandhiji told them to continue in their chosen profession. He said that once the country became free, it would require the services of experienced soldiers.

Prem had been raising 484 Field Company at Dighi near Kirkee. In mid-1943 the unit was moved to Chhindwara in the Central Provinces. It was now under 14 Indian (Training)

Division, located at Nagpur, which was training troops in jungle warfare for operations on the Burma front. Chhindwara was a remote place, without even the basic amenities, and the troops lived in *bashas* (a *basha* is a mudwalled hut with a thatched or tin roof) or tents. Mohini stayed on in Poona with her parents. Prem started preparing for the Staff College examination, since he thought that this would give him a chance to stay with his family in Quetta for five months. Ultimately, he did go to Staff College, but not in Quetta.

In January 1945, Prem was nominated to attend the last wartime course at Camberley in the UK. He and D.C. Misra of the Rajputana Rifles became the first Indians to be sent to Camberley. The course was of seven months duration, including attachment. Due to the uncertain transport arrangements, they took 10 days to reach England by a combination of air, sea, and rail journeys. Prem's first interview with the Deputy Commandant was a disaster. Having never served in India, the Deputy Commandant was not sure if Indians knew enough of the language to be able to follow instructions in English. He asked Prem, in halting English, speaking each word slowly: 'Can-you-speak-English?' Prem replied in the same manner: 'Yes-Sir-I-can.' A few days later, Prem had to give a talk, which was attended by the Deputy Commandant. When he heard Prem speaking flawlessly, he knew that the young Indian officer had taken him for a ride.

On his return to India, Prem along with five other Indian officers, was sent on a supplementary course at the School of Military Engineering, Roorkee. This was the first course after the war, and the six Indian officers were surprised to find that they had to dine in a separate mess and that the British officers were not keen to fraternise with them. Prem had to contend with another problem. His brother Tony had joined the Indian National Army, and was now facing trial at the Red Fort in Delhi. He was lucky to get off lightly, but had to resign his commission. Prem and Mohini invited him to stay with them, which he did for about a year before he was able to get a job as the Assistant Commissioner of Refugees.

In June 1946, Prem was again sent to England for a year to complete the engineering course, and this time, Mohini accompanied him. Momentous events were taking place in India during this period, and there was talk about partitioning the country. Prem was deeply disturbed, and wrote a monograph entitled '*My Land Divided*', in which he pleaded against attempts to divide the country on communal lines. He cited the example of the United States of America and Russia, where people of different ethnic groups had been able to join hands, and which had gone on to become powerful nations. Collins was interested in publishing the monograph, but when permission to do this was sought from the Indian government, it was refused.

In June 1947, Prem returned to India and was assigned to the Punjab Boundary Force, which was commanded by Major General T.W. Rees and had its HQ in Lahore. Soon after Partition, communal violence and riots ripped the subcontinent, and India and Pakistan realised that each would have to assume responsibility for maintaining law and order within its respective borders. On 1 September 1947, the Punjab Boundary Force was wound up, and Prem was posted as Commander Royal Engineers, 4 Infantry Division, in the rank of Lieutenant Colonel. The division was located at Jullunder, with Major General K.S. Thimayya as its GOC. His old friend, Raj Batra, was the Commander Signals, having moved his unit from Rawalpindi to Jullunder at the time of Partition.

Mohini Bhagat was then at Mussoorie, staying at Bhagat Kot. However, she and Prem's stepmother fell out with each other, and in October 1947 she suddenly decided to join him in Jullunder. One of her lady friends heard that she was planning to travel by truck, along with her baby and servant. She offered to give them a lift in her car, and they left Mussoorie accompanied by one of Prem's cousins. At this time, Punjab was in turmoil and the mass exodus of refugees had begun. By the time they reached

Ambala, it was dark. They were stopped at several places, including a picket manned by soldiers of the Baluch regiment, who were escorting Muslim refugees awaiting repatriation to Pakistan. At each place, they announced that they were part of Major General Thimayya's family. This worked like a charm, and ensured their safe passage. They reached Jullunder at midnight, to find Prem distraught with worry. He scolded all of them for taking such a risk. According to his wife, this was the only time she ever saw him lose his temper.

In July 1948, Prem was posted as GSO 1 at the Armed Forces Academy at Dehradun. He remained there for only eight months. Colonel A.P. Nanda, who was Commandant of the Bombay Engineer Group, died in November 1948, and someone was needed to replace him. Prem was offered the job, which he readily accepted, though many of his friends and well-wishers felt that he should stay with the troops and go to an active formation rather than a training centre. But Prem had always aspired for this job. On 15 February 1949, he achieved his ambition, and was appointed Commandant of the Bombay Sappers at Poona. He remained there for four-and-a-half years, and in many ways this was his best and most satisfying tenure. It was also during this period that the Bhagat legend was born. He carried out many innovations and improvements, which made the training centre the envy of all others. He took immense pride in being a Bombay Sapper, and whenever he was asked if he was a Sapper, he always replied: 'No, I am a Bombay Sapper'.

There is an interesting anecdote about Prem as the Commandant of the Bombay Sappers. Once, he heard that the Area Commander, who was based in Bombay, planned to pay a surprise visit to the centre. He promptly gave orders to all sentries that on that particular day, no visitor, irrespective of rank, was to be allowed in without his express permission. When the Area Commander arrived, he was stopped by the sentry, who refused to let him enter. After some argument, the General had to telephone the Commandant and identify himself.

Prem immediately expressed his regrets and apologised, saying that since he had not received any advance notice of the visit, he had been unable to receive the general. Prem then invited him to dinner at the officers' mess, where he played the gracious host to perfection.

Prem was a go-getter, who believed in getting things done. He had a way of getting around obstacles, and this penchant became more and more evident as he rose in rank. During the early 1950s, most states had introduced prohibition in deference to the views of Mahatma Gandhi. The rule did not apply to the armed forces, which continued to get their quota of liquor through the canteen, and were also allowed to serve it in officers' messes. However, the Area Commander directed that army units and establishments were also to comply with the order and go 'dry'. This caused some consternation, but Prem was unperturbed. He ordered the bar in the mess to be closed, and the entire stock of liquor distributed among officers, for safe-keeping. The residence of one of the officers, which was near the mess, was earmarked for socialising. Since there was no ban on drinking in one's residence, this solved the problem. Before parties, everyone would 'call' on the officer, and be suitably 'entertained'. Afterwards, the entire congregation would walk over to the mess for dinner.

After some time, when their stock needed replenishing, Prem discovered that liquor could be obtained if a doctor certified that it was required on health grounds. Orders were promptly issued to all battalion commanders to send the men on sick report to the military hospital, and request a 'prescription'. A roster was made to ensure that sufficient 'prescriptions' were obtained, and these were kept centrally and used to replenish the dwindling liquor stock. As a result, while the rest of Poona was dry, Bombay Sappers remained relatively 'wet'.

In 1954, Prem was posted to the Staff College at Wellington as the Chief Instructor (Army Wing). The Commandant was Major General W.D.A. Lentaigne, who had achieved fame in

Burma, with the Chindits. He had taken over from Brigadier S.D. Verma, who had moved the Staff College from Quetta to Wellington in October 1947. He remained the Commandant for over seven years, from March 1948 to May 1955. 'Joe' Lentaigne, as he was popularly called, brought up the Staff College during its fledgling years, and gave it the unique character and ethos for which it is well known even today. Prem was the fourth Chief Instructor (Army Wing), having been preceded by Leslie Sawhney, H.C. Badhwar and S.S. Malik. The first thing he did was to scrap all existing exercises and replace them with new ones. When the fresh course started, the students got a shock. Most of them had come armed with solutions to the previous exercises, since these were rarely changed. Another new innovation was the introduction of outdoor camps. The earlier practice was to go to the exercise area in the morning, and return to Wellington in the evening. Apart from the expense, a lot of time was wasted in travelling. Prem decided to establish a camp in the exercise area, where everyone stayed in tents until the exercise was over. Joe Lentaigne once remarked: 'He is the best CI this college ever had, or is likely to have. I predict that Prem will become the Indian C-in-C in time.'

In June 1956, Prem was invited to the Victoria Cross Centenary Celebrations in the UK. The Royal Air Force offered to airlift all the awardees, as well as their spouses. Prem and Mohini attended the celebrations in London, which comprised a grand parade in Hyde Park, a garden party at Marlborough, and several other functions. The couple were in England for almost a month, going on to Europe for a holiday accompanied by their hosts, the Dewans. Madan Dewan was the Military Attaché in London, and he and his wife Guddo were close friends of Prem and Mohini. After a very enjoyable holiday, they returned to India. It had been an excellent trip and had given both of them a much needed break.

In March 1957, Prem was promoted Brigadier and posted as Commander, 165 Infantry Brigade, located at Ramgarh.

This was to be a turning point in his career, as he had now joined the general cadre, and therefore would be automatically eligible for command of a division, corps or an army. Though no Engineer officer had risen to the rank of General, technically this was possible, and Prem could well be the first one to achieve this distinction. By all accounts, his performance as a brigade commander was well above par. His style of functioning made a refreshing change from the typical armchair commander, who rarely ventured out of his office and did everything by the book. Prem believed in running a happy team, based on mutual trust and confidence. He delegated authority to his subordinates and interfered only when it became absolutely necessary. This applied to operational, training, as well as administrative matters.

Prem's brigade was part of 20 Infantry Division, being commanded by Major General Henderson-Brooks. Once, a two-sided exercise was held, in which 165 Infantry Brigade was required to effect an opposed river crossing. Another brigade of the division was in defence, holding the opposite bank. Prem made a plan which involved a silent crossing away from the expected crossing point, and then concentrating his force at the enemy's rear. When Henderson-Brooks heard of the plan, he thought it was too ambitious and would probably result in heavy casualties since the surprise element would be lost. 'You must be expecting a miracle,' he told Prem, who took this as a challenge and was therefore even more determined to succeed.

True to his word, Prem managed to get his brigade across and behind the 'enemy' without loss of surprise. The exercise, which was to last a week, had to be called off on the fourth day. During the summing up, Major General Henderson-Brooks lavished praise on Prem and his brigade, saying that they had 'succeeded in achieving what appeared to be the impossible.'

In August 1959, Prem was posted to Army HQ as Director, Military Intelligence (DMI). At this time, Thimayya was the Army Chief and Krishna Menon the Defence Minister. Though his appointment was at Thimayya's behest, Prem soon found that he had little say in the higher echelons of power. Military intelligence had been devalued over the years and civilian intelligence agencies, particularly the Intelligence Bureau (IB), called the shots. The situation was not improved by the presence of B.N. Mullick, the Director of the IB, and B.M. Kaul, the QMG, who became the CGS after Thimayya's retirement in 1961. Both Kaul and Mullick were powerful men, and had the ear of the Prime Minister.

Soon after his arrival in Delhi, Prem was a mute witness to the chain of events that resulted in Thimayya's resignation and its subsequent withdrawal. Prem and Mohini had known 'Timmy' and Nina for several years, and were frequent visitors to White Gates, Thimayya's official residence. They were shocked and deeply hurt by the change it brought about in Thimayya, who withdrew into a shell. He was no longer the irrepressible Timmy, who could raise everyone's spirits by his very presence. More than his low morale, what worried Prem was the gradual erosion of his authority and the creation of new power centres in Army HQ, which did not bode well for the army.

Within a fortnight of his taking over as DMI, Prem produced a 30-page appreciation, highlighting the threat from the Chinese and making specific recommendations regarding deployment of troops, strengthening the intelligence set-up, and improving communications in the north-east. At that time, his recommendations were not given any serious consideration, but as later events were to prove, he was correct in his assessment.

In October 1959, a border incident took place in Ladakh, in which a police party led by Karam Singh of the IB was fired upon by the Chinese and 10 policemen were killed. Karam Singh and several others were taken prisoner. There was an outcry in Parliament, accompanied by a demand for more effective security measures at the border, which at that time was controlled by the IB under the Home Ministry. The Prime Minister played down the incident, saying that 'not a blade of grass' grows in the region, conveying the impression that the area was of no importance.

The opposition was quick to catch on to this phrase, and grilled Nehru for his unfortunate choice of words.

Shortly thereafter, Dr Rajendra Prasad, who, as President of India was also the Supreme Commander of the Armed Forces, summoned the DMI for a briefing on the incident. While he was briefing the President at Rashtrapati Bhawan, Prem also apprised him of the assessment he had made in his appreciation. After the briefing, the President told him to give a similar briefing to the Prime Minister. But when Prem approached the Ministry of Defence for an appointment, Krishna Menon expressed his displeasure and turned him down.

In May 1961, Thimayya retired and was succeeded by P.N. Thapar as COAS. 'Bogey' Sen was sent to Eastern Command as GOC-in-C, and Kaul replaced him as CGS. Prem was lucky enough to be nominated for the National Defence College (NDC) course, which was to commence in June 1961. The NDC had been established in April 1960, and Prem was to undergo the second course. Had he not been nominated for the course, it is doubtful if he would have survived in the army with Kaul as his new boss. He was not one of the 'Kaul boys'—a term coined by Sam Manekshaw for officers who were members of Kaul's 'court'—and his reluctance to attend the 'durbars' held at Kaul's residence would soon have put paid to his future in the army.

In May 1962, when he had completed the NDC course, Prem was posted as Commandant of the IMA at Dehradun. When the Chinese attacked India in October that year, Prem was at Dehradun. In fact, in spite of his war experience, Prem missed all the major action after Independence. In 1962, he was the Commandant of the IMA. In 1965, he was commanding 9 Infantry Division, but it did not take part in the battle. In 1971, he was the Army Commander at Lucknow, and again missed the show since the Central Army was not directly involved in the war.

During Prem's tenure at the IMA, several memorable events took place. In the wake of the Chinese invasion, there was a massive increase in the intake of officers. The duration of training for the cadets already in the IMA was curtailed, and emergency commissions were introduced. The strength of the regular courses was also substantially increased. From 720, the number of cadets increased to 1,800 within a year. This necessitated the construction of new facilities, such as classrooms, lecture halls, firing ranges, obstacle courses, living accommodations, and dining halls. Prem had his hands full, supervising the new projects. But when Army HQ proposed that the training period of regular officers at the IMA be shortened to six months, and that they be granted commissions after undergoing the balance of training at their respective schools of instruction, Prem put his foot down. He felt that this would create a second class officer, and would be detrimental to the Indian Army in times to come. Fortunately, his view prevailed and the situation that was created by having two types of officers— KCIOs and ICOs—during the days of the British was not repeated. Another important event was the presentation of colours to the IMA. The Academy was holding the King's Colours, with which it had been presented soon after its establishment in 1932. After India became a Republic in 1950, these could not be carried on parade and had been laid up. The President, Dr S. Radhakrishnan, presented new colours to the IMA at an impressive ceremonial parade on 10 December 1962. They were received by Gentleman Cadet V.B. Batra of the thirtieth (twenty-first NDA) course on behalf of the IMA. The old colours were laid up in Chetwode Hall with due ceremony, along with the King's Colours of various other regiments of the Indian Army.

Prem introduced the custom of inviting parents of the passing out cadets to the 'pipping ceremony' and the dinner held afterwards. Earlier, they had been invited only to the Passing Out Parade, which is held in the morning. In the old days, the pipping ceremony was accompanied by a ball, and only the families of officers on the staff were invited to attend. The passing-out cadet was permitted to invite a girlfriend, if he had one, and she did the honours of putting the star on his epaulette. Prem's scheme was opposed by many, on the grounds that due to the diverse backgrounds from which the cadets were drawn, the presence of their parents might affect the formality and solemnity of the occasion. Prem disagreed, and the glow of pride on the faces of the cadets who brought their parents to be introduced to him proved that he was right. He thus brought a truly Indian flavour to the passing out ceremony, making it an occasion to be shared and cherished by the cadets and their families.

Prem gave considerable attention to the training of gentleman cadets, or GCs as they are called. Even more than military training, he laid great stress on what are known as OLQ or 'officer like qualities'. Perhaps no one else has defined these as well and as succinctly as he did. In his address to the GCs when they passed out, he said: 'Do nothing petty, selfish or mean. Be magnanimous, be loyal, be courageous, and be a gentleman. You will then be an officer in the true sense.'

During his stint at the IMA, Prem had to perform another task which was to have wide-ranging repercussions. After the 1962 debacle in NEFA, there was a public outcry at the humiliation suffered by the nation, and Prime Minister Nehru agreed to institute an enquiry. The NEFA Enquiry, as it came to be known, was to be headed by Lieutenant General Henderson-Brooks, who was then GOC 11 Corps at Jullunder. Prem Bhagat was to be the sole member, and in January 1963 was attached as Brigadier General Staff to Headquarters 11 Corps for this purpose. During the next three months, he travelled extensively to the areas where the operations had taken place. He met hundreds of officers, JCOs and men to get a first-hand account of the events that had taken place. He also had to study thousands of operational orders and instructions, war diaries and other documents to piece the story together.

The Enquiry Report was submitted to the COAS on 12 May 1963, and he in turn forwarded it to the Defence Minister on 2 July 1963. Though it had been ordered by the Army Chief, the Ministry of Defence decided that its contents should not be made public, and it was graded 'Top Secret'. This was probably because it showed certain failings on the part of Nehru, Krishna Menon and a few others in the government, as well as the army. However, Defence Minister Y.B. Chavan made a statement in Parliament on 2 September 1963, in which he referred to certain portions of the report and its recommendations.

The four specific terms of reference which the enquiry had been asked to examine were shortcomings in training and equipment; system of command; physical fitness of troops; and capacity of commanders at all levels to influence the men under them. The enquiry decided to include three other points pertaining to operational aspects in order to come up with a more comprehensive picture. It thus also covered intelligence; staff work and procedures; and the higher direction of operations. Though the report was never made public, Neville Maxwell was somehow able to lay his hands on it, and he has written about it in his book, *India's China War*.

Prem's exposure to the real story of the NEFA debacle had a profound effect on his thinking, especially with regard to the shortcomings in training, equipment, system of command and intelligence. He spent the rest of his career trying to correct the shortcomings that had been identified. He also wrote about them extensively in his book, *Forging the Shield: A Study of the Defence of India and South East Asia*. Though he did not refer to the findings of the NEFA Enquiry, his views were clearly influenced by them. He dwelt at length on the subject of civilian control over the military and the division of responsibility between the political and the military leadership. As a result of the enquiry, far-reaching changes took place in the army. Many new organisations were created, and existing ones strengthened. New weapons, equipment and clothing were ordered, and systems of command were altered. The effect of these changes was felt in 1965, when India had to go to war again, with Pakistan, and was able to redeem the honour of her arms.

In May 1963, Prem was promoted Major General and posted as Chief of Staff, HQ Eastern Command, at Lucknow. The Army Commander was Lieutenant General P.P. Kumaramangalam, who later became COAS. Eastern Command was in the process of reorganisation and expansion in the aftermath of the Indo–Chinese War. One of the first tasks given to Prem was to prepare an administrative plan in keeping with the Army HQ directive issued recently. Within a fortnight, Prem had produced an administrative appreciation which outlined details of facilities required in Eastern Command. When Kumaramangalam read it, he was astonished at the size and cost of the maintenance infrastructure recommended. He told Prem that perhaps he had exaggerated his requirements. Prem's reply was that the Army Commander had obviously not read the appreciation thoroughly. Kumaramangalam read it again, more deliberately, and found that everything that had been included was justified. He ordered the appreciation to be sent to Army HQ without any modification, even though it was far in excess of the figures catered to in the directive. Even Army HQ could not find any fault in the calculations, and had to modify its instructions.

Prem also wrote for the Army Commander an appreciation of the Chinese threat in Eastern Command. Having worked on the NEFA Enquiry, he was familiar with every aspect of the subject and produced a comprehensive document, remarkable for its lucidity and attention to detail. He also planned a massive project for the accommodation of troops in forward areas. With his experience and background as a Sapper, he was able to work out the plan of accommodation at each station, and also the method of accounting for the expenditure, in consultation with the audit and finance authorities. Though he stayed at HQ Eastern Command for just over a year, his contribution was immense. Kumaramangalam was sorry to see him leave, and described him as the perfect example of a Chief of Staff, doing all the donkey work and leaving the boss to take credit.

On 1 August 1964, Prem was posted as GOC 9 Mountain Division. The division had fought in World War II as an infantry division, and had been disbanded afterwards. It was now to be re-raised, as a mountain division at Saugor in Central India. In November 1964, it was moved to Ramgarh in Bihar. After a year, it was again redesignated as an infantry division due to a change in its operational role. On 3 September 1965, India and Pakistan went to war. Though 9 Infantry Division was not directly involved, it was kept in readiness for operations against East Pakistan. However, after 22 days, a ceasefire was declared and the war ended. Prem had been following the events closely, and was somewhat disappointed at not being directly involved. However, he was elated by the performance of the Indian Army, and wrote a paper shortly after the war, entitled 'A Reputation is Redeemed', in which he said: 'The black mark against the Army in general, and the Officer Corps in particular, has been washed clean.' Later, when he wrote *The Shield and the Sword* in 1967, he included this paper as a chapter, under the heading 'Honour Redeemed'.

In August 1966, Prem was promoted Lieutenant General and appointed GOC 11 Corps at Jullunder. The Army Commander was Lieutenant General Harbaksh Singh, who had blunted the Pakistani attack in 1965. Prem spent four years in Jullunder, where he carried out extensive changes in tactical doctrine and training. From a purely defensive role, he visualised a mixed offensive and defensive role for 11 Corps, and trained the troops accordingly. He also planned the construction of fixed defences on the border, to prevent being surprised by Pakistani armour in future wars. He was an exponent of the ditch-cum-bund (DCB) defences, which now form part of the fixed defences in Punjab.

The welfare of troops had always been of major concern to Prem, and he paid attention to this aspect at Jullunder too. He spent a lot of time visiting the living accommodations of officers and men, and came down heavily if he found them in a state of disrepair. Several new projects were sanctioned, and he was rarely deterred by rules and regulations. An incident which occurred in 1970 is typical. There was a young captain who had recently gotten married, but could not bring his wife to the station due to the acute shortage of accommodation for married couples at Jullunder. His CO advised him to seek an interview with the Corps Commander, which he did. On hearing this, two of his colleagues, who were in a similar predicament, followed suit. When the requests reached Prem, he called the three officers to his office. He made them sit down and treated them to a lavish high tea. In the meantime, he had asked his ADC to call the Station Commander and the Brigadier in charge of administration. When the two officers arrived, Prem asked them if they had houses for themselves. When they replied in the affirmative, Prem wanted to know why the young officers, all newly married, did not have any houses. He said:

> If we go to war tomorrow, it is these youngsters who will die, while you and I will be twiddling our thumbs in the Corps HQ. I am not interested in excuses. If you do not have MES accommodation, hire it from civilians. If these youngsters don't have a house by next week, I will ask both of you to vacate yours and allot it to them.

Needless to say, the officers got the accommodation, and three joyful brides joined their husbands soon afterwards.

In August 1970, Prem became Army Commander and was appointed GOC-in-C Central Command at Lucknow. He had now reached the highest echelons of the profession, just one rung from the very top. He now had the authority and the wherewithal to put into practice many of his ideas, and improve the living and working conditions of the troops. Soon after taking over, he visited Jabalpur. When he visited the single officers' quarters, he was shocked to find them living in a barrack, without any furniture or furnishings. Furious, Prem asked the Area and Sub-

Area Commanders, who were present, to explain. When he heard the usual excuses about MES procedures and shortage of funds, he blew up.

> You expect these officers to be leaders of men, and yet you make them live like pigs . . . If these youngsters do not get proper accommodation in three months, I will make you vacate the Flag Staff House and allot it to these officers.

The officers were provided with proper accommodations well before the deadline.

By now, Prem was a well-known figure in army circles, but very few civilians had heard of him. All this changed in September 1971, when the city of Lucknow was ravaged by unprecedented floods and the army was asked to provide assistance. Under his directions, the army provided immediate aid and was able to plug the breach, thus saving a large part of the city from inundation. There are several stories about how he saved the city. A large embankment, built on the western bank of the Gomti river to protect the city, had been breached. Prem who was present at the site, could see that all attempts to plug the breach were proving futile. The force of the gushing water was just carrying away the large boulders and sandbags being thrown in. There were several Public Works Department (PWD) trucks that were loaded with stones and boulders and waiting to be unloaded. Prem called the Sapper officer who was in charge and explained to him what he wanted done. As several hundred people looked on, aghast, the first truck was driven up to the edge of the embankment and then pushed over the brink. This was followed by the next truck, which settled on top of the first one. Due to their heavy weight, the trucks sank into the breach and the flow of water was checked.

The next day, all newspapers reported the incident, calling Prem the 'Saviour of Lucknow'. Thereafter, whenever his car drove through the city, policemen stopped all traffic the moment they heard his pilot's siren, a privilege not extended even to the governor or chief minister. When he was transferred to Udhampur a few months later, the citizens of Lucknow were genuinely sorry to see him leave.

Prem's concern for the welfare of his men is well known, and is the subject of several anecdotes. Once, during a visit to an infantry battalion, he asked one of the men what time he got up in the morning.

'At three o'clock,' replied the soldier.

'Why so early?' asked Prem. 'I thought the PT parade is at six thirty.'

The soldier hesitated before blurting out the reason: The men had to spend a long time waiting in a queue to use the lavatory. Prem promptly asked the soldier to lead him to the lavatories. He found there were only 20 lavatories for the 800 men in the battalion. Naturally, there were long queues in the morning. Taking the CO aside, Prem gave him a dressing down. He asked the CO if he had ever visited the lavatories. When the CO said no, Prem literally blew his top. 'No wonder you don't know what is happening in your battalion,' he boomed. 'Well, I want you to not only visit the men's lavatory, but to use it tomorrow morning. And then confirm to me on telephone.'

Next morning, the hapless CO got up at 2 a.m., so that he could visit the lavatory before the men did. Then he returned to his room and phoned the Army Commander. Of course, the battalion got additional lavatories within a month.

While he was GOC-in-C Central Command, Prem visited Mhow, where a large number of training institutions are located. There were several officers doing long courses at the Infantry School and the Military College of Telecommunication Engineering (MCTE). Due to shortage of married accommodation, they were not allowed to bring their families to the station. When Prem heard of this, he was very angry. But he was told that additional married quarters would cost a lot of money and take several years to build.

'If we can't give them proper houses, let us give them tents,' he said. He sanctioned, on the spot, accommodation for 80 officers, comprising a plinth with walls and covered with tents. This would serve as the drawing-cum-dining room, as well as a bedroom. The kitchen and bathroom would be built alongside, and covered with asbestos sheets. He allotted three months' time for the task to be completed, and said that he would come and inspect the accommodation when it was ready.

After three months, Prem returned to Mhow. By now, the two tented colonies of 40 houses each were ready and occupied. While he was going around the two colonies, he met the wife of an officer who was doing a course at the MCTE.

'How long have you been married?' he asked.

'Two weeks' she replied.

'Then you are on your honeymoon. I hope you are enjoying it?' asked Prem.

'Hardly,' replied the young lady, who had never seen a general before. 'These tents are so hot, I have to sit under a tree the whole day.' Prem apologised to her for the inconvenience, and assured her that he would put it right. He asked the Garrison Engineer, who was accompanying him, why there were no fans in the tents. The engineer replied: 'But Sir, how can we put fans in the tents? The ceiling is so low, and there is nothing to hang them from.'

'Who is asking you to put ceiling fans? Get two table fans for each tent by tomorrow. I want a completion report before I leave,' said Prem, and stomped off. That evening, all the table fans in Mhow were bought up by the MES. But they did not add up to 160, so someone had to go to Indore and purchase the balance. Next morning, each officer had two brand new fans in his tent, thanks to General Bhagat and the outspoken young lady.

After the 1971 Indo–Pak War, about 90,000 soldiers who had been taken prisoner had to be housed in camps in Central Command. This was a major task, which Prem had to undertake at extremely short notice. Apart from the construction of camps, it involved arrangements for housing, security, feeding and administration. Prem insisted that the prisoners be given all the facilities authorised to them, and be treated exactly like Indian soldiers. He ensured that they had access to canteen stores, postal facilities and medical cover, and that they were given a portion of their salary, as provided by the Geneva Convention. In some cases, he got the accommodation occupied by our own troops vacated for the prisoners. As a result, Pakistani prisoners had only praise for the way they were treated in India, and often remarked that they wished their own officers were like the Indian officers in their concern for the welfare of men.

After the 1971 Indo–Pak War it was decided to form a new Army Command to look after Jammu and Kashmir, and Northern Command came into being with its headquarters at Udhampur. Prem was appointed its first GOC-in-C in June 1972. Having been an Army Commander for the last two years, he was eminently suited for his new assignment. His priorities remained the same—improvement of defences and the working and living conditions of troops. By this time, he had also developed a certain style which was often regarded as ostentatious. As an Army Commander, he expected the best—in accommodation, food, drink, or in terms of other facilities. He was fond of parties, and entertained often and lavishly. He wooed both the civilian officials and the IAF officers posted in Udhampur, and they were frequent guests at functions held at the club or the officers' mess. He smoked a particular brand of cigarettes and drank only Vat 69 whisky. Some of his staff officers did not see eye to eye with him on these matters, but Prem insisted that it was necessary to maintain standards. If he himself accepted low standards, how could he expect others to keep them high, he argued. When he had been in Lucknow, he had usually travelled by rail in the Army Commander's saloon, which was luxurious. He found air travel painful because of the damage he had suffered to his ear in East Africa. In Northern

Command, he did most of his travelling by road, since there was no railway in Jammu and Kashmir.

One of his first tasks as GOC-in-C was delineating the Line of Control after the 1971 war with Pakistan. He was appointed the leader of the Indian team, which also included his Chief of Staff, Major General M.R. Rajwade, and the Director of Military Operations at Army HQ, Major General I.S. Gill. The Pakistani team was led by Lieutenant General Abdul Hamid Khan. The main task of the teams was to delineate a Line of Control along the entire border in Jammu and Kashmir. The first meeting was held at Wagah on 3 September 1972. This was followed by others at Lahore, on 28 November and 7 December, between the two Chiefs, Sam Manekshaw and Tikka Khan. The final meeting, at which the agreement was signed, took place on 11 December 1972 at Suchetgarh. Prem carried out the task with distinction, winning the admiration of the Pakistani officers for his forthright manner.

During his tenure in Udhampur, which also proved to be his last, he undertook a large number of welfare-oriented projects. While visiting an infantry battalion in the Rajauri sector, he found the men in high spirits and complimented the CO for this. When Prem asked him if he could do something for his unit, the CO, after some hesitation, asked for some transistor radios for the men on the pickets.

'You will get them,' said Prem. 'What else?'

The CO looked at his Subedar Major and then, very diffidently, wondered if they could have a cinema projector.

'Okay. What else?' asked Prem.

By this time the CO was in a sweat. He was not sure if he had already exceeded the limits of good manners, and a scowl on the face of his brigade commander did little to bolster his confidence. He shook his head and said: 'Nothing, Sir.'

'Nothing, my foot,' said Prem. 'You chaps don't even know what to ask from an Army Commander. Tell me, how much time and effort do your men spend fetching water from the *nullah*? Wouldn't you like to have piped water in each post?'

'Yes, Sir. But it would cost a lot of money.'

'That is no concern of yours. If it can make life easier for the men, it is money well spent,' said Prem.

After a month, the CO received a letter saying that the Army Commander had sanctioned a project costing Rs 10 lakh for water supply to the pickets of his battalion.

Prem's propensity to spend money often annoyed the auditors, and there is a story, the veracity of which is suspect, that it was the Finance Ministry which scuttled the proposal for his appointment as COAS. While this may not be true, there is no doubt that during his tenures as Army Commander in Central and Northern Commands, he sanctioned more new projects than any of his predecessors. He felt that his first duty was towards the safety and well-being of the men, and no expenditure was too much to achieve this.

When he was in Northern Command, work had started on building residential accommodation for officers at Udhampur. The land used for the project had still to be acquired, but Prem nevertheless ordered the construction to commence, since there was an acute shortage of accommodation. In 1972, as part of the general stringency measures after the 1971 war, the government imposed several restrictions on new projects. This placed a ban on all new construction. For projects which had already commenced, only those which had reached roof level were to be completed; the rest were to be aborted.

Prem was informed by his staff that construction of the officers' accommodation would also have to be stopped, since only the foundation had been laid. When he heard about the roof-level stipulation, he gave a reply that became legendary and is still quoted. 'Make out a certificate that it has reached roof level, and I will sign it. Nobody can tell an Army Commander that he is a liar.'

There is no doubt that his methods were unorthodox, and sometimes legally untenable. But there is also no denying the fact that the troops have to thank Prem Bhagat for making them more comfortable. If it were not for him, the accommodation at Udhampur, aptly named Bhagat Enclave, would not have come up, since the proceedings for land acquisition were never completed.

The Army Chief, General G.G. Bewoor, was due to retire on 11 April 1974 (at that time, the retirement age for the Chief was 58, and 56 for Lieutenant Generals). Since Prem was the seniormost officer, and was going to be 56 years old only on 13 October 1974, he was almost certain to become the next Chief. But the bureaucrats in the Defence Ministry had other ideas. Having dealt with an intractable Chief like Sam Manekshaw for four years, they did not want another strong Chief on their hands. Officers due to retire are usually sent a routine letter advising them of their retirement about six months in advance. This was done in Prem's case as well. In order to pressure him to resign, news of the letter was leaked to the press, which speculated that he would now seek premature retirement. Prem was furious, and made it clear that he had no intention of doing so.

The government now realised that the only way to deny Prem the post of COAS was to supersede him. However, by now he had become immensely popular, and his supersession would have had wide-ranging repercussions. So they adopted another ploy. Due to the extension granted to Manekshaw, Bewoor's tenure had been reduced, and he had been Chief just for a year-and-a-half. To compensate him, it was decided that he should be given a year's extension. This would have the added advantage of ensuring that Prem would retire as a Lieutenant General without technically being superseded.

When this was announced, there was consternation in army circles. For Prem, it was a mortal blow, but like a good soldier, he did not utter a word. There were many who felt that if Bewoor had refused the extension, he would have considerably enhanced his stature, both within and outside the service. What is more, he would have thwarted an attempt by politicians and bureaucrats to play around with senior-level appointments in the army. It may be recalled that earlier attempts to interfere with top-level promotions had been scuttled by the army by virtue of the esprit de corps and camaraderie that prevailed among senior officers. Both Nathu Singh and Rajendra Sinhji had refused the appointment of C-in-C when it was offered to them, on the grounds that Cariappa was their senior, thus paving the way for his promotion.

In July 1974, Prem accepted the chairmanship of the Damodar Valley Corporation (DVC). True to his word, he did not resign, but proceeded on his new assignment as a serving officer. With his characteristic vigour and no-nonsense approach, he got the sluggish behemoth moving, and soon the results were there for all to see. From 45 MW in August 1974, the production rose to 700 MW by October 1974, an increase of more than 15 times in just two months. During the 10 months that Prem was at DVC, production increased twenty-fold, and he became the toast not only of Calcutta, but the whole of West Bengal. To begin with, the bureaucrats at DVC had been skeptical about an army officer with no previous experience being able to manage such a large organisation; but Prem Bhagat's achievements soon turned them all into his most ardent admirers.

On his very first visit to the office, he insisted on meeting all the staff. When he shook hands with an old junior employee, the man had tears in his eyes. When Prem asked him why he was crying, he replied that this was the first time he had seen the face of the Chairman, let alone shake hands with him. Very soon, Prem was visiting not only the power plants, but also the houses where the employees lived. Soon, his arrival at the family quarters became a much awaited event. Needless to say, after each visit, there was a visible improvement in the amenities and living conditions of the employees.

Prem achieved spectacular results by using unorthodox methods. Once, he was visiting a power plant that was showing very low productivity. A little bit of investigation showed that the drop in productivity was due to the shortage of certain spare parts. The file containing the requisition had been shuttling between various departments for six months. Bhagat was shocked. He got hold of the file, and picking up a pencil, wrote 'sanctioned' and signed his name below it. 'Now get on with it,' he said, not even bothering to ask about the total amount involved. After going back to his office, he issued instructions increasing the financial powers of the plant managers, so that they would not have to refer to him for making urgent purchases. At another power station, he found that some generators were not working, and that replacements were expected to be shipped out from Japan. When Prem asked how long it would take for the generators to arrive, he was given an estimate of six months. 'That is too much,' he said.'Why can't we fly them down?' His staff looked incredulous, and wondered how much it would cost. 'Much less than the losses we are incurring due to shortage of power,' said Prem, and ordered that an aircraft be chartered to fly the generators to India.

Soon after he took over as Chairman of DVC the union leaders came to meet him. When they mentioned that the welfare of workers was one of their main concerns, Prem told them that in the army, this was one of the prime responsibilities of the officers, and that he would ensure that this was emulated by DVC as well. The union, therefore, would not have much to do. Sometime later, he was told that there was usually a strike before the Puja holidays, with the workers demanding a bonus. Prem declared an 8 per cent bonus on his own, several months before the Puja. The union leaders were completely baffled, as Prem had pre-empted them and removed the only grounds they had to go on a strike.

Unfortunately, Prem did not live long enough to savour his success at the DVC, and died prematurely on 23 May 1975. On his return from a visit to Delhi, he came down with a fever. He was taken to the military hospital, where, his condition deteriorated. The cause of death was officially listed as Klebsiella Pneumonia. However, his wife Mohini feels that it was more likely due to a reaction caused by an injection of penicillin, to which Prem was allergic. During his 10-month stint at DVC, he had endeared himself to everyone, and there was genuine grief at his passing among the workers as well as their families. In fact, his name had become a household word in Calcutta; thanks to him, Calcuttans had almost forgotten about power cuts.

Prem had written his last will and testament on 16 September 1968. Characteristically, he ended with the following lines:

> . . . Finally, I wish to thank officers and men of the Army for all the happiness that has been given to me. I would place on record the happiness that I have derived from my family and my wife.

Prem's biography, written by Mathew Thomas and Jasjit Mansingh, carries a foreword by Sam Manekshaw, in which he wrote:

> As a senior officer the characteristics I admired in him, both as a Staff Officer and Commander, were his friendliness, outgoing and fun-loving attitude, his generosity, loyalty to his subordinates and colleagues, his outspokenness, and that he did not mince his words. He was well read, militarily sound and a thinker. I had considered him as my NATURAL SUCCESSOR as the Army Chief, but then the Government must have felt it would be uncomfortable having two successive strong Army Chiefs. SO THE ARMY MISSED A FIRST-RATE CHIEF.

Prem Bhagat is still remembered fondly, not only by all those served under him, but even those who had met him only once. He was truly a soldiers' general, who always had his feet firmly on the ground. He took enormous risks, not for personal gain, but for the welfare of his troops. He did not believe in regulations and red tape, and often cut through them like bulldozer. He wanted to get things done quickly, and did not worry if he trod on a few toes, especially those of the auditors. To his eternal glory, it can be said that he lived by the maxim of Field Marshal Lord Chetwode, and always kept the interests of the country uppermost, followed by those of his men. His own were last, always and every time.

9

Lieutenant General
Sagat Singh,
PVSM

9

Lieutenant General Sagat Singh, PVSM
India's Finest Combat Leader

Sagat Singh was one of India's most brilliant and audacious military leaders. Though not as well known as some of his contemporaries, his record as a combat leader is unmatched. He not only succeeded in every operation, but went beyond victory, always achieving more than he had been asked to do. Imbued with an aggressive spirit and the ability to take risks, he was the epitome of the combat leader who leads from the front. A brilliant tactician and strategist, he was known for his unconventional and creative manoeuvres, which are the key to success in battle. Tales about his wartime exploits abound, and are studied by students in military training institutions. Though he did not reach the top of the military ladder, he is better known than many who did. He was the most successful corps commander during the 1971 Indo–Pak War, but surprisingly, he was given neither a decoration, nor a promotion. He was a difficult subordinate, and his penchant for the unconventional and scant regard for rules and regulations did not help his career. Viewed purely from the military angle, Sagat's performance as a combat leader was par excellence. His standing among Indian military leaders is the same as that of Patton in the US Army, and of Rommel in the Wehrmacht.

Sagat was born on 14 July 1919 in Bikaner. His father, Thakur Brij Pal Singh, was a Rathore Rajput from the vassalage of Bikaner, which was one of the two important Indian states ruled by the Rathores, the other being Marwar (Jodhpur). He was with the famous Camel Corps of Bikaner, and fought in World War I in Mesopotamia (now Iraq). Sagat was the eldest of three brothers, and had his early education at Walter Nobles' School in Bikaner. After school, he joined Dungar College, also in Bikaner. However, he did not finish his graduation, and after passing the Intermediate examination, joined the Bikaner State Forces.

Soon after World War II started, Sagat joined the IMA as an Indian State Forces cadet. Passing out in 1941, he returned to the Bikaner State Forces after a short attachment with a British battalion, the South West Borders, which was then at Bannu in the NWFP. He joined the Bikaner State Forces at Secunderabad, from where the unit moved to Chaman on the frontier and, later, to Faizabad in the United Provinces. Finally, in October 1941, the unit was moved to Iraq to suppress the Rashid Ali revolt. After a few months in Iraq, the unit was moved to Kut-el-Amara, and then to Syria and Palestine before returning to Iraq as part of 6 Indian Division. In 1943, Sagat was nominated to attend the junior staff course at the Staff College in Haifa.

When Sagat reported to the Staff College, he found that the waiters serving in the mess were all Italians and did not understand English. Sagat asked the British Major, an old re-employed officer who was in charge of the mess, to instruct the waiters that he should not be served beef. The Major called the Staff Sergeant, and told him to ensure that the waiters were given the message. The Sergeant nodded his head and told Sagat not to worry: the waiters were familiar with the eating habits of Indians as they had had an Indian on the previous course. When Sagat was served his first meal, he thought the meat did not look like mutton. When he asked a colleague, he was informed that it was indeed beef. After a great deal of expostulation, it was discovered that the 'Indian' on the previous course was the son of Sir Sikander Hayat Khan. The waiters had been told that he did not eat pork, and they assumed that Sagat, being an Indian, would have the same preferences. To be on the safe side, Sagat decided to stay away from meat altogether, and remained a vegetarian for the rest of his stay in Haifa.

The course at Haifa, though of seven months' duration, was called the junior staff course, and did not have the same weightage as the full staff course at Camberley or Quetta. In 1945, he was nominated to the staff course at Quetta, and thus had the chance to attend two staff courses, within three years. After the course, Sagat returned to Bikaner to join his unit. However, after the merger of the Indian States with the Indian Union in 1947, he decided to opt for the Indian Army. His application was accepted, and on 15 January 1949, he was granted a permanent commission. His service in the Bikaner State Forces was taken into account, and he was given seniority from 27 October 1941 and assigned to the 3rd Gorkha Rifles. Since he was one of the few officers in the Indian Army who had done the staff course, he was posted to HQ Delhi Area as GSO 2 (Ops). The GOC was Major General Tara Singh Bal, and the tactical HQ was in the Red Fort.

After a short tenure in Delhi, Sagat was posted as Brigade Major to 168 Infantry Brigade, which was then in Chhamb. From this appointment, he was reverted to regimental service in 1954, and posted as second-in-command, 3/3 Gorkha Rifles, then being commanded by Lieutenant Colonel P.S. Thapa. The battalion was located at Bharatpur in Rajasthan, which was Sagat's home state. In November 1954, it moved to Dharamsala as part of a brigade which was under the command of Brigadier (later Lieutenant General) P.O. Dunn, who was from the same regiment and had commanded 1/3 Gorkha Rifles earlier.

In February 1955, Sagat was promoted Lieutenant Colonel and given command of 2/3 Gorkha Rifles, which was then at Ferozepore in the Punjab. He relieved Lieutenant Colonel Nand

Lal Kapur, who had come to the regiment from the Rajputana Rifles. Before Independence, Gurkha regiments were officered only by the British. In fact, British officers seemed to feel that Gurkha troops would refuse to serve under Indian officers. After Independence, four of the 10 Gurkha regiments were transferred to the British Army, while the rest remained in India. However, all Gurkha soldiers were given the choice of serving either in the British or the Indian Army. It came as a surprise to the British that 90 per cent opted to serve in India, under Indian officers. The 2nd, 6th, 7th and 10th Gurkhas became part of ' The Brigade of British Gurkhas'. The 1st, 3rd, 4th, 5th, 8th and 9th Gurkhas remained in the Indian Army, and were renamed the 'Gorkhas', which was their correct ethnic name. Officers from other regiments of the Indian Army were posted to replace the British officers, who left for home. The majority came from regiments that had been transferred to Pakistan, such as the Frontier Force and the Baluch Regiment.

2/3 Gorkha Rifles was then part of 167 Infantry Brigade, which was being commanded by Brigadier Badshah. In October 1955, the battalion moved to Jammu, and soon thereafter Sagat was nominated to the senior officers' course at the Infantry School, Mhow. In December 1955 he handed over command to Lieutenant Colonel J.P. D'Cunha, who came from his erstwhile battalion, 3/3 Gorkha Rifles. After completing the course, on which he was awarded instructor's grading, Sagat was posted as CO 3/3 Gorkha Rifles, in which he had served as the second-in-command. The CO of 3/3 Gorkha Rifles had been removed in February 1956, and Major P.J. Heffernon, the second-in-command, was officiating, till Sagat assumed command in April 1956. The battalion was still in Dharamsala, and Sagat set about improving the standard of training and the morale of the troops in right earnest. As a result, the battalion performed exceedingly well and won the divisional competitions in football, boxing and skill-at-arms. During an exercise, while performing the role of an Advance Guard, it moved at such a blistering pace that the Corps Commander, Lieutenant General (later General) J.N. Chaudhury commented: 'The rate of advance by the Advance Guard was so rapid that it could not be accepted as normal for planning purposes.'

An interesting incident that occurred during Sagat's command relates to the *khud* race.* 3 Sikh was located nearby, and there was great rivalry between the two battalions in games and sports. One day, the CO of the Sikhs remarked that his boys could outpace the Gorkhas anytime, and challenged them to a *khud* race. He had probably said it a joke, but Sagat took the challenge seriously. He invited the Corps Commander and the Divisional and Brigade Commanders to the race, at which Justice G.D. Khosla of the Punjab High Court was also present. When the Gorkhas won the race, the Corps Commander said: 'Well, there is no doubt as to who is superior up and down the hills.' Justice Khosla, for whom it was a unique experience, remarked: 'It is the most thrilling sport I have ever seen. To see a Gorkha coming down the hill is a pleasure indeed.'

The battalion moved in August 1957 to an operational area in the Poonch sector, in Jammu and Kashmir. In November 1957, Sagat handed over command of 3/3 Gorkha Rifles to Lieutenant Colonel P. Raghavan and proceeded to the Infantry School, where he had been posted as a Senior Instructor. After about a year in this capacity, Sagat was appointed GSO 1 of the Training Team. He was now responsible for the preparation of the training materials that were used for instruction. This involved the revision of outdoor as well as indoor exercises and updating the syllabus to incorporate new concepts and tactical doctrine. In 1959, he was promoted Colonel and posted to Delhi as Deputy Director, Personnel Services, in the Adjutant General's Branch at Army HQ. He now had to deal with a large number of subjects, such as salaries, pension, ceremonials, welfare, and

---

* *Khud*, loosely translated, means a valley or steep incline; a khud race is a cross-country race across hills and valleys.

terms and conditions of service. He replaced Colonel (later
Major General) D.K. 'Monty' Palit, who was promoted and
given command of a brigade.

After a short stint in Delhi, Sagat was promoted Brigadier
and given command of 50 Parachute Brigade at Agra in
September 1961. This was unprecedented, since he was not a
paratrooper and would have to earn his 'wings' before he could
become one. He was then over 40 years old, and few people had
started jumping at that age. But Sagat knew that he had to get
the coveted wings before he was accepted into the fraternity of
paratroopers, and could wield any authority. He had to undergo
a tough probation course before he could begin his jumps.
To save time, he sometimes did two jumps a day and got his
'wings' in record time. For a person of his age, this was no mean
achievement. Paratroopers place a high premium on courage
and physical toughness, and his success hiked up his stock in
the brigade as nothing else could have done. At the time, 50
Parachute Brigade had only two battalions, 1 Para and 2 Para,
with the latter having recently joined the formation from Jammu
and Kashmir. To get to know his command and gauge the state
of training, Sagat set tactical exercises for both battalions. This
was to prove useful subsequently in the Goa operations, where 2
Para had to perform a similar operational task.

It was while commanding 50 Parachute Brigade that Sagat
really blossomed, and his genius as a combat leader became
apparent. During the Goa operations, he displayed tactical
brilliance and the ability to seize opportunities in battle—
qualities that few commanders are gifted with. Sagat proved the
adage that the timorous rarely succeed in war, while the bold
invariably triumph, even against heavy odds. His exploits during
the Goa operations are now part of the Indian Army's folklore,
and are often used as examples for students of military science.

At this point, a brief history of Goa is in order. Of the three
Portuguese enclaves in India, Goa was the largest, with an area
of 3,635 square kilometres and a population of approximately

600,000—of whom over half were Hindus. The other two enclaves were Daman and Diu, located more than 500 kilometres to the north of Goa. Daman, including the parganas (a pargana is a subdivision of a district) of Dadra and Nagar Haveli, had an area of 213 square kilometres and a population of about 60,000. Diu was even smaller, measuring just 39 square kilometres, with a population of about 20,000. As in the rest of India, freedom movements had sprung up in these colonies, and when the British left in 1947, the demand for independence by the people of Goa also intensified.

In July 1954, volunteers of the United Front of Goans liberated Dadra and Nagar Haveli. A year later, on 15 August 1955, about 3,000 people entered Goa to offer 'satyagraha' (a non-violent form of protest, practised by Mahatma Gandhi). The police opened fire, killing and wounding a large number of the protesters. This led to a wave of anger among the Indian people, and considerable public pressure on the Indian government to liberate Goa. The Government of Portugal rejected all offers made by the Indian government, and refused to even discuss the matter. The issue was raised in the United Nations in 1960, but Portugal refused to provide any information about its colonies. This resulted in a resolution by the UN Trusteeship Council in November 1961, condemning Portugal's refusal and asking all member-states to 'deny any help to Portugal, which could be used for the subjugation of the people of the non-autonomous territories under Portuguese administration'. In October 1961, during a seminar on Portuguese colonialism held in New Delhi, Prime Minister Nehru indicated that India had now started thinking of using 'other methods' of liberating the colonies. The army was accordingly warned about the possibility of a military operation, so that it could begin preparations. When, on 18 November 1961, the Portuguese fired on an Indian vessel—SS Sabarmati—from Anjidiv island, wounding the Chief Engineer, the Indian government decided to act and the army was ordered to go in. Two warships of the Indian Navy—the Kirpan and the

Rajput—were sent from Bombay to the Karwar coast, on 28 November. On 30 November 1961, the government took the decision to liberate Goa and all other areas under Portuguese control through a combined operation involving all three services.

On 29 November 1961, Sagat received a telephone call from 'Monty' Palit—who was the Director of Military Operations (DMO) at Army HQ—asking him to rush to Delhi. Sagat commandeered a Dakota of the Paratroopers' Training School, and was in Palit's office in less than an hour. There, he learnt about the operation for the liberation of Goa and his own role in it. He was informed that the CGS, Lieutenant General B.M. Kaul, would be holding a meeting later in the day to finalise the plans. Sagat spent the next few hours studying the terrain and acquainting himself with a brief history of Goa. At the meeting in the evening, Sagat was informed that a battalion group from his brigade would be used in an airborne role. Since time and the riverine obstacles were the main considerations, Sagat suggested that 2 Para be dropped at night in the Ponda area, so that the water obstacles of the rivers Sanquelim, Bicholim, Usgaon and Candepar could be overpassed. The AOC-in-C Operational Command, who was also present, expressed his inability to undertake a drop at night. Sagat then suggested that one company be dropped at dawn, another at first light, and the rest of the battalion by day. This was accepted and Sagat returned to Agra in high spirits. The next day, when they heard about the proposed drop, there was considerable excitement and jubilation in the brigade. 2 Para was moved to Begumpet (Hyderabad) and immediately began training for the drop.

The terrain in Goa favoured the defender, and precluded the use of armour due to the large number of rivers and inland creeks. The Portuguese had about three battalions of infantry and one squadron of wheeled armoured cars. The naval element consisted of one frigate, the Albuquerque, equipped with 120 mm cannons. There was no air force worth the name, except for two transport planes of the Portuguese civil airline TAIP. The total number of soldiers, including Goans serving in the Portuguese forces, was about 5,000 in Goa and 750 each in Daman and Diu.

The operation for the liberation of Goa, code-named 'VIJAY', was planned for 14 December 1961. Lieutenant General J.N. Chaudhury, GOC-in-C Southern Command, was entrusted with the task. In order to pre-empt international intervention and prevent reinforcements from Portugal reaching Goa, it was essential for the operation to be quick and decisive. After a quick appreciation, Chaudhury decided to mount a two-pronged attack. The main force, comprising 17 Infantry Division, was to move into Goa from the east, while 50 Parachute Brigade, under Brigadier Sagat Singh, was to mount a subsidiary thrust from the north. Major General K.P. Candeth, GOC 17 Infantry Division, was placed in overall command of the taskforce. Daman and Diu were to be simultaneously tackled by a battalion each, while the Indian Navy was to capture Anjidiv island and blockade the ports of Margao, Vasco and Daman. The Indian Air Force was assigned the task of destroying the airfield at Dambolim and the wireless station at Bambolim, in addition to providing close support to the ground troops. To ensure that the Indian troops were not held up on the obstacles, a large amount of bridging equipment was grouped with the main column. A paradrop by a battalion group of the Parachute Brigade was also planned near Panjim, to capture vital bridges before they could be destroyed by the Portuguese.

50 Para Brigade began its move from Agra on 2 December, and reached Belgaum on 6 December. By now, with the IAF backing out, the drop by 2 Para had been cancelled, and the battalion, which had moved to Begumpet earlier, also joined the brigade in the concentration area. Another battalion joined the brigade in Belgaum and became its third battalion. This was 2 Sikh Light Infantry, which had been performing garrison duties in Madras and had no collective training for a considerable

period. They were also not fully equipped, and lacked even boots. Also, being a non-para unit, the battalion was not imbued with the characteristic esprit de corps and elan of the 'red berets'. However, Sagat welcomed them and tried his best to make them feel at home. Since an encounter with some Portuguese armour was expected, Sagat was allotted 7 Light Cavalry, less a squadron, equipped with Stuarts, and B Squadron ex-8 Cavalry, which had AMX tanks. However, being designed for an airborne role, the brigade was woefully short of transport. After much cajoling, Sagat managed to get some Nissan one-ton trucks. The brigade moved to Savantvadi on 13 December, and thence to its assembly area east of Dodamarg on 16 December. Meanwhile, 17 Infantry Division had also commenced its move from Ambala on 2 December, and had concentrated in Belgaum by 12 December. A tactical headquarters was established by HQ Southern Command at Belgaum on 13 December, from where the Army Commander and his staff functioned. The D-Day for the operation was initially set for 14 December, but was later postponed due to an attempt to avert the conflict and resolve the problem by diplomatic means. It was finally decided that the operation would commence on the night of 18 December.

Three days before D-Day, the COAS, General P.N. Thapar, accompanied by Lieutenant General P.P. Kumaramangalam, the Adjutant General, and Lieutenant General J.N. Chaudhury, the Army Commander, visited the brigade, and Sagat went through his plan for the operation with them. At the end of the presentation, the Army Commander expressed some reservation. He felt that Sagat's timings were too optimistic and that it may not be possible to keep to them. But Sagat insisted that the timings were feasible, and the visitors left after wishing the brigade good luck. On his return to tactical HQ, the Army Commander conveyed his doubts to his staff. However, Air Vice Marshal Pinto and the Chief of Staff, Major General P.O. Dunn, as well as G.N. Handoo of the IB, who knew Sagat well, supported him and he was allowed to proceed with his plan. As it happened, Sagat had already kept four hours in reserve, and was able to remain well ahead of the estimated timings when the operations took place.

50 Parachute Brigade had been given the subsidiary task of advancing from the north, primarily to tie down the Portuguese troops in that area. However, Sagat was not one to be tied down by orders, and had already visualised a larger role for himself. He had decided to move on a wide front on two axes, with a vehicle-mounted battalion group on each, supported by armour and artillery. He reasoned that if he was held up on one axis, he would continue the advance on the other, and using the reserve battalion advance deeper into Goa, either through Bicholim–Mapuca–Panjim Creek, or via Sanquelim–Usgaon–Ponda–Velha–Goa, on to Panjim. The 2 Sikh Light Infantry group, supported by a squadron of 7th Cavalry and a troop of 8th Cavalry, was tasked to advance on the Bicholim axis. 2 Para, supported by the rest of 7th Cavalry and a troop of 8th Cavalry, was assigned the Sanquelim axis, 1 Para was kept in reserve.

Though the operation was to commence on the night of 18 December, Sagat decided to launch fighting patrols the previous night to overcome the border outposts. This would facilitate the entry of the main column across the border the following morning. Accordingly, Sagat had tasked 1 Para to capture two border outposts, and 2 Para to proceed along the 'smugglers route' and capture the single span 110-foot-long bridge over the Sanquelim river on the previous night. Unfortunately, while these preliminary operations were going on, All India Radio gave the game away by announcing shortly after midnight that Indian troops were crossing into Goa. This alerted the Portuguese and the element of surprise, so important in such operations, was lost. One company of 2 Para, after a swift night approach, had reached within 200 yards of the bridge, when barking dogs alerted the defending troops, who quickly fired the demolitions and fled. The Portuguese Governor General and C-in-C, Major General Vassalo De Silva, was from the Engineers, and had made demolition chambers in all the bridges, with explosives attached for rapid demolition. However, the company of 2 Para managed to find a safe crossing point and secured the home bank, enabling Indian tanks, guns and vehicles to cross the river. The Portuguese had not been able to fire all the demolition charges, and only those at the two ends had exploded. The single span had fallen down but was undamaged. Using marine jacks, the span was lifted, and with the addition of abutments at both ends, the bridge was soon recommissioned. 1 Para also managed to capture the villages of Ibrampur, Maulinguem and Doromaoga by first light on 18 December, though it suffered some casualties.

The advance of 17 Infantry Division commenced from its assembly area south of Belgaum at dawn on 18 December, with 63 Infantry Brigade in the lead. The plan was to advance up to Ponda by way of Mollem. 48 Infantry Brigade, which was following it, was to pass through at Ponda and go for Panjim— the final objective. Because the advance had to be made on foot and due to the abnormally large size of the bridging column that was following the leading brigade, 48 Infantry Brigade could not keep up its advance, and when it reached the Candepar river in the evening, found that it was already occupied by paratroopers. Two battalions of 50 Parachute Brigade, 2 Para and 2 Sikh Light Infantry, had also commenced their advance at first light on 18 December. Moving on converging axes, they did not let the blown-up bridges deter them and simply swam across. The absence of heavy equipment and light opposition from the enemy, coupled with the initiative of the leaders, made this possible. As a result, the paratroopers made excellent progress and achieved more than was expected from them. By 0830 hrs, 2 Sikh Light Infantry had taken Bicholim; 2 Para reached Sanquelim by 1030 hrs, and by 1730 hrs they occupied Ponda. They did this despite two major obstacles—the Usgaon and Candepar rivers— which they crossed by means of improvised rafts and fording.

After the Usgaon river had been crossed, Sagat felt that there was now no need to hold 1 Para in reserve, and he ordered them to head straight for Banasterim after crossing the ferry at Piligao. According to his initial plan, on reaching Panjim 2 Para was to establish a firm base close to the city, with 1 Para tasked to clear the expected resistance in the built-up area. However, the lack of enemy resistance and the speed of advance had altered the situation. Another development took place at the tactical HQ of Southern Command at Belgaum. A wireless intercept indicated that the Portuguese Governor General had called for a meeting at 0800 hrs next morning to consider surrender. When informed of this, the Army Commander realised that the Portuguese had lost the battle. And when he saw the slow progress of 17 Infantry Division and the rapid advance of 50 Para Brigade, he decided to change the plan. The task of capturing Panjim, that had earlier been assigned to 17 Division, was now given to the paratroopers, who were asked to resume advance during the night. Due to a breakdown in signal communications, this order could not be passed on to HQ 17 Infantry Division, which had ordered 50 Para Brigade to firm in at Ponda and tasked 48 Brigade to capture Panjim. However, Lieutenant General Chaudhury personally spoke to the Brigade Major of 50 Para Brigade since Sagat was away visiting 2 Para at that time and gave him the instructions. Incidentally, 50 Para Brigade was able to maintain contact with Belgaum throughout the operation, thanks to a radio relay detachment that Sagat had managed to get from Major General R.N. Batra, the SO-in-C, on the 'old boy' net.

The advance of 2 Sikh Light Infantry was initially slow, even though it was led by the squadron of 7 Cavalry and a troop of AMX tanks. Sagat felt that they had a tendency to hug the ground, which slowed down their progress. He had to push them hard to speed up their advance and reach the Betim ferry on Panjim Creek by last light. By this time, 1 Para had reached the outskirts of Panjim. With two battalions around it by the evening of 18 December, 50 Para Brigade was now poised to capture the town from the east as well as the north. However, it was almost dark, and Sagat did not want to enter the built-up area of Panjim by night. He ordered 1 Para and 2 Sikh Light Infantry to halt and establish harbours for the night.

On the morning of 19 December, using the Betim ferry, some troops of 2 Sikh Light Infantry crossed the Panjim Creek and arrived in Panjim at 0800 hrs. Shortly afterwards, 1 Para also reached Panjim. Except for some firing from the customs house, there was no effective resistance and the city was in Indian hands by 0900 hrs. By a remarkable coincidence, the COs of both battalions bore the same name: Sucha Singh. However, Lieutenant Colonel Sucha Singh of 1 Para had been awarded the VrC and MC. But it was Lieutenant Colonel Sucha Singh of 2 Sikh Light Infantry who won the race by an hour and had the honour of accepting the surrender of the Portuguese troops who had assembled in the officers' mess. Major General Vassalo De Silva, the Governor General and C-in-C, escaped to Marmagao and surrendered later. The navy had already taken Anjidiv island the previous day, as well as sunk the Portuguese frigate, the Albuquerque. At 1100 hrs, Lieutenant General Chaudhury, accompanied by Air Vice Marshal Pinto, arrived in a helicopter and hoisted the tricolour on the secretariat building. Goa had been liberated in an operation that lasted a little over 24 hours.

Contrary to popular perception, the Portuguese did not surrender their enclaves without a fight. In Goa, the opposition was limited, but in Daman and Diu they put up stiff resistance. The destruction of the Indian wireless station had disrupted communications between Goa and the other enclaves, and this may have accounted for the spirited defence put up by the Portuguese. However, both Daman and Diu were occupied on 19 December, with the support of the IAF and the Indian Navy and accompanied by heavy artillery shelling. This resulted in several casualties among troops as well as civilians.

Before the operations, there had been considerable speculation about the parachute brigade and its chances of success in a ground role. In fact, Air Vice Marshal Pinto and

Mr Handoo, the Director of IB, had started a betting book, and wagers were made on the timings that the paratroopers had set for themselves. After the surrender, when Pinto came to Panjim with Chaudhury, he told Sagat that thanks to him, he had lost Rs 500. The Army Commander, who had laid three bets, lost all of them. Another interesting sidelight of the Goa operations was the propaganda about Indian troops being barbaric and indisciplined, spread by the Portuguese authorities in the hope of hardening the resolve of their troops. In fact, it had exactly the opposite effect. After the surrender, when 1 Para arrived at Altinho military camp, they found a large number of Portuguese officers and soldiers in their vests and underpants, cowering with fright. When asked why they were dressed so strangely, they confessed that they had been told that the Indian troops would kill all those found in uniform. Lieutenant Colonel Sucha Singh, VrC, MC, and his men had a good laugh at this absurdity.

Though the Goa operations were conducted along expected lines, the speed of the Indian advance surprised many observers. The credit for this goes to Sagat and his troops, who exceeded their brief and managed to reach Panjim, which they had not been asked to do. The fact that 17 Infantry Division, in spite of the vastly superior resources at their disposal and almost no opposition from the enemy, could make little headway, shows that the going was not easy. If the paratroopers succeeded, it was because of their better fighting spirit, morale and leadership. The ability to take risks and seize fleeting opportunities are the hallmark of a successful military leader, and Sagat proved beyond doubt that he had these qualities in ample measure. The failure of Indian troops barely a year later when facing the Chinese only served to underline the point that, irrespective of the fighting capabilities of the soldiers, it is the quality of leadership that tilts the balance in a war.

By the middle of June 1962, 50 Para Brigade was back in Agra. One day, Sagat was at the Clarkes Shiraz Hotel in civilian clothes. Also present was a group of American tourists, who kept looking at him intently. Finally, one of them came up to him and asked him if he was Brigadier Singh. Sagat said yes, and then asked the American how he had recognised him. The American replied that they had recently visited Portugal, where they had seen his photograph in several cafes and restaurants, with the caption that anyone who would capture and hand him over to the Portuguese government would be rewarded $10,000. Sagat had a hearty laugh and offered to be captured, but the Americans declined, saying that they were not going back to Lisbon.

While Operation VIJAY was a full-fledged military operation for the participating troops, the Indian government called it a police action. Several officers, including Sagat, were recommended for gallantry awards, but Krishna Menon, who was the Defence Minister, ruled that since it was a police action, no awards could be given. Of course, no one was fooled. Many years later, when Sagat was commanding 4 Corps, B.K. Nehru, who was then Governor of Assam, told him an interesting story. In 1961, Nehru was the Indian Ambassador in Washington. After the liberation of Goa, he met President Kennedy to explain the circumstances that had forced the Indian government to undertake the operation. Kennedy told Nehru that he understood that India had to do what it did for geo-political reasons. What he did not understand was the manner in which the Indian government tried to justify a military operation as a police action, and at the same time kept preaching non-violence to all and sundry. He laughed, and said that it was like a priest being caught in a brothel.

In January 1964, Sagat handed over command of 50 Para Brigade to Brigadier A.M.M. Nambiar, and proceeded to attend the fourth course at the National Defence College in Delhi. After a year on the course, he was posted as Brigadier General Staff 11 Corps in January 1965. He had served in this appointment for barely six months when, in July 1965, he was promoted Major General, and replaced Major General Har Prasad as GOC 17

Mountain Division. The division was then in Sikkim, and soon after he took over, there was a crisis. In order to help Pakistan during the 1965 war, the Chinese had served an ultimatum, demanding that the Indians withdraw their posts at Nathu La and Jelep La. According to the Corps HQ, the main defences of 17 Mountain Division were at Changgu, while Nathu La was only an observation post. In the adjoining sector, manned by 27 Mountain Division, Jelep La was also considered an observation post, with the main defences located at Lungthu. In case of hostilities, the divisional commanders had been given the authority to vacate the posts and fall back on the main defences. Accordingly, orders were issued by Corps HQ to both divisions to vacate Nathu La and Jelep La.

Sagat did not agree with these orders. Nathu La and Jelep La were passes on the watershed which comprised the natural boundary. The MacMahon Line, which India claimed as the International Border, followed the watershed principle, and India and China had gone to war over this issue three years earlier. Vacating the passes on the watershed would give the Chinese the tactical advantage of observation and fire into India, while denying the same to our own troops. Nathu La and Jelep La were also important because they were on the trade routes between India and Tibet, and provided the only means of ingress through the Chumbi Valley. Younghusband had used the same route during his expedition 65 years earlier, and handing it over to the enemy on a plate was not Sagat's idea of sound military strategy. Sagat also reasoned that the discretion to vacate the posts lay with the divisional commander, and he was not obliged to follow instructions from Corps HQ in this regard.

In the event, 27 Mountain Division vacated Jelep La, which the Chinese promptly occupied. However, Sagat refused to vacate Nathu La, and when the Chinese became belligerent and opened fire, he also opened up with guns and mortars, though there was a restriction imposed by Corps on the use of artillery. Lieutenant General (later General) G.G. Bewoor, the Corps

Commander, was extremely annoyed, and tried to speak to Sagat and ask him to explain his actions. But since Sagat was with the forward troops and not at his headquarters, his GSO 1, Lieutenant Colonel Lakhpat Singh, had to bear the brunt of Bewoor's wrath.

The Chinese had installed loudspeakers at Nathu La, and warned the Indians that they would suffer as they did in 1962 if they did not withdraw. However, Sagat had carried out a detailed appreciation of the situation and reached the conclusion that the Chinese were bluffing. They took up threatening postures, such as advancing in large numbers, but on reaching the border always stopped, turned around and withdrew. They also did not use any artillery for covering fire, which they would have certainly done had they been serious about capturing any Indian positions. Our own defences at Nathu La were strong. Sagat had put artillery observation posts on the adjoining high features called Camel's Back and Sebu La, which overlooked the Yatung valley for several kilometres. This allowed Sagat to bring down accurate fire on the enemy, an advantage that the Chinese did not have. Vacating Nathu La and gifting it to the Chinese would have been a tactical blunder. Ultimately, Sagat's fortitude saved the day for India and his stand was vindicated, two years later, when there was a showdown at Nathu La. Today, the strategic pass of Nathu La is still held by Indian troops, while Jelep La is in Chinese hands.

During the crisis, the Chinese managed to occupy Jelep La, but had gained nothing in the sector under Sagat's division. This was galling, and they continued to pressurise the Indians by making threatening gestures. In December 1965, the Chinese fired on a patrol of 17 Assam Rifles in North Sikkim, at a height of 16,000 feet, killing two men. Though the patrol was in Indian territory, the Chinese claimed that it had crossed over to their side. They made regular broadcasts from loudspeakers at Nathu La, pointing out to Indian troops the pathetic conditions in which they lived, and comparing their low salaries and lack of amenities to those enjoyed by officers. It was a form of psychological warfare at which the Chinese were adept, and had to be countered. Sagat had similar loudspeakers installed on the Indian side, and tape-recorded messages in the Chinese language were broadcast everyday. He kept looking for a chance to avenge the Indian soldiers who had fallen to Chinese bullets. Throughout 1966 and early 1967, Chinese propaganda, intimidation and attempted incursions into Indian territory continued. The border was not marked, and there were several vantage points on the crestline to which both sides claimed ownership. Patrols walking along the border often clashed, resulting in tension and sometimes even casualties.

In 1967, Sagat discussed the problem with the Corps Commander, Lieutenant General J.S. Aurora. He suggested that the border at Nathu La be clearly marked to prevent such incidents, and offered to walk along the crestline to test the Chinese resolve. If they did not object, the line along which he walked could be assumed as being acceptable to them. The suggestion was cleared and, accompanied by an escort, Sagat began his walk along the crest. The Chinese commander also walked alongside, accompanied by a photographer who kept taking pictures. However, there was no confrontation and the 'walk' ended peacefully.

Sagat then sought Aurora's permission to mark the crestline along which he had walked. He ordered a double wire fence to be erected from Nathu La towards the North and South Shoulders. However, as soon as work on the fence began on 20 August 1967, the Chinese became agitated and asked the Indians to stop. One strand of wire was laid that day, and two more were added over the next two days. On 6 September, a patrol of 2 Grenadiers, the battalion holding the defences at Nathu La, was going towards the South Shoulder, when it was surrounded and threatened by about 70 Chinese soldiers. On the following day, the Chinese tried to physically obstruct the construction of the fence, which resulted in a scuffle. However, work continued over the next two days and was almost finished by 10 September.

Since the Chinese appeared determined to prevent completion of the fence, it was decided to start early on 11 September, and finish the job before first light. All available manpower, including a platoon each of Engineers and Pioneers, was deployed for the task. A company of 18 Rajput was also brought in to reinforce the position and protect the men working on the fence. As soon as they started the Chinese tried to stop them. There followed a heated discussion between the Chinese commander, who was accompanied by the political commissar, and Lieutenant Colonel Rai Singh, CO 2 Grenadiers. Having foreseen this eventuality, Sagat had warned Rai Singh not to expose himself, but remain in his bunker with the Brigade Commander, Brigadier M.M.S. Bakshi. But Singh ignored the warning and came out into the open to stand face-to-face with the Chinese officers. Tempers rose and the arguments became more heated, but both sides stood their ground. Then suddenly the Chinese opened fire on the troops working on the wire fence. Among the many casualties was Lieutenant Colonel Rai Singh.

Seeing their CO fall, the Grenadiers were enraged. In a fit of fury, they came out of their trenches and, led by Captain P.S. Dagar, attacked the Chinese post. The company of 18 Rajput under Major Harbhajan Singh and the Engineers working on the fence had also suffered a few casualties. Realising that the only way to neutralise the Chinese was by physical assault, Harbhajan shouted to his men and led them in a charge on the Chinese position. Several of the Indian troops were mowed down by Chinese machine-guns, but those who reached the Chinese bunkers used their bayonets, and accounted for many of the enemy. Both Harbhajan and Dagar lost their lives in the action, which developed into a full-scale battle lasting three days. Sagat asked for some medium guns, which were moved up to Kyangnosa La, at a height of over 10,000 feet. The artillery observation posts, which Sagat had cited earlier, proved their worth in bringing down effective fire on the Chinese. Because of lack of observation, and the steep incline west of Nathu La, most Chinese shells fell behind the forward defences and did not harm the Indians. At one stage, soon after their CO was wounded, there was a dip in the morale of 2 Grenadiers, and some troops occupying the South Shoulder had started upsticking (pulling out). Sagat borrowed a sten from another officer, and with the help of the Subedar Major, pushed the men back into the trenches.

The Indian casualties in the action numbered just over 200—65 dead and 145 wounded. The Chinese are estimated to have suffered about 300 casualties. Though Sagat's attempt to mark the border with a wire fence had been approved by the higher authorities, the large number of casualties suffered by both sides created a furore. Of course, the casualties among Indian troops would not have occurred if they had remained in their defences and not exposed themselves by coming out of their trenches and rushing at the Chinese post. But seeing their CO fall, the troops had lost their cool and rushed forward under the orders of the young officer who lost his life in the action. Lieutenant General J.S. Aurora visited Nathu La to assess the situation, and advised Sagat to prevent further escalation of hostilities and avoid casualties among Indian troops. The Chinese had already announced that it was the Indians who had begun the conflict, and the large number of Indian bodies and wounded soldiers they had taken seemed to support their claim. However, Sagat was not perturbed. The Chinese had been instigating him, for the last two years, and had killed several Indian soldiers during this period. The specter of the 1962 Chinese attack still haunted the military and political leadership in India, preventing them from taking effective action against them. This was the first time the Chinese had got a bloody nose, and the myth of their invincibility was broken.

At the time that Sagat was commanding 17 Mountain Division, the author was also serving in the divisional signal regiment as a young captain. The entire formation seemed to have imbibed the aggressive spirit of the Divisional Commander, and morale was very high. The author recalls an incident that took place when Sagat visited the signal regiment to carry out his annual inspection. The Quarter Master (QM), Captain Balakrishnayya, was an old hand and knew what would impress Sagat. The cable held by the unit was stored in a tin shed with a little notice outside that said. 'Line Stores'. Bala, as he was known, had the words 'OP LHASA' painted above it in bold letters. When Sagat reached the shed and read the board, he asked the CO, Lieutenant Colonel P.K. Roy Chowdhury, what it meant. This was the first time the CO had seen the board and he looked askance at Bala, who promptly replied: 'Sir, this is the cable which will be used when we advance to Lhasa.' Sagat slapped Bala on the back, and exclaimed: 'This is the spirit I want in every officer of my division. PK, I need not see anything else in your unit. Let's go to the mess for a glass of beer.' And that was the end of the inspection.

In December 1967, Sagat was posted as GOC 101 Communication Zone Area in Shillong. He had been serving in a non-family station for almost two-and-a-half years, and deserved a peace posting. He had requested a posting to Delhi, and had been told that he would be sent to Army HQ as Director of Military Training. So he was surprised when he was asked to move post-haste to 101 Communication Zone Area, which was involved in counter-insurgency operations against Mizo hostiles. He came to know later that the Army Commander, Sam Manekshaw, had specifically asked for him to sort out the Mizo Hills problem. Sagat had no choice but to accept the assignment like a good soldier.

The Mizo Hills (the area was given statehood and renamed Mizoram in 1971) lay in the north-east of India. The region was bounded by foreign territory on three sides—Burma (now Myanmar) in the east and south, and East Pakistan (now Bangladesh) in the west. In the north, it touched Manipur and

Tripura, as well as Assam, the state of which all these territories then formed a part. The Mizos have close racial links with the Chins of Burma. They are a hardy tribe of hill people who love their freedom. They were being supplied with arms and ammunition by East Pakistan, which encouraged them to revolt against India and ask for freedom. They had formed a parallel government, and the Mizo National Army (MNA) had invested, or occupied, the southern part of the Mizo Hills. The Border Security Force and the Assam Rifles, which were operating in the area, could not control the situation, and in 1966 the army was inducted.

Shortly before Sagat's posting to 101 Communication Zone Area, a mixed Naga–Mizo gang had been formed in Manipur to collect weapons and ammunition from East Pakistan. The gang attacked a platoon outpost of 16 Jat, and after inflicting heavy casualties, got away with their weapons and ammunition. The gang then advanced towards Burma and ambushed a company column of 8 Sikh, again causing heavy casualties and taking away their weapons. It then overran a platoon outpost of 30 Punjab, and took their weapons as well. Subsequently, the gang ambushed a column of 2/11 Gorkha Rifles, and another of 5 Para, before crossing over into Burma. It was at this juncture that Sagat was asked to take charge and retrieve the situation.

Soon after taking over, Sagat decided to visit the battalions to assess the situation at close quarters. He visited every battalion deployed in the Mizo Hills, spending a night with each. After talking to everyone and analysing the encounters that had taken place, he was able to pinpoint three major reasons for the reverses suffered by our troops. These were lack of intelligence, lack of attunement of the infantry battalions to insurgency situations, and ill-treatment of the locals by a few post commanders. Sagat immediately set about remedying these weaknesses, and issued directions towards this end.

In his typical style, he devised his own intelligence gathering system by compromising some of the key members of the Naga–

Mizo gang. Instead of sending them to jail, he kept them near the base at Aizawl, where he had already moved his tactical headquarters. Their families were also brought there, and they began to help our troops by giving intelligence reports, identifying hostiles during cordon and search operations, and translating captured documents. Sagat also realised that the underground hostiles must be having their own systems for getting information and passing orders. From the few letters that had been recovered by the battalions, he was able to lay his hands on the stationery, letterheads and seals used by them and had them copied in Calcutta. More information about the organisation and the routine followed by its messengers was acquired. Thereafter, small ambushes were laid, the messengers intercepted, their bags searched and the papers they were carrying replaced with fakes.

The next problem was to adjust the training of the infantry battalions to suit the peculiar requirements of counter-insurgency operations. An ad hoc training camp was started with a few officers who had been serving in the area for long, and had the experience of fighting the hostiles. This later became the Counter Insurgency and Jungle Warfare School at Vairangte. All units inducted into the area had first to undergo an orientation course at this school. This proved very useful, and resulted in considerable reduction of casualties among the troops. Today, it is one of the premier training establishments of the Indian Army, which trains officers as well as entire units in jungle warfare and counter-insurgency techniques.

Sagat realised that ethnic and linguistic differences alone do not cause rebellion. More often than not, it is the discontent caused by the repression and neglect of minorities that leads to an uprising. He issued strict orders against harassment and ill-treatment of the population, meting out exemplary punishment to erring post commanders. To reduce the feeling of neglect by providing food, medical care and other facilities, and also to improve security, Sagat decided to group the villages astride the only road in the region that ran between Aizawl and Lungleh.

There were strong objections from the civil administration on legal and administrative grounds. Fortunately, Sagat's excellent rapport with Assam's Chief Minister, B.P. Chalia, and the Governor, B.K. Nehru, enabled him to have his way and he could carry out the grouping as planned.

Being a paratrooper, Sagat knew the value of helicopters and made extensive use of them in Special Helicopter Borne Operations (SHBOs). These were mounted at short notice whenever there was a tip-off by an agent, and enabled troops to reach and intercept guerrilla bands in remote areas as soon as their presence was detected. This experience was to pay rich dividends a few years later, during the operations for the liberation of Bangladesh. By the time Sagat left Mizo Hills, peace had returned to the area, with all hostile gangs either being liquidated, or having taken shelter in East Pakistan. In recognition of his splendid performance in controlling the insurgency in Mizo Hills, Sagat was awarded the PVSM, the highest non-gallantry award for soldiers in India.

After a long tenure of three years, Sagat was promoted Lieutenant General in November 1970, and given command of 4 Corps, which had its headquarters at Tezpur. This was his third successive tenure in the East. By this time, Sam Manekshaw had taken over as COAS, and it was again at his behest that Sagat was chosen for this assignment. It proved to be a serendipitous choice since, under Sagat's command, 4 Corps was to play a pivotal role a year later. The liberation of Bangladesh in 1971 was one of the Indian Army's finest achievements. The lightning campaign, lasting just 14 days, resulted in the total annihilation of Pakistani forces and a magnificent victory for India. There were many acts of valour and fortitude in the face of adversity. Units and sub-units fought with courage, dash and elan, and there was not a single reported incident of loss of morale or cohesion. More than individual or collective gallantry, the unique—and decisive—feature of the campaign was the quality of military leadership. Among the leaders who made a significant contribution to the success of the operation was Sagat Singh. In fact, it was in 1971 that Sagat displayed, for the last time, his skills as a tactician, and conclusively proved his worth as a combat leader par excellence.

The task of liberating Bangladesh, then called East Pakistan, was given to Lieutenant General Jagjit Singh Aurora, GOC-in-C Eastern Command. He had under him 2 Corps, commanded by Lieutenant General (later General) T.N. Raina; 33 Corps, commanded by Lieutenant General M.L. Thapan; 4 Corps, commanded by Lieutenant General Sagat Singh; and 101 Communication Zone Area, commanded by Major General G.S. Gill. The terrain in Bangladesh was riverine, which usually favours the defender. The rivers were interspersed with rice fields and marshes, which made cross-country movement very difficult, especially after the monsoons. Major troop movements had to be confined to the roads, and ferries or bridges over the rivers, if defended or destroyed, could hold up advancing columns for long periods. Inland water transport was also used for transportation of goods. Pakistan had three infantry divisions, comprising about 42 battalions of regular troops, and five squadrons of armour for the defence of the region and over 2,000 kilometres of border. Lieutenant General A.A.K. Niazi, who was in charge of the Eastern Command of the Pakistan Army, had appreciated that the Indian advance would have to be along the major road axes, and had deployed his troops accordingly. Strong points had been created along the likely axes, and it was visualised that unless these were cleared, the advancing enemy could make little headway. This proved to be a costly mistake.

The territory in East Pakistan was divided by major riverine obstacles into four distinct parts. The first part comprised all territory east of the Meghna river, including Sylhet, Brahmanbaria, Comilla, Noakhali, Chittagong and Cox's Bazaar; the second comprised the territory between the rivers Jamuna (Brahmaputra) to the east and Padma (Ganges) to the west, including Rangpur,

Bogra and Rajashahi; the third comprised territory west of the Padma, including Kushtia, Jessore and Khulna; and the fourth was the Dacca Bowl, surrounded by rivers on all sides—the mighty Meghna and Lakhaya to the east, the confluence of Meghna and Padma to the south, Padma and Burhi Ganga to the west, and a branch of the Jamuna, which joins the Meghna, to the north. Due to its geo-strategic importance, Dacca had always been chosen as the capital by successive rulers.

The task allotted to Eastern Command by Army HQ was to destroy the bulk of Pakistani forces in the theatre and occupy a major portion of East Pakistan. The capture of Dacca was not included in these instructions. Based on this, Eastern Command evolved its operational plan and allotted tasks to its subordinate formations. 2 Corps was given the task of advancing from the west and capturing all territory west of the river Padma; 33 Corps was to advance from the north-west and capture all territory up to the confluence of the Padma and the Jamuna; and 4 Corps was to advance from the east and capture all territory east of the river Meghna. The task of capturing the area of Mymensingh, between the Meghna and Jamuna rivers, was allotted to 101 Communication Zone Area.

Though this had not been spelt out in the instructions issued by Army HQ, Sam Manekshaw had visualised that after all three corps had achieved their tasks, the forces would be regrouped and launched for the capture of Dacca from the west, after crossing the Padma at Golundo Ghat. For this regrouping, 4 Corps was to shed 23 Mountain Division, all its medium artillery, and two squadrons of PT-76 tanks. In the event, there was no regrouping since 2 Corps could not cross the Madhumati and 33 Corps could only reach Bogra. Dacca was captured purely by chance, by forces that had never been intended to reach there.

The operation commenced on 4 December 1971, after Pakistan had launched airstrikes on a number of Indian airfields in the early morning hours of the previous day. According to plan, 2 Corps entered East Pakistan from the west, 33 Corps from the north, and 4 Corps from the east. Under Sagat's command, in 4 Corps were three mountain divisions, with their normal complement of supporting arms and services. In addition, he had been allotted two ad hoc squadrons of light PT-76 tanks, and a medium battery of 5.5-inch guns. The divisional commanders were Major General (later General) K.V. Krishna Rao (8 Mountain Division); Major General R.D. 'Rocky' Hira (23 Mountain Division); and Major General B.F. Gonsalves (57 Mountain Division). The main task given to 4 Corps was to destroy Pakistani forces east of rivers Meghna and Bulai.

Sagat decided to send in three divisional thrusts across the 250-kilometre stretch of border on which his corps was deployed. In the north, 8 Mountain Division was to advance along the line Dharmanagar–Kulaura–Maulvi Bazar, and head for Sylhet; 57 Mountain Division was to advance along the axis Akhaura–Ashuganj, and capture Daudakandi; and 23 Mountain Division, in the south, was to capture Maynamati, Comilla and the major river port of Chandpur. Subsidiary tasks were allotted to 61 Mountain Brigade Group and Kilo Force, to assist the corps operations. There was a rail bridge over the Meghna at Ashuganj, but the road alignment did not follow the railway. Though not spelt out in the Corps Operation Orders, Sagat was determined to 'bounce' the river if he got the opportunity, and race for Dacca.

A number of preliminary operations had been carried out in November to clear out Pakistani elements that could interfere with the advance once it began. A Pakistani post at Dhalai was cleared by 61 Brigade after two attempts and some casualties. The Belonia bulge, a tongue of Pakistani territory which jutted about 10 kilometres into Tripura and was a constant irritant, was cleared by 23 Mountain Division. And a Pakistani post at Atgram, on the north-eastern approach to Sylhet, was eliminated by 59 Brigade after heavy fighting.

Operations began on the intervening night of 3 and 4 December 1971. In the North, 81 Mountain Brigade secured

Shamshernagar, and 59 Mountain Brigade captured Ghazipur, followed by Kulaura on 6 December. On the same day, 81 Brigade captured Munshi Bazar. In this sector, Maulvi Bazar was held by a Pakistani brigade that was occupying a strongly defended position on a prominent high-ground. From the very beginning, Sagat tasked the Hunter aircraft, operating from Kumbhigram airfield, to constantly bomb Maulvi Bazar with napalm. He appreciated that this would prove very costly to the Pakistani brigade in terms of casualties as well as morale. At this stage, Sagat was informed by intelligence sources that the Pakistanis were pulling out of Sylhet in a bid to reinforce Ashuganj. Sagat saw in this an opportunity to seize Sylhet. On 7 December, 4/5 Gorkha Rifles were landed south-east of Sylhet by a special heli-borne operation. This so unnerved the Pakistani Command that the Maulvi Bazar brigade group was moved away to Sylhet, which already had a brigade group of four battalions. This was reported by the IAF, which flew a tactical reconnaissance mission over Maulvi Bazar the next day. Sagat immediately ordered Krishna Rao to occupy Maulvi Bazar, which he did. In a Pakistani officers' mess, they found lunch laid on the table, uneaten.

This was the first time an 'air bridge' had been employed by the Indian Army. Being a paratrooper, Sagat knew the potential of a heli-borne force and the immense advantages that could accrue from its employment at the opportune moment. The enemy was demoralised, and made no efforts to attack 4/5 Gorkha Rifles. As he had visualised, the noise of the helicopters misled the Pakistanis, and they overestimated the strength of the troops that had landed by helicopter. By resorting to a clever, unorthodox ploy, Sagat was able to capture Maulvi Bazar without a single shot being fired.

In the central sector of 4 Corps, 57 Mountain Division commenced its advance with two brigades: 73 Mountain Brigade, under Brigadier M.L. Tuli, went for Gangasagar, while 311 Mountain Brigade, under Brigadier Misra, attacked Akhaura. It was during the battle for Gangasagar, which was captured after a stiff battle, that the only PVC of the Bangladesh campaign was won by Lance-Naik (a naik is the Indian equivalent of a corporal) Albert Ekka of 14 Guards. Akhaura also fell on 5 December to 4 Guards and 18 Rajput of 311 Mountain Brigade. At this stage, it was reported by patrols that one pair of lines of the double track railway line running to Brahmanbaria had been removed, making it usable by vehicles, and that the captured bridge over the Titas was intact. Sagat promptly changed the task of 57 Mountain Division and ordered it to head to Ashuganj by way of Brahmanbaria, instead of going for Daudkandi. This was a crucial decision and led to a quickening of the operations of 4 Corps and its crossing of the Meghna.

Brahmanbaria, which was in the loop formed by the river Titas, was strongly defended by the Pakistanis. However, the troops holding it were expecting a frontal assault from the south-east, and when 73 Brigade sent columns to the west and south, they evacuated the town and began to withdraw towards Ashuganj. 311 Brigade of 57 Division pursued the withdrawing enemy upto the east bank of the Meghna, and the leading elements of 57 Division contacted Ashuganj on 9 December. By now, the Pakistanis were well entrenched at Ashuganj and not prepared to give it up without a fight. They let the Indian troops enter the built-up area and then opened fire. Taken by surprise, the Indians were forced to fall back after suffering heavy casualties and losing four tanks. The Pakistanis also blew up the bridge over the Meghna, leaving the Pakistani brigade commander and some troops on the east bank of the river.

At this stage, it was clear to Sagat that the enemy was in dire straits. Having blown up the Ashuganj bridge, the Pakistanis intended to fall back across the river and hold Bhairab Bazar with whatever little they had left. Chandpur and Daudkandi had also fallen, and Pakistani resistance in the eastern sector had almost ceased to exist. Sagat flew over Daudkandi, Chandpur and Ashuganj in a helicopter on 9 December, and discussed the situation with the local commanders. He then decided to heli-lift his troops across the Meghna and make for Dacca. He appreciated that the capture of Dacca would end the war, and the only way to achieve this would be to contain Bhairab Bazar and cross the Meghna further to the south, where no opposition was expected. He had only 12 MI-4 helicopters, but he reckoned that the element of surprise would more than make up for the deficiency in numbers. Having used helicopters in Mizo Hills for the last three years, he knew their worth and had already planned for just such a contingency, making his troops and helicopter pilots practise night landings using torches. Fortunately, Gonsalves, who was commanding 57 Mountain Division, was also a pilot and well-versed with their use in Mizo Hills, where his division had been deployed. Sagat had also commandeered several steamers from the river port at Chandpur and the Titas river, which had been fuelled and positioned for the crossing.

The airlift began on the afternoon of 9 December, and continued for the next 36 hours. A total of 110 sorties were flown from the Brahmanbaria stadium, and crossed the Meghna, which was 4,000 yards wide, to land at helipads that had been marked by torches, with their reflectors removed. During the day, the troops landed in paddy fields, with helicopters hovering low above the ground. The first battalion of 311 Mountain Brigade, 4 Guards, landed in Raipura, while 9 Punjab crossed the river using country boats. On the following day, the troops landed directly at Narsingdi. Meanwhile, 73 Brigade had started to cross the Meghna, using the boats that had been rounded up. The ferrying of artillery and tanks posed a serious problem, and required considerable ingenuity on the part of the Engineers. By 11 December, both 311 and 73 Mountain Brigades had crossed the Meghna, and were ordered to advance to Dacca on different axes. Using all modes of transport, including bullock carts and cycle rickshaws, both brigades advanced rapidly, and on 14 December, the first artillery shell was fired on Dacca. On 15 December, 311 Mountain Brigade was poised to enter Dacca when orders were received from HQ Eastern Command to halt further advance. Tactical HQ 101 Communication Zone Area, 95 and 167 Mountain Brigades and 2 Para were placed under the command of 4 Corps the same day. On the night of 15–16 December, Dacca was subjected to shelling by Sagat's artillery, which hastened its surrender, and ceasefire was declared on 16 December.

In the southern sector of the Corps, 23 Mountain Division commenced its advance towards Comilla and the Lalmai Hills. On 4 December, 301 Brigade captured over 200 prisoners of the 25 Frontier Force, including the battalion commander, near Comilla. Simultaneously, 181 Brigade cut the road and rail links between Laksham and Lalmai, enabling 301 Brigade to capture Mudfarganj on 5 December. The Pakistanis made an attempt to recapture the town on 7 December, but failed. Comilla was taken on 8 December, as were the Daudkandi ferry site and the major river port of Chandpur. The brigade group garrison at Laksham, comprising four battalions, had been encircled by 8 December. It disintegrated and headed for Maynamati on 9 December. Almost a thousand of them were captured before they could reach the brigade group defences in Maynamati, which was heavily defended and defied capture until the ceasefire and surrender on 16 December.

As had happened in the Goa operations, it was not the main column but a subsidiary thrust that claimed the final prize. In Goa, Sagat's 50 Para Brigade had been given a secondary role, but he managed to reach Panjim before the troops of 17 Mountain Division. In the Bangladesh operations, 2, 4 and 33 Corps constituted the main thrusts, while 101 Communication Zone Area had been assigned a complementary role in the Mymensingh–Tangail area. Ultimately, it was this column that reached Dacca first and won the race. However, this was only made possible by the crossing of the Meghna and the minor rivers of Balu and Satlakhya by 4 Corps, and its imminent entry into Dacca. After the crossing of the Meghna, 120 Pak

Brigade, which was facing 101 Communication Zone Area, was hurriedly withdrawn for the defence of Dacca. The Pakistanis had prepared defences around Dacca that had been christened 'Fortress Dacca'. Pak 120 Brigade disintegrated after Tungi was occupied by 73 Mountain Brigade of 57 Mountain Division. Niazi's predicament can be gauged from the fact that he had to employ the 'walking wounded' from military hospitals to occupy positions on the perimeter of 'Fortress Dacca'.

The rapid advance of 101 Communication Zone Area under the command of Major General G.S. Nagra, who had replaced Major General G.S. Gill after the latter was wounded, was also facilitated by the paradrop at Tangail on 11 December. On that day, 4 Corps was in Narsingdi, 35 kilometres from Dacca, while the leading elements of 95 Infantry Brigade, commanded by Brigadier H.S. Kler, were in Jamalpur, 160 kilometres from Dacca. Two days later, on 13 December, 95 Infantry Brigade and 2 Para were still at Tangail, almost 100 kilometres from Dacca, while Sagat's troops had reached the Satlakhya river and were just 10 kilometres from Dacca. Nagra was lucky to find a tarmac road running south, a few miles west of Safipur, which led to Dacca via Sabhar without having to cross the water obstacles of Turag and Dhaleshwari. Even at midnight on 14 December, when 95 Infantry Brigade was still on the Turag river, elements of the 57 Infantry Division of 4 Corps had crossed the Satlakhya, and had started shelling Dacca. Sagat would have reached Dacca first, but this honour went to Nagra, who had been placed under Sagat's command on 15 December and was thus technically a part of 4 Corps when he entered Dacca. However, though Nagra was the first across the finish line in the race for Dacca, the real winner was undoubtedly Sagat. If the Pakistanis had not surrendered, there is no way 101 Communication Zone could have taken Dacca earlier, since it would have required a major assault. Since Sagat had firmed in at Narsingdi and already planned the attack for 16 December, in all likelihood, the honour of taking the city would have gone to him. That he lost the chance does not in any way detract from his brilliant performance. Sagat was also anxious to avoid entering the built-up area of the city, where the Pakistanis would have had an advantage over Indian troops.

Sagat's decision to cross the Meghna proved to be crucial to the entire operation. This was also the first instance in military history of an 'air-bridge' being used to cross a major water obstacle by a brigade group. In his book, *Victory in Bangladesh*, Major General Lachhman Singh, who commanded 20 Mountain Division, which was part of 33 Corps during the campaign, writes:

> It was here that Sagat Singh exhibited the genius and initiative of a field commander. It was this decision which finally and decisively tilted the scale in our favour and led to the early surrender of the Pakistani forces at Dacca.

It was a bold decision, fraught with risk, and if he had failed, the responsibility would have been entirely his. However, battles are not won by those with weak hearts, as military history has proved time and again. Every military operation is a gamble, and the stakes are invariably high. Sagat was one of those who played for the jackpot, and won.

After the war, B.B. Lal, who was the Defence Secretary, told Sagat an interesting story. On 10 December 1971 at 1300 hrs, there was a meeting being held in South Block, chaired by Sardar Swaran Singh, the Minister for External Affairs. Attending the meeting were the Defence, Home and Foreign Secretaries, the IB Director and the Principal Secretary to the Prime Minister. The meeting had just commenced when the message arrived that Sagat had crossed the Meghna. Defence Minister Babu Jagjiwan Ram rushed in soon afterwards, while Prime Minister Indira Gandhi's principal private secretary ran to her office to inform her of this. Soon afterwards, according to Lal, Indira Gandhi was seen running down the corridor, her hair and saree flying. They were all surprised to see the Prime Minister bubbling with joy, and for him, this was the most unforgettable moment of the 1971 war. This was also the one day that Sam Manekshaw could not take credit for having ordered the operation, quipped Lal.

Sagat's contribution to the liberation of Bangladesh was recognised by the award of a Padma Bhushan, a non-gallantry award that is usually given to civilians. (The three awards in the Padma series are the Padma Vibhushan, which ranks just below the Bharat Ratna, the highest in the land; the Padma Bhushan; and the Padma Shri.) The majority of awardees are artists, writers, scientists, bureaucrats and politicians. Soldiers are rarely given the award, and when they are, it is for their contribution in non-military fields. Thimayya was awarded the Padma Bhushan and Thorat the Padma Shri for their performance in United Nations assignments in Korea. Sagat's sterling performance in 1971 was in military operations against the enemy and a gallantry award would have been more appropriate. Perhaps the military hierarchy did not recommend him for one, and as a compromise, the political leadership decided to compensate him with a civilian award, since he had already been awarded the PVSM just two years earlier. It was ironic that the most successful Corps Commander in the 1971 war had to be content with a civilian award, while several others, whose performance was much below par, were decorated for gallantry and became war heroes.

In November 1973, after commanding 4 Corps for exactly three years, Sagat was transferred and given command of 1 Corps. He had been serving in the East for more than eight years, and wanted to go to some place nearer home, from where he could look after his family. His request was accepted and he was posted to 1 Corps, which was in Mathura. He retired in November 1974 and moved to Jaipur, where he had decided to live after his retirement. He built a farmhouse on the outskirts of the city, aptly named 'Meghna Farm', and settled down. Shortly after his retirement, he became a director of the State Bank of Bikaner and Jaipur, as well as several other companies.

Sagat had four sons, two of whom joined the army. His eldest son, Ran Vijay, was born in February 1949. He was commissioned into 1 Garhwal, which was later mechanised and redesignated as 6 MECH. He retired as a Brigadier in March 2003 and lives in Jaipur. The historical association between the Garhwal Rifles and 2/3 Gurkha Rifles lies in the fact that the original 2/3 Gorkha Rifles, raised in 1887, started with a nucleus of Garhwalis, and in 1890 was renamed 39th Garhwali Regiment, the forbears of the present Garhwal Rifles. Based on this historical association, the Colonel of the Garhwal Rifles claimed Sagat's eldest son when he was to get his commission. His second son, Dig Vijay, was born in October 1950, and was commissioned into 2/3 Gorkha Rifles, the battalion his father had commanded. Unfortunately, he died an untimely death on 4 March 1976—while serving as a captain with the battalion in Poonch, the jeep he was travelling in met with an accident. Sagat's third son Vir Vijay was born in August 1954. An ill-fated scooter accident in Delhi claimed his life just eight months before that of his elder brother. The loss of two sons in the prime of their lives within a short span of eight months was a terrible blow for Sagat and his wife. Their youngest son, Chandra Vijay was born in April 1956. He is a business executive.

In November 1998, Sagat lost his wife. He lived alone in Jaipur, where his children and grandchildren visited him whenever they could. About two-and-a-half years after the death of his wife, he was operated for cancer of the prostate in Delhi. He returned to Jaipur in July 2001 and seemed to have recovered. But the heavy medicines he was taking had fatal side effects. He was infected with Hepatitis A and once again had to be moved to Delhi. He breathed his last at the army hospital on 26 September 2001.

Sagat was a soldier, but like everyone else, he also had his foibles. One of these was his proclivity for affaires de coeur. A burly six-foot-two, he was a handsome man in his prime and women found him irresistible. There are many stories about his peccadilloes, not all of which are true. But even if they were, they never affected his performance as a combat leader. In any case, he is in honourable company: Caesar, Napoleon, Nelson, and Wellington, all had the same weakness. In his book, *On the Psychology of Military Incompetence*, Norman Dixon writes: 'He (Wellington) shared with Nelson a predilection for the fairer sex, which could on occasion invite some fairly adverse comments from his contemporaries.' The views of Sam Manekshaw, India's most popular military leader, on this subject are well known.

Sagat was a commander who led from the front. He epitomises the traditional image of the military leader who fights and leads by example. If he had been born a few centuries earlier, or in America or Europe, and had been given the opportunity to operate on a larger canvas, he would perhaps have been one of the Great Captains of War. Unfortunately, the nation did not recognise his talents or value his contribution, and lesser mortals were given the rewards that he deserved. However, for those who knew him intimately, or have had the fortune to serve under him, Sagat Singh was the type of military leader whom soldiers followed willingly and gave their lives for.

10

Lieutenant General
Z.C. Bakshi,
PVSM, MVC, VrC, VSM

10

Lieutenant General
Z.C. Bakshi, PVSM, MVC, VrC, VSM

India's Most Decorated General

Zorawar Chand Bakshi is one of the most distinguished soldiers of the Indian Army, having won laurels both in peace and war. He took part in every war fought by the Indian Army after Independence, except for the Indo–China War of 1962, when he was in the Congo. He also has the unique distinction of being the most highly decorated officer of the Indian Army, having won awards for gallantry at every level, from company to division. A rare combination of a fighting and thinking soldier, he is as well known for his achievements as for his reluctance to talk about them. Rules regarding seniority and age prevented him from reaching the top, and the army was deprived of a first-rate Army Commander and Chief. Despite this, Bakshi is more widely known and admired in the army than many other soldiers who attained higher ranks. A perfect blend of a soldier and a gentleman, 'Zoru' Bakshi—as he is affectionately known throughout the army—is an icon who was a source of inspiration for an entire generation of officers.

The son of Sardar Bahadur Bakshi Lal Chand, Bakshi was born on 21 October 1921, in Gulyana village in Rawalpindi district of the Punjab, which is now in Pakistan. After graduating from Gordon College, Rawalpindi, he joined the IMA in 1942. He was commissioned on 27 June 1943 into the Infantry. After a short attachment with a British battalion, he was posted to 16/10 Baluch, which was then in the Arakan in Burma, and part of 51 Infantry Brigade under 25 Indian Division. The battalion was being commanded by Lieutenant Colonel John Fairlay, who was very fond of Indian officers, having earlier been an instructor at the IMA in Dehradun. The second-in-command was Major Mohammed Usman, who later became Brigadier and was posthumously awarded the MVC in 1948, after the capture of Jhangar. The battalion had two companies of Pathans, one company of Punjabi Mussalmans, and one of Dogras. Unlike the Dogras in most other regiments, the Baluch Dogras were not Rajputs, but Brahmins. Bakshi was assigned to one of the Pathan companies.

When Bakshi joined the battalion, the monsoon had just finished and operations had resumed after a long gap. Usman sent Bakshi with a patrol through the No Man's Land to probe the Japanese defences. Since Bakshi had just joined the battalion and was inexperienced, the patrol was led by a Junior Commissioned Officer (JCO), who had been told to keep an eye on the young officer. As they were climbing a hill, the Japanese opened fire. Everyone immediately went to the ground. The JCO asked Bakshi what they should do. They could either withdraw or bypass the enemy position. However, there was a sheer drop on one side, and a steep climb on the other. If they withdrew, they could walk into an ambush. Bakshi thought for a moment, and then decided that they should go down. They were able to bypass the enemy position and returned safely after completing the task.

The JCO reported to Usman and told him about the firing, and how the young subaltern had handled the patrol. On the following day, Usman sent another patrol to check out a hill feature held by the Japanese, and asked Bakshi to lead it. Zoru took some men from his own company, which comprised

Pathans, and returned with some useful information about the feature. The CO, Lieutenant Colonel Fairlay, was leaving on transfer next day, but before he left he gave orders for the hill to be captured, and assigned the Dogra company to carry out the task. Fairlay had begun his career in the Dogras, and had a soft corner for them. However, he did not have much faith in the British officer who was commanding the Dogra company, and ordered Bakshi to lead the attack. Zoru would have preferred to take his own company, but he had no choice in the matter. Since the Dogra company was not up to full strength, he decided to include a few non-combatants, such as cooks. One of these was Sepoy Bhandari Ram.

Bakshi launched the attack on the feature from three sides, using a platoon from each direction. There was a bloody fight, at the end of which the feature was captured. After the company had reorganised, it was found that Bhandari Ram was missing. Bakshi had seen him during the assault, and had been impressed by his gallantry. Later, Bhandari Ram was located and evacuated to the Regimental Aid Post. He had sustained several bullet wounds, besides which a grenade had burst right in front of him, and he was seriously wounded. The Regimental Medical Officer was a South Indian, who was fond of drinks and rarely sober. He promptly said that Bhandari Ram would be lucky to survive. But he was wrong. Bhandari Ram not only lived, but became a hero.

After the operation, Bakshi reported to Major Usman, who was officiating as CO since Fairlay had left and the new incumbent, Lieutenant Colonel L.P. 'Bogey' Sen, had yet to arrive. Usman decided that Bhandari Ram deserved a VC, and when the new CO joined next day, requested him to forward Bhandari's name for the award. Sen did forward Bhandari Ram's name, but for the Indian Order of Merit (IOM), which ranked much lower than the VC. Usman felt that this was not fair, and since he had been in command when the action took place, insisted that his opinion be taken into account. In the end,

Usman went to the Brigade Commander, who agreed with him and Bhandari Ram was awarded the VC.

In January 1945, 51 Infantry Brigade took part in the Battle of Kangaw, which was one of the hardest fought battles of the Burma Campaign. The Brigade Commander, Brigadier R.A. Hutton, was awarded the DSO, as were all three Commanding Officers of the famous 'All Indian Brigade', i.e., S.P.P. Thorat, K.S. Thimayya and L.P. Sen. Zoru Bakshi was mentioned in dispatches, and this was the first in a string of gallantry awards that he was to win in different wars over the next 30 years. After cessation of operations in Burma, the battalion was sent back to India for rest and refit, and was located at Pollachi near Madras. But it did not stay in India for long, and was soon moved to Malaysia with the rest of the division. However, the Japanese surrendered soon after they landed, and the battalion was given the task of looking after prisoners of war. It remained in Malaysia for about a year before being repatriated to India.

In August 1947, Bakshi was posted to the Punjab Boundary Force, which had been set up to maintain peace in the Punjab. The task of dividing the state had been entrusted to Sir Cyril Radcliffe, who was expected to finalise the alignment of the boundary by 15 August 1947, when Partition would come into effect. Anticipating that the announcement of the boundary award would be accompanied by large-scale disturbances, a special force was set up to maintain order when this happened. With its HQ at Lahore, the Punjab Boundary Force was placed under Major General T.W. Rees, who was commanding 4 Indian Division. It comprised a force of about 25 battalions, drawn from different regiments, with the staff and troops of 4 Indian Division forming the nucleus. Rees had senior officers of the rank of brigadier from both countries to act as his advisers. They were K.S. Thimayya and D.S. Brar from India, and Mohammad Ayub Khan and Nasir Ahmad from Pakistan.

As a member of the Boundary Force, Bakshi witnessed the horrors of Partition at close quarters. The exodus of people from both sides was accompanied by violence that quickly escalated from individual acts of looting and revenge to full-scale attacks by armed gangs. Instances of carnage, accompanied by looting and rape, became an everyday occurrence. Entire villages, columns of walking refugees, and trains were attacked by armed mobs driven by hatred and vengeance. The brutality of these attacks surprised even the battle-hardened soldiers of the Boundary Force, whose officers had to strive hard to ensure that they themselves remained unaffected by the virus of communalism. In his report, General Rees was to remark: 'The killing was pre-medieval in its ferocity. Neither age nor sex was spared. Mothers with babies in their arms were struck down, speared or shot.'

It was soon apparent that the Boundary Force would not be able to maintain peace with the meagre resources at its disposal. Civil administration had virtually ceased to exist, and the force had to look after not only law and order, but also the arrangements for transportation, shelter and food for the refugees, whose numbers had swelled to over 2 million. There was also the additional danger of the troops themselves becoming biased, as they came to know of atrocities against their own families and relatives. Rees told the Supreme Commander that the situation was critical, and recommended that responsibility for maintaining peace in their areas should be taken over by the respective governments. This was approved by the Joint Defence Council and, on 1 September 1947, the Punjab Boundary force ceased to exist. Ten battalions of the force, which belonged to regiments that had been allotted to Pakistan, left to join their new formations. The remainder, comprising units which were to stay on in India, were formed into the East Punjab Area. General Rees was appointed Military Assistant to Governor General Lord Mountbatten, and moved to Delhi, taking Bakshi along with him. In his new assignment, Bakshi had to man the operations room in the Governor General's House (now Rashtrapati Bhawan).

As a result of Partition, Bakshi's parent unit, 16 /10 Baluch, was allotted to Pakistan. Bakshi was transferred to the 5th Gurkha Rifles, which was one of the six Gurkha regiments that were to remain in India, while four were transferred to the British Army. Till then, Indian officers had not served in Gurkha regiments, and the sudden departure of British officers left a void that had to be quickly filled by posting officers from other regiments. Initially, these officers had a difficult time, since none of them knew anything about the customs and background of the men, nor could they speak Gurkhali. Unlike other regiments, where the VCOs knew English and could therefore act as a link between the officers and the men, very few of the Gurkha officers (as the VCOs in Gurkha regiments were then called) knew English. The Regimental Centre of the 5th Royal Gurkhas, which was at Abbotabad, was moved to Dehradun, where most of the other Gurkha regimental centres were located. After joining the Indian Army, the appellation 'Royal' was dropped, and the spelling of the word 'Gurkha' was also changed to 'Gorkha' in February 1949. Bakshi joined the Centre at Dehradun, where Lieutenant Colonel (later Major General) Niranjan Prasad was posted as the Centre Commandant.

In March 1948, Bakshi was posted as Brigade Major of 163 Infantry Brigade. The coveted appointment of Brigade Major is normally given to officers who perform well on the staff course. Bakshi had not done this course, but he was given the prestigious appointment due to the shortage of staff-trained officers after the British departed. 163 Infantry Brigade had been initially raised as 'Z' Brigade at Srinagar in the spring of 1948. At that time, there were three brigades in the Kashmir valley, which were part of the Sri (later 19) Division under the command of Major General K.S. Thimayya. 161 Infantry Brigade had been inducted in October 1947, soon after Pakistani tribesmen had entered Kashmir. After pushing back the tribesmen, it had remained there throughout the winter. 77 Parachute Brigade had arrived in May 1948, and 163 Brigade had been raised at about the same time. In the summer of 1948, after the snows melted, a general offensive had been planned to drive the enemy out of Kashmir valley. According to this plan, 161 Brigade was to advance on the Uri–Domel axis, and 163 Brigade on the Handwara–Tithwal axis. The commanders of 161 and 163 Brigades were L.P. Sen and Harbaksh Singh respectively, while 77 Brigade was under Hira Lal Atal.

163 Infantry Brigade was given the task of advancing towards Tithwal, clearing enemy opposition en route and recapturing lost territory, including the strategic town of Tithwal. The brigade comprised four infantry battalions, i.e., 1 Sikh, 1 Madras, 6 Rajputana Rifles and 3 Garhwal, during various stages of the battle. It also had a squadron of 7 Cavalry equipped with armoured cars, and two batteries of artillery guns. The brigade commenced operations from Handwara on 18 May 1948, and by 20 May had taken Chowkibal. The next day, the 10,000-foot high Nastachun Pass had been captured, and by 23 May Tithwal was in Indian hands. In five days, 163 Brigade had advanced 65 kilometres, killed 67 of the enemy and taken many prisoners. It was poised to advance to Muzaffarabad, which was just 30 kilometres away, when operations were halted on orders from Army HQ following the United Nations resolution. This severely jolted the morale and spirits of the soldiers, who were all set to drive the invaders out of the Kashmir valley.

The loss of Tithwal was also a severe blow to the Pakistanis, who reacted violently and launched several counter-attacks to recapture the feature. These attacks were supported by heavy shelling and resulted in many casualties. There were also several individual acts of bravery, including that of Company Havildar Major Piru Singh of 6 Rajputana Rifles, who was posthumously awarded the Param Vir Chakra, the country's highest award for gallantry. Bakshi played a prominent part in the battle, and displayed exceptional gallantry and leadership, for which he was awarded the Vir Chakra. This was remarkable, because Bakshi was a staff officer in the Brigade HQ, and was not commanding troops. Unlike commanders, staff officers rarely get a chance to display gallantry on the battlefield. The fact that he was recommended for the Vir Chakra and won the decoration was truly a brilliant achievement.

Shortly afterwards, Bakshi notched up another feat that resulted in his being awarded the MacGregor Memorial Medal. This medal was instituted in 1888 in memory of Major General Sir Charles Metcalfe MacGregor, the founder of the United Service Institution of India. It is awarded every year for the best military reconnaissance or journey of exploration or survey in remote areas of India. However, it is awarded only if the journey or expedition is exceptional, and in case there have been none, no award is given that year. In fact, the award has been given only about a dozen times during the 50 years since Independence. Bakshi was assigned the task of carrying out an important strategic military reconnaissance of certain areas in Tibet. Dressed as a Buddhist monk, Bakshi went from Nathu La into the Chumbi valley, and then to Gyantse and Lhasa. He covered a distance of 400 kilometres in 80 days, and traversed some of the highest passes in the Himalayas. For this feat, he was awarded the medal in 1949, and became the first recipient of the medal after Independence.

After completing his tenure in 163 Infantry Brigade, Bakshi was posted back to the Regimental Centre at Dehradun in July 1949. Early in 1951, he was posted to 2/5 Gorkha Rifles, which had moved to Dehradun recently, after short tenures in Meerut and Jhansi. The battalion was under the command of Lieutenant Colonel Niranjan Prasad, who had brought it to Jhansi from Hyderabad, where it had taken part in the Police Action in 1948 and then stayed on for internal security duties. In April 1951, the battalion moved to Jandiala Guru in Punjab, as part of the 43 Lorried Brigade. While he was with the battalion, Bakshi appeared for the entrance examination for Staff College, and after qualifying, was nominated to the Fourth Course at the Defence Services Staff College, Wellington, which commenced in October 1951. He performed exceptionally well and was recommended for an instructional appointment in his course report. After completing the course in August 1952, he was posted as Brigade Major of 123 Infantry Brigade. He remained in this appointment till October 1955, a posting of well over three years. He thus had the distinction of not only completing two tenures as Brigade Major, but also an unusually long stint in this coveted staff appointment.

After his tenure with 123 Infantry Brigade, Bakshi was posted to 2/5 Gorkha Rifles, which was then located at Mahura in the Uri sector of Jammu and Kashmir. In April 1958, he was posted as an instructor to the Infantry School, Mhow, where he remained for almost two years. In January 1960, he was promoted Lieutenant Colonel and posted to the Staff College in Wellington as an instructor. During his tenure there, Major General (later Field Marshal) S.H.F.J. Manekshaw, who was the Commandant, had to undergo an inquiry ordered at the behest of Lieutenant General B.M. Kaul, the CGS. The charges related to Manekshaw's so-called anti-Indian views, and Bakshi was among the officers who were questioned by the Court of Inquiry headed by Lieutenant General Daulet Singh. None of the charges could be proved, and the inquiry was dropped.

Bakshi had completed about a year-and-a-half at Wellington when, in August 1961, he received orders posting him as CO 2/5 Gorkha Rifles, which was then in Calcutta. The battalion had been ordered to move to Silchar, but these orders were cancelled and they were sent to the Congo instead. At that time, the battalion had two Victoria Cross winners—Subedar Major Gaje Singh Ghale and Subedar Agansing Rai. According to army rules, holders of the VC and PVC are not permitted to go into areas where there is likelihood of action. However, both Ghale and Rai were adamant about accompanying the battalion, and Bakshi had to refer the matter to Army HQ, which agreed to make an exception in their case.

In January 1962, they left Calcutta for Ahmednagar, en route to Bombay. They embarked on the US naval ship, General

Blatchford, on 10 March 1962, and reached Dar-es-Salaam after a voyage of nine days. From there the troops were flown to Elizabethville, while their baggage was transported first by barges across Lake Tanganyika, and then by train. By 25 March, the battalion had concentrated in Elizabethville as part of the Indian Brigade, which was in the Katanga province. The Indians formed part of the 27-nation United Nations Force called the Organisation des Nations Unies au Congo (ONUC), which had its headquarters at Leopoldville.

After independence from Belgium, tribal disunity and a breakdown of law and order plunged Congo (now Zaire) into a civil war. The army mutinied, and one of the tribal leaders, Tshombe, seized power. The task of the United Nations' peace-keeping force was to maintain law and order, and protect vital installations from sabotage. The battalion frequently had to fight the Katangese Gendarmerie, and there were several skirmishes as well as some hard fought battles resulting in heavy casualties to both sides. By the end of the year, 2/5 Gorkha Rifles had cleared Elizabethville—and the surrounding area within a radius of about 20 kilometres—of all enemy positions and minefields. After a year the battalion returned to India in March 1963 on-board the same ship on which it had sailed to Congo. It was awarded two Sena Medals and four 'mentioned-in-dispatches'. Bakshi had missed the Indo–China War of 1962—in fact, this was the only operation he missed—but was awarded a Vishist Seva Medal (VSM) for his role in the Congo. Upon its return, the battalion moved to Almora.

In August 1963, Bakshi was posted to the Military Operations Directorate in Delhi. The MO is the most important branch in Army Headquarters, responsible for operational planning, and only officers with the highest rating are posted to this directorate. From December 1964 onwards, he officiated as the Director of Military Operations. Early in 1965, Pakistan had launched operations in the Rann of Kutch to regain control of territory which she claimed as her own. Indian troops were rushed to the sector and the offensive was blunted. As a result of the efforts of British Prime Minister Harold Wilson, who acted as a mediator, a ceasefire was accepted by both sides on 1 July 1965. An agreement was signed to this effect, returning to the situation as on 1 January 1965. However, as was subsequently discovered, the Kutch operations had been launched by Pakistan with a view to tie up Indian reserves, and test the weapons and equipment that had been supplied to her by the USA. The operations had also been intended to gauge Indian reaction, both political and military. After the debacle against China in 1962, India's defence capability was not held in high esteem, and Pakistan's new President, Ayub Khan, saw this as a golden opportunity to wrest Kashmir, an attempt in which Pakistan had failed in 1947.

Preparations for the operations began in early 1965. Thousands of guerrillas were trained and armed by Pakistan. By mid-1965, a force of 8,000 Razakars, a lightly armed volunteer force, was raised. In addition, about 150,000 Mujahids (crusaders) were trained to support the regular army and militia. Anti-India propaganda was stepped up, and Kashmiris were exhorted to rise against the 'alien' rule of India. A special organisation, called the Gibraltar Forces, was created to undertake the operations in Kashmir. Each force was to have about 30,000 men, divided into small groups of about a 100 each, with a hard core of regular troops supported by Mujahids and Razakars. The forces were given the names of famous Muslim warriors, such as Salauddin, Ghaznavi, Babar and Khilji, to inspire the guerrillas and induce religious fervour. They were concentrated at Murree, and placed under the command of Major General Akhtar Hussain Malik, General Officer Commanding 12 Division in Pak Occupied Kashmir.

In July 1965, Bakshi was promoted Brigadier and given command of the newly raised 68 Infantry Brigade, in Jammu and Kashmir. Though the brigade formed part of 3 Infantry Division in Ladakh, it was located in the Kashmir valley. Pakistani infiltration began a few days after he assumed command. Crossing the border at several places, the guerrillas began to blow up bridges, establish roadblocks, and destroy administrative installations. Though the Indian troops had no inkling of the planned infiltration, they were well prepared and their reaction was swift. The infiltrators were dealt with wherever they were encountered, and soon most were either liquidated or made to surrender. In some places, the Pakistanis used artillery to support the guerrillas, thus escalating the operations. To prevent further ingress by guerrillas and to block the routes that were being used by them, it was decided to capture some key tactical features. One of these was the Hajipir pass.

The road connecting Uri and Punch passed through the Hajipir pass at a height of 8,650 feet. The pass was strategically very important, and provided one of the main routes of ingress into the Kashmir valley. The pass had been given to Pakistan after the ceasefire agreement in 1948. In order to capture the pass, a pincer attack from two directions was planned, with one brigade ex-19 Infantry Division launching an attack from the north along the road from Uri, and another brigade ex-25 Infantry Division from the south, along the road coming from Punch. The task of capturing the feature from the north was assigned to 68 Infantry Brigade. By this time, Bakshi had already proved his worth as a commander, and won decorations in Burma during World War II, in Jammu and Kashmir in 1947–48, and in Congo in 1962. As an indication of the confidence the higher command of the army placed in him, the operation for the capture of Hajipir was code-named Operation Bakshi. Zoru Bakshi more than justified the faith reposed in him by his superiors. In one of the most brilliant and successful operations of the 1965 War, he captured the Hajipir pass and wrote his name into Indian military history.

Bakshi had only one battalion, 6 Dogra, which had been raised just six months earlier. For the operation, almost all the troops allotted to him were new to him. He concentrated his brigade at Uri in the third week of August 1965, where most of his units joined him. He had three infantry battalions: 1 Para, 19 Punjab and 4 Rajput. Another battalion ex-161 Infantry Brigade was placed under his command for the operation. He also had an artillery regiment, 164 Field Regiment, equipped with 25-pounder field guns, 144 Mountain Battery, and a troop of medium guns ex-39 Medium Regiment. In addition, he had the usual complement of Engineers and Signals. The artillery ammunition was restricted—the field guns had five first line scales, and the medium guns four first lines. Information about the exact dispositions of the enemy was scanty. Bakshi was not permitted to carry out any ground reconnaissance or visit the area held by troops of 161 Infantry Brigade, through which he had to pass to launch the attack. The Hajipir pass and the subsidiary features covering its approaches, were known to be held by 20 Punjab of the Pak Army. To distract the enemy's attention and prevent them from reinforcing their position, troops deployed all along the Cease Fire Line in the 19 Infantry Division sector were ordered to put in small-scale attacks to coincide with the main attack of 68 Infantry Brigade. Strange as it may seem, Bakshi was not told about the pincer movement, or the attack by 93 Infantry Brigade from the south.

Bakshi's plan for the operation envisaged a two-pronged attack from the north, to be conducted in three phases. In the first phase, 1 Para was to attack from the right and capture Sank Ridge, Sawan Pathri and Ledwali Gali by 0500 hours on 25 August 1965. Simultaneously, 19 Punjab was to attack from the left and capture Ring Contour and Pathra by 0100 hours the same day. In phase two, 19 Punjab was to capture Point 10330 and Point 11107, two features on the left axis, by 0600 hours, while in phase three, 4 Rajput was to capture Hajipir pass along the right axis by 1430 hours on the same day. D-Day for the operation was set for 24 August 1965.

Bakshi met the COs of the infantry battalions and the artillery regiment for the first time on 23 August at Uri, when he issued his orders for the operation. He had not met any of

them before, nor had he had a chance to see the officers and
men under their command. He was also unaware of the plan
of 93 Infantry Brigade, which was to link up with him from
the south. Undeterred by these handicaps, Bakshi went ahead
with his orders, during which he explained not only his plan,
but also his philosophy for the conduct of the attack. He stressed
the need for surprise, speed, flexibility, offensive action, and the
necessity for officers to lead from up front.

On 24 August, the Army Commander flew to HQ 25
Infantry Division, and was briefed on the plan for attack from
the south. He was surprised to learn that the scope of the
operation had been drastically reduced by 25 Infantry Division,
with the permission of the Corps Commander. He ordered that
the minimum strength to be employed for the attack should be
a battalion, and the objective should be as far towards Kahuta
as possible. He then flew to HQ 19 Infantry Division, where he
found things more to his liking. Bakshi was ready to undertake
the operation as planned, but recommended postponement by
a day, since there had been heavy rain throughout the day and
night, and all the nullahs (streams) along the right axis were
flooded. Bakshi had also decided to switch over 4 Rajput to the
left axis, i.e., Ring Contour–Pathra instead of the Sank–Ledwali
Gali approach. In the revised plan, there were two converging
arms of the pincer meeting at Hajipir pass. The left column,
comprising 4 Rajput and 19 Punjab, was to advance along Point
10048–Point 10944–Bedori–Kuthnar di Gali–Hajipir pass. The
right column, comprising 1 Para, was to advance along Uri–
Sank–Ledwali Gali–Hajipir pass.

The attack was launched on the night of 25 August. By 0130
hrs on 26 August, 19 Punjab had captured Pathra. However,
it could not proceed further to Bedori due to the rugged and
precipitous terrain and stiff resistance by the enemy, and fell
back to Pathra by first light. On the right axis, 1 Para launched
their attack on Sank as planned. Initially, the assaulting troops
lost their way due to lack of topographical information about the

feature. In a subsequent attempt the same night, they were held up by intense enemy fire and suffered about 30 casualties. The forward companies were pinned down, and had to be extricated the next morning with great difficulty. Bakshi was now in a dilemma, since the attacks on Bedori and Sank had both failed. He decided to attack Sank again, using 1 Para, and requested Divisional HQ to assign the task of capturing Bedori to 161 Infantry Brigade. To add to his worries, at about midday on 26 August, he received a 'personal for' message from the Army Commander, expressing dissatisfaction at the heavy expenditure of artillery ammunition, which 'was not commensurate with the results'. After the failure of his initial attacks, Bakshi knew that if he failed again, he was unlikely to remain in command for long. Hence it was all the more important that the enemy positions be softened up by a heavy barrage of artillery before the attack went in. If he succeeded, no one would hold the heavy ammunition expenditure against him. If he failed, he would be sacked in any case. He decided to disregard the signal, and go ahead with the attack as planned.

At about 1500 hrs on 26 August, Bakshi got a telephone call from the General Staff Officer Grade 1 (GSO 1) from Headquarters 19 Infantry Division, who informed him that Bedori had been captured by 161 Infantry Brigade. Bakshi was skeptical, since none of his troops had reported any movement or battle noises. When he expressed his doubts, the GSO 1 connected him to Commander 161 Infantry Brigade, who confirmed the news. Bakshi then decided to modify his plan, and asked 4 Rajput to resume the advance along the left axis and proceed to Kuthnar Di Gali, skirting around the western slopes of Bedori. The attack of 1 Para on Sank would go ahead as planned.

The attack by 1 Para on Sank went in at 2230 hrs after a heavy artillery barrage. To break up the assault, the enemy opened up with automatic weapons. The artillery forward observation officers accompanying the assaulting troops adjusted the artillery fire on the enemy, who had come out of his defences. In spite of heavy opposition, 1 Para continued its attack, and by first light on 27 August Sank had been captured. The enemy vacated the feature, leaving 15 dead and a large quantity of arms and ammunition. Keeping up the momentum, 1 Para continued to press on and by midday had secured Sar and Ledwali Gali.

While the capture of Sank raised the brigade's spirits, Bakshi was in for a shock on the Bedori approach. 4 Rajput came under fire from Bedori while going around its western slopes, and asked for artillery fire to neutralise the 'enemy fire'. Bakshi did not permit this, believing that Bedori was held by troops of 161 Infantry brigade. He spoke to the Divisional HQ and Commander 161 Infantry brigade, who again confirmed that Bedori had been captured. In the meantime, 4 Rajput was suffering casualties. Bakshi ordered them to fall back.

Bakshi now decided to exploit the success he had achieved on the Sank approach, and ignore the Bedori approach till the situation became clearer. Hajipir pass, being in depth, was not expected to be occupied by the enemy ab initio. However, the enemy had by now been alerted and would have started moving additional troops to reinforce the feature. Once it was reinforced, it would no longer be within the capability of a brigade to capture the pass. He decided to go for the pass directly, without waiting for Bedori to be cleared. Of course, this meant a frontal assault from the north, which would necessarily have to be under enemy observation and fire, and could result in heavy casualties. He knew that the men were physically and mentally exhausted, having spent two days on the move in rough terrain and abominable weather. The attack would succeed only if pressed home, and needed resolute leadership.

Bakshi spoke to Lieutenant Colonel Prabhjinder Singh, the Commanding Officer of 1 Para, and told him that he was looking for a suitable officer who could deliver the goods. Prabhjinder suggested the name of his Second-in-Command, Major (later Lieutenant General) Ranjit Singh Dayal. Dayal was summoned to the Brigade Headquarters, and Bakshi personally briefed him on the mission. He explained that Dayal would have to avoid the direct approach along the ridge from Ledwali Gali to the Western Knoll. Instead he would have to capture the knolls on either side of the pass from an unexpected direction. He was told to take an infantry company, with an additional platoon. An artillery officer would accompany him as the FOO. Another company of 1 Para was earmarked to reinforce Dayal as soon as he had captured the pass. At the end of the briefing, Bakshi told Dayal: 'If you succeed, the credit will go to you. If you don't, I will accept responsibility for the failure.'

While all this was going on, Bakshi received another call from the GSO 1 of 19 Infantry Division, who informed him that Bedori had not been captured, as reported earlier, but was still in enemy hands. Shortly afterwards, the Divisional Commander spoke to Bakshi, and told him that Bedori must be captured at the earliest, and had priority even over Hajipir pass. Bakshi was flabbergasted and protested strongly, saying that the diversion of troops from the Sank axis to Bedori would take time. More importantly, any delay in the capture of Haji Pir would give the enemy time to occupy and strengthen the defences at the pass. But the Divisional Commander would have none of it. The earlier news of Bedori's capture had been announced on All India Radio on 26 August, and its immediate capture was therefore essential to avoid embarrassment.

Bakshi was forced to modify his plans again. However, he decided to make no change in the plan for the capture of Hajipir. The problem was finding troops for the capture of Bedori. At this stage, Lieutenant Colonel Sampuran Singh, the Commanding Officer of 19 Punjab, volunteered to capture Bedori using the subsidiary axis Kaunrali–Burji–Bedori Spring–Bedori. Bakshi readily granted permission, and instructed 4 Rajput to maintain pressure on the enemy from the north and north-west to divert their attention when the attack went in on the night of 28/29 August.

Major Ranjit Singh Dayal left with his column at last light on 27 August. He was accompanied by Captain Vaswani as his secondin-command, and Second-Lieutenant JS Talwar of 164 Field Regiment as the FOO. As the company was descending from Ledwali Gali into the Haidarabad nullah, it came under machinegun and mortar fire from the western shoulder of the pass, which overlooked the nullah. But this was more of a nuisance than a threat. Soon the column came under fire from a different direction. A party of Pathans withdrawing from Sawan Pathri had seen the force, and concluding that they were being encircled, had opened fire. Dayal despatched a platoon to deal with the Pathans, and asking them to join up with him later, continued the advance. In case it was delayed, the platoon was told to join the battalion at Ledwali Gali. Dayal also ordered the FOO to register the eastern and western shoulders of the pass, which dominated the surrounding area.

After registration had been completed, the company moved along the left bank of the Haidarabad nullah, hugging the hillside. By about 1800 hrs it had started to rain, and the valley was covered with low clouds and mist. This made movement difficult, but it also concealed their movement, and the enemy lost touch with the company till the morning. Crossing the nullah, the column began to climb, avoiding the track. At about 2000 hrs, they reached a house which appeared to be occupied. Resting there for the night were 10 Pakistani soldiers who had fallen back from Bedori. After they were disarmed, they were pressed into service for carrying loads. Soaked to the skin and utterly exhausted, the men kept on moving throughout the night, weighed down by heavy loads. Dayal knew that soon it would be first light, and he had to reach the pass before that happened. He kept up the pace and did not allow the men to rest, except after crossing a difficult stretch, when they were halted and counted before resuming advance. Dayal had taken the precaution of hiring a local porter as a guide, who led them to the pass without losing his way even once.

At about 0430 hrs on 28 August, when the company hit the old Uri–Punch road, Dayal decided to give the men a much-needed break. After a few hours of rest, the advance was resumed at 0700 hrs. When they had advanced for about an hour, the leading platoon negotiated a turn and came under intense machine-gun fire from the western shoulder of the pass. The area was open, and the objective was almost 1,200 yards away. Leaving the leading platoon and the forward observation officer to keep the enemy engaged from the front, Dayal took the balance of the company to the right and began climbing up the western shoulder of the pass. On reaching the top, they rolled down, completely surprising the Pakistani soldiers, who took to their heels without offering any resistance. By 1100 hrs on 28 August, Hajipir pass had been captured. Twelve Pakistanis, including one officer, were taken prisoner. There was not a single Indian casualty.

After the capture of Hajipir, Bakshi turned his attention to the capture of Bedori, which was to be attempted by 19 Punjab. Bedori is a rocky feature, where it was difficult to dig trenches. The enemy had constructed stone 'sangars' to improve their defences, on the pattern used in the North West Frontier. During the frontier campaigns, mountain guns had proved very effective in direct shooting at such defences. Bakshi decided to use similar tactics, and ordered one 3.7-inch howitzer to be deployed forward for the destruction of sangars on Bedori by direct shooting. While 19 Punjab was getting ready for the attack, the howitzer picked up one sangar after the other, and before last light on 28 August, had knocked down most of them. The attack was launched during the night, and Bedori pass was captured in the early hours of 29 August. The position was occupied by two companies of the enemy, supported by five medium machine-guns. However, the Pakistanis were so shaken by the ferocity of the assault by 19 Punjab that they did not launch a counter-attack, and left behind a large quantity of arms and ammunition.

After the loss of Hajipir, the enemy began to bring up fresh troops on to Ring Contour, a feature about 1,500 yards south–west of the pass. When Bakshi got wind of this on 29 August, he ordered 1 Para to dislodge the enemy before it could build up in larger numbers and launch a counter-attack. The same night, a platoon patrol was sent up from 'D' company that had joined 'A' company on the pass. However, the platoon found the task beyond its capacity. Dayal then set off himself, at about 0730 hrs, with a platoon of 'D' company and Major A.S. Baicher, the company commander. He told the remainder of 'D' company and a platoon of 'A' company to follow, along with the FOO.

The assault involved a descent of about 1,000 and then an ascent to the same height. It was now broad daylight, and when the enemy saw the assaulting troops, they reacted violently and opened fire with all weapons, including artillery. As the platoon was climbing the last 100 feet the firing intensified. The platoon was composed entirely of 'Ahirs' (a sub-caste of Hindus found in North India, especially in the region around Delhi. They are simple and hardy folk, mostly engaged in agriculture and dairying, who worship Krishna). Suddenly, the Ahirs raised their battlecry—*Krishan Maharaj ki Jai* (Glory to Lord Krishna)—and then charged. Hand-to-hand fighting followed, in which nine men were killed and 26 wounded, including the platoon commander. The enemy lost eight men, and the rest ran away. During the next three hours, the enemy launched three counter-attacks, all of which were beaten back. Major Baicher was wounded in the leg, and Major Dayal had a narrow escape—a machine-gun burst shot off the sten gun slung on his left shoulder. By 1600 hrs on 30 August the enemy had given up, and the feature was firmly in Indian hands. Soon afterwards, 19 Punjab linked up with 1 Para, and the entire area between Bedori, Ledwali Gali and Hajipir pass was free of the enemy. On 1 September, Bakshi moved his tactical HQ to Hajipir pass.

The battle of Hajipir pass is a saga of courage, determined leadership and valour. Its capture was an important victory for

India, and a big blow for Pakistan. The credit for the success went to Dayal, who had led his men resolutely, and to Bakshi, who had not only conceived the bold plan, fraught with risk, but had executed it brilliantly. Had the attack failed, there is little doubt that he would have been held responsible, since he had gone ahead with it without permission from the higher authorities. He had taken a grave risk, but it had paid off. In battle, a commander must be prepared to take risks, and Bakshi proved this quite conclusively. He was awarded the Maha Vir Chakra (MVC), the country's second highest gallantry award. Having already won the Vir Chakra earlier, he became the only Indian to have won both the awards. Major Ranjit Singh Dayal was also awarded the MVC for his courage and gallantry in capturing the Hajipir pass. Incidentally, the Muslim porter who had guided Dayal to the pass continued to work for the Indian Army for several decades as a mate (supervisor) in the Labour Procurement Organisation, which provides porters and ponies to carry stores for troops operating in difficult areas in Jammu and Kashmir.

After the capture of Hajipir pass, 68 Infantry Brigade expected to get some time off, but this was not to be. On 2 September, the divisional commander ordered Bakshi to capture Bisali (Point 11229), which was the highest feature on the western side of the road joining Uri and Hajipir. However, it had little tactical significance, and Bakshi requested that he be permitted to press on to Kahuta. His request was denied and he was told to capture Bisali first. 6 Dogra had relieved 1 Para at Hajipir pass on 3 September, and was now available for further operations. The CO of 4 Rajput, Lieutenant Colonel Sudershan Singh, requested that the task of capturing Bisali be assigned to him, since the other two battalions, 1 Para and 19 Punjab, had already had their share of glory during the Hajipir battle. This was accepted by Bakshi, who also gave 4 Rajput two additional companies from 6 Jammu and Kashmir Rifles. 1 Para was to be used in phase two of the brigade attack.

4 Rajput launched the attack on Bisali at 2200 hours on 4 September, with artillery support. At about 0330 hrs on 5 September, the Commanding Officer reported that he had captured the objective and phase two could be cancelled. The assaulting troops were exhausted, and having captured the objective, flopped down for a well-earned rest. But the FOO with the leading company realised that what they had captured was not the top of the feature, and expressed his doubts to the company commander, who had been his batchmate at the Academy. The latter's response, accompanied by a choice expletive, was to advise the FOO not be afraid and go to sleep. When dawn broke, the enemy began firing from the top, and then counter-attacked. 4 Rajput withdrew in disorder, leaving behind a large quantity of weapons. The casualties were substantial—two officers and 63 other ranks killed, and four officers and 47 other ranks wounded.

Soon afterwards, the divisional commander visited 68 Infantry Brigade and discussed the plan for the link-up with 93 Infantry Brigade, which was undertaking an offensive from Punch towards Kahuta. Bakshi was ordered to advance southwards towards Kahuta. Once again, there was a disagreement, since Bakshi would have preferred to operate along the eastern ridge of Kuthnar–Ziarat, while the divisional commander ordered an advance along the western side. 1 Para was tasked to capture Ring Contour south of Point 8786 in phase one, while 19 Punjab was to capture Point 8777 in phase two. Both attacks failed.

Bakshi then decided to switch to the eastern approach, which he had in any case preferred. On 8 September he ordered 1 Para to relieve 6 Dogra. The revised plan was to capture Point 9270 with 19 Punjab and Point 7720 with 6 Dogra. Both attacks were successful, and operations continued further south. On 9 September, 19 Punjab secured Ziarat, while 6 Dogra captured Halan Zanubi the next day. On 10 September, Major Megh Singh, with a platoon of commandos from Punch, made contact with 19 Punjab at Ziarat. Kahuta, an important town north of Punch, was captured on 11 September, and this opened the road link between Uri and Punch, which had not been in use since 1947. However, the enemy was still holding strong positions around Gitian, from where they could interfere with the movement on the Uri–Punch road. On 15 September, the enemy attacked 19 Punjab positions between Kahuta and Gitian three times without success. On 18 September, Bakshi ordered 6 Dogra to capture enemy positions south of Gitian, consisting of Left Knoll, Tree Hill and Hut Hill. It was to be a silent attack with a prearranged fire plan on call. 6 Dogra was to attack Tree Hill and Hut Hill, while one company each from 1 Para and 19 Punjab were to divert the enemy's attention by simulating attacks on Ring Contour and Point 8777 respectively.

On the night of 20/21 September, 6 Dogra launched their attack and the forward companies managed to capture their objectives. But the enemy brought down effective artillery fire, causing some disorganisation, and Bakshi ordered a company of 19 Punjab to pitch in. This was one of the most expensive battles of the campaign, with three officers losing their lives—Major Lalli of 6 Dogra, Major Ranbir of 19 Punjab, and the artillery FOO from 164 Field Regiment. In addition, one JCO and 32 OR were also killed. The list of wounded included five officers, three JCOs and 80 OR.

By this time, Pakistan had launched a full-scale attack, code-named GRAND SLAM, in the Chhamb-Akhnur sector, and the conflict between India and Pakistan had escalated into a full-scale war. The focus shifted to the plains of the Punjab, where the decisive battles of the 1965 war were fought. On 23 September, a ceasefire was declared after a resolution in the UN Security Council, and hostilities came to an end. As a result of the agreement signed in Tashkent between President Ayub Khan of Pakistan and Prime Minister Lal Bahadur Shastri of India, troops of both countries had to withdraw to positions held by them before 5 August 1965. For the second time, Hajipir pass, captured at great cost, was returned to Pakistan.

In March 1967, Bakshi was posted as Brigadier General Staff, HQ Eastern Command, in Calcutta. Lieutenant General Sam Manekshaw was the Army Commander, and he found Bakshi to be a pragmatic, efficient and competent staff officer. At that time, Eastern Command was engaged in building up defences in the Northeast, which had become the Indian Army's top priority after the debacle of 1962. The situation in the Naga and Mizo Hills had also begun to deteriorate, and this too required deft handling. Bakshi did not stay in Eastern Command for very long. In December 1967, he was selected to do the course at the Imperial Defence College, London. This was a prestigious course, on which only highly rated officers of the rank of brigadier were sent. He stayed in London for a year and qualified on the course with distinction. The Imperial Defence College has now been renamed the Royal College of Defence Studies, and one Indian officer is still nominated on the course, even though India now has its own institution of the same level, called the National Defence College, in Delhi.

On his return from England in February 1969, Bakshi was posted to the Military Training Directorate at Army Headquarters. In June 1969, he was promoted Major General and appointed GOC 8 Mountain Division in Nagaland, where insurgency had become a serious problem. His previous experience in Eastern Command, as well as the fact that Sam Manekshaw was still the Army Commander, probably played a part in his appointment. Soon after the announcement of his appointment as COAS, Sam came to Nagaland on a farewell visit. He told Bakshi, perhaps in a lighter vein, that Brigadier (later Lieutenant General) S.K. Sinha, who was commanding 71 Brigade, had reached his limit, and had not acquitted himself well as a brigade commander. He hoped that Bakshi would duly reflect this in Sinha's Annual Confidential Report. Bakshi replied that on the basis of performance, he considered Sinha to be the best brigade commander among the six he had in his division. As the reviewing officer, Manekshaw could always disagree with Bakshi's assessment and write whatever he liked in Sinha's report. Manekshaw smiled and said that Bakshi was showing his regimental loyalty, since he and Sinha were from the same regiment. Bakshi replied that it was not a question of loyalty but of conscience. Sam was soon to take over as the Army Chief, but this did not deter Bakshi from expressing his views, even though he knew that they were contrary to those of the Chief designate. Fortunately, Sam admired men who had the courage to speak their minds, and did not take it amiss.

Bakshi was a strict disciplinarian and ensured that the troops maintained the highest standards of behaviour, especially with the local population. He also did not believe in the adage that the end justifies the means, and had given strict orders that atrocities would not be tolerated, even against insurgents. There was an incident in a battalion that was part of Sinha's brigade, involving the death of two Nagas in custody, during interrogation. Initially, the battalion denied the allegations, and the Brigade HQ supported them. But Bakshi was not convinced and ordered an independent inquiry by one of the other brigade commanders. He had been an instructor at the Academy when the CO of the battalion was a cadet, and he was soon able to get the truth out of him. One of the company commanders, in a bid to impress his CO and notch up a high score in captured weapons, had picked up the two Nagas, who were suspected to be hostiles. Based on the advice of a JCO, who claimed to have supernatural powers, he had tortured them to elicit information about hidden weapons. In the process, the two suspects died and their bodies were disposed of.

When the truth came out, Bakshi was very upset and conveyed his displeasure to Sinha, who had been badly let down by one of his battalions. He told Sinha that he was about to put him up for the award of an AVSM, but could no longer do so after this incident. He had the battalion commander removed from command and demoted to the rank of major. The two officers who were directly involved were courtmartialled and sentenced to be dismissed from service and undergo varying terms of imprisonment. The JCO was also dismissed from service.

In September 1970, Bakshi was posted as GOC 26 Infantry Division, which was responsible for the defence of Jammu. In 1971, operations against Pakistan became imminent, after it was realised that the problem of refugees from East Pakistan could not be solved by other means. Since the primary aim of the operations was the liberation of Bangladesh, the government had decided that only a defensive posture would be maintained in the west. However, limited offensive operations were planned with the intention of drawing out Pakistani reserves, so that they could not be used for major offensives against India. Lieutenant General K.P. Candeth, General Officer Commanding-in-Chief, Western Command, had accordingly planned an advance by 1 Corps in the Shakargarh bulge, and a two-pronged offensive by 15 Corps, with 10 Infantry Division advancing north of the river Chenab, and 26 Infantry Division advancing south of the river, to threaten Sialkot. Pakistan's 15 Infantry Division, under Major General Abid Ali Zahid, was holding defences in the Sialkot sector. To its rear, Pakistan's strongest strike formation, 1 Corps, had its headquarters at Sialkot. Considering the importance of the task assigned to 26 Infantry Division, Zoru Bakshi had been selected by Sam Manekshaw to command the division.

The operations commenced on 3 December 1971 after air-strikes by Pakistan, and orders were issued for the planned advances by Indian troops to commence. However, due to the Pakistani offensive in Chhamb, 10 Infantry Division had to fall back and could not undertake any offensive action. A brigade of 26 Infantry Division was sent to 39 Infantry Division to make up the loss of 33 Infantry Brigade, which had been despatched to Punch to counter the Pakistani offensive in that sector. This resulted in the cancellation of the all-important offensive of 26 Infantry Division towards Sialkot. However, Bakshi was not deterred by this setback and proceeded to capture Chicken's Neck, an important gain of the 1971 operations, which compensated to some extent the loss of Chhamb by 10 Infantry Division.

The name 'Chicken's Neck' was coined by Zoru Bakshi. To the South of Akhnur, there is a narrow strip of territory that belongs to Pakistan and measures about 170 square kilometres in area. It is actually an islet between the river Chenab and Chander Bagha, one of its subsidiary channels. It has a small neck in the south, and a jagged head, with a beak shaped like a dagger extending towards the north. The beak points towards the Akhnur bridge, and because of its shape and the threat it posed to Akhnur, the area had long been known as 'the dagger'. Bakshi felt that the name indicated a defensive mentality and promptly informed everyone that henceforth it would be called the 'Chicken's Neck', which could be wrung at will by India. It is known by this name even today.

The Chicken's Neck, referred to as the Phuklian salient by the Pakistanis, was strategically important for Pakistan as it provided the shortest route to the bridge over the Chenab at Akhnur. It enabled operations to be developed towards Jammu, and also uncovered the flanks of troops deployed in the Jaurian sector. It was used by them for infiltration into Indian territory from their base at Marala, which lay to the south of the salient. To enter the salient, they had to cross the Chenab, using ferries. Intelligence reports indicated that the area was held by four companies of Rangers, supported by a regular battalion and some armour. Protective minefields had been laid around the defended localities. Except during the monsoon, the area was dry, and could be negotiated by tanks and motor vehicles.

Bakshi's main task was to defend Jammu, and almost his entire division was deployed in a defensive posture. He had been allotted an armoured brigade and an additional infantry brigade for the operation. Though his role was defensive, Bakshi had to undertake the advance towards Sialkot, as part of the limited offensive planned by 15 Corps. As soon as operations commenced, Bakshi had planned to carry out certain preliminary operations to facilitate his task. In order to remove the Pakistani threat to the Akhnur bridge, he decided to capture Chicken's Neck. This would release the troops employed in the close defence of the bridge, which he could then utilise for the advance towards Sialkot. It was essential that this be done swiftly, immediately after hostilities broke out.

Since the Pakistani defences were oriented towards the north and north-east, Bakshi decided to infiltrate the salient from the south, from where the enemy least expected an attack. This would achieve surprise, cut off the enemy's route of withdrawal and demoralise him even before his main defences were contacted. He tasked 19 Infantry Brigade, commanded by Brigadier Mohinder Singh, to carry out the operation, for which he was given 9 Para Commando and some armour as support. He decided not to use the bulk of the armour, since he realised that it would take several days to ferry the tanks across the river, and once in the salient, it would be extremely difficult to retrieve them for the subsequent advance towards Sialkot, which was his main task.

19 Infantry Brigade commenced infiltration on the evening of 5 December 1971. The operation achieved complete surprise, and the leading battalion found well-prepared defences, which were not occupied as they had been vacated by the Pakistanis. In spite of this, the leading troops made slow progress, since they insisted on following set-piece battle drills, losing precious time. The situation called for bold and audacious action, but the commanders were overcautious and refused to exploit the factors of surprise and demoralisation of the enemy. The motor vehicles of the follow-up battalion kept getting bogged down in the soft sand of the rivulets and streams that they had to cross, and this further slowed down their pace.

Bakshi arranged to set up roadblocks, using his tanks and the para commandos. However, most of the enemy was able to withdraw before the roadblocks were in place. In one case, some armour that had been inducted into the salient to hasten its clearance, clashed with the roadblock armour, which mistook them for withdrawing Pakistani tanks. Timely intervention by the Brigade HQ staff averted what could have been a disaster. The para commando roadblock at one of the ferries was attacked by a large body of withdrawing Pakistani troops, and had to be rescued by tank-mounted infantry which was rushed to their aid. By the evening of 7 December, the salient was cleared of the enemy and Chicken's Neck had been captured. Enemy casualties were 32 killed, four wounded, and 28 captured, including two officers. Leaving a battalion to hold the salient, Bakshi withdrew the remainder of the brigade for other tasks.

The capture of Chicken's Neck within 48 hours did a lot to raise the morale of the Indian forces in the sector. The operation was brilliantly conceived, and had it been pursued with greater vigour by the leading elements a large number of prisoners would have been captured. In an operation reminiscent of the capture of Hajipir pass in 1965, Zoru Bakshi had once again proved that in war, it is not numerical superiority but daring and audacity which bring success. After the capture of Chicken's Neck, 26 Infantry Division had little to do and had to content itself with small raids on border outposts opposite its area. It was unfortunate that higher commanders found no use for the gallant commander or the troops of 26 Infantry Division, which had been relieved after the operation, for the rest of the war. Since Bakshi had already won both the MVC and the VrC earlier, he was awarded the Param Vishisht Seva Medal (PVSM), for this operation. This made him the most highly decorated soldier in the army, who had won awards at every level, from company to division.

After completing his tenure in 26 Infantry Division, in October 1973, Zoru was appointed the Director of Military Operations (DMO), at Army Headquarters. He remained for a year in this important appointment, which carries a lot of respect and authority. In September 1974, he was promoted Lieutenant General and appointed the Military Secretary, at

Army Headquarters. He was now responsible for the promotions and transfers of all officers of the army. Bakshi performed this job with credit, and was known for being fair and impartial.

In May 1975, Bakshi was given command of the Strike Corps, which is perhaps the most coveted assignment for a lieutenant general. He replaced Lieutenant General T.N. Raina, who moved on promotion as Western Army Commander, and later became the Army Chief. Bakshi remained in command of 2 Corps for more than three-and-a-half years, till he retired on 31 January 1979. He thus had the longest tenure as a Corps Commander in the Indian Army. Though he had all the qualifications to become Army Commander, the rules stipulated that only Lieutenant Generals who had at least two years residual service could be given this appointment. Age was against Bakshi, and he had to retire as a Corps Commander. If he had been younger, there is little doubt that he would have become not only an Army Commander, but probably the Army Chief as well.

After retirement, Bakshi did not take up a job in either the private or public sector. With his drive and determination, he was ideally suited for a challenging assignment, such as breathing new life into a sick public sector undertaking. Had he been given such a job, there is no doubt that he would have done it well, as Prem Bhagat did in the Damodar Valley Corporation. But because of his modest and unassuming nature, he was not very well known outside the army, and perhaps this is why his services were not in demand. However, he continued to take keen interest in the profession of arms, and was a regular visitor to the United Service Institution of India in Delhi.

Zoru Bakshi is one of the most well-known generals of the Indian Army. A highly decorated soldier, he possesses all the qualities one would expect in a successful military leader. A thorough professional, he epitomises the classic image of an officer and a gentleman. In battle, he displayed, time and again, his brilliance as a strategist and a tactician. In all the operations he undertook, he tasted defeat not once, nor did he lose an inch of territory to the enemy. This is a unique record, unequalled by any other Indian military leader except Lieutenant General Sagat Singh. His courage on the battlefield was matched by his sense of fair play, upright behaviour, morality and the courage to stand by his convictions and his subordinates. Zoru Bakshi is a true son of the soil, who defended the honour of his motherland and of his command, always and every time.

Lieutenant General S.K. Sinha, PVSM

11

Lieutenant General S.K. Sinha, PVSM

The Solider–Statesman

S.K. Sinha is unique among our military leaders, in that while he was well known in the army during his service, most of his countrymen came to know of him only after his retirement. He had all the credentials to reach the top, but missed doing so by a hair's breadth. In 1983, as the Vice Chief of Army Staff, he resigned when his junior A.S. Vaidya was appointed the Army Chief, leading to an uproar in Parliament and the press. Though his career ended in a blaze of controversy, Sinha had always avoided discord, preferring to live by the book. He was known as an upright soldier who did his job without fear or favour. He did not win any battles or gallantry awards, but his achievements, insofar as they affected the Indian Army, are not small. Few will forget his contribution to the wellbeing of the soldier by improving his living conditions, salary and allowances. His forceful arguments before the Pay Commission in 1971 are still remembered, and became a model for subsequent presentations by the armed forces. His contribution to military history is also considerable. He is a prolific writer, and his books and articles on military matters have earned him esteem and recognition from soldiers as well as civilians. He was also a successful diplomat, and was responsible for improving relations between India and Nepal while he was the Indian Ambassador in Kathmandu.

S.K. Sinha was born on 7 January 1926 at Gaya in Bihar, in the home of his mother's parents. His father, M.K. Sinha, who was in the police, rose to the rank of Inspector General of Police (IGP) of Bihar State, an office he held for 11 years, from 1949 to 1960.

M.K. Sinha's father, A.K. Sinha, had also been IGP of Bihar, and the first Indian to reach the top police appointment. Sinha lost his mother when he was just four years old, and spent most of his childhood with his grandparents. He began his schooling at St. Joseph's Convent, in Patna, and later moved to the Patna Collegiate School, where his father and grandfather had both studied.

Sinha matriculated in 1939, and joined Patna College, from where he graduated in 1943. By this time, World War II had been going on for four years. At college, Sinha had joined the University Training Corps, which put him in contact with several British officers. The nationalist movement was also at its height, and students in Bihar were actively involved, thanks to leaders like Jayaprakash Narain and Rajendra Prasad. Two of his uncles were already in the army, serving in Burma and North Africa, and Sinha decided to follow in their footsteps. The Indian Military Academy had been established in 1932, and Indians were being granted regular commissions since 1934. However, the grant of regular commissions was suspended in 1939, when World War II began, and emergency commissions began to be given after a short period of training at one of the four training institutes located at Dehradun, Bangalore, Mhow and Belgaum. Sinha applied, and after being screened by the provincial board, was asked to appear before the final selection board at Dehradun. He was among the 12 selected from a group of 60 candidates. He was then 18 years old.

Sinha joined the Officers' Training School in Belgaum in March 1944. Arun Vaidya was also in the same batch, but left after a few months to join the Armoured Corps Training School at Ahmednagar. He was commissioned two months after Sinha, and thus became his junior. Almost 40 years later, when Vaidya was appointed COAS superseding Sinha, the latter resigned. Even if Vaidya had continued at Belgaum, Sinha would have been his senior as he passed out at the top of his batch, earning the Commandant's Baton, which was the wartime equivalent of the Sword of Honour. On 10 December 1944, Sinha was granted an emergency commission in the Infantry, and posted to the Jat Regiment.

Sinha joined the Jat Regimental Centre at Bareilly, where he stayed for six weeks before being sent to 7/9 Jat Regiment, which was part of a jungle training division located at Saharanpur. After three months of intensive training in jungle warfare, he was posted to 6/9 Jat in Burma. Travelling to Calcutta by train, he embarked on a troopship which took him to Rangoon. There he was told that his battalion, which had been part of 17 Indian Division, had been sent back to India, but would be returning to Burma after a few weeks. Meanwhile, he was told to take a newly arrived draft to 17 Division, which was somewhere north of Pegu. Since most of the men were to go to 4/12 Frontier Force, he decided to stay on with them till his own battalion fetched up.

After spending a fortnight with 4/12 Frontier Force, which was engaged in intercepting the retreating Japanese across the Salween, Sinha returned to Rangoon. His battalion, 6/9 Jat, arrived after a few days and was moved to Prome as part of the Lushai Brigade. In August 1945, after the US atomic bombing, Japan surrendered and World War II officially came to an end. A large number of Japanese were taken prisoner and kept in POW camps. Part of Sinha's battalion was given the task of guarding one such camp, which held about 10,000 prisoners, and he was appointed the Adjutant. After two months, when the POW camp was wound up, Sinha was promoted Captain and posted as GSO 3 in the Brigade HQ.

In March 1946, the brigade was ordered to return to India. However, Sinha had to appear before a Services Selection Board at Singapore, which was screening officers granted emergency commissions during the war for grant of permanent commissions. Sinha was one of the 450 selected from 13,000 such officers. He now received orders posting him as GSO 3 (Operations) to HQ 15 Indian Corps, which was then in Batavia (now called Jakarta), the capital of Indonesia. A few months later, Indian troops were replaced by Dutch troops, and Sinha was posted to the Military Operations Directorate at GHQ in Delhi. Yahya Khan, who later became President of Pakistan, and Sam Manekshaw were also posted to MO, which had hitherto been the exclusive preserve of British officers.

Sinha was posted to MO 2, the section that dealt with internal security. He was soon up to his ears in work due to the communal riots that had flared up at several places after the carnage in Calcutta in August 1946. On 3 June 1947, the date for Partition was announced as 15 August, and work became even more hectic as the day drew nearer. Army HQ India was created and moved to Red Fort, while GHQ remained in South Block. Sinha was sent to Simla, along with another officer who was to go to Pakistan, to divide the old records. As the task had to be completed within a week, a large amount of material that could not be clearly identified as pertaining to either of the two countries was destroyed. A few days before the actual date of Partition, a party was held at the Imperial Gymkhana Club to bid farewell to British and Pakistani officers leaving India. It was an emotional parting, and some officers wept openly.

On 15 August 1947, British rule ended and India became a free nation. There was widespread jubilation, even though the holocaust of Partition continued for some time. Thousands of refugees from India and the newly-born nation of Pakistan poured into each other's territory to escape the wanton carnage that was sweeping across the land like a raging fire. To establish law and order and control the flow of refugees, a neutral force, called the Punjab Boundary Force, was set up under the control of the Supreme HQ. However, this was found to be ineffective and was soon wound up, with both nations being asked to look after law and order in their respective dominions. In India, a new Command, designated the Delhi and East Punjab (DEP) Command, was set up with its HQ in Delhi, under Lieutenant General Sir Dudley Russell, commonly known as Russell Pasha. In September 1947, Sinha was promoted Major, and posted as GSO 2 (Operations), HQ DEP Command.

Besides maintaining law and order in Delhi and East Punjab, DEP Command was also tasked with organising the evacuation of refugees from both sides. This was mostly done in refugee trains, which had to be suitably escorted to protect the refugees from being attacked en route. Russel Pasha decided to establish a mobile HQ, for which he was allowed the use of the Viceregal train, and he spent several weeks in it, moving between Delhi and Lahore to supervise the evacuation. As a result, several hundred thousand refugees were evacuated without mishap. The bloodbath that had occurred before DEP command was set up could not be undone, but it proved effective in preventing further loss of lives.

On 26 October 1947, Sinha attended what he was later to recall as the most momentous meeting of his career. He was at the club when, at about 9 pm, a staff car was sent to fetch him to the office. When he reached there, he found himself in the midst of a high-level meeting being chaired by the Army Commander. Pakistani raiders had entered Kashmir, and were advancing on Srinagar even as they spoke. It had been decided to send Indian troops into the valley to defend Srinagar. A brigade was to be sent by air, and another to follow by road. The airlift was to commence next morning, and 1 Sikh, located at Gurgaon, was to be moved first. Sinha was given the task of organising the airlift.

Considering the time and resources available, the task appeared almost impossible. The IAF could muster up only two Dakotas, and the remaining had to be requisitioned from private airlines. Sinha's first task was to warn the troops, and emergency signals were sent to 1 Sikh at Gurgaon and 50 Parachute Brigade at Gurdaspur, which was to move by road. Only two companies of 1 Sikh were then in Gurgaon, the rest being deployed elsewhere. The CO, Lieutenant Colonel Dewan Ranjit Rai, was asked to concentrate with his battalion, less two companies, at Palam airfield by 4 a.m. on 27 October 1947, with the rest following on the subsequent day. He was to be briefed about his task, and the battalion issued with rations, ammunition and warm clothing at the airfield before emplaning.

Sinha spent the next few hours writing out orders and issuing instructions for the move of ammunition and stores. He reached the airfield soon after midnight and when Rai arrived at the airfield at about 3 am, he found that Sinha had not only been able to collect the aircraft and stores, but had also arranged for a hot cup of tea for his troops. He went through the operational instructions that Sinha handed over to him, and after issuing orders to his sub-unit commanders, decided to have a short nap until they took off. Given the circumstances, Sinha could not help but admire his composure.

Since only seven Dakotas were available on the first day, they were to do two sorties each to airlift the battalion less two companies. At dawn, the first sortie took off, landing in Srinagar a few hours later. As it happened, this was none too soon, and Kashmir would have been lost if 1 Sikh had not landed in Srinagar on 27 October 1947. The raiders were then sacking Baramulla, and would have reached Srinagar the next day. After landing, Ranjit Rai left a company at the airfield and rushed towards Baramulla with the remainder of his force. He was able to intercept and delay the raiders, so that reinforcements could be flown in. Within the next few days, a brigade was airlifted, and the threat to Srinagar was averted. Rai did not live to see the fruits of his efforts. On 28 October, while withdrawing from Baramulla to Pattan under enemy pressure, he was hit by automatic fire and lost his life. He was posthumously awarded the MVC for his gallantry.

Within three days, the whole of 161 Brigade, under Brigadier J.C. Katoch, had been inducted into Kashmir, with 30 Dakotas doing 60 sorties each day. On 30 October, Brigadier Katoch was wounded by a sniper's bullet and had to be evacuated to Delhi. The situation seemed to have stabilised, but it was not very clear. Since there was a ban on British officers going to Kashmir, Sinha, who was then the only Indian officer on the Command staff, was deputed by Russell to bring a first-hand account of the situation. On 31 October, Sinha flew to Srinagar, and was given a detailed briefing at the Brigade HQ by Major Dilbagh Singh, the Brigade Major. After visiting 1 Sikh at Pattan and 4 Kumaon at Srinagar, he returned to Delhi to update the Army Commander on the situation. He also briefed Colonel L.P. 'Bogey' Sen, who was to move on promotion the next day as Commander 161 Brigade.

As the situation in Jammu and Kashmir worsened, it became difficult for the Army Commander, Russell Pasha, to exercise control over the operations from Delhi. After the fall of Mirpur and Rajauri, he decided to go to Jammu despite the ban on British officers visiting Jammu and Kashmir.* The British High Commissioner protested, Russell resigned, and on 20 January 1948, was replaced by K.M. Cariappa, who was then the senior Indian officer in the army. Sinha continued as the GSO 2 (Ops) and served under Cariappa for a year, until the latter became C-in-C in January 1949. Cariappa was a human dynamo, and Sinha found him to be a staff officer's nightmare. He was full of energy and was constantly rattling off instructions to his staff, with which they found it difficult to keep pace. He would spend at least 15 days in a month touring the forward areas, and Sinha invariably accompanied him on these visits. Since the General's ADC was left behind to look after Cariappa's household, including his two children, Sinha had to take on his responsibilities as well.

---

* After Independence, British officers were serving in the armies of India and Pakistan. At the behest of the British government, this ban was imposed, to obviate the possibility of British officers fighting each other in the J&K operations.

Sinha accompanied Cariappa on the memorable trip to Naushera, where the Army Commander asked Brigadier Mohd Usman for a present: the capture of Kot. It was also during this visit that Cariappa addressed the troops and made his famous speech about the country having become *muft* (free). As part of Cariappa's staff, Sinha was deeply involved with all facets of the operations in Jammu and Kashmir, and was a witness to many historical events. In June 1948, he had the opportunity to fly to Leh in a Dakota very soon after Thimayya and Mehar Singh made the first historic landing at the highest airfield in the world. He was again with Cariappa on 3 September 1948, when the first attack on Zojila was launched, albeit unsuccessfully. Sinha was also present at the historic meeting in Srinagar, where the crucial decision to use tanks at Zojila was taken. In fact, it was his suggestion to use tracked weapon carriers with improvised superstructures to carry the infantry accompanying the tanks.

During the attack on Zojila, Cariappa sent Sinha from Baltal to Matayan, a trek of some 12 miles in the mountains, to get an update about the latest situation from the brigade commander, Brigadier K.L. Atal. On his way back, Sinha decided to take a shortcut and got lost. He soon found himself in the middle of the attack that had commenced on Batkundi. He quickly destroyed the secret papers he was carrying, and had to march at night for many hours in heavy snow before he reached an Indian post at Gumri. He was lucky that he did not get frostbitten, and even more fortunate to escape capture by the enemy.

On New Year's day in 1949, a ceasefire came into effect and all hostilities in Kashmir ceased. Fifteen days later, Cariappa was promoted General and appointed the C-in-C of the Indian Army. Cariappa offered to take Sinha as his military assistant, an appointment, which carried considerable authority and perks. However, when the Military Secretary told him that the appointment was for the rank of a lieutenant colonel, and as per the rules no officer with less than six years' service could officiate as one (Sinha had less than five), Cariappa changed his mind. He did not want to bend rules. (Today, the appointment is held by a brigadier, an indication of the devaluation of ranks and responsibility in the army.)

Soon afterwards, a high-level delegation, headed by Lieutenant General S.M. Shrinagesh, who succeeded Cariappa as GOC-in-C Western Command, was sent to Karachi for a conference convened by the United Nations to delineate the Cease Fire Line. The secretaries in the Department of Kashmir Affairs and in the Ministry of Defence were members of the delegation, which also included Major General K.S. Thimayya and Brigadier S.H.F.J. Manekshaw.

Sinha was appointed secretary of the delegation—even though he was only a major—because of his knowledge of and familiarity with the operations in Kashmir. After a briefing by Prime Minister Jawaharlal Nehru, the delegation left for Karachi, where an entire week was spent delineating almost 400 miles of the border in the presence of UN representatives. Ultimately, an agreement was signed that gave India about 600 square miles of additional territory, including the Lolab and Tilel valleys in Kashmir. However, Ledigalli and Pirkanthi were awarded to Pakistan. India's claims to these features were not upheld because on 1 January 1949, the day the ceasefire came into effect, Indian troops had withdrawn from these two features and Pakistani patrols had occupied them.

In June 1949, Sinha married Premini, the daughter of H.P. Verma, an industrialist from Uttar Pradesh. The match was arranged by his parents, and Sinha did not meet his prospective bride until his wedding, which was held according to Hindu rites and included a large dowry from the bride's father. In January 1950, Sinha was posted as Brigade Major, 123 Infantry Brigade, then located at Amritsar. There was an acute shortage of married accommodation, but the brigade commander, Brigadier Sarda Nand Singh, permitted Sinha the use of the MES Inspection Bungalow for two months, so that he could bring his wife to the station. Soon afterwards, Sinha received orders transferring him to 3/4 Gorkha Rifles. Before Independence, no Indian officers were posted to Gorkha regiments, and the departure of British officers had left a vacuum. As a result, a large number of officers had to be imported from other regiments and Sinha was one of them. He joined the battalion at Gurais in Kashmir, where it was occupying pickets at high altitudes. He was given command of a company located at a height of 13,000 feet, which was about a six-hour climb from the roadhead.

In 1952, Sinha qualified for the Staff College in Wellington. Before he left for Wellington, he was detailed to undergo the junior commanders' course at the Infantry School, where he was awarded the rare 'distinguished' grading. After completing the course at Wellington, he was reverted to regimental duty and joined 3/5 Gorkha Rifles, then located in Jammu and Kashmir, in August 1953. He served with the battalion for two years before being posted as an instructor at the Junior Command Wing of the Infantry School. The Commandant of the school was Brigadier Sam Manekshaw, with whom he had served earlier at the MO Directorate in Delhi. Sinha was now able to settle down with his family. He had a long tenure of three years at Mhow, and it was here that his son, Yashwardhan, was born.

In 1958, Sinha was posted back to 3/5 Gorkha Rifles, which was then in Shillong. After a few months, he moved with the battalion to Dalhousie. However, after another two years with the battalion, he was moved to Delhi as DAQMG (Operations) in the QMG's Branch at Army HQ. The QMG was Lieutenant General B.M. Kaul, who had been promoted by Krishna Menon, the Defence Minister, against the advice of the Army Chief, General Thimayya. Sinha soon found that Kaul was a very powerful man and was virtually running the Army, thanks to his proximity to Nehru and Krishna Menon. Kaul seemed to be happy with Sinha and, after a year, when Thimayya retired and Kaul took over as CGS, he rewarded Sinha by getting him detailed on a course at the Joint Services Staff College (JSSC) in the UK. Normally, only officers of the rank of brigadier or at least lieutenant colonel were sent on this course, and Sinha was still a major. However, Kaul could bend rules and he not only had Sinha nominated but also arranged for him to get a month's attachment to the Naval and Air Wings of the Staff College in Wellington before he left for the JSSC.

While Sinha was doing his attachment at Wellington, Kaul sent an emissary to collect evidence against the Commandant, Major General Sam Manekshaw, for his 'anti national' activities. Sinha was asked to give evidence, but he declined. When Kaul heard of this, he threatened to have Sinha's nomination on the JSSC course cancelled. But Sinha insisted that he had no knowledge of any anti-national act committed by Manekshaw. Ultimately, he was able to proceed on the course, and sailed from Bombay with his wife and three children in July 1961.

Sinha spent a pleasant year with his family in Latimer, and as he could afford to hire a car, they managed to see a lot of the English countryside. During the course, he was invited to attend the Gorkha Brigade Dinner. Sinha went in his *sherwani*, wearing his miniatures, which included the Burma Star. Field Marshal Slim was then President of the Gorkha Brigade. Recognising the Burma Star, and seeing Sinha's dress, he assumed that he was a JCO who had served in Burma in the ranks. He asked Sinha in Hindustani: *'Sahib, aap Burma mein kis rank mein thei?'* (Sahib, in which rank did you serve in Burma?) Slim was taken aback when Sinha told him that he had served in Burma as a lieutenant and a captain, and was now doing the JSSC course. Slim apologised for his gaffe, explaining that since he had heard that officers in the Indian Army were getting very quick promotions, he had thought that anyone who had been in Burma as an officer would by now be a general.

While Sinha was in England, Goa was liberated by Indian troops, and there was a lot of criticism of India's action in the British press. A junior minister in the British government, who had been a member of the British delegation to the United Nations, came to give a talk on the problems being faced by the UN, including its failure to ensure peace in Goa. Though he avoided making direct references to Goa, one of the students raised the issue and termed India's action as nothing short of international brigandry. In reply to the question, the minister criticised Nehru and Menon, and warned that India would have to face the consequences of her action. Sinha got up and put up a spirited defence of his country, citing the American Civil War, the Bay of Pigs and the Suez and Hungary crises. He questioned Portugal's moral and legal rights to hold on to Goa in violation of the UN resolutions, and felt that the international community, instead of criticising India, should be supporting her.

Sinha's stand was appreciated by the audience, as well as the Commandant, who mentioned that if he had been the only British officer doing a course in India, and if the subject of British action in Suez had come up, he would not have dared to defend that action as stoutly as Sinha had defended the Indian action in Goa. Later, Sinha sent a written report of the incident to the Military Attaché at the Indian High Commission, in London. It was shown to the High Commissioner who directed that a copy be sent to Delhi.

After the course, Sinha did an attachment with a British regiment, the King's Own Hussars, which was then part of the British Army on the Rhine in Germany. When he returned to India in July 1962, he was promoted Lieutenant Colonel and posted as an instructor at the Defence Services Staff College in Wellington. Sam Manekshaw was still the Commandant, and he objected to Sinha's posting on the grounds that he had still not commanded a battalion. Since there were other instructors at the college who had not commanded battalions, and Manekshaw had himself not done so, he was on a weak wicket, and Kaul overruled him. Soon afterwards, the Chinese attacked the Indian positions in NEFA, and the Indo–China War started, resulting in an ignominious defeat for India. The Indian Army had no experience of fighting in the mountains, and this was one of the reasons for its poor performance. Mountain warfare was now given top priority at all training institutions, and Sinha was given the task of writing out an exercise on the subject. To gain first-hand experience, he was sent on an extensive tour where he also had the opportunity to meet several officers who had taken part in the operations. Later, he wrote an exercise in the form of a telephone battle on mountain warfare. This was the first time the subject had been covered at the Staff College, and his efforts were appreciated by everyone.

In December 1964, Sinha was posted back to 3/5 Gorkha Rifles, as its CO. The battalion was at Fort William in Calcutta. Sam Manekshaw was GOC-in-C Eastern Command, and Sinha found that he continued to be cold towards him, even though this was the fourth time Sinha was serving under him. The battalion was later moved to Kachrapara, about 25 miles from Calcutta. During the Indo–Pakistan War, which broke out soon afterwards, the battalion was moved to the border with East Pakistan, and was part of the force earmarked to capture Jessore. Major General P.S. Bhagat, VC, was the GOC, and he had selected Sinha's battalion to lead the advance. The advance was to commence before dawn, but soon after midnight orders were received from Army HQ to hold up the operation. Ultimately, ceasefire was declared on 23 September 1965, and the battalion moved back to barracks in Kachrapara.

In June 1966, the battalion was moved to Ladakh. It was located at Khatpadambophu at a height of 14,500 feet. During winter, the temperature fell to minus 30 degrees centigrade, but the Gorkha troops, being hillmen, had little trouble adapting to the cold climate. After spending two cold winters in Ladakh, Sinha was promoted Brigadier and posted as Commander 71 Mountain Brigade, which was located at Ramgarh in Bihar. This was the first time he would be serving in his home state, and both he and his family were overjoyed. Ironically, this was destined to be one of his shortest tenures. Just five months after his arrival in Ramgarh, the brigade was ordered to move to Nagaland, to combat insurgency which had recieved a fillip by Naga gangs returning from China through Burma, after having been trained and armed by the Chinese. As it happened, two brigades were inducted, one in Nagaland and the other in Manipur—167 Mountain Brigade, under Brigadier Arun Vaidya, moved to Kohima in Nagaland, and Sinha's brigade to Imphal, in Manipur.

During this period, Prime Minister Indira Gandhi decided to visit Imphal. The Lieutenant Governor of Manipur, Baleshwar Prasad, asked Sinha to coordinate arrangements for her security with the police and civil administration. When Sinha approached the civil officials, they told him that they were quite capable of looking after the arrangements themselves, and did not need the army's help. Nonetheless, Sinha took the precaution of moving two infantry battalions to Imphal, and a third one to a nearby location. He also moved his own tactical HQ to Imphal.

When Indira Gandhi arrived, there was an agitation staged by Meiteis, who were demanding statehood for Manipur. The police had to lathi-charge a section of the crowd that had gathered in the open ground where the Prime Minister was scheduled to address a public meeting. As soon as she arrived, the crowds became violent and started pelting her with stones. She could not address the meeting, and had to leave the rostrum and return to Raj Niwas (Government House). Riots and arson broke out in the town and the situation became critical. Without waiting for a formal requisition from the civil administration, Sinha ordered his troops to rush to the meeting ground, where he could see that police vehicles had been set on fire and some people had opened fire from the housetops. Seeing soldiers with fixed bayonets rushing towards them, the miscreants ran away. In the melee, seven policemen were killed and some police vehicles completely burnt.

The Lieutenant Governor summoned Sinha to Raj Niwas and asked him to take over the situation, as well as the responsibility for the Prime Minister's security. The IGP, who was also present, confessed that he had no faith in his men. Since most of them were Manipuris, they sympathised with the agitating

Meiteis. Sinha assured the Lieutenant Governor that he would do the needful, and ordered the two battalions already in town to begin vigorous patrolling. A curfew was ordered, and the third battalion was also brought in. Within a few hours, Sinha had the situation under control. In the evening, All India Radio broadcast details of the disturbances. He received a message from the Army Commander in Calcutta that the security of the Prime Minister was his personal responsibility. Next morning, the Prime Minister left Imphal. She was seen off at the airport by the Lieutenant Governor, Sinha, and senior civil and police officials, who looked visibly embarrassed.

Early in 1971, Sinha was posted to Delhi as Director of the Pay Commission Cell. The Third Pay Commission had been set up by the government, and the cell had been formed as part of the Adjutant General's Branch to present the army's case. Though Sinha had little experience in financial matters, he had excellent credentials for the job. He had written an article in the *USI Journal* on the service conditions of army officers, comparing them with those of the civil officers. The article had been referred to by Stephen Cohen in his book about the Indian Army, and also formed the basis of a question in parliament. Sam Manekshaw was now the COAS, and he selected Sinha for this assignment, which turned out to be one of the most important that Sinha was to fulfil during his career.

This was the first time that the army and the other two services were being allowed to present their cases to the Pay Commission directly. The earlier two commissions had not examined the case of the defence services, and the Ministry of Defence had taken decisions regarding them, following the commssion's recommendations for the civil services. In the process, the interests of the defence services had suffered. The civil services had unions and associations to look after their interests, while the Defence Services had none. This was the main reason for establishing pay commission cells in the Service HQs. The Ministry of Defence wanted to screen their proposals, but the Service Chiefs did not accept this, and it was finally agreed that they could send their proposals directly to the Pay Commission, with a copy to the Defence Ministry, which could forward their comments if necessary.

Sinha had to interact closely with his counterparts in the navy and the air force. The first obstacle was to get the others to agree not to raise issues of disparities within the defence services. For instance, the other two services were sore that army officers were entitled to orderlies, while they were not. The army had a genuine grouse that its soldiers got inferior scales of rations, compared to sailors and airmen. In the end, the three services agreed not to raise these issues, as they could be used by bureaucrats to create divisions among them, resulting in long-term losses rather than gains. Sinha managed to ensure consensus among the three services. He put in a lot of research, studying the pay scales and other perquisites for the past hundred years or so. Questionnaires were sent to military attachés in Indian missions abroad to determine the service conditions of soldiers in foreign countries. To find out what attracted the Indian youth to a military career, questionnaires were also sent to students through the National Cadet Corps. Senior serving and retired officers were asked whether they would like their sons to take up the same career. From the responses to all these questionnaires, a databank was built up, which proved to be of great help in formulating the proposals.

After a lot of deliberation, Sinha decided to base his recommendations on four broad principles. The first was parity of army officers with the IAS officers in terms of pay and allowances. The second was Class II status for JCOs. The third was the equation of the infantry soldier with a skilled worker, and the fourth was treating the erstwhile non-combatants, such as cooks, washermen and barbers, as combatants and giving them the status and emoluments of soldiers. The proposals were presented to the service chiefs, as well as the army commanders, who fully endorsed them. It was then forwarded to the Pay

Commission, which complimented the army on presenting most forceful and well-researched proposals, backed by cogent arguments. Copies of the proposals, running into 300 printed pages, were sent by Sinha, under Manekshaw's signature, to all formations in the army. This was done to apprise them that their interests had been well looked after, and if the government did not give them their due, it would not be because their case had not been presented properly. As a result, Sinha became a well known figure in army circles.

In March 1971, after the military crackdown in East Pakistan, preparations began for the inevitable showdown. Sinha's work with the Pay Commission was almost done, and he wanted to move to an active formation. He went up to the Chief and said: 'The old G-1 is going to war with the old G-2, and the old G-3 is being left out.' Manekshaw understood what he meant. In 1947, Manekshaw had been GSO-1; Yahya Khan, who was now the President of Pakistan, had been the GSO-2; and Sinha had been GSO-3 in the MO Directorate at the General HQ in Delhi. Manekshaw told Sinha that he could not let him go till the Pay Commission had completed its work. He also hinted that Sinha might be retained in the Adjutant General's Branch to carry out various important tasks in preparation for the imminent operations. Sinha was due for promotion, and when the Deputy Adjutant General, Major General T.N. Raina, left to take over a corps, he was asked to officiate in his place.

The conflict with Pakistan started on 3 December 1971, and was over by 16 December. Dacca had fallen and 93,000 Pakistani soldiers had been taken prisoner. A new nation, Bangladesh, was born. Early in 1972, Sinha was promoted Major General and formally appointed Deputy Adjutant General. He had his hands full, dealing with cases of pensions for the widows of men killed in action, and for the soldiers who had been disabled. In addition, the prisoners of war had to be housed and looked after. One of his major achievements was the grant of liberalised pensions for war widows, which was sanctioned by the government.

They would now get three-fourths of the pay of their deceased husbands, and would continue to get it even after they remarried. In addition, their children would get free education, including reimbursement of tuition and boarding fees, as well as the cost of school uniforms and books.

Perhaps the biggest problem he faced related to the POWs, whose large number necessitated the creation of over a dozen camps, at very short notice. The Indian Army had almost no previous experience of handling prisoners, and Sinha's stint as the Adjutant of a POW camp in Burma stood him in good stead. The camps were provided with all amenities, sometimes taking these away from Indian troops, who had to go without them. The Geneva Convention was strictly followed, and the prisoners were treated extremely well. On the occasion of Eid, a message was sent to all prisoners from Manekshaw, hoping that they would soon be reunited with their families. A *bara khana* (feast) was organised for the prisoners on that day, and Sinha was at the camp in Faizabad when the message from the Chief was read out. With tears in his eyes, a Pakistani JCO sitting next to him said:

> Sahib, I now know why we lost the war. Indian Army officers care so much for the soldiers. In my own army, I never sat next to a general before. Our generals and other senior officers were too busy playing politics and lived like nawabs (noblemen). They had little time for us.

In early 1973, Sinha was sent to Italy as the head of an Indian delegation to a Convention on Application of Humanitarian Rights to Warfare, organised by the United Nations and the International Red Cross. Sinha had to cross swords with Professor Tom Crabb, the leader of the American delegation, who bitterly criticised India for her action against East Pakistan, and also in Kashmir and Goa. Sinha was able to refute the arguments, and Crabb was gracious enough to apologise for basing his remarks on wrong facts. Sinha also gave a detailed account of the POW camps, and the laudatory references of the foreign press, including a report in the *Washington Post*, which had said that never in history had any country treated POWs in a better manner. On his return to India, Sinha was congratulated for his speech by Manekshaw as well as Jagjiwan Ram, the Defence Minister.

One of Sinha's major contributions towards the welfare of troops was the introduction of the Army Group Insurance Scheme. This was on the pattern of a similar scheme in vogue in the US Army during the Vietnam War. According to the scheme, a fixed sum is deducted from the salary of each officer, JCO and soldier. In return, he is insured for a certain sum of money, which is given to his dependant in case he dies while in service. The scheme also has a savings element: the deductions are suitably invested, and a large sum is paid to the individual on retirement. This scheme has proved very successful and is still in operation.

In January 1973, Manekshaw was to retire. But on New Year's day, the government announced that he was being promoted to the rank of Field Marshal. The rank was conferred on him by the President of India at a special investiture held at Rashtrapati Bhawan on 3 January 1973. As Deputy Adjutant General, Sinha was responsible for getting the new badges of rank and the Field Marshal's baton, for which no design was specified, since this was the first time that rank was being conferred in India. He relied on the *Encyclopaedia Brittanica* for the design, and got badges fabricated in black metal at the army workshop, in Delhi. For the baton, he had to innovate. He used a smaller, but suitably embellished version of the baton normally carried by the stick orderly who stands outside the office of the CO. The investiture went off without a hitch, but Sinha failed to get the bureaucrats to agree to give Manekshaw the status, salary and privileges that Field Marshals are entitled to in the UK, or any of the other countries in Europe where this rank exists.

Shortly afterwards, Sinha received his posting orders as GOC 23 Mountain Division, which had its HQ at Rangia in Assam. The division was deployed along the Brahmputra valley, and was part of 4 Corps, which had performed extremely well during the 1971 operations in Bangladesh. Lieutenant General Sagat Singh, who had led the corps brilliantly during the war, was still commanding it. Unfortunately, Sinha had a short tenure of just over a year in command of the division, and was posted back to Delhi in 1974 as the Director of Military Intelligence (DMI). A few months later, General G.G. Bewoor retired as COAS and was succeeded by General T.N. Raina. Shortly afterwards, Indira Gandhi imposed the Emergency.

During his tenure as DMI, Sinha visited several foreign countries to inspect the offices of military attachés in Indian embassies. He first went to Afghanistan, Iraq and Iran, and then on another trip to the UK and France, followed by Sweden and Sri Lanka, where he accompanied the Chief. Much against his will, he found himself in Delhi's cocktail circuit, as he had to attend parties at all embassies as part of his duties. However, his appointment had some advantages as well. Almost 20 years earlier, as a major, he had written a book, *Operation Rescue*, about the Kashmir operations in 1947–48. He had sent the manuscript to the MI Directorate for security clearance, but this had not been granted by the government for political reasons. Now, Sinha used his influence with the IB and Ministry of External Affairs, and was able to get their concurrence for its publication. The book turned out to be a bestseller, running into four editions.

In December 1976, Sinha was posted as GOC 10 Infantry Division. His earlier command of a division had been truncated, and he was keen to complete the mandatory period which would make him eligible for further promotion. He moved to his new assignment, leaving his family in Delhi. The division was located in the Jammu sector, with its HQ at Akhnur, on the banks of the Chenab. The Corps Commander, Lieutenant

General K.V. Krishna Rao, later became the Army Chief. A little after his arrival at Akhnur, Indira Gandhi lost the elections and the Emergency ended. Sinha's tenure as divisional commander was again cut short. His turn had come up for promotion to Lieutenant General, and he was posted back to Delhi as the Adjutant General.

Sinha had worked earlier as Deputy Adjutant General, and was conversant with the issues related to his new job. One of his first tasks was to convince the government to remove disparities in rank, pay and status between the civil services and the army, which had gradually crept in after Independence, and were causing demoralisation in all ranks. He submitted a proposal for a cadre review for the three services to the Chiefs of Staff Committee, which endorsed it. The proposal was then forwarded to the Cabinet under the signature of the three Chiefs. To improve promotion prospects, Sinha had proposed that additional appointments be created in all selection grade ranks, as had been done for the civil services. He proposed the grant of a second lieutenant's rank, with pay, to officer cadets during training, as was being done for IAS and IPS (Indian Police Service). On commission, the officer would get the rank of Lieutenant, and the CO's rank would thus automatically be upgraded from lieutenant colonel to that of colonel. The army commanders were to be upgraded to the four-star rank of full general, to differentiate them from corps commanders, who were lieutenant generals with a three-star rank.

After the proposal was accepted in principle, Sinha was asked to prepare a detailed proposal and present it to the Defence Minister. The presentation was attended by the Cabinet Secretary, the Secretaries of Defence and Finance and the three Service Chiefs. Sinha made comparisons, with a lot of statistical data, between the Indian Army and those of foreign countries, as well as with the pre-Independence Indian Army. He also compared the conditions prevailing in the defence services with those among their counterparts in foreign countries, as well as the civil services in India. At the end of the presentation, the Defence Minister as well as the secretaries were convinced of the anomalies and the need for correction. Mr Subramaniam, the Defence Minister, told Sinha: 'General, you joined the wrong profession. You should have been a lawyer.'

Most of Sinha's recommendations were accepted, except two important ones dealing with the grant of the rank of lieutenant to cadets and the upgradation of army commanders to four-star rank. (The first proposal, however, was accepted 20 years later, and officers are now commissioned as lieutenants.) Sinha also tried to resolve the issue of protocol, and the relative precedence of ranks, between the armed forces and the civil services. However, his efforts did not meet with much success. For major generals and above, the Order of Precedence was issued by the Central Government. For brigadiers and below, state governments were asked to decide the issue on their own, based on guidelines issued by the central government. Most of them did not follow these guidelines, causing misunderstandings and unpleasant incidents, which sometimes still occur.

Another project that bore fruit due to Sinha's efforts was the Army Welfare Housing Organisation (AWHO). A chance meeting with the Secretary of the Housing Ministry, who had lived with him in the same officers' mess 30 years earlier when he was a naval officer, enabled him to get five acres of land in R.K. Puram, New Delhi, allotted to the AWHO. About 400 flats were built in the complex, which was named Som Vihar after Major Som Nath Sharma, the first recipient of the PVC. Similar complexes were made at several other stations, where land was acquired from state governments. The AWHO envisaged the deduction of a small sum of money from the salaries of officers, JCOs and men who joined the scheme. After contributing for about 20 years, they would be given a house around the time they retired. This way, it would be possible for them to own a house, without heavy expenditure or the headache of constructing one themselves. It would also provide the soldiers and their families a sense of security. Unfortunately, the scheme has been drastically amended and is now similar to the self-financing schemes of various government housing boards, where the entire cost of the house has to be paid within two to three years before allotment.

Sinha was also responsible for establishing the Army Welfare Education Society (AWES). After the 1971 war, the Indian Army received a crore of rupees as its share of prize money for goods seized on the high seas. Sinha decided to use this sum to open schools for the children of army personnel. The Army Public School was established in Delhi, and an army school was set up in each command. Today, there is a string of army schools all over the country, where the fees are subsidised, and children of army personnel given admission even during mid-session. This has considerably eased the problems of soldiers, who are frequently transferred.

After two-and-a-half years as Adjutant General, Sinha was posted as GOC of the Strike Corps, then located at Chandimandir. His immediate superior, once again, was Lieutenant General Krishna Rao, who was GOC-in-C Western Command. In mid-1981, Krishna Rao took over as COAS, and Sinha replaced him as Army Commander in Simla. During his tenure as Army Commander, Sinha witnessed momentous events that were later to change the nation's history. During the Asian games held in Delhi in 1982, there were reports that Sikh extremists were planning to disrupt the games. As a precautionary measure, all Sikhs travelling towards Delhi were subjected to body searches and harassed when passing through Haryana. Surprisingly, even army officers were subjected to this treatment. Sinha took up the matter with Army HQ, but did not receive any support.

Shortly after this, Lala Jagat Narain, a prominent editor based in Punjab, was assassinated. Sant Jarnail Singh Bhindranwale, a militant Sikh leader, was suspected of being involved in the murder. He was staying in a gurudwara at Mehta Chowk, between Amritsar and Jullunder. The Punjab police was reluctant to arrest him and asked the army for help. The army refused. The Chief Minister of Punjab then spoke to the Prime Minister, who ordered the army to arrest Bhindranwale. These orders were passed on to Sinha, who spoke to the Chief, pointing out that it was wrong for the army to undertake a task that was the responsibility of the police. If the police failed, then, as provided by law, the army could be called out in aid of civil power. He also said that he would need more time for reconnaissance before undertaking the operation. Krishna Rao spoke to the Prime Minister, and she rescinded the order.

When the police went to arrest Bhindranwale at Mehta Chowk, he told them that he would come out after 48 hours. The police waited outside the gurudwara for two days, by which time a sizable crowd had collected. When Bhindranwale came out, the Nihangs (members of an armed Sikh sect) attacked the police, who had to open fire, killing several people. Bhindranwale was taken to Ferozepore, but was released after a few days due to lack of evidence. His release was celebrated throughout Punjab, where he was treated like a hero. He moved to Amritsar, where he took refuge in the Golden Temple. The rest is history.

In January 1983, Sinha was posted to Delhi as Vice Chief of Army Staff. Since there were just six months left for Krishna Rao to retire, and Sinha was the senior Army Commander, it was assumed that he would be the next Chief, and his move to Delhi only served to reinforce this impression. After he took over as Vice Chief, Krishna Rao indicated that since Sinha would be taking over from him in a few months, all other Principal Staff Officers should work through him, so that he was kept fully in the picture. During the next five months, Sinha and Krishna Rao worked closely together, and everyone took it for granted that Sinha would step into Rao's shoes when he retired.

On 29 May 1983, Krishna Rao informed Sinha that the government had decided to appoint Arun Vaidya, who was GOC-in-C Eastern Command, as the next Army Chief. Sinha was taken aback, and told Krishna Rao that he had decided to put in his papers. Rao tried to dissuade him, but Sinha had made up his mind. He returned to his office, and after dictating a letter of congratulations to Vaidya, wrote out his application for premature retirement and handed it over to the Military Secretary on the same day. While Vaidya's appointment as Army Chief was announced on the radio in the afternoon, the story appeared in the newspapers the following morning. It made the front page in most newspapers, along with the news that Sinha had resigned.

Though Parliament was not in session, some MPs buttonholed R. Venkataraman, the Defence Minister, in the Central Hall, and questioned him on the reasons for Sinha's supersession. Later that day, P.K. Kaul, the Defence Secretary, sent Ram Mohan Rao, the Director of Public Relations, as an emissary to Sinha, advising him to withdraw his resignation. Kaul also indicated that the government was ready to make an amicable settlement with him. Sinha refused, and told the emissary that he was not interested in a settlement, which probably meant a gubernatorial or a diplomatic appointment. Shortly afterwards, Sinha was requested by Ram Mohan Rao to meet some press correspondents, who wanted to see him. Sinha initially refused, but subsequently agreed to meet them.

When questioned by the press, he declined to comment on his supersession and said that, as a disciplined soldier, he had accepted the government's decision. The press asked him if he felt that appointments in the army were being made based on political considerations, and whether it was his family's proximity to Jayaprakash Narain which had been responsible for his supersession. Sinha refused to be drawn into a controversy, and requested the press to keep politics away from the army. Next morning, Sinha's statement was prominently reported in all newspapers. His assertion that he had chosen to retire from the army after accepting the decision of the government to supersede him, and his reference to Arun Vaidya as a dear friend and a competent general, won him many admirers. It created a wave of sympathy for him in the army as well as among civilians, most of whom felt that he had been unfairly treated. He received a large number of letters, appreciating his stand, from several retired officers, which included two former Chiefs, Cariappa and Kumaramangalam. Apart from the officers who had served with him, he was surprised to get letters from soldiers and civilians who had come to know of him only after reading the newspapers.

A few days later, there was a joint statement in the press, by six prominent MPs, which included Charan Singh, Jagjiwan Ram, L.K. Advani, H.N. Bahuguna, George Fernandez and Dharam Vir Sinha. They severely criticised the government for its interference in the professionalism of the army for short-term political gains, and praised Sinha's dignified reaction to his supersession. They demanded a debate on the subject in the forthcoming session of the Parliament. However, the speaker of the Lok Sabha did not permit a discussion on grounds of security. In the Rajya Sabha, too, the Chairman disallowed a debate, leading to angry exchanges between the treasury benches and the Opposition, some of whom brought up the issue of Thimayya's resignation and the debate in Parliament that followed.

Though the official reason cited by the government for Sinha's supersession was his relative lack of combat experience, the actual reason could have been one of many others. Some felt that his proximity to Jayaprakash Narain, whose very name was anathema to Indira Gandhi, had sealed his fate. Others felt that his views on the role of civil servants in the higher defence organisation, and the need for a Chief of Defence Staff (CDS), were not appreciated by bureaucrats, who lobbied to get him sidelined. Another reason could have been his penchant for wresting concessions from the government, which had made him popular with the soldiers. A senior journalist, Kuldip Nayar, wrote: 'Sinha's brilliance was his undoing.'

Sinha's request for premature retirement was accepted by the government. Before he left Delhi, he called on the Naval and Air Force Chiefs, who greeted him warmly. However, when he went to call on Venkataraman, the Defence Minister, he was given the cold shoulder and not offered even a cup of tea. Instead, he was advised that he should stay away from politics for his own good. Sinha's last call was on President Gyani Zail Singh, who was also the Supreme Commander of the Armed Forces. He was extremely affable, and related to Sinha the story behind his supersession, which he claimed had been done at the instance of the Prime Minister.

Though the IAF offered a service aircraft to take him to Patna, Sinha declined, and decided to go by a scheduled Indian Airlines flight. He had planned to depart quietly, but when he reached the airport, he was surprised to find a large crowd of officers and men, including some from his own battalion, who had come from Meerut. There were also a large number of press correspondents, who were surprised that several of his senior colleagues had come in uniform to see him off. When his plane landed in Patna, the crowd that had gathered to receive him was even larger. It included several prominent politicians, including Karpoori Thakur and Raj Narain. The Sub-Area Commander was also there, and he escorted Sinha to his house in a manner befitting a Vice Chief, with outriders and a pilot jeep. Sinha's retirement was to come into effect the next day, and he was entitled to these courtesies, though he had not expected them.

Unlike most other retired generals, Sinha did not fade away. He was invited by a large number of universities to deliver lectures on a variety of subjects. He also continued to write for almost all major newspapers and journals. Major Opposition leaders, such as Charan Singh of the DMKP, Chandra Shekhar of the Janata Party, and Atal Behari Vajpayee of the BJP, invited him to join their parties, but he declined. He decided to take a holiday, and accompanied by his wife, went to Spain, where one of his daughters was living with her husband. His other two daughters, who were in the USA, joined them for a family reunion. Sinha and his wife spent a pleasant month with their children and grandchildren in Spain.

In the 1984 General Elections, Sinha stood as an independent candidate from Patna. He was supported by three Opposition parties, and it was expected that he would win. After the polling was over, the ballot boxes were kept in a strongroom. Next morning, it was discovered that the room had been opened during the night by the District Magistrate, and a number of ballot papers bearing Sinha's name were found strewn about. At the same time, ballot papers with the name of the Congress (I) candidate were found stacked in the box. When the votes were counted, Sinha was found to have polled about 117,000 votes, while the ruling party candidate had 200,000. Sinha complained to the Election Commission, and later even filed a writ petition in the High Court, but to no avail. That was the end of his foray into politics, though he campaigned for V.P. Singh in 1988, when the latter contested the bye-election from Allahabad and won by a handsome majority. During the 1989 General Elections, Sinha actively campaigned for the Janata Dal led by V.P. Singh, which won and came to power, defeating the Congress (I).

Soon after becoming Prime Minister, V.P. Singh offered Sinha the appointment of India's Ambassador to Nepal, with whom relations had deteriorated during Rajiv Gandhi's tenure. The treaty on trade and transit had lapsed in March 1989, and Nepal's economy had been badly affected. Most people blamed India for trying to stifle the growth of her smaller neighbour. Landlocked and lacking in resources, Nepal was economically dependent on her for almost everything. Not surprisingly, there was considerable resentment in Nepal against India, which soon became a convenient whipping boy for its political parties.

When Sinha arrived in Kathmandu on 20 February, the King was in Pokhra and not due to return for a month. However, Sinha was surprised when he was invited to present his credentials to the King at Pokhra within two days of his arrival. Sinha had served for over 30 years with the Gorkhas, who were citizens of Nepal, and could speak Gurkhali fluently. He soon developed an excellent rapport with the King, as well as with the people in Kathmandu. As a result, Indo–Nepal relations soon started improving, and after a few months, an agreement was signed in Delhi between the Prime Ministers of the two countries. The 20 trade and transit points on the border, which had been closed, were reopened with much fanfare, and India gave a number of concessions to Nepal.

In 1990, V.P. Singh's government fell and Chandra Shekhar became Prime Minister. Since Sinha was a political appointee and not a career diplomat, he resigned. The Prime Minister of Nepal requested him to continue for some more time, and even spoke to the Indian Prime Minister about it. Unfortunately, the new government did not accede to this request, and Sinha returned to India after having served as ambassador for just 11 months. However, his short tenure in Nepal had been momentous. When he left, Indo–Nepal relations had improved to a new level of cordiality, and democracy had been established in the Himalayan kingdom. The Prime Minister of Nepal wrote: 'General Sinha was a true friend of Nepal. He was as much India's ambassador to Nepal as Nepal's ambassador to India.' Sinha returned to Patna, where he remained active, and his name continued to appear regularly in the columns of major newspapers. He was also invited to deliver lectures at various universities and institutions, including the United Service Institution and the National Defence College.

In July 1997, Sinha was appointed the Governor of Assam. The situation in Assam had deteriorated, with the United Liberation Front of Assam (ULFA) almost running a parallel government. There were frequent kidnappings of senior officials of the Oil India Corporation and the tea gardens, which resulted in large sums of money being paid as ransom. The political leadership of the state was unable to cope, and the central government had to deploy a large force of paramilitary as well as regular army troops to control the situation. Sinha was a well-known and respected figure, whose impartiality was beyond reproach. He had also done a commendable job as India's High

Commissioner in Nepal. His appointment was widely welcomed by almost everyone, including most political parties. A measure of his popularity is the fact that when the BJP government came to power in Delhi in March 1998, one of the few governors about whom there was no talk of changing was Sinha.

S.K. Sinha did not rise to the top in the military profession, but is perhaps better known than most of those who did. He was a military leader with a difference—a 'thinking' General. What he lacked in charisma and flamboyance, he made up in erudition and integrity. His military career was eventful, though he missed the opportunity to play an active part in the three major wars that the country fought in 1962, 1965 and 1971, which is ostensibly why he was denied the post of Army Chief. However, his contribution to the Indian Army, in terms of improving the service conditions of troops, was immense. No less was his accomplishment in the only diplomatic assignment that he undertook as India's ambassador to Nepal. In the final analysis, he emerges as a military leader who has lived by the highest traditions of the Indian Army, and more important, a man of character, an approbation few men can claim.

12

Lieutenant General
Hanut Singh,
PVSM, MVC

12

Lieutenant General Hanut Singh, PVSM, MVC

A Brilliant Tactician

If one were asked to describe Hanut Singh in just a word, the one that would fit the bill is 'soldier'. He epitomises courage, both moral and physical, fair-mindedness, a high standard of morality, discipline and professionalism. Though he did not reach the highest rank—he retired as Lieutenant General—Hanut had become a legend even as Lieutenant Colonel, when he was commanding the most prestigious cavalry regiment in the Indian Army, 17 Horse. Also called the Poona Horse, this unit has the unique distinction of winning four VCs and two PVCs. Hanut was himself decorated with the MVC in 1971, when he was in command of the regiment. His subsequent tenures with the Armoured Division and the Strike Corps only reinforced his claim as the best armour commander India has produced, and the only one the Pakistani Army feared and respected.

To understand Hanut, one must know his background and early life, which were instrumental in shaping his unique character and values. Hanut is the scion of a proud clan of Rathore Rajputs from Jasol, in Barmer district of Rajasthan. The Jasol Rajputs are known for their valour, patriotism, courage, and highly individualistic nature, born out of centuries of independent existence. After losing Kanauj, a branch of the Rathores led by Rao Siaji, the son of Raja Jai Chand of Kanauj, established a kingdom at Khed, near Jasol. It was from here that the Rathores branched out and established the kingdoms of Jodhpur, Bikaner and Idar. For this reason, the Rathores of Jasol consider themselves as the senior house of the Rathores. They have maintained their independent status ever since, defending it against all comers. Hanut's father, Lieutenant Colonel Arjun Singh, was himself a great soldier who served in the Jodhpur Lancers, and later commanded the famous Kachawa Horse.

Hanut was born on 6 July 1933 in Jasol. He was sent to Colonel Brown's School at Dehradun for his early education, where he was exposed to Western values, some of which conflicted with those held for centuries by the Rajputs. Hanut tried to resolve the contradiction by adopting what was best in both traditions. A brilliant student, Hanut earned a double promotion from Class 7 to Class 9. He was a voracious reader, who made an extensive study of Rajput history and tradition, in which he took immense pride. His choice of the martial profession was almost natural, as was his predilection for the Cavalry, which he later joined.

On 1 January 1949, the Joint Services Wing (JSW) of the IMA was established, at Clement Town in Dehradun. This was later shifted to Khadakvasla, near Poona, and renamed the National Defence Academy. Hanut joined the first course at JSW, along with S.F. Rodrigues, who later became COAS; Ram Das, who rose to be the Chief of Naval Staff; and N.C. Suri, who retired as the Chief of Air Staff. At the Academy, he was seen as a loner. His fellow cadets could not help but notice his strict self-discipline, moral values and strength of character, and held him in high regard. Unfortunately, this regard turned to jealousy in later years, when some of his colleagues used these very qualities to sideline him, calling him arrogant and stubborn.

Hanut was commissioned on 28 December 1952 into 17 Horse—or the Poona Horse—one of the elite cavalry regiments of the Indian Army. This was not surprising, given his background and inclination. In the early 1900s, Maharaja Sir Pratap Singh of Jodhpur, the famous Sir 'P', had funded the raising of two Rathore Rajput squadrons in the Poona Horse. Sir 'P' was appointed Honorary Colonel of the Regiment, and ever since then, the Maharajas of Jodhpur have continued to hold this appointment. Hanut's father and uncle, who were in the Jodhpur Lancers, did attachments with the Poona Horse. So it was only natural that Hanut should also join the Poona Horse.

The Poona Horse was one of the last regiments to be Indianised. As a result, it had very few Indian officers at the time of Independence. To make up the shortfall after the British left, several officers from other regiments were transferred to Poona Horse. This heterogeneous collection of officers, most of whom were of average calibre, did little to enhance the reputation of the regiment. For some reason, most officers from the IMA who joined after Independence were from a feudal background, and the Poona Horse came to be known as 'Kanwar Sahib's Regiment', where the accent was on high living rather than professionalism. (In Rajasthan, the name of a highborn Rajput is prefixed with 'Thakur', that of his son with 'Kanwar', and grandson with 'Bhanwar'.) It was only in the 1950s, after a new breed of officers began to be commissioned into Poona Horse, that the tide turned and the regiment once again began to regain its lost glory and place of honour in the Indian cavalry.

Hanut took immense pride in his regiment, which he considered to be the best in the Indian Army. In those days, however, it was not as highly regarded as it deserved to be, and Hanut was pained to hear certain senior officers pass disparaging remarks about it. He decided that it was not enough for him to consider his regiment to be the best—every good regimental officer should also feel the same. It was only when the Poona Horse was acknowledged as the best by others that it could legitimately claim this distinction. And so it became his personal mission to ensure that the Poona Horse was accepted and universally acclaimed as the best cavalry regiment of the Indian Army. He worked with missionary zeal towards achieving this goal, and motivated and inspired other officers of the regiment to do likewise. The success of these efforts can be gauged from the fact that the exploits of the Poona Horse during the Indo–Pak Wars of 1965 and 1971 became legends. It emerged as the most highly decorated regiment in both wars, winning a PVC in each. In 1965, the Commandant, Lieutenant Colonel A.B. Tarapore was awarded the PVC; and in 1971, the youngest officer in the unit, Second Lieutenant Arun Khetarpal, won the coveted award. This is a unique distinction, unmatched by any other unit in the Indian Army. To cap it all, the Pakistani Army acknowledged the regiment's valour on the battlefield by conferring on it the title *Fakhr-e-Hind* (Pride of India). Hanut's pride and faith in his regiment were vindicated.

As a young officer, Hanut developed a deep admiration for the German General Staff, particularly their total dedication to the profession of arms, and their unmatched expertise in the art of war. He sought to emulate these qualities himself, and encouraged other officers in the regiment to do the same. As a result, qualities like professionalism, personal rectitude and total dedication to the regiment and the service became the hallmarks of the Poona Horse officers, and continue to be so even today. In fact, a group of officers in the regiment jokingly referred to themselves as the 'PH General Staff', and being admitted to this group was a coveted honour for the others. A whole generation of Poona Horse officers was directly influenced by Hanut's ideas and views, and it is interesting to note that almost all of them rose to become General officers—just one more of the many unique distinctions earned by the regiment. Many of them, such as Ajai Singh, Surrinder Singh, Amrik Virk, Neville Foley and Moti Dar, who joined the regiment after Hanut, recall with nostalgia the days spent under his tutelage.

Describing his first meeting with Hanut in July 1956, Lieutenant General Ajai Singh who later became a Governor, has written in the book, *Fakhr-e-Hind*: The Story of the Poona Horse:

It was after two to three days of my stay in the Regiment that I met him. I was sitting in the C Squadron office after the Maintenance Parade when a tall, thin, smartly turned out officer entered the office. What struck me most about him was his prominent hooked nose and the very proud and penetrating look in his eyes. He walked to me and met with such enthusiasm, warmth and affection that I felt as though we had known each other for ages . . . Thereafter, without further ado, he took me to the Squadron and introduced me to all members of his troop, which I was to take over. Having done this at the garages itself, he gave me a programme for my training which I was to commence from the next day; he also gave me a large bundle of books and precis which I was to read in my own time. I went through all this businesslike activity in a state of total shock because, till then, such a serious approach to professional matters had neither been seen or heard during the few days I had spent in the Regiment.

So this was Hanut—stoic, businesslike and upright. Being a senior subaltern he had full authority over the Young Officers (YOs), which he exercised with ruthless impartiality, whether it was in the Officers' Mess, or on the playgrounds. Some of the senior YOs, of course, resented this attitude but Hanut would not compromise. Irrespective of what the juniors and seniors felt about this remarkable man, one thing was universally true; he was loved by the men and admired and respected by all officers. Even then, as a youngster, I could foresee that he might just be the right man to usher in a new era in the Poona Horse—an era of regenerated Regimental spirit, professionalism and high spirits. As time passed, my anticipation proved more than correct. His influence on all the officers that were to follow was so complete that some of them went so far as to emulate him even in talk, gestures and mannerisms. This also explains why, in the course of time, he came to be nicknamed 'Gurudev' (teacher, or master).

Writing in a similar vein in the same book, Lieutenant General Surrinder Singh, who joined the Poona Horse in January 1958, reminisces:

> Amongst this lot, the officer who was to have the most profound influence was Hanut Singh, who had joined the Regiment in January 1953. A tall, lean and ascetic figure, uncompromising in his beliefs and convictions yet gentle and considerate to his juniors and subordinates, possessed with an exuberant sense of humour and a pungent, ready wit, he was an extremely dedicated and devoted professional. His forte was instruction, delivered in a modulated and compelling tone which carried conviction and understanding. A man of sterling character combined with a forceful personality, he had no time for fools—a fact which was soon apparent to those in this category.

An amusing sidelight was Hanut's strong belief that a married officer could not devote himself whole-heartedly to his profession, as his family would demand some of his time and attention. He himself was a bachelor, and encouraged others to follow his example. As a result, the Poona Horse had a fair number of rather senior bachelors. This added great zest to mess life, but also caused considerable anxiety and consternation to the other officers' parents, who naturally blamed Hanut for the continued refusal of their sons to enter into matrimony.

Hanut devoted his spare time to spiritual pursuits, and to his favourite hobby of reading. He had an abiding love for books, and read extensively on a wide variety of subjects. But what he loved to read most was spiritual literature and the biographies of great men, particularly the great 'Captains of War'. He found socialising, and the meaningless small talk that goes with it, painfully boring. He liked nothing better than to be left alone with a good book. In the extroverted army environment, this was considered odd and he was soon dubbed as being anti-social. But Hanut couldn't care less, and was quite happy as long as he was left to himself and his books.

In the mid-1950s, the Poona Horse was issued with Centurion tanks. In 1958, Hanut, who was then a young Captain, was selected to attend a Centurion tank gunnery course in the United Kingdom, for which he was awarded a 'distinction'. On his return, he was appointed a gunnery instructor at the Armoured Corps Centre and School, Ahmednagar, in May 1959. There, he rewrote the General Staff pamphlet on the 'Technique of Shooting from Armoured Fighting Vehicles'. He also introduced revised techniques of shooting and new tank gunnery training methods, and prepared precis for disseminating instructions on these subjects. These techniques continued to be the bedrock of gunnery training in the Armoured Corps for as long as the Centurions were in service, and enabled them to outshoot the Pakistani pattons and establish their supremacy on the battlefield during the Indo–Pak wars of 1965 and 1971.

When Hanut joined the Armoured Corps, there was no tactical doctrine available on armour, nor were there any publications on armour tactics at unit level. The tactics that were taught at the Armoured Corps Centre and School were basically Infantry-oriented, based on precis issued by the Infantry School in Mhow. Hanut felt that armour must have its own tactical doctrine, based on the principles of mobile warfare. So he decided to evolve such a doctrine and, based on that, develop unit-level tactics for armoured troops, squadrons and regiments. Since he believed that only the Germans had a thorough understanding of mobile warfare, he studied in detail the campaigns and battles fought by the Panzer formations and units during World War II. Based on these principles, he developed unit-level tactics, which he tried out with his troop and squadron during training. After making the appropriate modifications, he disseminated them to other officers of the regiment. He kept detailed notes of the entire process, updating them over the years.

In December 1960, Hanut returned to the regiment. After attending the junior command course at the Infantry School in 1961, he began to prepare for the Staff College entrance examination. He qualified and proceeded to Wellington to attend the course in 1963. His colleagues in Wellington remember him as a thoroughly dedicated professional, who had little time for distractions like the races at Ooty or the weekly dances at the Gymkhana Club. Even as a student, his leadership qualities were obvious to both his instructors and colleagues.

There is an interesting anecdote related to Wellington, which brings out Hanut's character and style. During the telephone battle, he was given the appointment of a divisional commander. As is customary, he was wearing the badges of rank of a major general, though he was actually a major. This was done to make the exercise seem more realistic. After he had given his orders, the actual 'battle' commenced. At about 9 p.m., after the 'enemy' had made his opening moves, Hanut told his staff that he was retiring for the night, and was not to be disturbed unless there was a situation that required his decision or personal intervention. This caused some surprise, since it was contrary to the normally accepted, nail-biting image of a GOC, supposedly under pressure, who remained on tenterhooks and kept harassing his staff and subordinates, instead of leaving them alone to get on with their jobs. This meant that by the time he was actually required to do something, he was already bleary-eyed and his mind fogged for want of rest and sleep.

After delivering his instructions, Hanut went to his allotted office and went to bed on the camp-cot, which he had placed there. He slept soundly, and awoke next morning to the twittering of birds. It seemed strangely quiet, so he went out to see what was going on. He found all the rooms locked, with no sign of the other student officers or directing staff. He later learnt that as the 'enemy' had failed to make any headway, the exercise had been prematurely called off at 1 a.m. The senior instructor had told the others to go home without disturbing Hanut, in accordance with the instructions he had given to his staff! This incident became the subject of much amused comment during the summing up, and was remembered for years.

Hanut performed exceptionally well on the course, and when it was over, he was posted as Brigade Major of 66 Infantry Brigade. During the 1965 war, when Poona Horse wrote its name into history books by destroying 60 enemy tanks (and losing only nine of its own), and Lieutenant Colonel Tarapore won a posthumous PVC, Hanut was not with the regiment. After a tenure of a little over two years in this appointment, he was reverted to his regiment in October 1966. He had spent only two years with it when he was given a prestigious staff appointment as GSO 2 in the MO Directorate at Army HQ. This was the first of his many stints at the MO, where he was to serve again as a Brigadier and then as a Major General.

In August 1970, Hanut was promoted Lieutenant Colonel and posted as Officer Commanding Tactical Wing in the Armoured Corps Centre and School. Hanut had retained the notes he had made during his earlier tenure at the school, which he had updated periodically during his subsequent tenures in the regiment and on staff. He used them to bring out books on the tactical handling of armoured units and sub-units. These remain the basic books on armour tactics even today, and are still used by the Armoured Corps Centre and School. In April 1971, he was nominated to the senior command course at the College of Combat (now called Army War College), which had recently been established at Mhow. In September 1971, Hanut was posted as Commandant, 17 Horse. (The Commanding Officer, or CO, is called the 'commandant' in cavalry regiments.) The regiment was located at Sangrur and was part of 16 Independent Armoured Brigade, which was then commanded by Brigadier A.S. Vaidya, MVC, who later became COAS.

By then, war clouds had begun gathering and within days of his assuming command, Hanut had to move his regiment to battle locations. On 8 October 1965, 17 Horse was carrying out its annual field firing at Naraingarh ranges when it received a message asking it to return at once to its permanent location. On his way back to Sangrur, Hanut reported to HQ 16 Independent Armoured Brigade, where he was briefed by the Brigade Commander. Vaidya informed him that 17 Horse had been placed under the command of 323 Infantry Brigade at Dinanagar, and that Hanut should move the regiment to its concentration area immediately. The regiment began moving by road and rail on 10 October, and within four days had concentrated at Sujanpur, a small village near Madhopur. After reaching its new location, Hanut was called to HQ 39 Infantry Division and briefed on his task.

Hanut learned that his regiment had been temporarily placed under the command of 323 Infantry Brigade for a defensive task. There were reports of an impending attack by Pakistan in the general area of Gurdaspur–Dinanagar, and 323 Infantry Brigade was to be deployed to contain this thrust with 17 Horse in a supporting role. Hanut was subsequently briefed by Brigadier G.S. Grewal, Commander 323 Infantry Brigade, who told him to base himself at Dinanagar and select suitable dispersal areas for his regiment. By the time Hanut reached the resthouse at Dinanagar, which he had selected as his regimental HQ, it was almost 10 p.m. As he was entering the resthouse, he sensed that he was being followed. He stopped and loudly asked what was going on. It transpired that the men following him were part of a reconnoitering party, led by an officer, from 36 Infantry Division. On hearing the tanks of 17 Horse enter the area, they had assumed that it was the spearhead of the Pakistani offensive. Hanut's aquiline nose and handlebar moustache had led them to mistake him for a Pathan. They were profusely apologetic when they realised that they had been stalking the Commandant of the Poona Horse instead of a Pakistani officer.

Next morning, orders were received that the Scinde Horse, which had just arrived, would relieve the Poona Horse, which was to revert under the command of 39 Infantry Division and move to Malichak. After spending almost a month there, the regiment moved to a forward concentration area near Dinai, just short of Samba, on the Pathankot–Jammu road. By this time, all personnel on leave, courses and extra-regimental employment had rejoined, and the regiment was up to full strength. The period spent in Malichak had been put to good use, in training and reconnaissance.

In 1971, the Indian Army's main task was the liberation of Bangladesh, then called East Pakistan. On the western front, it was decided to maintain an offensive–defence posture, primarily because of the commitment of troops in the east, where there was a possibility of Chinese intervention. However, it was expected that Pakistan would undertake a major offensive either in the Punjab, Jammu and Kashmir, or Rajasthan. As part of his overall strategy, Lieutenant General K.P. Candeth, GOC-in-C Western Command, had planned certain offensive operations with the intention of drawing out Pakistani reserves and weakening their ability to undertake major offensives against India. An advance by 1 Corps into the Shakargarh bulge was part of these plans.

Lieutenant General K.K. Singh, GOC 1 Corps, had been the DMO at Army HQ before assuming command of 1 Corps in October 1971. He was thus familiar with the overall strategy and plans for the operations. He had three infantry divisions (36, 39 and 54), two independent armoured brigades (2 and 16), two independent artillery brigades and two engineer brigades. He also had a locating battery and an air observation post squadron. 36 Infantry Division, under Major General B.S. Ahluwalia, was initially deployed south-east of the Ravi river, in the Thakurpur–Gurdaspur–Dinanagar area; 39 Infantry Division, under Major General B.R. Prabhu, was north of the Ravi, in the Madhopur–Bamial–Dayalchak area; and 54 Infantry Division, under Major

General W.A.G. Pinto, was deployed around Samba, between the Bein river and the Degh Nadi.

Lieutenant General K.K. Singh, known as 'KK', had commanded 1 Armoured Brigade during the 1965 War, and Poona Horse had been under his command at that time. In 1971, he was given the task of containing the enemy offensive, and then forcing them back by delivering a riposte against their lines of communication. In case the enemy did not launch an offensive, KK was to advance into the Shakargarh bulge east of the Degh Nadi, and capture Zafarwal, Dhamtal and Narowal. Subsequently, he was to secure the line Marala–Ravi link canal–Degh Nadi and later take Pasrur. KK appreciated that the best way to carry out the allotted tasks was to go on the offensive. He planned to do this in the central sector of the corps zone, retaining a strong defensive posture on the flanks. According to the plan, 54 Infantry Division was to advance between the Degh Nadi and the Karir Nadi, led by 16 independent Armoured Brigade less 16 Cavalry. 39 Infantry Division, led by 2 Independent Armoured Brigade was to advance between the Bien river and the Karir Nadi and guard the western flank. The eastern flank was to be guarded by two brigades (one each from 26 and 39 Infantry Divisions), supported by 16 Cavalry. 36 Infantry Division, supported by Scinde Horse, was to hold a defensive position along the Ravi river.

Based on the information available, it had been appreciated that the enemy would have laid three or four tiers of minefields, starting from the international border. In the 54 Infantry Division sector, the first minefield was visualised to be at the border; the second along the general line Bhoi Brahma–Thakurdwara–Nagwal; the third along the general line Ghamrola–Barkhanian; and the fourth in conjunction with the Basantar Nala. The enemy was also expected to have advance positions based on the Basantar Nala, with covering troops operating ahead of it to delay the advance of Indian troops, and deny crossings over the minefields.

On the basis of the enemy's anticipated deployment, it was planned that two infantry brigades ex-54 Infantry Division, with a squadron each of 17 Horse under command, would secure a bridgehead across the first minefield in the area Dandaut–Gola–Mawa–Mukhwal and establish a firm base for the divisional advance. The third brigade of 54 Infantry Division and 4 Horse would then advance between the Basantar river and Karir Nadi, with a view to secure crossings across the second minefield at Thakurdwara. Thereafter 4 Horse with one brigade would make another bridgehead across the third minefield at Barkhanian. Once the third minefield had been breached, a combat group comprising 17 Horse and 18 Rajputana Rifles less two companies would break out and secure an encounter crossing over the Basantar Nala in the general area of Pinjori, for a subsequent advance to capture the Zafarwal–Dhamtal complex.

While the various contingencies were being worked out, Hanut was dismayed to find that in each one of these plans, his regiment had been kept in reserve and not allotted any operational task. When this happened for the third time running, Hanut met the brigade commander and asked him why his regiment had not been given any task. 'From this,' said Hanut, 'I can only conclude that you do not have confidence in me, or in my regiment, or both.' Vaidya was initially nonplussed at being confronted in this way by one of his COs, but had to agree that he was right. He explained that he had just taken over the brigade, and being unfamiliar with the units, was going by the information his predecessor, Brigadier K.K. Kaul had given him. Hanut pointed out that because of a personality clash between Lieutenant Colonel Shiv Raj Singh, the previous Commandant of 17 Horse, and the brigade commander, the latter's opinion about the regiment was biased. He therefore requested Vaidya not to give it too much weightage. Vaidya agreed, and assured Hanut that in the future he would ensure that his regiment got its rightful due.

After air-strikes against Indian airfields on the evening of 3 December 1971, Pakistan attacked Indian positions in Chhamb the same night, preceded by heavy artillery bombardment of border outposts. The next day, 4 December 1971, Yahya Khan formally declared war. Indian counter-offensive plans were immediately put into motion, in the eastern as well as the western sectors. In the evening, 17 Horse received orders to deploy for the protection of the firm base of 54 Infantry Division. This entailed moving the regiment from east to west across the Samba T-junction. Simultaneously, 7 Cavalry was asked to move from west to east across the same choke point, to its forward assembly area west of Samba. The two columns reached the choke point at the same time, and got stuck in a traffic jam. Fortunately, the enemy artillery and air did not take advantage of this disaster, and the chaos was sorted out only after the two COs personally intervened. It was primarily the initiative of the junior leaders of both regiments, who worked overtime to disentangle their respective tanks, which enabled the regiments to reach their forward assembly areas by first light.

At the border post of Galar Tanda, there was a 30-foot high observation tower, which provided the Pakistanis a view of the Indian territory, and could be used to bring down artillery fire over the concentration areas of our troops. B Squadron was located at Gala, right opposite the tower, and Hanut ordered them to destroy it. An accurate shot from one of B Squadron's tanks brought down the tower, signalling the start of the battle in the 54 Infantry Division sector. A troop of Pakistani tanks, hidden behind the tall grass, emerged on hearing the shot, and then pulled back in panic. Hanut calculated that since the enemy tanks were moving freely along the border, there were no minefields in that area. He conveyed this information to Commander 16 Armoured Brigade, but Vaidya did not respond. The full-scale attacks went ahead as planned.

91 and 74 Infantry Brigades launched their attacks for the capture of Dandout–Chamana, Khurd–Chhahal and Mukhwal

at 2000 hrs on 5 December. The infantry did not encounter any enemy, nor did the trawls find any mines when they went through the anticipated minefield. Both brigades secured their bridgeheads, and two squadrons of 17 Horse were moved to protect their flanks. Shortly after midnight, 4 Horse was inducted into the bridgehead, but commenced its breakout only at first light. By 0800 hrs, leading elements of 4 Horse had contacted the minefield astride Thakurdwara. Surprisingly, the regiment waited until last light before the leading squadron commenced breaching the minefield. Once again, no enemy was encountered, and a firm base was secured across the minefield. A squadron of 17 Horse was moved up to take over the firm base and relieve 4 Horse for further advance.

Unknown to Indian troops, Pakistani armour was present in the area. B Squadron of Pak 20 Lancers had withdrawn behind the first defensive minefield at Thakurdwara on the night of 5–6 December, and the next day, when 4 Horse was advancing, the squadron was strafed by the IAF and withdrew to the next minefield at Barkaniyan by last light on 6 December. It was joined by a squadron of 33 Cavalry (Pattons), and soon thereafter, the rest of 20 Lancers had also concentrated behind the second minefield. On the morning of 7 December, 17 Horse was moved from Bhoi Brahmana to guard the western flank. To the east, the operations of 39 Infantry Division with 7 Cavalry in support, had not made much progress and were still to cross the first minefield. The enemy had developed Dehlra and Chakra as a strong defensive position, and a squadron ex-Poona Horse was sent to Dadwan Kalan to mask Chakra and secure Bari, while 4 Horse was ordered to clear Darman and Ghamrola. After completing its task, 4 Horse moved forward to Barkaniyan, and Poona Horse less two squadrons was moved from Rayian to Gala, with the other two squadrons at Bhoi Brahmana and Sadwal–Dadwan Kalan.

Information of a likely enemy counter-attack at Mukhwal was received on the afternoon of 8 December. 17 Horse less two squadrons, with a company of 18 Rajputana Rifles under command, was ordered to secure Mukhwal. As the column was moving along a high embankment, it came under air attack. Only the leading tanks could get off the road, while the rest of the 2-kilometre-long column continued to move in single file along the narrow road. Hanut was in the leading tank, and had managed to get off the road and into the tall elephant grass. However, he saw sortie after sortie of enemy aircraft coming in to attack the column with bombs and rockets. Expecting most of his tanks to have been destroyed, he asked all stations to report casualties after the attack was over. Everyone was surprised and relieved to find that there were none. Having witnessed their shooting skills, the Poona Horse treated the Pakistani Air Force with contempt for the rest of the war.

After reaching Mukhwal, Hanut deployed the company of 18 Rajputana Rifles on the high ground ahead of the village, with their armoured personnel carriers (APCs) in close support. The armour was held in reserve, hidden from view in the village itself. The plan was that when the enemy launched their attack, the infantry would mount their APCs and withdraw towards Mukhwal, firing their machine-guns. Once the enemy assumed that they had captured the area and began to reorganise, the tanks and APCs would mount a combined assault. Shortly after the deployment had been completed, the enemy started shelling the area, and Hanut thought that they were just registering targets before launching the attack. However, the infantry and armour waited in vain. The enemy did not attack, causing all-round disappointment.

While the operations of 54 Infantry Division had progressed well, 39 Infantry Division had not been able to capture Dehlra. Major General W.A.G. Pinto, GOC 54 Infantry Division, realised that unless the Dehlra–Chakra complex was cleared, his own operations would not progress. He therefore decided to clear it using his own troops, and allotted the task to Brigadier Ujagar Singh, Commander 74 Infantry Brigade, who was given a squadron ex-4 Horse for this purpose. This was completed by first light on 11 December. Pinto now ordered Brigadier A. Handoo, Commander 91 Infantry Brigade, to establish a bridgehead across the Barkaniyan minefield. 17 Horse was placed under command 91 Infantry Brigade for this operation, with the further tasks of breaking out from the bridgehead, contacting the enemy positions along the Basantar nullah, and if opportunity offered, establishing an encounter crossing across the Basantar. The regiment moved forward from Mukhwal and concentrated at Tarakwal by 1400 hrs on 12 December. 18 Rajputana Rifles less two companies, mounted on APCs, was placed under command 17 Horse for the encounter crossing, in addition to an Engineer taskforce with trawl and bridge layer tanks.

Hanut planned to carry out the encounter crossing under cover of darkness, as soon as the bridgehead across the minefield had been established by 91 Infantry Brigade. However, Commander 91 Infantry Brigade did not permit this, since he was worried about his own security. Hanut knew that the Basantar would be heavily defended, and a daylight encounter crossing would not succeed. Finally, it was agreed that a squadron of 4 Horse would take over the defence of the bridgehead, allowing 17 Horse to break out the same night. The operation began on the night of 13 December, and 91 Infantry Brigade secured a bridgehead across the minefield. The Engineers began trawling and, by 2330 hrs, a safe lane for tanks had been cleared. At 0230 hrs, the combat group commenced the breakout.

After going some distance, the combat group came across some tank tracks. They conjectured that the tracks belonged to enemy tanks that had withdrawn from the Barkaniyan minefield, and would lead to a suitable crossing place over the Basantar. The regiment had made an elaborate navigation plan—with compass bearings and night charts—showing the route from point to point, but it was felt that following the tracks would speed up their movement and save time. Abandoning the navigation plan, the combat group began to follow the tracks. This proved to be a mistake since the enemy tanks, instead of crossing the Basantar, had veered off east and crossed a tributary of the Basantar. When the combat group reached the nullah in the early hours of 14 December, they found the crossing unmined and undefended. Only then did it dawn on the two COs that they had hit a tributary rather than the main Basantar nullah. The combat group quickly swung round to get back on the original axis, but it was soon daylight, and the area was found to be boggy. They decided to defer the attempt, and the tanks were dispersed. As it turned out, the Basantar was heavily defended and too formidable to have been breached by an encounter crossing, so the failure to reach the correct place turned out to be a blessing in disguise. Though the regiment suffered a number of casualties due to air attacks during the day, these were nothing compared to what they would have suffered had the encounter crossing been attempted.

Over the next two days, enemy resistance on the home side of the obstacle was systematically cleared, and on 15 December, a deliberate operation was launched across the Basantar nullah. 47 Infantry Brigade, under Brigadier A.P. Bhardwaj, was made responsible for securing a bridgehead. The brigade had three battalions, 13 Grenadiers, 6 Madras and 16 Madras, in addition to 17 Horse and 18 Rajputana Rifles less two companies. The plan involved the capture of area 2r in the Ghazipur reserve forest, including Saraj Chak by 16 Madras in phase one, followed by the capture of Jarpal and Lohal by 13 Grenadiers in phase two. 17 Horse and 18 Rajputana Rifles less two companies were to protect the bridgehead against enemy counterattack. On the following day, 13 Grenadiers, supported by a squadron of 17 Horse, was to capture Barapind, while 16 Madras, supported by another squadron of the regiment, was to capture Ghazipur.

The infantry attack went in as planned, and the bridgehead was secured by 16 Madras at 2030 hrs. The breaching of the minefield commenced, and the armour was waiting for safe lanes to be cleared. The second phase of the brigade attack also went in, and at 2330 hrs 13 Grenadiers reported that it had secured Jarpal. Meanwhile, there were frantic calls from Lieutenant Colonel V. Ghai, CO 16 Madras, reporting that he was being threatened by enemy armour, which was building up for the counter-attack. At about 0230 hrs, there was another desperate appeal from Ghai, indicating that the situation was critical, and that if he did not get any armour, he would not be able to hold out. Hanut realized that waiting for safe lanes could mean destruction of the infantry and loss of the bridgehead. Crossing the minefield, still unbreached, could result in a large number of his tanks being written off.

Hanut decided to take the risk and send at least one squadron across to relieve the beleaguered infantry. He gave the task to C Squadron, which was led by the second-in-command, Major Ajai Singh, who had taken over after the squadron commander Major Moti Dar had been wounded when his tank received a direct hit. Captain Ravi Deol was transferred to C Squadron from B Squadron, since he was familiar with the area, having seen it during daylight. The squadron began to negotiate the minefield, with Deol as the navigating officer and Ajai in the following tank. Miraculously, the squadron crossed the minefield without a single casualty and successfully secured the bridgehead. The next day, a jeep and an APC, which tried to follow the tank tracks, blew up on the enemy mines. Hanut attributes the luck of the squadron in crossing 600 metres of unbreached minefield without a single casualty to the 'Hand of Allah'. (The Standard of the Poona Horse is surmounted by a silver hand, which was captured by the regiment from the 1st Khusgai Regiment of Fars during the Persian War in 1857. The hand bears the inscription, dated AD 1066, 'Yad Ullal Fauk Idehim', which means 'The Hand of God is above all things.')

There was a fierce tank battle on 16 December, followed by another one on the next day, when the full weight of Pakistan's 8 Armoured Brigade was brought to bear on the Poona Horse.

Inspired by Hanut's leadership, the regiment fought like lions and in a single day's battle, destroyed 50 enemy tanks, losing 13 of its own. In the Battle of Basantar, one of Pakistan's oldest and proudest cavalry regiments—13 Lancers—was decimated, while another, 31 Cavalry, was crippled. It was during this action that Second Lieutenant Arun Khetarpal, a young officer with barely six months' service, sacrificed his life and was awarded a PVC. The incident is now a legend and merits recounting.

During the battle, Major Amarjit Bal, the officer commanding (OC) B Squadron, who had only two of his troops with him, requested reinforcements. Hanut called Major Man Singh, OC A Squadron, on the radio, but he had gone to the Regimental Aid Post (RAP) with a casualty. He ordered the squadron's second-in-command, Captain V. Malhotra, to reinforce B Squadron with two troops. Malhotra immediately took off with Number 3 Troop under Avtar Ahlawat and Number 4 Troop under Arun Khetarpal. With their guns blazing, the six tanks rushed towards the enemy, destroying several tanks, and taking some prisoners, who were carried piggy-back until they were handed over to the infantry. In fact, A Squadron's tanks had raced ahead of the positions occupied by B Squadron and had to be pulled back in line by Hanut on the radio. They had barely got into fire positions when the enemy's main attack was delivered, and they were smack in the middle of it. Whereas three tanks managed to find some cover, the three being commanded by Malhotra, Ahlawat and Khetarpal were out in the open.

Very soon, Malhotra's tank became inoperative due to a mechanical defect, and that of Ahlawat was shot up. Now only Arun Khetarpal was left in the fray. Hanut had just passed a net call on the radio ordering 'All tanks will fight it out from where they are; no tank will move back even an inch.' Arun's tank had received a hit, but it had ricocheted. Now he received a second hit and the tank caught fire. Malhotra ordered him to abandon his tank but Arun, realising that he was the only one left who could stop the enemy, refused, saying: 'My gun is still functioning. I will get the remaining lot.' When Malhotra insisted that he abandon his tank or pull back, Arun switched off his radio set. The driver, Prayag Singh, remonstrated with Arun, saying that it would take them only a few minutes to pull back, put out the fire, and rejoin the battle. Arun replied: 'Didn't you hear the CO's transmission? No tank will pull back even an inch.'

By this time most of the enemy squadron, commanded by Major Nissar, had been destroyed, but four or five tanks were still left. Arun systematically began knocking them out, and the last tank he hit, at a range of barely 75 metres, was that of Major Nissar himself. At this stage, his own tank suffered a fourth hit, killing the radio operator and severely wounding Arun and the gunner. The driver, Prayag Singh, showing great presence of mind, reversed his tank behind cover and evacuated the gunner to another tank. Though he was himself wounded, he tried to pull Arun out of the tank with the help of the crew of another tank. In the process, the gallant officer breathed his last.

Arun Khetarpal's sacrifice was more than an act of personal courage and valour. It was a manifestation of 'the PH spirit', which Hanut had inculcated amongst his officers. Twenty years later, when Hanut wrote the book *Fakhr-e-Hind*, he dedicated it to 'The PH Spirit', which, according to him, is 'an intangible compendium of many qualities that defies description, but infuses every Poona Horseman and guides and sustains him both in peace and in war'. In simpler terms, it is a rare combination of comradeship, loyalty and total dedication to the profession of arms. Arun's refusal to abandon his tank, at grave personal risk, on the grounds that the CO had forbidden it, is a manifestation of the fierce sense of loyalty which Hanut commanded from his subordinates. It is this sort of mutual trust and loyalty that wins battles, and the ability to inspire it is the true hallmark of a leader, which Hanut undeniably was. Another oft-repeated tale about the Battle of Basantar concerns Hanut's habit of daily meditation. It is said that during the thick of the battle, Hanut did not answer when the brigade commander Brigadier A.S. Vaidya called him on the radio. When Vaidya questioned him about it later, Hanut is reported to have said that he was doing his 'puja'. The story is only partly true. Hanut did switch off his radio set to HQ 16 Independent Armoured Brigade, but this was because his unit was placed under command of 47 Infantry Brigade for the bridgehead operation. Also, he did not want any distraction or interference during the tank battle, where the rapidly changing situation required his undivided attention. According to Hanut, Vaidya did not call him during the battle, and only learned about the action much later, from the After Action Report.

Even before the operations commenced, Hanut had anticipated that his regiment would be involved in a major battle with Pakistani armour as soon as they crossed the Basantar river. Accordingly, he had rehearsed his unit with a map and a sand model. An aspect that he repeatedly stressed was that once they beat back the inevitable counter-attack, the enemy would be in complete disarray. At this decisive moment, they would have to sally forth and finish off the remnants of enemy armour. As he had foreseen, this opportunity presented itself at 1100 hrs on 16 December, when the counterattack by Pakistan 8 Armoured Brigade was decisively repulsed. Some of the more enthusiastic officers of Poona Horse asked Hanut on the radio when he was going to launch them into action, as had been planned. But the enemy response was far stronger than Hanut had anticipated, and he did not want to risk leaving the bridgehead undefended. The brigade and divisional commanders were listening in on the radio, but did not react. Hanut told his Adjutant to convey a message to the brigade commander on the brigade net, requesting him to 'build up sister unit fastest'. Since the enemy was monitoring the net, the message could not be made more explicit. But Vaidya failed to grasp its significance and did nothing. The second armoured regiment—4 Horse—was moved to the bridgehead only after last light on 16 December, on the instructions of the corps commander. Thus, a magnificent opportunity was lost, and the ceasefire saw them still confined to the bridgehead.

On 16 December, there were six major units in the bridgehead, three from 47 Infantry Brigade, and three from 16 Armoured Brigade. However, none of the brigade commanders was there to issue orders. Hanut was the senior CO, and his orders for readjustment and redeployment were issued on his own initiative, in consultation with the others. In fact, as Hanut recounts, the first time he saw any senior officer during the battle was just a few hours before the ceasefire on 17 December, when the Corps Commander, Lieutenant General K.K. Singh, came to visit and congratulate the regiment, accompanied by the Divisional Commander, Major General W.A.G. Pinto, and Brigadier A.P. Bhardwaj, Commander 47 Infantry Brigade.

In the various post-mortems carried out after the war, and in the After Action Reports, commanders at all levels glossed over their lapses and weaknesses. In the euphoria of victory, everyone indulged in mutual praise and congratulations. Hanut brought up these weaknesses during discussions and debriefings, and also mentioned them in his After Action Report. This caused a lot of resentment among some senior officers, who felt that he was being unnecessarily critical. But Hanut had very definite ideas about command in battle and the responsibility that goes with it. In armour battles, command has to be exercised from 'up front', and he always made sure that his own tank was positioned at the point of contact. This enabled him to see and assess the action as it developed, and issue orders according to the exigencies of the situation. He did not like to look back over his shoulder, and strongly rebuffed attempts at backseat driving by his superiors. He found it distracting to have to answer meaningless queries from staff officers at higher HQ, and frequently switched off his rearward radio, leaving the second-in-command or Adjutant to deal with them. This allowed him to concentrate on his command and conduct the battle without interference.

After two years as Commandant of the Poona Horse, Hanut was posted as GSO 1, HQ 31 Armoured Division in September 1973. Two years later he was promoted brigadier, and appointed Commander 14 (Independent) Armoured Brigade, which he commanded with distinction. Shortly after he assumed command, a discussion was held at the Corps HQ to evaluate the concept of the crossing of a water obstacle by an armoured division and the subsequent breakout. This concept had been worked out by the Armoured Division, and after endorsement by the Command and Corps HQ, had been forwarded to Army HQ for approval. The Military Training Directorate had come up with a draft training note, which was sent to the Corps HQ for comments and approval before it was issued. At this time, Lieutenant General Z.C. 'Zoru' Bakshi was the Corps Commander, and Lieutenant General I.S. Gill was the Army Commander. Bakshi wanted the concept to be discussed and evaluated before any decision was taken. It was a high-level discussion, in which almost all senior formation commanders of Western Command participated or attended as observers. The Army Commander was also present.

When Hanut read through the paper, he found that the concept was totally impractical. He felt that it had been conceived by some armchair tactician, and was surprised that it had been accepted all the way up to Army HQ without anyone questioning its basic assumptions. When he tried to raise the issue within his syndicate, he was overruled by his syndicate leader on the grounds that it had already been approved. When the discussion got under way, almost everyone lauded the concept as brilliant. During tea-break, Hanut spoke to the Chief of Staff HQ 2 Corps, who was conducting the discussion, and told him that he wished to express a personal opinion on the issue, as his syndicate was not in agreement with his views. When the discussion was resumed, Hanut was invited to give his comments. He began by saying: 'Though I find myself in the position of being one man against the house, yet I have some very major and serious reservations about the proposed concept.' He went on to outline his objections and finished by declaring that the concept could not be executed in even a full-scale 'Exercise with Troops', let alone in war.

There was a stunned silence, and everyone started looking at the Army Commander, Lieutenant General Gill, who intervened, to say: 'Hanut, you are not one man against the house. I too do not agree with this concept.' He then asked him whether he had any alternative to suggest. Hanut presented what he thought was a workable solution. During the summing up that followed, both the Army and Corps Commanders agreed with his views, and the proposed concept was scrapped.

A few months later, an Exercise with Troops was held in which his brigade was tasked to execute a breakout. At the planning stage itself, Hanut pointed out to the commander of the infantry division which was establishing the bridgehead, that the site selected was incorrect. Because of the presence of lakes on two sides, the armour would have to break out through a defile, which could be blocked very easily by the enemy. Hanut was overruled, and was assured that his tanks would be given safe passage. When the exercise began, the situation developed exactly as he had predicted. Hanut immediately called off the breakout and ordered his tanks to deploy. Next morning, when the Army and Corps Commanders asked Hanut why he had aborted the manoeuvre, he replied: 'I am not prepared to order my leading regiment to undertake a mission which I know to be suicidal.' They left without a word. Subsequently, Hanut was given a clear passage through the defile, and the armoured brigade broke out as planned.

In January 1978, Hanut was nominated to attend the course at the National Defence College, after which he was posted to the MO Directorate, where he remained for an unprecedented three-and-a-half years. In May 1982, he was promoted Major General and given command of 17 Mountain Division in Sikkim. Hanut's first brush was with Talyarkhan, the State Governor, a man with an enormous ego. He never tired of telling anyone he met how close he was to the Nehru family, particularly Mrs Indira Gandhi, who had specially selected him to oversee the transition of Sikkim from an independent kingdom to a state of the Indian Union. Hanut found that Talyarkhan behaved more like a colonial ruler than a constitutional head of government. He demanded various perks and privileges that were beyond his entitlement. One of these was that he expected to be received by the divisional commander, or at least one of the brigade commanders, whenever he visited any part of the state. Hanut's predecessor, Major General 'Tich' Sharma, had extended these courtesies to the Governor, but Hanut decided to put a stop it. Shortly after he took over, the Governor decided to visit North Sikkim, and the brigade commander requested Hanut's permission to receive him. Hanut told him that there was no need for him to do this since the Governor's visit was at the behest of the civil administration, and the army had nothing to do with it. However, if he visited any place where an army unit was located, the local unit commander could be present at the time of his arrival and departure.

When Talyarkhan landed at the helipad he was incensed because, as he put it, 'only a lieutenant colonel' was present to receive him. On his return to Gangtok, he immediately rang up Hanut, who was not available because he was at his prayers. This further enraged the Governor, who threatened to complain about this to the COAS. He tried to speak to the Army Chief over the Post and Telegraph circuit, but could not do so because the lines were down. When Hanut heard about this, he directed that the Governor's call be conveyed on army channels, which was done. Naturally, nothing came out of it. When Hanut was asked about the incident, he pointed out that there was no protocol requiring an army representative to receive the Governor, unless he was visiting army units. In fact, he made it clear that this time one of the battalion commanders had been asked to receive him because it had become an established practice, and he did not want to make any abrupt changes. In the future, no army officer would be present. When Talyarkhan found that Hanut could not be browbeaten, his attitude changed and relations between them, though formal, became more cordial thereafter.

However, Hanut's relations with Lieutenant General Surjit Singh Brar, the Corps Commander, were not so cordial. They had differences of opinion on almost everything, which included operational and administrative aspects. Hanut found the operational plans very passive, and wanted to introduce a more aggressive form of defence. This called for substantial reserves at every level, and the only way these could be created was by restructuring the deployment. As was his practice, Hanut ran a sand model exercise, which he conducted personally, in order to apprise the division's officers of the concept. Brar, who attended the discussion, was openly critical. In order to avoid an unseemly argument in front of junior officers, Hanut terminated the discussion, saying: 'So long as I am the GOC, this is how I will fight the defensive battle.' And that was that.

During his visits to the forward defences, Hanut found the officers and men living under appalling conditions. The men were in sheds that had no insulation, and had to huddle around *bukharie*s (stoves used for heating), as the shed never really got warm. Once the bukhari was put out, it became unbearably cold inside. The tin roofs of the sheds had holes, letting in rain and melted snow, causing permanent slush inside. There were no toilets and bathrooms—just a hessian cloth enclosure, flapping in the wind. There was no lighting, so the day ended as soon as the sun went down. Hanut thought it was shameful that even after spending 20 years in the same locations, the troops were being made to suffer in this manner. He berated the officers for timidly accepting this state of affairs, and told them that unless they insisted on certain minimum standards in facilities for troops, no one would do anything about it.

Hanut raised the issue at the next Operational Works Conference. He pointed out that they already had surplus defence works in almost all defended localities, and suggested that for the next few years, the funds for operational works be used for providing decent living accommodation for troops. To his surprise, Brar replied that he too, had visited the forward defences, and found the state of accommodation to be quite satisfactory. Obviously, either the standards used by the Corps Commander were very low, or he was deliberately trying to snub Hanut.

When Hanut realised that he would get no help from Corps HQ in the form of funds, he requested some engineer effort. However, even this was refused. Hanut then decided to procure the necessary material using the funds and engineer resources of the division. Wood was locally available at cheap rates, and this was used for insulating the living accommodation. When the Corps HQ objected on the ground that it would increase the risk of fire, Hanut said that he would take the responsibility. Bathrooms were made using hollow cement blocks, and each post was provided with a generator for lighting, as well as a radio, so that their day did not end at sunset. Naturally, the troops were delighted, and when Hanut left after a year, the 'Water Shed Brigade' recorded their appreciation and thanks by presenting to him a memento inscribed with the words: 'You have done more for improving our operational preparedness, administrative facilities and our living conditions in one year, than others have done in twenty.' Hanut cherished the gift, as it came from the heart.

During Hanut's tenure in Sikkim, there was no lavish hospitality laid out for VIPs, for which the division had acquired a dubious reputation. During summer, there was usually a large influx of visitors who expected to be looked after along with their families and relatives. Once they found that they were expected to pay for the hospitality, their numbers began to dwindle. Soon, the stream of visitors dried up, as word went around that social life in Gangtok had become dull after the new GOC had taken over. Hanut took this as a compliment, since it was a welcome relief for his harassed staff, who had to make all the arrangements, including accommodation, transport and sightseeing. Not surprisingly, this led to further deterioration in the relations between Hanut and the Corps Commander. After a year, General K.V. Krishna Rao, the COAS, selected him to command the prestigious Armoured Division, an appointment that every cavalry officer dreams about. Hanut was happy to leave, both for personal and professional reasons. He would now have a chance to put into practice his ideas on armoured warfare.

Soon after he took over as GOC 1 Armoured Division in May 1983, Hanut found that there were several shortcomings in training and equipment. He stopped all other work for the next few months, and had the entire division carry out equipment maintenance. Then one day he announced that they were all going to the desert for training. Before sending them out, he taught them the operational concepts and tactics that he wanted them to practice, so that they knew exactly what was required of them. First, all regiments were sent out under their COs. Brigade commanders were forbidden to visit them till after a month. He himself would visit them after exactly six weeks and observe them for a week. If satisfied, he would order them to return. If not, they would continue to train in the desert.

Whenever Hanut arrived in the training area, he came with his own caravan and a small mess detachment. He would park it near the unit or formation he was visiting, and ask for a telephone line. In all other respects, he would be independent. He never taxed the units for mess facilities, accommodation, manpower and so on, leaving them free to concentrate on training. He ensured that this procedure was followed by his brigade commanders as well. Of course, there were no parties, and he would flare up if he saw sofa sets, carpets and curtains being carried to the exercise area, as was the custom in the Armoured Division before Hanut assumed command.

During his tenure, an operational discussion was held at the Corps HQ. General K. Sundarji, GOC-in-C Western Command, was also attending, along with most of the senior commanders. Exercise 'Chetak', a large scale exercise with troops, had just finished, and had thrown up a large number of concepts regarding the employment of the Armoured Division. Hanut did not agree with these concepts, and though the main theme of the discussion was slightly different, he decided to take advantage of the gathering and raise the issues that were bothering him.

When Hanut expressed his reservations, Sundarji invited the other divisional commanders to also give their views. Though most of them had agreed with Hanut in private discussions, no one dared to admit this openly, since most of the issues raised had been advocated by Sundarji or had his endorsement. This led to a verbal duel between Sundarji and Hanut. Finally, Hanut ended the argument by making it clear that as long as he was in command of the Armoured Division, he would fight the battle in the way he thought best.

Having said this, Hanut sat down. There was a stunned silence. Sundarji was the Army Commander, and his promotion and appointment as the Army Chief was almost a certainty. Crossing swords with him was tantamount to professional suicide, and Hanut seemed to have done just that. Soon afterwards, someone remarked: 'After this, Hanut may as well plan his retirement and start growing roses.'

But as usual, the prophets of doom were proved wrong. Sundarji was one of the few senior officers in the army, who would not only tolerate a professional difference of opinion, but appreciate it, provided it was backed by sound reasons. In December 1984, Hanut was posted to the MO Directorate at Army HQ. This was his third tenure in MO, and it was expected that he would soon be promoted Lieutenant General and given command of a corps. At this time, General A.S. Vaidya was the COAS. Though he was also from the Armoured Corps and Hanut had served under him earlier, the two did not see eye to eye on many matters. Fortunately, Sundarji had by now taken over as Vice Chief of Army Staff, and he acted as a buffer between them.

After a year in MO, Hanut was promoted Lieutenant General, but side-stepped as Director General of Armoured Corps, in December 1985. His promotion was not without impediment. Though he had been approved by the selection board, Vaidya was not favourably inclined and tried to block his promotion. However, Arun Singh, the Minister of State for Defence, overruled him, reportedly at the behest of Sundarji, who was slated to succeed Vaidya. When Sundarji took over as Chief on 1 February 1986, he called Hanut and told him that he wanted him to command the Strike Corps for Exercise 'Brass Tacks', which was to be the largest and most ambitious series of exercises undertaken by the Indian Army till then. Sundarji wanted to try out certain new concepts, including the Air Assault Division and the Reorganised Assault Plains Infantry Division (RAPID), which were both ideas introduced by him for the first time.

On 29 April 1986, Hanut took over as GOC 2 Corps. Naturally, he was delighted at the chance to command the prestigious Strike Corps. Here was an opportunity to put into practice the concepts of mobile warfare that he had studied and evolved, but which had remained at the level of theory for want of an opportunity to put them into practice. Hanut set about his task in right earnest, to educate and inculcate the troops, and more so the formation commanders who would have to implement the concepts. He held a series of talks, followed by map and sand model exercises, followed by training exercises without troops (TEsWT), and finally full-scale exercises with troops. By the time Exercise 'Brass Tacks-4' began, his corps was keyed to a pitch of training that is seldom achieved.

It is now well known that during Exercise 'Brass Tacks', India and Pakistan almost went to war. Due to various reasons, the crisis was averted and the troops withdrawn from the border. By Hanut's own reckoning, if he had been allowed to continue, his corps would have executed offensive operations that would be rated among the classics of mobile warfare. His officers and men were itching for a fight and a chance to put into practice all that they had been learning and practising for the last few months. When the whole thing fizzled out, most of them were bitterly disappointed. If Hanut had been given the 'go ahead', there is little doubt that he would have changed the map, given his past record of bold and brilliant handling of armour.

Hanut feels that second only to the rare privilege of commanding his regiment in battle, the command of 2 Corps provided him the greatest professional satisfaction. He had the unique opportunity of being able to personally train and handle the corps in a full-scale exercise with troops, complete with the opposing defending forces. This was the first time that an exercise of such magnitude had been held, and it was also likely to be the last time. For not only is the cost of holding such exercises prohibitive, it is also rare to come by a Chief who, like Sundarji, has the vision and perception to conceive such an exercise.

Hanut remained in command of 2 Corps for over two years. The fact that he had been selected for this appointment by Sundarji, with whom he had crossed swords a few years earlier, had surprised many of his contemporaries. In fact, Hanut's career disproves the theories often put forward of the Indian Army being a 'one mistake' army, with a 'zero error syndrome'. Hanut fell out with his immediate superior officer in almost every rank and appointment. Yet he was never denied a promotion. In spite of personal differences, not one of his superiors could fault his professional competence, dedication and loyalty to the organisation.

While in service, Hanut led a Spartan life. He shunned parties, and if forced to attend one, left after a short while. He was deeply religious, and never missed his daily meditation. Because of his reserved temperament, he gave the appearance of being distant and aloof, and was a strict disciplinarian. Yet, his concern for the welfare of men was legendary. He had forbidden the prevalent custom of employing working parties of men to do cleaning or gardening on Sundays and holidays, and in the evenings. He was always sympathetic towards the men and their problems, and spared no effort to better their living conditions. He expected high standards, but forgave errors of judgement. Whenever he saw a mistake being made, he corrected it without losing his temper. In fact, he would personally teach not only officers but even JCOs and jawans. But he would get angry if he found someone sleeping during a professional lecture or discussion.

There were many facets to Hanut's personality, some of which were seen only by his closest associates. He was a very humane and level-headed person, who went out of his way to help people in distress. With the ladies, he was extremely charming, but his behaviour was always respectful and correct. Contrary to popular belief, he had many admirers among the fairer sex. His sense of humour, both in conversation and in writing, was unmatched. However, in many other respects, his behaviour and style were not in consonance with the generally accepted norms of the Indian Army. He found the widely prevalent practice of prefixing every sentence with 'Sir' when talking to a superior, disconcerting. He gave up the habit and encouraged his subordinates to do so as well. He was upright, truthful, and knowledgeable, and had a mind of his own. He did not hesitate to express his views, even when he knew they would not be accepted. However, he never became argumentative, or forced his ideas on his subordinates. This personality was later used by his detractors to brand him as anti-establishment.

A lot has been said about Hanut's religious beliefs. Religion and the military profession appear to be a contradiction in terms, but Hanut did not see it that way. Religion has always formed an integral part of Rajput culture and ethos. Hanut believed that religion gave soldiers the inner strength to rise above the mundane and achieve self-actualisation. In fact, Hanut found religion a great motivating factor. He did not practise religion in the traditional manner of rituals and fasts, but as an intellectual who had explored and found a new dimension to it. His wide reading enabled him to grasp its true meaning, and he abided by the tenet of the Bhagwad Gita, which equates Dharma or religion with Karma or righteous living. Hanut realised that for a soldier, the two are synonymous, and this became the basic philosophy of his life.

Hanut's attitude towards his profession was a subject of intense debate. His dedication to the profession of arms was so complete that he never married, as he felt that this would compromise it. He made it a subject of deep study, research and experimentation in order to become perfect. In the process he developed professional acumen of unmatched brilliance in all military matters. When he spoke, it was with an authority born out of years of experience and study. His inner strength and conviction were transparent, and had a hypnotic effect on his subordinates, who were ever ready to follow him, regardless of the consequences. He had an intense desire to teach whatever he knew to anybody who cared to learn. In the process, he got so involved that he would not spare himself or the student until he was satisfied that the learning process was complete.

Many of Hanut's contemporaries felt that he was eccentric and on a perpetual collision course with his superiors. Hanut knew this, but felt that since he always acted in the interests of the service and the men under his command, he was justified. Some of his superiors understood this and tolerated his idiosyncrasies, and a few even appreciated it. However, the larger majority could not stomach it and reacted adversely. Hanut was rarely perturbed by this reaction, since he knew the reason from which it stemmed, and did not hold it against the concerned officers.

Hanut's last assignment was as the Commandant of the Armoured Corps Centre and School at Ahmednagar, where he moved in July 1988. It was expected that he would be made an Army Commander, but this was not to be. By now, General Sundarji had retired and General V.N. Sharma, who was also from the Armoured Corps, had taken over as COAS. With a faultless service record, there was no reason for Hanut to be considered unsuitable for commanding a field army. Yet he was. There were two reasons put forward for this. The first, that he was a bachelor and shunned social life, was valid, but the second, concerning his religious beliefs, was not. He was branded a 'religious bigot', a charge that was blatantly untrue and unfair. Though he was a deeply religious man, Hanut could by no stretch of the imagination be called a bigot. He was extremely broad-minded and never interfered with those practising other religions. The fact that troops of all religious denominations literally worshipped him, should have been enough to give the lie to this insinuation made by one of his own ilk.

When a subordinate informed Hanut of his having been passed over, and expressed his sorrow, his reply was typical. 'Why should you be sorry? It is the army which should be sorry. If they don't want me, the loss is theirs.' Not many officers in uniform would take their supersession so philosophically. Hanut knew it was not a reflection on his professional competence, and felt no need to represent against it. He continued to do his job with the same dedication and loyalty till he retired on 31 July 1991.

In the final analysis, Hanut would like to be remembered as a 'soldier's General'. He always felt, and told other officers: 'We as officers do not deserve the men we command. We do so little for them, and they give us so much more in return.' Wherever he went, he tried to ameliorate and improve the working and living conditions of the common soldier. Often, a JCO, NCO or jawan would walk up to him and introduce himself, saying: 'You will not remember me, but I was serving in so and so unit under your command. I heard that you were around, and came to pay my respects.' (The word they usually used was 'darshan', which really has no equivalent in the English language.) In fact, one of Hanut's most treasured memories is of the soldier who walked up to his driver and asked him: 'Yeh wohi general sahib hain jo ki jawanon ka itna khayal rakha karte the? Maine darshan to nahin kiye hain, par nam bada suna hai.' (Is this the same general, who was known for his concern for the welfare of troops? I have never had the chance to see him, but have heard a lot about him.)

Today, Hanut lives in Dehradun. Having lived like a hermit even while in uniform, he has been able to make the transition to retired life smoothly, unlike several others who find the change traumatic. He spends most of his time meditating and reading. Having followed a rigid and spartan regime all his life, he is still in good health and has several years of active life before him. Though comparatively unknown outside army circles, Hanut will be remembered as one of the finest armour commanders of the Indian Army. His simplicity, courage, boldness, high sense of moral values and professionalism will always be a source of inspiration for generations of officers to come.

Select Bibliography

Ahmad, Lieutenant Colonel Mustasad. 1994. 'Cariappa: A Legend', *The Regimental Journal of the Rajput Regiment*, 1 January.

Bhagat, Lieutenant General P.S. 1967. *The Shield and the Sword*. Calcutta: The Statesman.

Brett-James, Antony. 1951. *Ball of Fire: The Fifth Indian Division in the Second World War*. Aldershot: Gale and Polden.

Chatterjee, Raj. 'Sam Bahadur'. *The Times of India*.

Chaudhuri, J.N. 1969. *Arms, Aims and Aspects*. Bombay: Manaktalas. Cohen, Stephen P. 1971. *The Indian Army: Its Contribution to the Development of a Nation*. Berkeley: University of California Press.

Cohen, Stephen P. and Richard L. Park. 1978. *India: Emergent Power*. New York: Crave Russak.

Dalvi, Brigadier John. 1969. *Himalayan Blunder*. Bombay: Thacker and Co.

Dhiman, Kuldip. 2000. 'Field Marshal S.H.F.J. Manekshaw', *The Tribune* (Chandigarh), 9 April.

Dixon, Norman. 1976. *On the Psychology of Military Incompetence*. London: Jonathan Cape.

Evans, Humphrey. 1988. *Thimayya of India*. Dehradun: Nataraj Publishers.

Gaylor, John. 1993. *Sons of John Company—The Indian and Pakistani Armies, 1903–1991*. New Delhi: Lancer Publishers and Distributors.

Jacob, Lieutenant General J.F.R. 1997. *Surrender at Dacca—Birth of a Nation*. New Delhi: Manohar.

Kadiyan, Rajesh. 1990. *India and its Army*. New Delhi: Vision Books.

Kapur, Brigadier T.B. 'Timmy, The Beloved Kumaoni General of the Indian Army', *The Kumaoni*, Journal of the Kumaon Regiment.

Kar, Lieutenant Colonel H.C. 1980. *Military History of India*. Calcutta: Firma KLB.

Kaul, Lieutenant General B.M. 1967. *The Untold Story*. New Delhi: Allied Publishers.

Khan, Field Marshal Ayub. 1967. *Friends, Not Masters*. London: Oxford University Press.

Khanduri. Brigadier C.B. 1995. *Field Marshal K.M. Cariappa—His Life and Times*. New Delhi: Lancer Publishers and Distributors.

Khera, P.N. 1974. *Operation Vijay*. New Delhi: Historical Division, Ministry of Defence, Government of India.

Lal, Air Marshal P.C. 1986. *My Years with the IAF*. New Delhi: Lancer Publishers and Distributors.

Longer, V. 1974. *Red Coats to Olive Green*. Bombay: Allied Publishers.

Malik, Harjit. 1993. 'The General Danced', *The Times of India* (New Delhi), 3 June.

Mason, Philip. 1985. *The Men Who Ruled India*. New York: Norton. Maxwell, Neville. 1971. *India's China War*. Bombay: Jaico Publishing House.

Muthanna, I.M. 1964. *General Cariappa*. Mysore: Usha Press.

———. 1972. *General Thimayya*. Bangalore: Orient Press.

Nath, Major General Rajendra. 1990. *Military Leadership In India: Vedic Period to Indo–Pakistani War*. New Delhi: Lancer Publishers and Distributors.

Niazi, Lieutenant General A.A.K. 1998. *The Betrayal of East Pakistan*. New Delhi: Manohar.

Palit, Major General D.K. 1972. *The Lightning Campaign*. New Delhi: Thompson.

———. 1991. *War in High Himalaya—The Indian Army in Crisis, 1962*. London: Hurst and Co.

Palsokar, Colonel R.D. 1980. *The Grenadiers—A Tradition of Valour*. Jabalpur: Grenadiers Regimental Centre.

———. 1987. *Defence Services Staff College, Wellington (India), 1947– 1987*. Wellington: The Commandant, Defence Services Staff College.

———. 1991. *History of the 5th Gorkha Rifles (Frontier Force) Volume III: 1858–1991*. Shillong: The Commandant, 58 Gorkha Training Centre.

Pannikar, K.M. *Problems of Indian Defence*. Bombay: Asia Publishing House.

Prasad, Sri Nandan. 1976. *The Military History of India*. Calcutta: K.P. Bagchi.

Prasad, S.N. and Dharampal. *History of the Operations in Jammu and Kashmir (1947–48)*. New Delhi: Historical Division, Ministry of Defence, Government of India.

Praval, Major K.C. 1987. *Indian Army after Independence*. New Delhi: Lancer Publishers and Distributors.

———. 1973. *India's Paratroopers: A History of the Parachute Regiment of India*. New Delhi: Thomson Press.

Proudfoot, Colonel C.L. 1984. *Flash of the Khukri—History of the 3rd Gorkha Rifles (1947–1980)*. New Delhi: Vision Books.

Puryear, Edgar F. 1971. *Nineteen Stars*. Orange, USA: Green Publishers. Rikhye, Ravi. 1981. *The Fourth Round*. New Delhi: ABC Publishing House.

Sen, Lieutenant General L.P. 1973. *Slender was the Thread*. New Delhi: Sangam.

Sharma, Lieutenant Colonel Gautam. 1996. *Nationalisation of the Indian Army*. New Delhi: Allied Publishers.

Singh, Major General Lachhman. 1979. *Indian Sword Strikes in East Pakistan*. New Delhi: Vikas Publishing House.

———. 1981. *Victory in Bangladesh*. Dehradun: Nataraj Publishers.

———. 1997. *Missed Opportunities—Indo–Pak War 1965*. Dehradun: Nataraj Publishers.

Singh, Lieutenant General Depinder. 2002. *Field Marshal Sam Manekshaw, MC—Soldiering with Dignity*. Dehradun: Nataraj Publishers.

Singh, Lieutenant General Hanut. 1993. *Fakhr-e-Hind—The Story of the Poona Horse*. Dehradun: Agrim Publishers.

Singh, Major General Sukhwant. 1980. *The Liberation of Bangladesh*. New Delhi: Vikas Publishing House.

Sinha, S.K. 1977. *Operation Rescue*. New Delhi: Vision Books.

———. 1987. *Of Matters Military*. New Delhi: Vision Books.

———. 1992. *A Soldier Recalls*. New Delhi: Lancer Publishers and Distributors.

Thomas, Lieutenant General Mathew and Jasjit Mansingh. 1994. *Lt Gen P.S. Bhagat, PVSM, VC*. New Delhi: Lancer Publishers and Distributors.

Thorat, Lieutenant General S.P.P. 1986. *From Reveille to Retreat*. New Delhi: Allied Publishers.

Verma, Major General Ashok Kalyan. 1998. *Rivers of Silence*. New Delhi: Lancer Publishers and Distributors.

Woodruff, Philip. 1965. *The Men Who Rule India, Volume II: The Guardians*. London: Jonathan Cape.

Other Sources

Film on Manekshaw by Jessica Gupta: *In War and Peace—The Life of Field Marshal Sam Manekshaw*. MC, UNESCO Parzor Project, New Delhi, March 2002.

Private papers of R.N. Batra, held by the Corps of Signals History Cell, New Delhi.

Private papers of Nathu Singh, held by Thakur Amarjeet Singh, Jaipur.

Souvenir on Bhagat: *Prem Bhagat—Commemorative Issue*, The Bombay Sappers, Poona, 23 May 1976.

Souvenir on Manekshaw: *In War and Peace—The Life of Field Marshal Sam Manekshaw*. MC, UNESCO Parzor Project, New Delhi, March 2002.

Scan QR code to access the
Penguin Random House India website